Marketing Plans

The Marketing Series is one of the most comprehensive collections of books in marketing and sales available from the UK today.

Published by Butterworth-Heinemann on behalf of the Chartered Institute of Marketing, the series is divided into three distinct groups: *Student* (fulfilling the needs of those taking the Institute's certificate and diploma qualifications); *Professional Development* (for those on formal or self-study training programmes); and *Practitioner* (presented in a more informal, motivating and highly practical manner for personal use).

Formed in 1911, the Chartered Institute of Marketing is now the largest professional marketing management body in Europe with over 60,000 members worldwide. Its primary objectives are focused on the development of awareness and understanding of marketing throughout UK industry and commerce and on the raising of standards of professionalism in the education, training and practice of this key business discipline.

Marketing Plans

How to Prepare Them
How to Use Them

Malcolm H. B. McDonald
MA (Oxon), MSc, PhD, FRSA, FCIM

Third Edition

Published on behalf of the Chartered Institute of Marketing and the CAM Foundation

Butterworth-Heinemann
Linacre House, Jordan Hill, Oxford OX2 8DP
A division of Reed Educational and Professional Publishing Ltd

ℛ A member of the Reed Elsevier plc group

OXFORD   JOHANNESBURG   BOSTON
MELBOURNE   NEW DEHLI   SINGAPORE

First published 1984
Reprinted 1984, 1985, 1986, 1987, 1988
Second edition 1989
Reprinted 1990 (twice), 1992, 1993
Third edition 1995
Reprinted 1995, 1996, 1997

British Library Cataloguing in Publication Data
McDonald, M. H. B.
Marketing Plans: How to Prepare Them, How to Use Them.
– 3 Rev. ed. – (Marketing Series: Professional Development)
I. Title II. Series
658.802

ISBN 0 7506 2213 X

Typeset by Pure Tech Corporation, Pondicherry, India
Printed in Great Britain by The Bath Press, Bath

Contents

Preface

This is the Third Edition of a book which, since its launch in 1984, has helped and encouraged hundreds of thousands of practising managers with the difficult task of marketing planning. Many of them have been kind enough to write to me and thank me for the book's practical, no-nonsense style and approach to the subject. This has encouraged me to up-date the book to incorporate the findings of my latest research and experience in this difficult domain of marketing. This support has also encouraged me to strengthen the book considerably by the addition of a chapter which incorporates a step-by-step, 'this is how you do it' approach to the preparation of marketing plans. The result is a book which takes the reader painstakingly through the process of marketing planning, while also providing a detailed means of implementing all the concepts and methodologies outlined. I have done this because, in working with companies ranging from world leaders in their fields to small domestic companies, there continues to be much confusion between the *process* and *methods* of marketing planning and the actual *output* of this process, i.e. the marketing plan. I hope you will find this addition to the book of considerable value.

I have also expanded the book to incorporate much of the latest thinking in the domain of marketing, without trying to make it a detailed, specialist book on any particular aspect of marketing. For example, while there are sections on database marketing, competitive strategies and marketing research, readers would be well advised to turn to specialist books in these subjects for detailed methodologies.

The purpose of this book is quite simply to explain and demonstrate how to prepare and use a marketing plan. It is equally relevant for consumer, service and industrial goods companies, since the process is universal, although I have now included in the CIM series specialist books on marketing planning for retailers and marketing planning for service businesses.

It is based on my research into the marketing planning practices of industrial, service and retail companies, which has revealed marketing planning as an area of major weakness. Almost without exception, companies that thought they were planning were in fact only fore-casting and budgeting, and suffered grave operational difficulties as a result. The problem, as companies face up to the opportunities and challenges of the new millenium is not that the *philosophy* of marketing is not believed; rather it is that most companies, particularly industrial goods companies, have difficulty in making it work.

This is largely because of ignorance about the process of planning their marketing activities, for which little help is provided in the extant body of literature. Books or articles often turn out to be about the management of the several elements of the marketing mix rather than about how the process of combining them into a coherent plan can be managed. Others treat marketing planning in such a generalized way that it is difficult to distil from them any guidance of operational significance. Finally, there are many excellent papers about individual aspects of the marketing planning process.

The truth is, of course, that the actual *process* of marketing planning is simple in outline. Any book will tell us that it consists of: a situation review; assumptions; objectives; strategies; programmes; and measurement and review. What other books *do not* tell us is that there are a number of contextual issues that have to be considered that make marketing planning one of the most baffling of all management problems.

Here are some of those issues:

When should it be done, *how often*, by *whom*, and *how*?
Is it different in a *large* and a *small* company?
Is it different in a *diversified* and an *undiversified* company?
Is it different in an *international* and a *domestic* company?
What is the role of the *chief executive*?
What is the role of the *planning department*?
Should marketing planning be *top-down* or *bottom-up*?
What is the relationship between *operational* (one year) and *strategic* (longer term) planning?

Since effective marketing planning lies at the heart of a company's revenue-earning activities, it is not surprising that there is a great demand for a guide which strips away the confusion and mystery surrounding this subject and helps firms to get to grips with it in a practical and down-to-earth manner.

This book explains what marketing is, how the marketing planning process works, how to carry out a marketing audit, how to set marketing objectives and strategies, how to schedule and cost out what has to be done to achieve the objectives, and how to design and implement a simple marketing planning system.

I believe my approach is both logical and practical. This belief has been confirmed by the hundreds of letters referred to above, and by the fact that this book is now a standard text on many marketing courses in universities, and in-company training programmes around the world.*

This book includes:

○ Exercises to enable practising managers to translate the theory into practice
○ Mini case studies to exemplify the points being made

Computer-based training software is also available, on request, from Butterworth-Heinemann.

Additionally, a comprehensive Tutors' Guide is available for those who wish to teach the subject to others. This Tutors' Guide contains lecture plans, overhead transparency masters, case studies, tutors' discussion points and additional assignments for use by tutors.

We have taken reasonable steps in writing this book to avoid any kind of prejudice, or sexism. Where possible, for example, we have used the expression 'they', rather than 'he', or 'she'. On occasions, however, to avoid irritating the reader by unnecessary and convoluted English, we have used the word 'he'. Please be assured, however, that no deliberate offence is intended.

Malcolm H. B. McDonald
Cranfield School of Management
January 1995

*Further details of the PhD research on which this book is based are available from Professor Malcolm H. B. McDonald, Chairman of the Cranfield Marketing Planning Centre, Cranfield School of Management, Cranfield, Bedford, England, MK43 0AL.

How to use this book to achieve the best results

At the end of each chapter, you will find a number of application questions. More importantly, there are also a number of exercises designed to help you translate the theory into practice in the context of your own organization.

As you work through this book, you will find that some of the exercises are diagnostic and enable you to 'plot' where your company is. Some will help you to understand what might be happening to your company. Other exercises are more concerned with generating factual information about your company, its products, its markets or its planning processes. We find this combination of exercises not only provides you with insights and learning about many aspects of marketing planning, but it also helps you to assemble information which can contribute to a marketing plan for your company.

Whenever scoring and interpretation are required for an exercise, you will find the answers are provided at the end of each chapter.

This book is written to fulfil three principal needs. The first relates to the *process* of marketing planning, which, while theoretically simple, is in practice extraordinarily complex, involving, as it does, people, systems and organizational structures. One purpose, then, is to ensure that readers fully understand the process, what the pitfalls are and how to negotiate them.

The second purpose is to ensure that readers know which are the appropriate marketing diagnostic tools, structures and frameworks to use at each stage of the process.

The third and most important purpose, however, is to give both students and managers a no-nonsense, practical, step-by-step guide on how to prepare a really good, strategic marketing plan that will help their organizations to create sustainable competitive advantage for themselves and for their customers.

Marketing planning fastrack

While we do not wish to discourage anyone from taking the time to understand both the process and the diagnostic tools, we can, nonetheless, suggest that readers start by quickly reading through the whole of Chapter 13, which provides a step-by-step system for producing a marketing plan.

This should ensure that everyone is fully aware of the difference between the *process* and the *output* (i.e. the strategic marketing plan). For, let no one ever forget that it is the output of the process that ultimately matters. Having this overall picture first should make Chapters 1 to 12 more meaningful and enjoyable.

A note from the author

STOP

Producing an effective marketing plan that will give your organiza-tion competitive advantage is not easy. It takes knowledge, skills, intellect, creativity and, above all, time.

Everything you need to succeed is in this book, but you must be prepared to devote time to it. It is most definitely not a quick read!

FAST TRACK

However, for those who need a fast track to producing a marketing plan, Chapter 13 will help you. Be careful, however:

A little learning is a dangerous thing. Drink deep, or taste not the Pierian Spring

(Alexander Pope)

Professor Malcolm McDonald
Cranfield, January 1995

1 Understanding the marketing process

Summary

In Chapter 1, we discuss the marketing concept, company cap abilities, the marketing environment, customer wants, the marketing mix, confusion about what marketing is, what the customer really wants, whether consumer service and industrial marketing are different, and finally, whether you need a marketing department.

Readers who are already wholly familiar with the role of marketing in organizations may wish to go straight to Chapter 2, which begins to explain the marketing planning process.

The marketing concept

In 1776, when Adam Smith said that consumption is the sole end and purpose of production, he was in fact describing what in recent years has become known as the *marketing concept*.

> The central idea of marketing is of a matching between a company's capabilities and the wants of customers in order to achieve the objectives of both parties.

It is important at this stage to understand the difference between the marketing concept (often referred to as 'market orientation') and the marketing function, which is concerned with the management of the *marketing mix*. The management of the marketing mix involves using the various tools and techniques available to managers in order to implement the marketing concept.

For the sake of simplicity, these are often written about and referred to as the four Ps, these being Product, Price, Promotion and Place.

However, before any meaningful discussion can take place about how the marketing function should be managed, it is vital to have a full understanding about the idea of marketing itself (the marketing concept), and it is this issue that we principally address in this chapter.

Company capabilities

We have said that marketing is a matching process between a company's capabilities and the wants of customers. In Chapter 4 we will explain what we mean when we talk about customer wants. But for now, it is important to understand what we mean when we talk about a company's capabilities. To explain this more fully, let us imagine that we have been made redundant and have decided to set ourselves up in our own business.

The first thing we would have to do is to decide what it is that we can actually *do*. In answering this question we would quickly realize that our actual knowledge and skills restrict us very severely to certain obvious areas. For example, it would be difficult for a former sales manager to set himself up in business as an estate agent, or for an estate agent to start a marketing consultancy, unless, of course, both had the necessary skills and knowledge. A little thought will confirm that it is exactly the same for a company.

> **Many commercial disasters have resulted from companies diversifying into activities for which they were basically unsuited.**

One such case concerns a firm making connectors for the military and aviation markets. When these traditional markets went into decline, the company diversified into making connectors for several industrial markets such as consumer durables, automobiles and so on. Unfortunately these markets were so completely different from the ones that the company had been used to that they quickly went into a loss-making situation. Whereas the connector which the company had previously manufactured had been a highly engineered product made to the specifications of a few high technology customers, the company now had to mass produce simple connectors for broad markets. This meant making for stock and carrying field inventory. It also meant low competitive prices. The sales force did not know how to cope with the demands of their new markets. They had been used to making one or two calls a day and to having detailed technical discussions with buyers, whereas now they were expected to make eight or nine calls a day and to sell against many competitive products. Furthermore, the company just did not have the right image to succeed in the market. The results of all this were very serious indeed.

The lesson simply is that all firms have a unique set of capabilities in the form of resources and management skills which are not necessarily capable of taking advantage of *all* market opportunities as effectively, hence as competitively, as other firms. To summarize, the matching process between a company's capabilities and customer wants is fundamental to commercial success. That this is so will become clearer as we get further into the task of explaining the role and the nature of marketing.

The role of marketing in business

What causes success in the long run, by which we mean a continuous growth in earnings per share and in the capital value of the shares, has been shown by research* to depend on four elements:

*'Business Orientations and Corporate Success', Veronica Wong and John Saunders, *Journal of Strategic Marketing*, Vol. 1, No. 1, March 1993.

1 An excellent core product or service and all the associated R and D. Clearly, marketing will have a heavy input into this process. All this is showing is that companies with average products deserve average success.
2 Excellent, world class, state-of-the-art operations. All this is saying is that inefficiency today is likely to be punished. Marketing should, of course, have an input to defining operational efficiency in customer satisfaction terms. Where it is not allowed to, because of corporate culture, quality becomes a sterile ISO activity.
3 A culture which encourages and produces an infrastructure within which employees can be creative and entrepreneurial within the prescribed company procedures. Bored and boring people, for whom subservience and compliance is the norm, cause average performance.
4 Professional marketing departments, staffed by qualified professionals (not failed engineers, sales people or, indeed, failures from any other function). All this means is that companies who recruit professionally qualified marketers with appropriate experience have a far greater chance of success than those whose marketing departments are staffed by just about anybody who fancies themselves as marketers.

Given these ingredients and, above all else, a corporate culture which is not dominated (because of its history) by either production, operations, or financial orientation, all the evidence shows that marketing as a function makes a contribution to the achievement of corporate objectives.

The marketing environment

The matching process referred to earlier takes place in what we can call the *marketing environment*, which is the milieu in which the firm is operating. Perhaps the most obvious constituent of the marketing environment is our competitors, for what they do vitally affects our own behaviour as a company.

The point is that, since what our competitors do so vitally affects our own decisions, it is necessary to find some way of monitoring this and other elements of the environment and of building this into our decision-making process. In Chapter 11 we show how this can be done.

The *political, fiscal, economic* and *legal* policies of the governments of the countries where we sell our goods also determine what we can do. For example, inflation reduces the discretionary spending power of consumers, and this can result in market decline. Legislation concerning such things as labelling, packaging, advertising, environmentalism, and so on, all affect the way we run our business, and all these things have to be taken account of when we make our plans.

Technology is constantly changing, and we can no longer assume that our current range of products will continue to be demanded by our customers. For example, the introduction of non-drip paint had a profound effect on what had traditionally been a stable market. People discovered that they could use paint without causing a mess, and eventually this product was demanded in new kinds of outlets such as supermarkets. One can imagine what happened to some of those paint manufacturers who continued to make only their traditional products and to distribute them only through the more traditional outlets.

Such a change would also call for a change in pricing, promotional and distribution policies, and failure to realize this and to act accordingly would probably result in commercial failure.

The point is that the environment in which we operate is not controlled by us, and it is dynamic. Hence, it must be constantly monitored.

So far, we have talked about the three constituent parts of what we have described as a matching process:

- O The capabilities of a firm
- O The wants of customers
- O The marketing environment

Diagrammatically, it is shown in Figure 1.1.

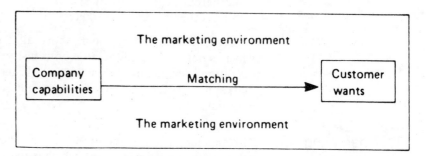

Figure 1.1

Customer wants

Although we shall be dealing with this subject in Chapter 4, let us briefly turn our attention to the subject of customer wants, so that we can complete our understanding of what marketing is.

Perhaps one of the greatest areas for misunderstanding in marketing concerns this question of customer wants. Companies are accused of manipulating innocent consumers by making them want things they do not really need.

If this were so, we would not have a situation in which a very high proportion of all new products launched actually fail! The fact is people have always had needs, such as, say, for home entertainment. What changes in the course of time is the way people satisfy this need. For example, television was only commercially viable because people needed home entertainment, and this was yet another way of fulfilling that need.

But let us not be fooled into believing that the customer, in the end, does not have the final say. All customer needs have many different ways of being satisfied, and wherever people have *choice* they will choose that product which they perceive as offering the greatest benefits to them at whatever price they are prepared to pay.

What this means, in effect, since all companies incur costs in taking goods or services to the market, is that profit, through customer satisfaction, is the only measure of efficacy or worth of what the commercial firm is doing.

> Cheapness, efficiency, quality (in the sense of international standards such as ISO) or, indeed, any other measure, are not criteria of effectiveness, since there is little point in producing anything cheaply, efficiently or perfectly if people don't actually want it.

Since costs are incurred in producing goods, it is necessary to find customers to buy those goods at a sufficiently high price and in sufficient volume (margin × turnover) to enable the company to cover its costs and to make a surplus (or profit). This is an economic necessity to enable the company to stay in business and means that, unless what is being offered is seen by customers as satisfying their wants, they will not buy it.

> Thus, in the commercial sector, research has shown that there is a direct link between long-run profitability and the ability of a firm to understand its customers' needs and provide value for them. For industries previously protected from competition, such as the airline industry and telecommunications, many now know that sustainable profitability can only come in the long run through continuous customer satisfaction.

In the not-for-profit sector, customer satisfaction is obviously a proxy for profitability.

To summarize, any organization that continues to offer something for which there is a long-term fundamental decline in demand, unless it is prepared to change so as to be more in tune with what the market wants, in the end will go out of business. Even less sensible would be for a government, or a parent company, to subsidize such an operation, since we know that to go on producing what people do not want is economically inefficient, especially when people will get what they want from abroad if they cannot buy it in their home country.

The same line of reasoning must also apply to those who continually counsel increased productivity as the only answer to our economic problems. Unfortunately any additional production would more than likely end up in stock unless people actually wanted what was being produced.

It would be different, of course, if there was only a temporary hiccup in demand, but, unfortunately, this is rarely the case, because markets are dynamic and we must learn as a company to adapt and change as our markets mutate.

Central to this question of customer wants is an understanding that there is rarely such a thing as 'a market'. To start with, it is clear that it is customers who buy products, not markets. A market is merely an aggregation of customers sharing similar needs and wants. In reality, most markets consist of a number of sub-markets, each of which is different. For example, the airline market consists of freight and passenger transport. The passenger side can be subdivided further into VFR (visiting friends and relatives), high rated (business travel), charter, and so on. Failure to understand the needs of these very different customer groups would result in failure to provide the desired services at an acceptable price.

Of course, it is not quite as easy as this, which is why we devote the whole of Chapter 4 to this very important aspect of what we call 'market segmentation'. But for now all that it is necessary to understand is that our ability to identify groups of customer wants which our particular company capabilities are able to satisfy profitably is central to marketing management.

The marketing mix

As we have already said, managing the marketing mix involves the use of the tools and techniques of marketing. Thus, in order for the matching process to take place, we need *information*. External and internal marketing information flows (marketing research) and database management are discussed further in Chapter 11.

Having found out what customers want, we must develop products to satisfy those wants. This is known as 'product management' and is discussed in Chapter 5. Obviously we must charge a price for our products, and this is discussed in Chapter 9.

We must also get our products into our customers' hands, thus giving a time and a place utility to our product. Distribution and customer service are discussed in Chapter 10.

All that remains now is to tell our customers about our products, for we can be certain that customers will not beat a path to our door to buy whatever it is we are making. Here we must consider all forms of communication, especially advertising, personal selling, and sales promotion. These are discussed in Chapters 7 and 8.

Finally we must consider how to tie it all together in the form of a marketing plan. This latter point is so important that the whole of the next two chapters are devoted to a discussion of the marketing planning process.

Confusion about what marketing is – veneer or substance?

It is a sad reflection on the state of marketing that in spite of almost fifty years of marketing education, ignorance still abounds concerning what marketing is.

The marketing function (or department) never has, nor ever will be, effective in an organization whose history to date is one of technical, production, operations or financial orientation. Such enterprises have long since adopted the vocabulary of marketing and applied a veneer of marketing terminology.

Thus, some of the High Street banks have spent fortunes on hiring marketing people, often from FMCG, producing expensive TV commercials and creating a multiplicity of products, brochures and leaflets. Yet still most customers would have difficulty in distinguishing between the major players (so where's the competitive advantage?) or even finding their branch open when they wish to visit it.

Is this marketing in the sense of understanding and meeting customers' needs better than the competition or is it old-fashioned selling with the name changed, where we try to persuade customers to buy what we want to sell them, how, when and where we want to sell it?

The computer industry provides perhaps even clearer examples. For years they have used the word 'marketing' quite indiscriminately as they tried to persuade customers to buy the ever more complex outpourings of their technology. At least one major hardware manufacturer used to call its Branch Sales Managers 'Marketing Managers' to create the illusion of a local process of understanding and responding to customer needs. Racked by recession, decline and huge losses, this is an industry which only now is going through the birth-pangs of marketing and having to change root and branch the way it goes about its business.

The following are the major areas of confusion about marketing:

1 Confusion with sales

One managing director aggressively announced to everyone at the beginning of a seminar in Sydney, Australia, 'There's no time for marketing in my company until sales improve!' Confusion with sales is still one of the biggest barriers to be overcome.

2 Confusion with product management

The belief that all a company has to do to succeed is to produce a good product also still abounds, and neither Concorde; the EMI Scanner, nor the many thousands of brilliant products that have seen their owners or inventors go bankrupt during the past twenty years will convince such people otherwise.

3 Confusion with advertising

This is another popular misconception and the annals of business are replete with examples such as Dunlop, Woolworths and British Airways who, before they got professional management in, won awards with their brilliant advertising campaigns, while failing to deliver the goods. Throwing advertising expenditure at the problem is still a very popular way of tackling deep-rooted marketing problems.

4 Confusion with customer service

The 'Have a nice day' syndrome is currently having its heyday in many countries of the world, originally popularized, of course, by Peters and Waterman in *In Search of Excellence*.

Many organizations now know, of course, that training staff to be nice to customers does not help a lot if the basic offer is fundamentally wrong. For example, in many railway companies around the world, while it helps to be treated nicely, it is actually much more important to get there on time!

It should by now be obvious that those people who talk about 'the sharp end', by which they usually mean personal selling, as being the only thing that matters in marketing, have probably got it wrong.

Selling is just one aspect of communication with customers, and to say that it is the only thing that matters is to ignore the importance of product management, pricing, distribution and other forms of communication in achieving profitable sales. Selling is just one part of this process, in which the transaction is actually clinched. It is the culmination of the marketing process, and success will only be possible if all the other elements of the marketing mix have been properly managed. Imagine having a horse that didn't have four legs! The more attention that is paid to finding out what customers want, to developing products to satisfy these wants, to pricing at a level consistent with the benefits offered, to gaining distribution, and to communicating effectively with our target market, the more likely we are to be able to exchange contracts through the personal selling process.

Likewise, it is naive to assume that marketing is all about advertising, since it is by now clear that advertising is only one aspect of communication. Many firms waste their advertising expenditure because they have not properly identified what their target market is.

> For example, one public transport company spent a quarter of a million pounds advertising how reliable their bus service was when, in reality, utilization of buses by the public was declining because they somehow felt that buses were working class! This was a classic case of believing that advertising will increase sales irrespective of what the message is. Had this company done its research, it could have decided to what extent and how advertising could be used to overcome this prejudice. As it was, the company spent a small fortune telling people something that was largely irrelevant!

In reality, many companies spend more on advertising when times are good and less on advertising when times are bad. Cutting the advertising budget is often seen as an easy way of boosting the profit and loss account when a firm is below its budgeted level of profit. This tendency is encouraged by the fact that this can be done without any apparent immediate adverse effect on sales. Unfortunately, this is just another classic piece of misunderstanding about marketing and about the role of advertising in particular. The belief here is that advertising is *caused* by sales! Also, it is naive in the extreme to assume that advertising effectiveness can be measured in terms of sales when it is only a part of the total marketing process.

What does the customer want?

Finally, we have to beware of what the words 'finding out what the customer wants', which appear in most definitions of marketing, really mean. The reality, of course, is that most advances in customer satisfaction are technology-driven. For example, the fabulous technological breakthroughs that occurred as a result of the Houston space programme, when the Americans put two men on the moon, have provided thousands of opportunities for commercial exploitation. The role of marketing has been to find commercial application for the technology.

The truth, of course, is that there are two kinds of research and development:

○ Technology-driven
○ Market-driven

From the kind of technology-driven programmes that take place on science parks and in laboratories around the world, come opportunities for commercial exploitation.

> From the kind of market-driven programmes that most companies engage in come incremental, and sometimes discontinuous, improvements to product performance. Both are legitimate activities. The former has been glamorized and popularized by companies such as 3M, who claim to encourage and institutionalize unfocused scientific research. This has led to the formation of a number of new businesses and product launches, the most famous of which is Post-It.

The main point to remember, however, is that customers do not really know what they want! All they really want are better ways of solving their problems, so one of the main tasks of marketing is to understand the customers and their problems in depth so that we can continuously work on ways of making life easier for them. Whether this happens as a result of serendipity or focused research and development is less important than the end result.

Are industrial, consumer and service marketing different?

The central ideas of marketing are universal and it makes no difference whether we are marketing furnaces, insurance policies or margarine. Yet problems sometimes arise when we try to implement marketing ideas in service companies and industrial goods companies. A service does not lend itself to being specified in the same way as a product, as it does not have the same reproducible physical dimensions that can be measured. Thus, with the purchase of any service, there is a large element of trust on the part of the buyer, who can only be sure of the quality and performance of the service after it has been completed. Largely because of this, the salesperson actually selling the service obviously becomes part of the service, since this is one of the principal ways in which the potential efficacy of the service can be assessed. Additionally, a service product cannot be made in advance and stored for selling 'off the shelf' at some later stage. Nonetheless, apart from some differences in emphasis, the principles of marketing apply to services in exactly the same way.

Industrial goods are simply those goods sold to industrial businesses, institutional or government buyers for incorporation into their own products, to be resold, or to be used by them within their own business. Principal types of industrial goods are raw materials, components, capital goods and maintenance, repair and operating goods and equipment.

The fact that the share of world trade enjoyed by some industrial countries has slumped so dramatically over the past thirty years is not generally because their products were not as good as those produced by other countries, but because they failed to *market* them as effectively as their competitors, and there is much government, university and trade body evidence to support this view.

One reason for this is that many industrial goods companies naively believe that the name of the game is making well-engineered products. Making well-engineered products is all some companies are concerned about, in spite of the fact that all the evidence points to the conclusion that more often than not it is for other reasons that the final choice is actually made. Failure to understand the importance of market segmentation (to be discussed in Chapter 4), market share, service, and repuration, among other things, is the principal reason why such companies fail to compete successfully in so many world markets. Making what they consider to be good products and then giving them to the sales force to get rid of is just not enough.

Failure to understand the importance of market segmentation is the principal reason for failure to compete effectively in world markets.

But, quite apart from the fact that there appears to be a sort of status about being in engineering which sometimes acts as a barrier to the consideration of marketing issues, it is also a fact that marketing is difficult in many industrial markets. This makes it inevitable that managers will resort to doing things they can understand. For example, demand for all industrial products is derived from the demand for consumer products, which adds greater uncertainty to decision-making and makes forecasting extremely difficult.

Figure 1.2

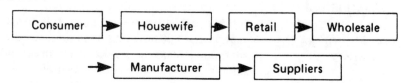

It can be readily appreciated from Figure 1.2 that the further a company gets from the eventual consumer, the less control it has over demand. Take the example of a brewer. He can communicate direct with his consumers whereas the company making his plant, and the suppliers in turn to the plant company, are, in the final analysis, dependent on the ultimate consumer and they are less able to influence what he does.

Also, information about industrial markets is not so readily available as in consumer goods markets, which makes it more difficult to measure changes in market share. There are other difficulties besides these, which make marketing in the industrial area more difficult.

Unfortunately, the answer to this problem by many companies has been to recruit a 'marketing person' and leave them to get on with the job of marketing. But it will now be obvious that such a solution can never work, because the marketing concept, if it is to work at all, has to be understood and practised by all executives in a firm, not just by the marketing manager. Otherwise everyone goes on behaving just as they did before and the marketing person quickly becomes ineffective.

Again, however, the conclusion must be that, apart from differences in emphasis, the principles of marketing apply in exactly the same way.

Do you need a marketing department?

This brings us finally to the question of whether it is necessary for a company to have a marketing department.

It is not essential to have a formalized marketing department for the analysis, planning and control of the matching process. This is particularly so in small, undiversified companies where the chief executive has an in-depth understanding of his customers' needs. Even in large companies it is not necessary to have a marketing department, because the management of products can be left to the engineers, pricing can be managed by the accountants, distribution can be managed by distribution specialists, and selling and advertising can be managed by the Sales Manager.

The dangers in this approach, however, are obvious. Technicians often place too much emphasis on the physical aspects of the products, accountants can be too concerned with costs rather than with market values, distribution people can often succeed in optimizing their own objectives for stock, yet at the same time sub-optimizing other more important aspects of the business, such as customer service, and selling and promotion can often be carried out in a way which may not be in the best interests of the firm's overall goals.

However, as a company's product range and customer types grow, and as competitive pressures and environmental turbulence increase, so it often becomes necessary to organize the management of marketing under one central control function, otherwise there is a danger of ending up with the kind of product which is brilliant technically, but disastrous commercially.

It is absurd to believe that marketing is the sole domain of those in the organization who happen to belong to the marketing department.

In professional organisations, great care is necessary in thinking about the appropriate organizational form for marketing. For example, in a postgraduate business school, the major role of the marketing department has traditionally been in the domain of promotion and information coordination. Whilst it does obviously act as a facilitator for strategy development, it is intellectually simplistic to imagine that it could be the originator of strategy. In some other service organizations, the central marketing function might also provide the systems to enable others to carry out effective marketing, but in such organizations marketing departments never have, nor ever will, actually do marketing.

The reasons are obvious. If the term 'marketing' is intended to embrace all those related activities, to demand creation and satisfaction and the associated intelligence, then it is clear that most marketing takes place during the service delivery and customer contact process, in all its forms. Marketing, then, reflects this process and it is absurd to believe that it is the sole domain of those people in the organization who happen to belong to the marketing department.

As Alan Mitchell said in the February 1994 issue of *Marketing Business*, 'To say the Marketing Department is responsible for marketing is like saying love is the responsibility of one family member.'

It is equally absurd to suggest that the personnel department should actually do personnel management, with all other managers in the organization having nothing to do with people. The same could be said for finance and information systems. Indeed, it is such myopic functional separation that got most organizations into the mess they are in today.

Much more important, however, than who is responsible for marketing in an organization, is the question of its marketing orientation, i.e. the degree to which the company as a whole understands the importance of finding out what customer groups want and of organizing all the company's resources to satisfy those wants at a profit.

Application questions

1 Describe as best you can what you think marketing means in your company.
2 Describe the role of your marketing department, if you have one.
3 If you do not have a marketing department, describe how decisions are made in respect of the following:

   ○ The product itself
   ○ Price
   ○ Customer service levels
   ○ Physical distribution
   ○ Advertising
   ○ Sales promotion
   ○ The sales force
   ○ Information about markets

4 How do you distinguish between marketing, promotion and selling in your organization?
5 Would you say your products are what the market wants, or what you prefer to produce?
6 Do you start your planning process with a sales forecast and then work out a budget, or do you start by setting marketing objectives, which are based on a thorough review of the previous year's performance? If the former, describe why you think this is better than the latter.

Review of Chapter 1

The marketing concept

Providing goods or services for which there is a known customer demand, as opposed to selling what the company likes to produce. By focusing on customers and their wants the company is better positioned to make a profit. The company is then said to be market-led, or to have a 'market orientation'. *Try Exercise 1.1*

Company capabilities

The company will not be equally good at all things. It will have strengths and weaknesses. The astute company tries to identify customer wants that best match its own strengths, be they its product range, relations with customers, technical expertise, flexibility, or whatever. Inevitably there is an element of compromise in the matching process, but successful companies strive to build on their strengths and reduce their weaknesses. *Try Exercise 1.2*

The marketing environment

No business operates in a vacuum; it has an environment which not only contains all its existing and potential customers and its competitors, but many factors outside its control. Changes in the environment in terms of

- customer wants
- fashions
- technology
- environmental concern
- legislation
- economic climate
- competition, etc.

present the company with both opportunities and threats. Keeping a finger on the pulse of the environment is essential for the successful company. *Try Exercise 1.3*

Questions raised for the company

1 Is it different marketing a product or a service?
 The central ideas of marketing are universal.
2 What do customers want?
 They don't always know, but dialogue with them and intelligent research can help to answer this question.
3 Do we need to bother with marketing?
 Some companies are very successful by chance. They happen to be in the right place at the right time. Most other companies need to plan their marketing. *Try Exercise 1.4*
4 Do we need a marketing department?
 Not necessarily. It will depend upon the size and complexity of the company's range of products and services. The higher the complexity, the more difficult it is to coordinate activities and achieve the 'matching' of a company to its customers.

Introduction to
Chapter 1
exercises

Exercise 1.1
Marketing
orientation

The exercises are intended to give you an opportunity to explore ways of looking at marketing. Exercise 1.1 enables you to make an assessment of your own beliefs about marketing; the remaining exercises can be applied to your organization.

Below are a number of definitions of marketing that have appeared in books and journals over the last twenty or so years. Read through them carefully and note on a piece of paper the numbers of those which most accurately reflect your own views.

While there is no upper limit to the number of definitions you can choose, try, if you can, to limit your choice to a maximum of nine or ten definitions.

1 'The planning and execution of all aspects and activities of a product so as to exert optimum influence on the consumer, to result in maximum consumption at the optimum price and thereby producing the maximum long term profit.'

2 'Deciding what the customer wants; arranging to make it; distributing and selling it at a profit.'

3 'Marketing perceives consumption as a democratic process in which consumers have the right to select preferred candidates. They elect them by casting their money votes to those who supply the goods or services that satisfy their needs.'

4 'The planning, executing and evaluating of the external factors related to a company's profit objectives.'

5 'Adjusting the whole activity of a business to the needs of the customer or potential customer.'

6 '. . . marketing is concerned with the idea of satisfying the needs of customers by means of the product and a whole cluster of things associated with creating, delivering and, finally, consuming it.'

7 'The total system of interacting business activities designed to plan, price, promote and distribute products and services to present and potential customers.'

8 '(Marketing is) the world of business seen from the point of view of its final result, that is from the customer's viewpoint. Concern and responsibility for marketing must therefore permeate all areas of the enterprise.'

9 'The activity that can keep in constant touch with an organization's consumers, read their needs and build a programme of communications to express the organization's purposes.'

10 'The management function which organizes and directs all those business activities involved in assessing and converting customer purchasing power into effective demand for a specific product or service and moving the product or service to the final customer or user so as to achieve the profit target or other objectives set by the company.'

11 'The marketing concept emphasizes the vital importance to effective corporate planning and control, of monitoring both the environment in which the offering is made and the needs of the customers, in order that the process may operate as effectively as is humanly possible.'

12 'The organization and performance of those business activities that facilitate the exchange of goods and services between maker and user.'

13 'The process of: (1) Identifying customer needs, (2) Conceptualizing these needs in terms of the organization's capacity to produce, (3) Communicating that conceptualization to the appropriate locus of power in the organization, (4) Conceptualizing the consequent output in terms of the customer needs earlier identified, (5) Communicating that conceptualization to the customer.'

14 '(In a marketing company) all activities – from finance to production to marketing – should be geared to profitable consumer satisfaction.'

15 'The performance of those business activities that direct the flow of goods from producer to consumer or user.'

16 'The skill of selecting and fulfilling consumer wants so as to maximize the profitability per unit of capital employed in the enterprise.'

17 'The economic process by means of which goods and services are exchanged and their values determined in terms of money prices.'

18 'The performance of business activities that direct the flow of goods and services from producer to consumer in order to accomplish the firm's objectives.'

19 'Marketing is concerned with preventing the accumulation of non-moving stocks.'

20 'The activity that can keep in constant touch with an organization's consumers, read their needs and build a programme of communications to express the organization's purposes . . . and means of satisfying them.'

Scoring for Exercise 1.1

You should have selected a number of definitions that you identify with. To work out your score, tick the boxes in the table below which equate to your chosen statements. Now add the number of ticks in each group and enter the total in the boxes at the end of each row.

| Group A | 1 | 2 | 4 | 7 | 10 | 12 | 15 | 17 | 18 | 19 | |
| Group B | 3 | 5 | 6 | 8 | 9 | 11 | 13 | 14 | 16 | 20 | |

For example, if you selected definitions 1, 3, 5, 6, 10 and 14, then 1 and 10 would score a total of 2 in Group A and 3, 5, 6 and 14 would score a total of 4 in Group B.

Interpretation of Exercise 1.1

If you study the various definitions, you will find that the essential difference between those in Group A and those in Group B is that *Group B definitions make an unambiguous reference about identifying and satisfying customer needs and building systems around this principle.* This is generally accepted as true marketing orientation, and is the stance taken throughout this book about marketing.

Group A definitions tend to focus far less on the customer (unless it is to *decide* what customers want, or to *exert influence* on the customer, i.e. to do things to the customer) and more on the company's own systems and profit motives. Thus Group A definitions could be described as being more traditional views about managing a business. Therefore the more Group B and the fewer Group A answers you have, then the higher your marketing orientation and the less at odds you should be with the ideas put forward in this book.

Please note that this is your personal orientation towards marketing and nothing to do with your company.

Exercise 1.2 Company capabilities and the matching process

1 Reflect on your company's recent history, say the last five years. Over that period, what would you say have been the key strengths that have carried the company to its present position?

(a) Make a list of these below. *Note*: In a small company, among the strengths might be listed key people. Where this happens, expand on what the person actually brings to the organization, e.g. sales director – his/her contacts in the industry.

(b) What would you say are the three main weaknesses at present?

(i) ....

(ii) ....

(iii) ....

2 Again, considering the last five-year period, has the company got better at matching its strengths to customers and to its business environment, or worse?

Often there are both positive and negative forces at work.

(a) Make a note of the factors which led to improvements in the space below.

(b) Make a note of the factors which led to a deterioration in the space below.

At this stage you do not need to draw any specific conclusions from this exercise, although you will probably find it useful to return to this information as you progress through the book.

Exercise 1.3 The marketing environment

You will be asked to consider the marketing environment in more detail later. For now, think back over the last five years of the company's history and answer these questions:

1 Which were the three most significant *opportunities* in the environment which contributed to the company's success/present situation?

(a) .... ( )

(b) .... ( )

(c) .... ( )

Put a score against each factor listed, in the bracket, using a 1–10 scale (where 10 is extremely significant).

2 Which were the three most significant *threats* which operated against the company over this period and which inhibited its success?

(a) .... ( )

(b) .... ( )

(c) .... ( )

Again, score these threats on a 1–10 scale as above.

3 Reflect on what you have written above and consider whether or not these opportunities and threats are increasing or decreasing in significance, or if new ones are on the horizon. Make notes below, looking ahead for, say, the next three years.

Opportunities → ....

Threats → ....

Again, at this stage, you do not need to draw any specific conclusions from this exercise, although you will probably find it useful to return to this information as you progress through the book.

Exercise 1.4 Marketing quiz*

Place a tick after each statement in the column which most accurately describes your company situation.

	Very true	True	Don't know	Un-true	Very untrue
1 (a) Our return on invested capital is satisfactory.					
(b) There is good evidence it will stay that way for the next 5 years.					
(c) Detailed analysis indicates that it is probably incapable of being materially improved.					
2 (a) Our market share is not declining.					
(b) This is a fact, based on objective evidence.					
(c) There is objective evidence that it will stay that way.					
3 (a) Our turnover is increasing.					
(b) At a rate faster than inflation.					
(c) But not at the expense of profitability.					

*Adapted by Professor M. H. B. McDonald from a questionnaire devised by Harry Henry Associates in 1971.

	Very true	True	Don't know	Un- true	Very untrue
4 I know for sure that our sales organization is only allowed to push less profitable lines at the expense of more profitable ones if there are rational reasons for doing so.					
5 (a) I understand why the company has performed the way it has during the past 5 years.					
(b) I know (apart from hoping) where it is heading during the next 5 years.					
6 (a) I am wholly satisfied that we make what the market wants, not what we prefer to produce.					
(b) Our production, marketing, selling and advertising strategies are developed for the profitability of the company as a whole rather than for the gratification of any personal ambitions.					
(c) I am satisfied that we do not use short-term tactics which are injurious to our long-term interests.					
7 (a) I know that sales and profit forecasts presented by operating management are realistic.					
(b) I know they are as exacting as they can reasonably be.					
(c) If I or anyone insists that they are raised, it is because a higher level is attainable not just because a better-looking budget is required.					
8 (a) The detailed data generated internally are analysed to provide timely information about what is happening in the key areas of the business.					
(b) Marketing research data which operating management acquires is synthesized into plain English and is actually needed and used in the key decision-making process.					
9 (a) We do not sell unprofitably to any customer.					
(b) We analyse our figures to be sure of this.					

	Very true	True	Don't know	Un- true	Very untrue
(c) If we do, it is for rational reasons known to us all.					
10 Our marketing policies are based on market-centred opportunities which we have fully researched, not on vague hopes of doing better.					

Join up the ticks down the page and count how many are to the left of the *don't know* position, and how many are at the *don't know* position or to the right of it.

Interpretation of Exercise 1.4

If you have 11 or more answers in the *don't know* position or to the right of it, then the chances are that your company isn't very marketing-orientated. It needs to take a closer look at itself in the ways suggested by this book.

Scores between 12 and 20 to the left of the *don't know* position indicate an organization that appears to have reasonable control of many of the significant ingredients of commercial success. Nonetheless, there is clearly still room for improvement, and this book should be useful in bringing about such an improvement.

Scores above 20 to the left of the *don't know* position indicate an organization completely in command of the key success variables. Are you *certain* that this is a true reflection of your organization's situation? If you are, then the chances are that its marketing skills are already highly developed. However, this book will still be useful for newcomers to the marketing function who wish to learn about the marketing process, and it will certainly help to maintain your high standards.

2 The marketing planning process: 1 The main steps

Summary

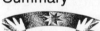

In Chapter 2, we discuss what marketing planning is, why it is essential, the difference between a tactical and strategic marketing plan, the marketing planning process, what a marketing audit is, why it is necessary, the form of the audit, its place in the management audit, when and who should carry out an audit, what happens to the results of an audit, how marketing planning relates to corporate planning, what assumptions, marketing objectives, marketing strategies and programmes are, how plans should be used, what a budget is, what should appear in a strategic plan, and, finally, what a mission statement is.

What is marketing planning?

Any manager will readily agree that a sensible way to manage the sales and marketing function is to find a systematic way of identifying a range of options, to choose one or more of them, then to schedule and cost out what has to be done to achieve the objectives.

This process can be defined as *marketing planning*, which is the planned application of marketing resources to achieve marketing objectives.

Marketing planning, then, is simply a logical sequence and a series of activities leading to the setting of marketing objectives and the formulation of plans for achieving them. Companies generally go through some kind of management process in developing marketing plans. In small, undiversified companies this process is usually informal. In larger, more diversified organizations the process is often systematized. Conceptually, this process is very simple and involves a situation review, the formulation of some basic assumptions, setting objectives for what is being sold and to whom, deciding on how the objectives are to be achieved, and scheduling and costing out the actions necessary for implementation.

> The problem is that, while as a process it is intellectually simple to understand, in practice it is the most difficult of all marketing tasks.

The reason is that it involves bringing together into one coherent plan all the elements of marketing, and in order to do this at least some degree of institutionalized procedures is necessary. It is this which seems to cause so much difficulty for companies.

Another difficulty concerns the cultural, organizational and political problems that surround the process itself. This will be dealt with in Chapter 3.

> The purpose of this chapter is to explain as simply as possible what marketing planning is, and how the process works, before going on to expand on the more important components of marketing planning in later chapters.

One reason for this difficulty is that there is not much guidance available to management on how the process itself might be managed, proceeding as it does from reviews to objectives, strategies, programmes, budgets and back again, until some kind of acceptable compromise is reached between what is desirable and what is practicable, given all the constraints that any company has.

Another reason is that a planning system itself is little more than a structured approach to the process just described. But because of the varying size, complexity, character and diversity of commercial operations, there can be no such thing as an 'off the peg' system that can be implemented without some pretty fundamental amendments to suit the situation-specific requirements of each company.

Also, the degree to which any company can develop an integrated, coordinated and consistent plan depends on a deep understanding of the marketing planning process itself as a means of sharpening the focus within all levels of management within an organization.

Why is marketing planning essential?

There can be little doubt that marketing planning is essential when we consider the increasingly hostile and complex environment in which companies operate. Hundreds of external and internal factors interact in a bafflingly complex way to affect our ability to achieve profitable sales. Also, let us consider for a moment the four typical objectives which companies set: maximizing revenue; maximizing profits; maximizing return on investment; and minimizing costs. Each one of these has its own special appeal to different managers within the company, depending on the nature of their particular function. In reality, the best that can ever be achieved is a kind of 'optimum compromise', because each of these objectives could be considered to be in conflict in terms of equivalences.

Managers of a company have to have some understanding or view about how all these variables interact and managers must try to be rational about their business decisions, no matter how important intuition, feel and experience are as contributory factors in this process of rationality.

Most managers accept that some kind of formalized procedure for marketing planning helps sharpen this rationality so as to reduce the complexity of business operations and add a dimension of realism to the company's hopes for the future. Because it is so difficult, however, most companies rely only on sales forecasting and budgeting systems. It is a well-known fact that any fool can write figures down! All too frequently, however, they bear little relationship to the real opportunities and problems facing a company. It is far more difficult to write down marketing objectives and strategies.

Apart from the need to cope with increasing turbulence, environmental complexity, more intense competitive pressures, and the sheer speed of technological change, a marketing plan is useful:

o For *you*	o To help identify sources of competitive advantage
	o To force an organized approach
	o To develop specificity
	o To ensure consistent relationships
o For *superiors*	o To inform
o For *non-marketing functions*	o To get resources
o For *subordinates*	o To get support
	o To gain commitment
	o To set objectives and strategies

Are wo talking about a tactical or a strategic marketing plan?

The author's own research has shown that, in peering into the murky depths of organizational behaviour in relation to marketing planning, confusion reigns supreme, and nowhere more than over the terminology of marketing.

Few practising marketers understand the real significance of a *strategic* marketing plan as opposed to a *tactical*, or operational marketing plan.

Why should this be so? For an answer, we need to look at some of the changes that have taken place during the past two decades. For example, the simple environment of the 1970s and early 1980s, characterized by growth and the easy marketability of products and services, has now been replaced by an increasingly complex and abrasive environment, often made worse by static or declining markets. For most, the days have gone when it was only necessary to ride the tidal wave of growth. There wasn't the same need for a disciplined, systematic approach to the market. A tactical, short-term approach to marketing planning seemed to work perfectly well in such conditions. But, by failing to grasp the nettle of strategic orientation in plans that identify and develop their distinctive competence, companies have become, or will increasingly become, casualties during the late 1990s.

The problem is really quite simple.

> Most managers prefer to sell the products they find easiest to sell to those customers who offer the least line of resistance. By developing short-term, tactical marketing plans first and then extrapolating them, managers merely succeed in extrapolating their own shortcomings.

It is a bit like steering from the wake – all right in calm, clear waters, but not so sensible in busy and choppy waters! Preoccupation with preparing a detailed one-year plan first is typical of those many companies who confuse sales forecasting and budgeting with strategic marketing planning – in our experience the most common mistake of all.

This brings us to the starting point in marketing planning – an understanding of the difference between strategy and tactics and the

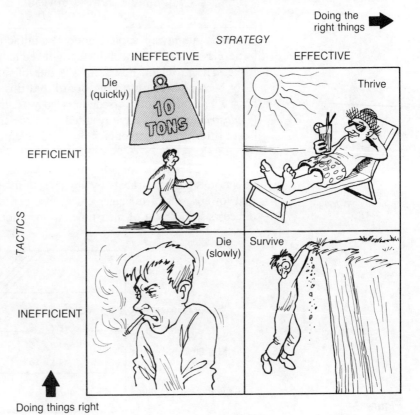

Figure 2.1

association with the relevant adjectives, 'effective' and 'efficient'. Figure 2.1 shows a matrix in which the horizontal axis represents strategy as a continuum from ineffective to effective. The vertical axis represents tactics on a continuum from inefficient to efficient. Those firms with an effective strategy and efficient tactics continue to thrive, while those with an effective strategy but inefficient tactics have merely survived. Many such firms have devoted much of their time and energy to shedding unnecessary and inefficient peripheral activities and are once more moving towards the top right-hand box. Many, of course, have gone bankrupt because they didn't move quickly enough.

Those firms to the left of the matrix are destined to die. It is in circumstances like this where the old style management fails. Unfortunately, companies place too much emphasis on tactics and not enough on strategy. The problem with this is that, if they become efficient but still fail to address the underlying strategic issues surrounding changing market needs and how to meet these needs to achieve growth, they tend to die more quickly. It's a little like making a stupid salesperson work twice as hard, the only effect of which would be to increase the chaos!

> Already, companies led by chief executives with a proactive orientation that stretches beyond the end of the current fiscal year have begun to show results visibly better than the old reactive companies with only a short-term vision.

> One Scandinavian capital goods manufacturer was devoting its energies to stock control, headcount reduction, cash-flow and the like. The problem, however, was one of falling demand. Had it not been pointed out to the Board that this underlying marketing issue had to be addressed, it is easy to imagine how *anorexia industrialosa* could have resulted (an excessive desire to be leaner and fitter, leading to emaciation and, eventually, death).

Figure 2.2 shows the old style of company in which very little attention is paid to strategy by any level of management. It will be seen that lower levels of management do not get involved at all, while the directors spend most of their time on operational/tactical issues.

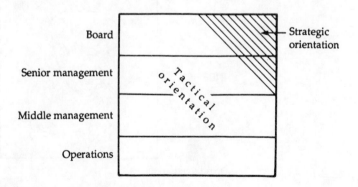

Figure 2.2

Figure 2.3 is a representation of those companies that recognize the importance of strategy and who manage to involve all levels of management in strategy formulation.

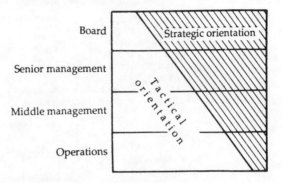

Figure 2.3

The rule, then, is simple:

○ Develop the *strategic* marketing plan first. This entails greater emphasis on scanning the external environment: the early identification of forces emanating from it, and developing appropriate strategic responses, involving all levels of management in the process.
○ A strategic plan should cover a period of between three and five years, and only when this has been developed and agreed should the one-year operational marketing plan be developed. Never write the one-year plan first and extrapolate it.

> The emphasis throughout this book is on the preparation of a *strategic* marketing plan. The format for an operational or tactical plan is exactly the same, except for the amount of detail. This will be dealt with in Chapter 13.

The marketing planning process

Figure 2.4 illustrates the several stages that have to be gone through in order to arrive at a marketing plan.

A recent major study of leading companies carried out by the author showed that a strategic marketing plan should contain:

○ A mission statement.
○ A financial summary of the revenue and profits to be achieved during the planning period.
○ A summary of the principal external factors which affected the company's marketing performance during the previous year, together with a statement of the company's strengths and weaknesses *vis-à-vis* the competition. This is what we call a SWOT (i.e. strengths, weaknesses, opportunities, threats) analysis.
○ A portfolio of the SWOT.
○ Some assumptions about the key determinants of marketing success and failure.

The ten steps of the strategic marketing planning process

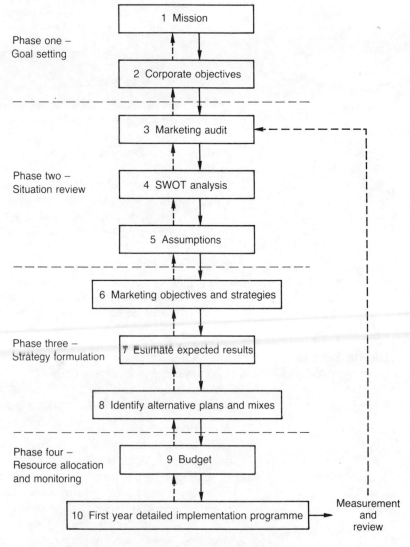

**The strategic plan
(output of the planning process)**

Mission statement
Financial summary
Market overview
SWOT analyses
Portfolio summary
Assumptions
MArketing objectives and strategies
Three-year forecasts and budgets

1 Mission

Phase one –
Goal setting

2 Corporate objectives

3 Marketing audit

Phase two –
Situation review

4 SWOT analysis

5 Assumptions

6 Marketing objectives and strategies

Phase three –
Strategy formulation

7 Estimate expected results

8 Identify alternative plans and mixes

Phase four –
Resource allocation
and monitoring

9 Budget

10 First year detailed implementation programme

Measurement
and
review

Figure 2.4

○ Overall marketing objectives and strategies.
○ Programmes containing details of timing, responsibilities and
costs, with sales forecasts and budgets.

Each of the stages illustrated here will be discussed in more detail later in this chapter.

The dotted lines are meant to indicate the reality of the planning process, in that it is likely that each of these steps will have to be gone through more than once before final programmes can be written.

Although research has shown these marketing planning steps to be universally applicable, the degree to which each of the separate steps in the diagram needs to be formalized depends to a large extent on the size and nature of the company. For example an *undiversified* company generally uses less formalized procedures, since top management tends to have greater functional knowledge and expertise than subordinates and because the lack of diversity of operations enables direct control to be exercised over most of the key determinants of success. Thus, situation reviews, the setting of marketing objectives, and so on, are not always made explicit in writing, although these steps still have to be gone through.

In contrast, in a *diversified* company, it is usually not possible for top management to have greater functional knowledge and expertise than subordinate management, hence the whole planning process tends to be more formalized in order to provide a consistent discipline for those who have to make the decisions throughout the organization.

Either way, however, there is now a substantial body of evidence to show that formalized marketing planning procedures generally result in greater profitability and stability in the long term and also help to reduce friction and operational difficulties within organizations.

Where marketing planning has failed, it has generally been because companies have placed too much emphasis on the procedures themselves and the resulting paperwork, rather than on generating information useful to and consumable by management. Also, where companies relegate marketing planning to someone called a 'planner', it invariably fails, for the single reason that planning for line management cannot be delegated to a third party. The real role of the 'planner' should be to help those responsible for implementation to plan. Failure to recognize this simple fact can be disastrous. Finally, planning failures often result from companies trying too much, too quickly, and without training staff in the use of procedures.

One Swedish company selling batteries internationally tried unsuccessfully three times to introduce a marketing planning system, each one failing because management throughout the organization were confused by what was being asked of them. Also, not only did they not understand the need for the new systems, but they were not provided with the necessary resources to make the system work effectively. Training of managers, and careful thought about resource requirements, would have largely overcome this company's planning problems.

> In contrast, a major multinational oil company, having suffered grave profitability and operational difficulties through not having an effective marketing planning system, introduced one over a three-year period that included a training programme in the use of the new procedures and the provision of adequate resources to make them work effectively. This company is now firmly in control of its diverse activities and has regained its confidence and its profitability.

We can now look at the marketing planning process in more detail, starting with a look at the marketing audit. So far we have looked at the need for marketing planning and outlined a series of steps that have to be gone through in order to arrive at a marketing plan. However, any plan will only be as good as the information on which it is based, and the marketing audit is the means by which information for planning is organized.

What is a marketing audit?

Auditing as a process is usually associated with the financial side of a business and is conducted according to a defined set of accounting standards, which are well documented, easily understood, and which therefore lend themselves readily to the auditing process. The total business process, although more complicated, innovative and relying more on judgement than on a set of rules, is still nevertheless capable of being audited.

> Basically, an audit is the means by which a company can understand how it relates to the environment in which it operates. It is the means by which a company can identify its own strengths and weaknesses as they relate to external opportunities and threats. It is thus a way of helping management to select a position in that environment based on known factors.

Expressed in its simplest form, if the purpose of a corporate plan is to answer three central questions:

○ Where is the company now?
○ Where does the company want to go?
○ How should the company organize its resources to get there?

then the audit is the means by which the first of these questions is answered. An audit is a systematic, critical and unbiased review and appraisal of the environment and of the company's operations. A marketing audit is part of the larger management audit and is concerned with the marketing environment and marketing operations.

Why is there a need for an audit?

> Often the need for an audit does not manifest itself until things start to go wrong for a company, such as declining sales, falling margins, lost market share, underutilized production capacity, and so on.

At times like these, management often attempts to treat the wrong symptoms. For example, introducing new products or dropping products, reorganizing the sales force, reducing prices, and cutting costs, are just some of the actions which could be taken. But such measures are unlikely to be effective if there are more fundamental problems which have not been identified. Of course, if the company could survive long enough, it might eventually solve its problems through a process of elimination! Essentially, the argument is that problems have to be properly defined, and the audit is a means of helping to define them.

To summarize, the audit is a structured approach to the collection and analysis of information and data in the complex business environment and an essential prerequisite to problem-solving.

The form of the audit

Any company carrying out an audit will be faced with two kinds of variables. Firstly, there are variables over which the company has no direct control. These usually take the form of what can be described as environmental, market and competitive variables. Secondly, there are variables over which the company has complete control. These we can call operational variables.

This gives us a clue as to how we can structure an audit. That is to say, in two parts:

○ External audit
○ Internal audit

The *external audit* is concerned with the uncontrollable variables, whilst the *internal audit* is concerned with the controllable variables.

The external audit starts with an examination of information on the general economy and then moves on to the outlook for the health and growth of the markets served by the company.

The purpose of the internal audit is to assess the organization's resources as they relate to the environment and *vis-à-vis* the resources of competitors.

The place of the marketing audit in the management audit

The term *management audit* (Figure 2.5) merely means a company-wide audit which includes an assessment of all internal resources against the external environment. In practice, the best way to carry out a management audit is to conduct a separate audit of each major management

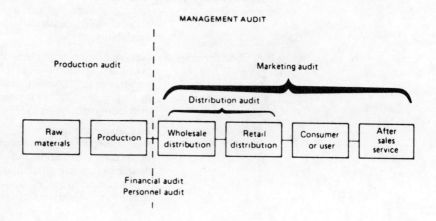

Figure 2.5

function. Thus the marketing audit is merely part of the larger management audit, in the same way that the production audit is.

Here is a checklist of areas which should be investigated as part of the marketing audit. This is shown in greater detail in Table 2.1.

External audit

Business and economic environment
Economic
Political/fiscal/legal
Social/cultural
Technological
Intra-company

The market
Total market, size, growth and trends (value/volume)
Market characteristics, developments and trends
  Products
  Prices
  Physical distribution
  Channels
  Customers/consumers

Communication
Industry practices

Competition
Major competitors
Size
Market shares/coverage
Market standing/reputation
Production capabilities
Distribution policies
Marketing methods
Extent of diversification
Personnel issues
International links
Profitability
Key strengths and weaknesses

Internal audit
Marketing operational variables
Own company
Sales (total, by geographical location, by industrial type, by customer, by product)
Market shares
Profit margins/costs

Marketing procedures
Marketing organization
Marketing information/research
Marketing mix variables as follows:
  Product management
  Price
  Distribution
  Promotion

Table 2.1 Marketing audit checklist (fuller details)

EXTERNAL (opportunities and threats)		
Business and economic environment		
Economic	Inflation, unemployment, energy, price, volatility, materials availability, etc.	as they affect your business
Political/fiscal/legal	Nationalization, union legislation, taxation, duty increases, regulatory constraints (e.g. labelling, product quality, packaging, trade practices, advertising, pricing, etc.)	as they affect your business
Social/cultural	Education, immigration, emigration, religion, environment, population distribution and dynamics (e.g. age distribution, regional distribution, etc.), changes in consumer life style, etc.	as they affect your business

Technological	Aspects of product and/or production technology which could profoundly affect the economics of the industry (e.g. new technology, cost savings, materials, components, equipment, machinery, methods and systems, availability of substitutes, etc.)	as they affect your business
Intracompany	Capital investment, closures, strikes, etc.	as they affect your business

The market
Total market Size, growth, and trends (value, volume).
Market characteristics Developments and trends.

Products: principal products bought; end-use of products; product characteristics (weights, measures, sizes, physical characteristics, packaging, accessories, associated products, etc.).

Prices: price levels and range; terms and conditions of sale; normal trade practices; official regulations, etc.

Physical distribution: principal method of physical distribution

Channels: principal channels; purchasing patterns (e.g. types of product bought, prices paid, etc.); purchasing ability; geographical location; stocks; turnover; profits; needs; tastes; attitudes; decision-makers, bases of purchasing decision; etc.

Communication: principal methods of communication, e.g. sales force, advertising, direct response, exhibitions, public relations, etc.

Industry practices: e.g. trade associations, government bodies, historical attitudes, interfirm comparisons; etc.

Competition

Industry structure: make-up of companies in the industry, major market standing/reputation; extent
of excess capacity; production capability; distribution capability; marketing methods; competitive arrangements; extent of diversification into other areas by major companies in the industry; new entrants; mergers; acquisitions; bankruptcies; significant aspects; international links; key strengths and weaknesses.

Industry profitability: financial and non-financial barriers to entry; industry profitability and the relative performance of individual companies; structure of operating costs; investment; effect on return on investment of changes in price; volume; cost of investment; source of industry profits; etc.

INTERNAL (strengths and weaknesses)
Own company
Sales (total, by geographical location, by industrial type, by customer, by product)
Market shares
Profit margins

Table 2.1. – *cont.*

Marketing procedures
Marketing organization
Sales/marketing control data
Marketing mix variables as follows:

Market research	Samples
Product development	Exhibitions
Product range	Selling
Product quality	Sales aids
Unit of sale	Point of sale
Stock levels	Advertising
Distribution	Sales promotion
Dealer support	Public relations
Pricing, discounts, credit	After-sales service
Packaging	Training

Operations and resources

Marketing objectives
Are the marketing objectives clearly stated and consistent with marketing and corporate objectives?

Marketing strategy
What is the strategy for achieving the stated objectives? Are sufficient resources available to achieve these objectives? Are the available resources sufficient and optimally allocated across elements of the marketing mix?

Structure
Are the marketing responsibilities and authorities clearly structured along functional, product, end-user, and territorial lines?

Information system
Is the marketing intelligence system producing accurate, sufficient and timely information about developments in the market place?
Is information gathered being used effectively in making marketing decisions?

Planning system
Is the marketing planning system well conceived and effective?

Control system
Do control mechanisms and procedures exist within the group to ensure planned objectives are achieved, e.g. meeting overall objectives, etc.?

Functional efficiency
Are internal communications within the group effective?

Interfunctional efficiency
Are there any problems between marketing and other corporate functions?
Is the question of centralized versus decentralized marketing an issue in the company?

Profitability analysis
Is the profitability performance monitored by product, served markets, etc., to assess where the best profits and biggest costs of the operation are located?

Cost-effectiveness analysis
Do any current marketing activities seem to have excess costs?
Are these valid or could they be reduced?

The marketing audit should not be a last-ditch attempt to define a company's marketing problem.

Each one of these headings should be examined with a view to isolating those factors that are considered critical to the company's performance. Initially, the auditor's task is to screen the enormous amount of information and data for validity and relevance. Some data and information will have to be reorganized into a more easily usable form, and judgement will have to be applied to decide what further data and information are necessary to a proper definition of the problem.

> Thus there are basically two phases which comprise the auditing process:
>
> 1 Identification, measurement, collection, and analysis of all the relevant facts and opinions which impinge on a company's problems.
> 2 The application of judgement to uncertain areas which are remaining following this analysis.

When should the marketing audit be carried out?

A mistaken belief held by many people is that the marketing audit should be a last-ditch, end-of-the-road attempt to define a company's marketing problem, or at best something done by an independent body from time to time to ensure that a company is on the right lines.

> However, since marketing is such a complex function, it seems illogical not to carry out a pretty thorough situation analysis at least once a year at the beginning of the planning cycle.

There is much evidence to show that many highly successful companies, as well as using normal information and control procedures and marketing research throughout the year, also start their planning cycle each year with a formal review, through an audit-type process, of everything that has had an important influence on marketing activities. Certainly in many leading consumer goods companies, the annual self-audit approach is a tried and tested discipline integrated into the management process.

Who should carry out the audit?

Occasionally, it may be justified to hire outside consultants to carry out a marketing audit to check that a company is getting the most out of its resources. However, it seems an unnecessary expense to have this done every year. The answer, therefore, is to have an audit carried out annually by the company's own line managers on their own areas of responsibility.

Objections to this usually centre around the problems of time and objectivity. In practice, these problems are overcome by institutionalizing procedures in as much detail as possible so that all managers have to conform to a disciplined approach and, secondly by thorough training in the use of the procedures themselves. However, even this will not result in achieving the purpose of an audit unless a rigorous discipline is applied from the highest down to the lowest levels of management involved in the audit. Such a discipline is usually successful in helping managers to avoid the sort of tunnel vision that often results from a lack of critical appraisal.

What happens to the results of the audit?

It is essential to concentrate on analysis that determines which trends and developments will actually affect the company.

The only remaining question is what happens to the results of the audit? Some companies consume valuable resources carrying out audits that bring very little by way of actionable results.

Indeed, there is always the danger that, at the audit stage, insufficient attention is paid to the need to concentrate on analysis that determines which trends and developments will actually affect the company. Whilst the checklist demonstrates the completeness of logic and analysis, the people carrying out the audit should discipline themselves to omit from their audits all the information that is not central to the company's marketing problems. Thus, inclusion of research reports, or overdetailed sales performance histories by product which lead to no logical actions whatever, only serve to rob the audit of focus and reduce its relevance.

Since the objective of the audit is to indicate what a company's marketing objectives and strategies should be, it follows that it would be helpful if some format could be found for organizing the major findings.

One useful way of doing this is in the form of a SWOT analysis. This is a summary of the audit under the headings, internal strengths and weaknesses as they relate to external opportunities and threats. Detailed analysis on how to complete a SWOT are contained in Chapters 4, 5 and 13.

This SWOT analysis should, if possible, contain not more than four or five pages of commentary focusing on *key* factors only. It should highlight internal *differential* strengths and weaknesses *vis-à-vis* competitors and *key* external opportunities and threats. A summary of reasons for good or bad performance should be included. It should be interesting to read, contain concise statements, include only relevant and important data, and give greater emphasis to creative analysis.

To summarize, carrying out a regular and thorough marketing audit in a structured manner will go a long way towards giving a company a knowledge of the business, trends in the market, and where value is added by competitors, as the basis for setting objectives and strategies.

How marketing planning relates to corporate planning

Before turning our attention to the other important steps in the marketing planning process, it would be useful to discuss how marketing planning relates to the corporate planning process.

There are five steps in the corporate planning process. As can be seen from Table 2.2, the starting point is usually a statement of corporate financial objectives for the long-range planning period of the company, which are often expressed in terms of turnover, profit before tax, and return on investment.

More often than not, this long-range planning horizon is five years although, more recently, three years is becoming increasingly the norm. However, the precise period should be determined by the nature of the markets in which the company operates. For example, five years would not be a long enough period for a glass manufacturer, since it takes that period of time to commission a new furnace, whereas in some fashion industries five years would be too long. A useful guideline in determining the planning horizon is that there should be a market for the company products for long enough at least to amortize any new capital investment associated with those products.

Nonetheless, for the purpose of putting in sufficient detail for a strategic plan to be of any practical use, it is advisable to keep the period down to three years if possible, since beyond this period, detail of any kind is likely to become pointless. There can certainly be scenarios for five to ten years, but not a plan in the sense intended by this book.

Table 2.2 Marketing planning and its place in the corporate cycle

Step 1	2 Management audit	3 Objective and strategy setting	4 Plans	5 Corporate plans
	Marketing audit Marketing	Marketing objectives, strategies	Marketing plan	
	Distribution audit Stocks and control; transportation; warehousing	Distribution objectives, strategies	Distribution plan	
Corporate financial objectives	*Production audit* Value analysis; engineering development; work study; quality control; labour; materials, plant and space utilization; production planning; factories	Production objectives strategies	Production plan	Issue of corporate plan, to include corporate objectives and strategies; production objectives and strategies, etc.; long-range profit and loss accounts; balance sheets
	Financial audit Credit, debt, cash flow and budgetary control; resource allocation; capital expenditure; long-term finance	Financial objectives, strategies	Financial plan	
	Personnel audit Management, technical and administrative ability, etc.	Personnel objectives, strategies		

The next step is the *management audit*, which we have already discussed. This is an obvious activity to follow on with, since a thorough situation review, particularly in the area of marketing, should enable the company to determine whether it will be able to meet the long-range financial targets with its current range of products in its current markets. Any projected gap can be filled by the various methods of product development or market extension.

Undoubtedly the most important and difficult of all stages in the corporate planning process is the third step, *objective and strategy setting*, since if this is not done properly, everything that follows is of little value.

One of the main purposes of a corporate plan is to provide a long-term vision of what the company is or is striving to achieve.

Later on, we will discuss marketing objectives and strategies in more detail. For now, the important point to make is that this is the time in the planning cycle when a compromise has to be reached between what is wanted by the several functional departments and what is practicable, given all the constraints that any company has. For example, it is no good setting a marketing objective of penetrating a new market, if the company does not have the production capacity to cope with the new business, and if capital is not available for whatever investment is necessary in additional capacity. At this stage, objectives and strategies will be set for three years, or for whatever the planning horizon is.

Step 4 involves producing detailed *plans* for one year, containing the responsibilities, timing and costs of carrying out the first year's objectives, and broad plans for the following years.

These plans can then be incorporated into the *corporate plan*, which will contain long-range corporate objectives, strategies, plans, profit and loss accounts, and balance sheets.

At this point it is worth noting that one of the main purposes of a corporate plan is to provide a long-term vision of what the company is or is striving to become, taking account of shareholder expectations, environmental trends, resource market trends, consumption market trends, and the distinctive competence of the company as revealed by the management audit. What this means in practice is that the corporate plan will usually contain at least the following elements:

○ The desired level of profitability
○ Business boundaries
 – what kinds of products will be sold to what kinds of markets (marketing)
 – what kinds of facilities will be developed (production and distribution)
 – the size and character of the labour force (personnel)
 – funding (finance)
○ Other corporate objectives, such as social responsibility, corporate image, stock market image, employer image, etc.

Such a corporate plan, containing projected profit and loss accounts and balance sheets, being the result of the process described above, is more likely to provide long-term stability for a company than plans based on a more intuitive process and containing forecasts which tend to be little more than extrapolations of previous trends. This process is further summarized in Figure 2.6.

The headquarters of one major multinational company with a sophisticated budgeting system used to receive 'plans' from all over the world and coordinate them in quantitative and cross-functional terms such as numbers of employees, units of sales, items of plant, square feet of production area, and so on, together with the associated financial implications. The trouble was that the whole complicated edifice was built on the initial sales forecasts, which were themselves little more than a time-consuming numbers game. The really key strategic issues relating to products and markets were lost in all the financial activity, which eventually resulted in grave operational and profitability problems.

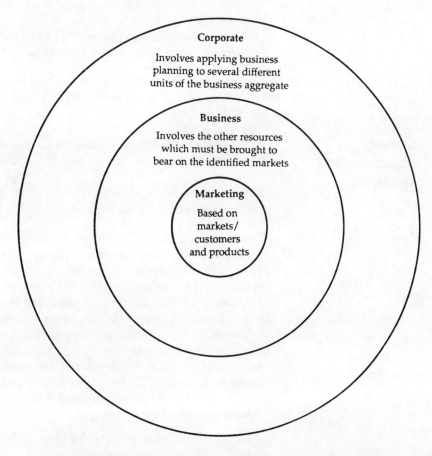

Corporate

Involves applying business planning to several different units of the business aggregate

Business

Involves the other resources which must be brought to bear on the identified markets

Marketing

Based on markets/ customers and products

Figure 2.6

Assumptions

Let us now return to the preparation of the marketing plan. If we refer again to the marketing planning process, and have completed our marketing audit and SWOT analysis, assumptions now have to be written.

> There are certain key determinants of success in all companies about which assumptions have to be made before the planning process can proceed.

It is really a question of standardizing the planning environment. For example, it would be no good receiving plans from two product managers, one of whom believed the market was going to increase by 10 per cent, while the other believed the market was going to decline by 10 per cent.

Examples of assumptions might be:

'With respect to the company's industrial climate, it is assumed that:

1 Industrial overcapacity will increase from 105 per cent to 115 per cent as new industrial plans come into operation.
2 Price competition will force price levels down by 10 per cent across the board.
3 A new product in the field of *x* will be introduced by our major competitor before the end of the second quarter.'

Assumptions should be few in number, and if a plan is possible irrespective of the assumptions made, then the assumptions are unnecessary.

Marketing objectives and strategies

The next step in marketing planning is the writing of marketing objectives and strategies, the key step in the whole process.

An *objective* is what you want to achieve. A *strategy* is how you plan to achieve your objectives.

Thus, there can be objectives and strategies at all levels in marketing. For example, there can be advertising objectives and strategies, and pricing objectives and strategies.

However, the important point to remember about marketing objectives is that they are about *products* and *markets* only. Common sense will confirm that it is only by selling something to someone that the company's financial goals can be achieved, and that advertising, pricing, service levels and so on are the means (or strategies) by which we might succeed in doing this. Thus, pricing objectives, sales promotion objectives, advertising objectives and the like should not be confused with marketing objectives.

Marketing objectives are simply about one, or more, of the following:

○ Existing products in existing markets
○ New products for existing markets
○ Existing products for new markets
○ New products for new markets

They should be capable of measurement, otherwise they are not objectives. Directional terms such as 'maximize', 'minimize', 'penetrate', 'increase', etc. are only acceptable if quantitative measurement can be attached to them. Measurement should be in terms of some, or all, of the following: sales volume; sales value; market share; profit; percentage penetration of outlets.

Marketing strategies are the means by which marketing objectives will be achieved and generally are concerned with the four Ps, as follows:

Product	The general policies for product deletions, modifications, additions, design, packaging, etc.
Price	The general pricing policies to be followed for product groups in market segments.
Place	The general policies for channels and customer service levels.
Promotion	The general policies for communicating with customers under the relevant headings, such as advertising, sales force, sales promotion, public relations, exhibitions, direct mail, etc.

Having completed this major planning task, it is normal at this stage to employ judgement, analogous experience, field tests, and so on, to test out the feasibility of the objectives and strategies in terms of market share, sales, costs, profits, and so on. It is also normally at this stage that alternative plans and mixes are considered, if necessary.

Programmes

In a strategic marketing plan, these strategies would normally be costed out approximately and, if not practicable, alternative strategies would be proposed and costed out until a satisfactory solution could be reached. This would then become the budget. In a one-year tactical plan, the general marketing strategies would be developed into specific sub-objectives, each supported by more detailed strategy and action statements.

A company organized according to functions might have an advertising plan, a sales promotion plan, a pricing plan, and so on.

A product-based company might have a product plan, with objectives, strategies and tactics for price, place and promotion as necessary.

A market or geographically based company might have a market plan, with objectives, strategies and tactics for the four Ps as necessary.

Likewise, a company with a few major customers might have a customer plan.

Any combination of the above might be suitable, depending on circumstances.

Use of marketing plans

A written strategic marketing plan is the backcloth against which operational decisions are taken on an on-going basis.

Consequently, too much detail should not be attempted. Its major function is to determine where the company is now, where it wants to go, and how to get there. It lies at the heart of a company's revenue-generating activities and from it flow all other corporate activities, such as the timing of the cash flow, the size and character of the labour force, and so on.

The marketing plan should be distributed on a 'need to know' basis only.

Finally, the marketing plan should be used as an aid to effective management. It cannot be a substitute for it.

The marketing budget

From a zero base, a hierarchy of objectives is built up so that every item of budgeted expenditure can be related directly back to the initial corporate financial objectives.

It will be obvious from all of this that the setting of budgets becomes not only much easier, but the resulting budgets are more likely to be realistic and related to what the *whole* company wants to achieve, rather than just one functional department.

The problem of designing a dynamic system for budget setting, rather than the 'tablets of stone' approach, which is more common, is a major challenge to the marketing and financial directors of all companies.

The most satisfactory approach would be for a marketing director to justify all marketing expenditure from a zero base each year against the tasks he or she wishes to accomplish. A little thought will confirm that this is exactly the approach recommended in this chapter. If these procedures are followed, a hierarchy of objectives is built up in such a way that every item of budgeted expenditure can be related directly back to the initial corporate financial objectives. For example, if sales promotion is a major means of achieving an objective in a particular market, when sales promotional items appear in the programme, each one has a specific purpose which can be related back to a major objective.

Doing it this way not only ensures that every item of expenditure is fully accounted for as part of a rational, objective and task approach, but also that when changes have to be made during the period to which the plan relates, these changes can be made in such a way that the least damage is caused to the company's long-term objectives.

> The incremental marketing expense can be considered to be all costs that are incurred after the product leaves the factory, *other than* costs involved in physical distribution, the costs of which usually represent a discrete subset.

There is, of course, no textbook answer to problems relating to questions such as whether packaging should be a marketing or a production expense, and whether some distribution costs could be considered to be marketing costs. For example, insistence on high service levels results in high inventory carrying costs. Only common sense will reveal workable solutions to issues such as these.

Under *price*, however, any form of discounting that reduces the expected gross income, such as promotional discounts, quantity discounts, royalty rebates, and so on, as well as sales commission and unpaid invoices, should be given the most careful attention as incremental marketing expenses.

Most obvious incremental marketing expenses will occur, however, under the heading *promotion*, in the form of advertising, sales salaries and expenses, sales promotional expenditure, direct mail costs, and so on.

The important point about the measurable effects of marketing activity is that anticipated levels should be the result of the most careful analysis of what is required to take the company towards its goals, while the most careful attention should be paid to gathering all items of expenditure under appropriate headings. The healthiest way of treating these issues is a zero-based budgeting approach.

What should appear in a strategic marketing plan?

A written strategic marketing plan is the backdrop against which operational decisions are taken. Consequently, too much detail should be avoided. Its major function is to determine where the company is, where it wants to go and how it can get there.

It lies at the heart of a company's revenue-generating activities, such as the timing of the cash flow and the size and character of the labour force. What should actually appear in a written strategic marketing plan is shown in Table 2.3. Further details and explanations about each of the components will be given in later chapters.

This framework should be borne in mind throughout the remainder of this book.

What is a mission or purpose statement?

Table 2.3 shows that a strategic marketing plan should begin with a mission or purpose statement. This is perhaps the most difficult aspect of marketing planning for managers to master, largely because it is philosophical and qualitative in nature. Many organizations find their different departments, and sometimes even different groups in the same department, pulling in different directions, often with

Table 2.3 What should appear in a strategic marketing plan

1 Start with a mission or purpose statement.
2 Next, include a financial summary which illustrates graphically revenue and profit for the full planning period.
3 Now do a market overview:
   ○ What *is* the market?
   ○ Has the market declined or grown?
   ○ How does it break down into segments?
   ○ What are the trends in each?
   Keep it simple. If you do not have the facts, make estimates. Use life cycles, bar charts and pie charts to make it all crystal clear.
4 Now identify the key segments and do a SWOT for each one:
   ○ Outline the major external influences and their impact on each segment.
   ○ List the key factors for success. There should be less than five.
   ○ Give an assessment of the company's differential strengths and weaknesses compared with those of its competitors. Score yourself and your competitors out of ten and then multiply each score by a weighing factor for each critical success factor (e.g. CSF1 = 60, CSF2 = 25, CSF3 = 10, CSF4 = 5). (Detailed instructions on how to do this are given in Chapters 5 and 13.)
5 Make a brief statement about the key issues that have to be addressed in the planning period.
6 Summarize the SWOTs using a portfolio matrix in order to illustrate the important relationships between the key points of your business.
7 List your assumptions.
8 Set objectives and strategies.
9 Summarize your resource requirements for the planning period in the form of a budget.

disastrous results, simply because the organization hasn't defined the boundaries of the business and the way it wishes to do business.

> Take the example of a high-technology company. One group of directors felt the company should be emphasizing technology, while another group felt technology was less important than marketing. With such confusion at the top of the company, it is not hard to imagine the chaos further down.

> A different example concerns a hosiery buyer for a department store group. She believed her mission was to maximize profit, whereas research showed that women shopped in department stores for items other than hosiery. They did, however, expect hosiery to be on sale, even though that was rarely the purpose of their visit. This buyer, in trying to maximize profit, limited the number of brands, colours and sizes on sale, with the result that many women visitors to the store were disappointed and did not return. So, it can be seen that, in this case, by maximizing her own profit, she was sub-optimizing the total profit of the group. In this case, the role of her section was more of a *service* role than a profit-maximizing role.

Here, we can see two levels of mission. One is a *corporate* mission statement, the other is a lower level, or *purpose* statement. But there is yet another level, as shown in the following summary:

Type 1 'Motherhood' – usually found inside annual reports designed to 'stroke' shareholders. Otherwise no practical use.

Type 2 The real thing. A meaningful statement, unique to the organization concerned, which 'impacts' on the behaviour of the executives at all levels.

Type 3 This is a 'purpose' statement (or lower level mission statement). It is appropriate at the strategic business unit, departmental or product group level of the organization.

The following should appear in a mission or purpose statement, which should normally consist of no more than one page:

1 *Role or contribution*
   ○ Profit (specify)
   ○ Service
   ○ Opportunity seeker
2 *Business definition* – define the business, preferably in terms of the *benefits* you provide or the *needs* you satisfy, rather than in terms of what you make.
3 *Distinctive competences* – these are the essential skills/ capabilities/resources that underpin whatever success has been achieved to date. It can consist of one particular item or the possession of a number of skills compared with competitors. If,

however, you could equally well put a competitor's name to these distinctive competences, then it is *not* a distinctive competence.

4 *Indications for the future*
   ○ What the firm *will* do
   ○ What the firm *might* do
   ○ What the firm will *never* do

This process and its relationship to the other issues discussed in this chapter, are summarized in Figure 2.7.

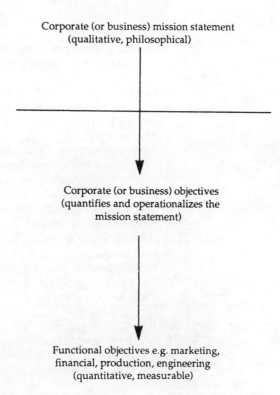

Corporate (or business) mission statement
(qualitative, philosophical)

Corporate (or business) objectives
(quantifies and operationalizes the
mission statement)

Functional objectives e.g. marketing,
financial, production, engineering
(quantitative, measurable)

Figure 2.7

Application questions

1 Describe your company's marketing planning system in detail.
2 List the *good* things and the *bad* things about it.
3 Say how you think it could be improved.

Review of Chapter 2

What is marketing planning?
A logical sequence of events leading to the setting of marketing objectives and the formulation of plans for achieving them.
   The sequence is:
   1 Mission statement.
   2 Set corporate objectives.
   3 Conduct marketing audit.
   4 Conduct SWOT analysis.
   5 Make assumptions.
   6 Set marketing objectives and strategies.

---

7 Estimate expected results.
8 Identify alternative plans and mixes.
9 Set the budget.
10 Establish first year implementation programmes.   *Try Exercise 2.1*

The plan itself contains:
1 Mission statement.
2 Financial summary.
3 Market overview.
4 SWOT analyses.
5 Portfolio summary.
6 Assumptions.
7 Marketing objectives and strategies.
8 Programmes with forecasts and budgets.   *Try Exercise 2.2*

Why do it?
As business becomes increasingly complex and competition increases, a marketing plan is essential.
The benefits are:
1 Better coordination of activities.
2 It identifies expected developments.
3 It increases organizational preparedness to change.
4 It minimizes non-rational responses to the unexpected.
5 It reduces conflicts about where the company should be going.
6 It improves communications.
7 Management is forced to think ahead systematically.
8 Available resources can be better matched to opportunities.
9 The plan provides a framework for the continuing review of operations.
10 A systematic approach to strategy formulation leads to a higher return on investment.   *Try Exercise 2.3*

Will it help us to survive?
All companies need to have a longer-term (strategic) marketing view as well as a short-term (tactical) marketing operation. Often the most potent short-term tactic is the use of the salesforce. These can combine thus:

Market planning

		Ineffective	*Effective*
Sales performance	*Good*	Die quickly	Thrive
	Poor	Die slowly	Survive

From this it can be seen that being good at implementing the wrong strategy can lead to a very quick death!   *Try Exercise 2.4*

Questions raised for the company

1 Can we 'buy' an 'off the peg' planning system?
Since all companies are different, the process has to be 'tailored' to fit individual requirements.

2 Are we talking about tactics or strategy?
A strategic marketing plan takes a long-term look (say 3 years) and is therefore strategic. A tactical, or operational, marketing plan is a detailed scheduling and costing out of the *first* year of the strategic marketing plan.

3 How is the marketing plan used?
The plan determines where the company is now, where it wants to go and how to get there. It therefore should be the backdrop against which all organizational decisions are made.

4 Does the plan have to be written?
The planning sequence is really a thinking process. However, key pieces of information are worth writing down because they reduce confusion and aid communication. The degree of formality depends on the size of the company and the complexity of its business.

5 How detailed?
Enough to be useful.

Introduction to Chapter 2 exercises

The first exercise enables you to make an objective analysis of your company's marketing planning process. If you choose, you can then take matters further by working out in what ways the planning process might be improved.

The second exercise helps to clarify an often misunderstood issue, that of the company's mission statement.

The third exercise explores the extent to which your company is receiving the benefits that are usually attributed to a marketing planning process.

The final exercise will enable you to plot your company's position on the 'survival matrix'. There are several benefits to be derived from knowing this:

1 It infers the relation between your company's focus on long-term versus short-term issues.

2 It can be a powerful means of communicating to your colleagues that all might not be well in the company.

3 It provides an unambiguous message about what the company needs to address for future survival.

Exercise 2.1 The marketing planning process questionnaire

This questionnaire enables you to make an objective assessment about the marketing planning process in your company. It is designed to enable you to take a 'helicopter view' of the way your company does its planning and then to home in on the areas where improvements can be made. This approach will also enable you to identify information gaps that might be unknown to you at present.

Although care has been taken to use generally accepted terminology in the wording of this questionnaire, there will always be the company that uses different words. For example, when we talk about return on investment (ROI), other companies might well use other expressions or measures, such as return on capital employed, etc.

With this caveat in mind, please respond to the questionnaire by putting a tick against each question in one of the four columns provided.

	Yes	No	Don't know	Not applic.
Section 1 Corporate issues				
1 Is there a corporate statement about:				
(i) The nature of the company's current business mission?				
(ii) Its vision of the future?				
2 Is there a target figure for ROI?				
3 Is there a corporate plan to channel the company resources to this end?				
4 Are there defined business boundaries in terms of:				
(i) Products or services (that will be offered)?				
(ii) Customers or markets (to deal with)?				
(iii) Production facilities?				
(iv) Distribution facilities?				
(v) Size and character of the workforce?				
(vi) Sources and levels of funding?				
5 Are there objectives for promoting the corporate image with:				
(i) The stock market?				
(ii) Customers?				
(iii) The local community?				
(iv) The employees?				
(v) Environmentalist/conservationist lobby?				
(vi) Government departments?				
(vii) Trade associations, etc.?				
Section 2 Marketing issues				
6 Is there a marketing plan?				
7 Is it compatible with the corporate plan?				
8 Does it cover the same period?				
9 Is the marketing plan regularly reviewed?				
10 Is the plan based on an assessment of market potential or past performance?				
11 Will the plan close the 'gap' if carried out?				
12 Is there a marketing plan by product/service?				
13 Do relevant managers have a copy of the marketing plan?				
14 Are the following factors monitored in a regular and conscious way, in terms of how they affect the company's business prospects?				
(a) *Business environment*				
(i) Economic factors?				

	Yes	No	Don't know	Not applic.
(ii) Political/legal factors?				
(iii) Fiscal factors				
(iv) Technological developments?				
(v) Social/cultural factors?				
(vi) Intra-company issues?				
(b) The market				
(i) Trends in market size/growth in volume? in value?				
(ii) Developments/trends in product use? product demand? product presentation? accessories? substitutes?				
(iii) Developments/trends in prices? terms and conditions? trade practices?				
(iv) Developments/trends in physical distribution? channels of distribution? purchasing patterns? stockholding? turnover?				
(v) Developments/trends in communications? use of salesforce? advertising? promotions? exhibitions?				
(c) Competition				
(i) Developments/trends of competitors? their marketing strategies? their strengths? their weaknesses? new entrants? mergers/acquisitions? their reputation?				
(d) The industry				
(i) Activities of trade association(s)?				
(ii) Inter-firm comparisons?				
(iii) Industry profitability?				
(iv) Investment levels of competitors?				
(v) Changes in cost structure?				
(vi) Investment prospects?				
(vii) Technological developments?				
(viii) Sources of raw materials?				
(ix) Energy utilization?				

	Yes	No	Don't know	Not applic.
Section 3 SWOT analysis				
1 Is there someone (individual or group) responsible for converting the analysis of factors in Section 2 into a summary which highlights:				
(i) The company's principal strengths?				
(ii) The company's principal weaknesses (in terms of relating to external opportunities/threats)?				
2 Does this person(s) have access to the necessary information?				
3 Is this person(s) sufficiently senior for his or her analysis to make an impact?				
4 Is the organizational climate such that a full and accurate analysis is seen as a striving for improvement rather than an attack on specific departments or vested interests?				
Section 4 Assumptions				
1 Is there a set of assumptions around which the marketing plan is formulated?				
2 Are these assumptions made explicit to senior company personnel?				
3 Do they cover:				
(i) The business environment?				
(ii) The market?				
(iii) The competitors?				
(iv) The industry?				
4 Are the assumptions valid in the light of current and predicted trading situations?				
Section 5 Marketing objectives/strategies				
1 Are the marketing objectives clearly stated and consistent with the corporate objectives?				
2 Are there clear strategies for achieving the stated marketing objectives?				
3 Are sufficient resources made available?				
4 Are all responsibilities and authority clearly made known?				
5 Are there agreed objectives about:				
(i) The product range?				
(ii) The value of sales?				
(iii) The volume of sales?				
(iv) Profits?				
(v) Market share?				
(vi) Market penetration?				

	Yes	No	Don't know	Not applic.
(vii) Number of customers?				
(viii) Introducing new products/services?				
(ix) Divesting of old products/services?				
(x) Organization changes to:				
(a) Develop company strengths?				
(b) Reduce company weaknesses?				
Section 6 Monitoring evaluation				
1 Is the planning system well conceived and effective?				
2 Do control mechanisms exist to ensure planned objectives are met?				
3 Do internal communications function effectively?				
4 Are there any problems between marketing and other corporate functions?				
5 Are people clear about their role in the planning process?				
6 Is there a procedure for dealing with non-achievement of objectives?				
7 Is there evidence that this reduces the chance of subsequent failure?				
8 Are there still unexploited opportunities?				
9 Are there still organizational weaknesses?				
10 Are the assumptions upon which the plan was based valid?				
11 Are there contingency plans in the event of objectives not being met/conditions changing?				

Scoring and interpretation for Exercise 2.1

1 Add up how many ticks were listed under 'not applicable'. It is our experience that if there are more than eight ticks, then some aspects of planning that are covered by most companies are being avoided. Reappraise those items you initially ticked as 'not applicable'. Try getting a second opinion by checking your findings with colleagues.

2 Look at those items you ticked as 'don't know'. Find out if those activities are covered in your company's planning process.

3 Having ascertained what is and what isn't done in your company, list:

    (a) The *good* things in your company's planning process.
    (b) The *bad* things about it.

4 Make a note, in the space below, or on a separate sheet of paper, of ways in which you think the planning process in your company could be improved.

**Exercise 2.2
The mission
statement**

The following should appear in a mission statement:

1 *Role or contribution*

- O Profit (specify), or
- O Service, or
- O Opportunity-seeker.

2 *Business definition*
This should be defined in terms of the *benefits* you provide or the *needs* you satisfy, rather than in terms of what you do or what you make.

3 *Distinctive competence*
What essential skills/capabilities/resources underpin whatever success has been achieved to date? (*Note*: These factors should not apply equally to a competitor, otherwise there is no distinctive quality about them.)

4 *Indications for the future*
- O What the company *will* do.
- O What the company *might* do.
- O What the company will *never* do.

Questions

1 To what extent does your company's mission statement meet the criteria listed above?
2 If you do not have a mission statement, try writing one, following the guidelines provided here. Try it out on your colleagues and see if they agree with you or if they can find ways to improve on what you have written.

Scoring and interpretation for Exercise 2.2
Use the following to gauge whether you feel you and your colleagues have developed a mission statement that is of real value:

- O What values are true priorities for the next few years?
- O What would make me professionally commit my mind and heart to this vision over the next 5 to 10 years?

○ What is unique about us?

○ What does the world really need that our company can and should provide?

○ What do I want our company to accomplish so that I will be committed, aligned, and proud of my association with the institution?

Exercise 2.3 The benefits of marketing planning

What follows is a list of the benefits of marketing planning. With your company in mind, score each benefit by means of the scale given below.

0	1	2	3	4	5	6	7	8	9	10
Never	*Sometimes*			*Frequently*			*Most of the time*			*Always*

1 Our approach to marketing planning ensures that we get a high level of coordination of our various marketing activities. . . . . . .

2 Our marketing planning process enables us to identify unexpected developments in advance. . . . . . .

3 Because of the way we approach marketing planning, there is an increased readiness for the organization to change, in response to the issues 'flagged up'. . . . . . .

4 When we are faced with the unexpected, our marketing planning process minimizes the risk of non-rational responses. . . . . . .

5 Having a marketing plan reduces the conflicts between managers regarding 'where the company should be going'. . . . . . .

6 Our marketing plan improves communications about market-related issues. . . . . . .

7 Because of our marketing planning process, management is forced to think ahead systematically. . . . . . .

8 Having a marketing plan enables us to match our resources to opportunities in an effective way. . . . . . .

9 Our marketing plan provides us with a useful framework for a continuing review of progress. . . . . . .

10 Our marketing planning has led us to develop more profitable marketing strategies. . . . . . .

TOTAL _____

Scoring and interpretation for Exercise 2.3

The maximum score for the exercise is 100. If you scored:

81–100: Marketing planning is really paying off in your company.

61–80: You are not receiving the benefits you should be receiving. What's getting in the way? (Exercise 2.1 might give some clues.)

41–60: You appear to be moving along the right lines, but there is still a long way to go.

0–40: Either your marketing planning process is inadequate, or your company is not really trying to make marketing planning work.

Exercise 2.4
Survival matrix

Before you tackle this exercise, it is important to remember that profitability and high market growth are nearly always correlated. In other words, the higher the market growth, the higher the profitability.

This phenomenon can sometimes obscure the fact that a company that appears to be doing well can still be losing ground in comparison with its competitors. While apparently thriving, it is in fact dying slowly. The crunch comes when the erstwhile buoyant market growth slows down, and the other companies demonstrate quite clearly their superior performance.

INSTRUCTIONS
Before coming to the matrix, please respond to the following statements by scoring them as follows:

0	1	2	3	4	5	6	7	8	9	10

Never   Sometimes   Frequently   Most of the time   Always

1 When it comes to recruiting salespeople, we seem able to pick the best candidates in the job market.   . . . . . .

2 The training we provide for salespeople is second to none.   . . . . . .

3 Our salespeople consistently meet or exceed their sales targets.   . . . . . .

4 Compared with our competitors, our salespeople have a better image.   . . . . . .

5 We actually have the most appropriate number of sales-people employed.   . . . . . .

6 Our sales staff are clear about the role they are expected to play.   . . . . . .

7 Our sales managers are very good motivators.   . . . . . .

8 Territory planning is a strong point of our salesforce.   . . . . . .

9 The salesforce has a good conversion rate in terms of number of visits per order.   . . . . . .

10 Our sales force is reasonably stable, i.e. there is not a labour turnover problem.   . . . . . .

TOTAL _____

Scoring and interpretation for Exercise 2.4
Enter the salesforce effectiveness score on the vertical axis on the matrix (Figure 2.8) and then draw a horizontal dotted line across the matrix. Take the marketing benefits score from Exercise 2.3 and enter this on the horizontal axis of the matrix. Draw a vertical dotted line up from this point.

Where the two dotted lines meet is where you position your company on the survival matrix.

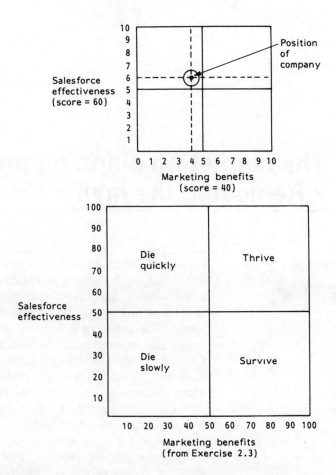

Figure 2.8 Survival matrix

Questions

1 What are the implications for your company?

2 What actions might be required if improvements are needed?

3 The marketing planning process: 2 Removing the myths

Summary

Having described the *process* of marketing planning, the purpose of this chapter is to highlight some of the problems you are likely to encounter on the way. It is an important chapter, as it will make you aware of some of the barriers that have to be overcome. If, however, you are certain that you can get straight on with the job unhindered by contextual problems, then go straight to Chapter 4. Chapter 3 describes the ignorance surrounding the process of marketing planning and the associated operational problems. There is a reminder about what marketing planning is, a discussion of the naivety surrounding the subject, and a list of marketing planning problems. These include: weak support from the chief executive and top management; lack of a plan for planning; lack of line management support; confusion over planning terms; numbers in lieu of written objectives and strategies; too much detail, too far ahead; once-a-year ritual; the separation of operational planning from strategic planning; failure to integrate marketing planning into corporate planning; and delegation of planning to a planner

Finally there is a discussion of requisite marketing planning systems.

Introduction

In spite of the apparent simplicity and logic of the process described in the last chapter, marketing planning remains one of the most baffling subjects, both for academics and practitioners alike.

The purpose of of this chapter is to remove some of the myths which surround this very complex area of marketing management and to explain why much of what passes for marketing planning in industry is largely ineffective. These conclusions are based on a four-year study by the author into how two hundred British goods companies carried out their marketing planning. Four hundred directors were interviewed, the companies being broadly representative of the complete spectrum of type and size of industrial company. These results have been confirmed by other recent studies carried out at universities in America, Europe and Australia.

Marketing's contribution to business success in manufacturing, distribution or merchanting activities lies in its commitment to detailed analysis of future opportunities to meet customer needs and a wholly professional approach to selling to well-defined market segments those products or services that deliver the sought-after benefits. While prices and discounts are important, as are advertising and promotion, the link with engineering through the product is paramount.

The process of marketing planning is concerned with identifying what and to whom sales are going to be made in the longer term.

> Such a commitment and activities must not be mistaken for budgets and forecasts. Those of course we need and have already got. Our accounting colleagues have long since seen to that.

No – put quite bluntly, the process of marketing planning is concerned with identifying what and to whom sales are going to be made in the longer term to give revenue budgets and sales forecasts any chance of achievement. Furthermore, chances of achievement are a function of how good our intelligence services are; and how well suited are our strategies; and how well we are led.

Ignorance of marketing planning and associated operational problems

The degree to which a company is able to cope with its operating environment is very much a function of the understanding it has of the marketing planning process as a means of sharpening the rationality and focus of all levels of management throughout the organization.

This requires further explanation.

> What most companies think of as planning systems are little more than forecasting and budgeting systems.

These give impetus and direction to tackling the current operational problems of the business, but tend merely to project the current business unchanged into the future – something often referred to in management literature as 'tunnel vision'.

The problem with this approach is that because companies are dynamically evolving systems within a dynamically evolving business environment, some means of evaluation of the way in which the two interact has to be found in order that there should be a better matching between them. Otherwise, because of a general unpreparedness, a company will suffer increased pressures in the short term, in trying to react and to cope with environmental factors.

Many companies, having gone through various forms of rationalization or efficiency-increasing measures, become aware of the opportunities for making profit which have been lost to them because of their unpreparedness, but are confused about how to make better use of their limited resources. This problem increases in importance in relation to the size and diversity of companies.

> There is widespread awareness of lost market opportunities through unpreparedness and real confusion over what to do about it. It is hard not to conclude, therefore, that there is a strong relationship between these two problems and the systems most widely in use at present, i.e. *sales forecasting and budgeting systems.*

Table 3.1 lists the most frequently mentioned operating problems resulting from a reliance on traditional sales forecasting and budgeting procedures in the absence of a marketing planning system.

Table 3.1 Most frequently mentioned problems

1 Lost opportunities for profit
2 Meaningless numbers in long-range plans
3 Unrealistic objectives
4 Lack of actionable market information
5 Interfunctional strife
6 Management frustration
7 Proliferation of products and markets
8 Wasted promotional expenditure
9 Pricing confusion
10 Growing vulnerability to environmental change
11 Loss of control over the business

It is not difficult to see the connection between all of these problems. However, what is perhaps not apparent from the list is that each of these operational difficulties is in fact a symptom of a much larger problem, which emanates from the way in which the objectives of a firm are set.

The meaningfulness, hence the eventual effectiveness, of any objective is heavily dependent on the quality of the information inputs about the business environment. However, objectives also need to be realistic, and to be realistic, they have to be closely related to the firm's particular capabilities in the form of its assets, competences and reputation that have evolved over a number of years.

The objective-setting process of a business, then, is central to its effectiveness.

If the process by which the key function of setting objectives is performed is inadequate it follows that operational efficiency will be adversely affected.

> What the research study demonstrated conclusively is that it is inadequacies in the objective-setting process which lie at the heart of most commercial problems.

Since companies are based on the existence of markets, and since a company's sole means of making profit is to find and maintain profitable markets, then, clearly, setting objectives in respect of these markets is a key business function. If the process by which this key function is performed is inadequate in relation to the differing organizational settings in which it takes place, it follows that operational efficiency will be adversely affected.

Some kind of appropriate system has to be used to enable meaningful and realistic marketing objectives to be set. A frequent complaint is the preoccupation with short-term thinking and an almost total lack of what has been referred to as 'strategic thinking'. This was referred to briefly in Chapter 2.

> Another complaint is that plans consist largely of numbers, which are difficult to evaluate in any meaningful way, since they do not highlight and quantify opportunities, emphasize key issues, show the company's position clearly in its markets, or delineate the means of achieving the sales forecasts.

Indeed, very often the actual numbers that are written down bear little relationship to any of these things. Sales targets for the sales force are often inflated in order to motivate them to higher achievement, while the actual budgets themselves are deflated in order to provide a safety net against shortfall. Both act as demotivators and both lead to the frequent use of expressions such as 'ritual', 'the numbers game', 'meaningless horsetrading', and so on. It is easy to see how the problems listed in Table 3.1 begin to manifest themselves in this sort of environment. Closely allied to this is the frequent reference to profit as being the only objective necessary to successful business performance.

This theme is frequently encountered. There is in the minds of many businesspeople the assumption that in order to be commercially successful, all that is necessary is for 'the boss' to set profit targets, to decentralize the firm into groups of similar activities, and then to make managers accountable for achieving those profits.

However, even though many companies have made the making of 'profit' almost the sole objective, many industries have gone into decline, and ironically there has also been a decline in real profitability.

> There are countless examples of companies pursuing decentralized profit goals that have failed miserably.

Many companies appear to be bad at determining strategies for matching what the firm is good at with properly researched market-centred opportunities.

Why should this be so? It is largely because some top managers believe that all they have to do is to set profit targets, and somehow middle management will automatically make everything come right. Indeed, there is much evidence to show that many companies believe that planning is only about setting profit goals. However, while this is an easy task for any company to do, saying exactly *how* these results are to be achieved is altogether a different matter.

Here it is necessary to focus attention on what so many companies appear to be bad at, namely determining strategies for matching what the firm is good at with properly researched market-centred opportunities and then scheduling and costing out what has to be done to achieve these objectives. There is little evidence of a deep understanding of what it is that companies can do better than their competitors or of how their distinctive competence can be matched with the needs of certain customer groups.

Instead, overall volume increases and minimum rates of return on investment are frequently applied to all products and markets, irrespective of market share, market growth rate, or the longevity of the product life cycle.

Indeed there is a lot of evidence to show that many companies are in trouble today precisely because their decentralized units manage their business only for the current profit and loss account, often at the expense of giving up valuable and hard-earned market share and running down the current business.

Thus, financial objectives, while being essential measures of the desired performance of a company, are of little practical help, since they say nothing about *how* the results are to be achieved.

The same applies to sales forecasts and budgets, which are *not* marketing objectives and strategies. Understanding the real meaning and significance of marketing objectives helps managers to know what information they need to enable them to think through the implications of choosing one or more positions in the market.

Finding the right words to describe the logic of marketing objectives and strategies is infinitely more difficult than writing down numbers on a piece of paper and leaving the strategies implicit.

This lies at the heart of the problem. For, clearly, a numbers-oriented system will not encourage managers to think in a structured way about strategically relevant market segments, nor will it encourage the collection, analysis and synthesis of actionable market data. And in the absence of such activities within operating units, it is unlikely that headquarters will have much other than intuition and 'feel' to use as a basis for decisions about the management of scarce resources.

This raises the difficult question of how these very complex problems can be overcome, for this is what baffles those who have been forced by market pressures to consider different ways of coping with their environment.

The problem remains of how to get managers throughout an organization to think beyond the horizon of the current year's operations. This applies universally to all types and sizes of company. Even chief executives of small companies find difficulty in breaking out of the fetters of the current profit and loss account.

The successes enjoyed in the past are often the result of the easy marketability of products, and during periods of high economic prosperity there was little pressure on companies to do anything other than solve operational problems as they arose.

Careful planning for the future seemed unnecessary. However, most companies today find themselves in increasingly competitive markets, and there is a growing realization that success in the future will come only from patient and meticulous planning and market preparation. This entails making a commitment to the future.

In today's increasingly competitive markets, there is a growing realization that success in the future will only come from meticulous planning and market preparation.

The problem is that, in large companies, managers who are evaluated and rewarded on the basis of current operations find difficulty in concerning themselves about the corporate future. This is exacerbated by behavioural issues, in the sense that it is safer, and more rewarding personally, for a manager to do what he knows best, which, in most cases, is to manage his *current* range of products and customers in order to make the *current* year's budget.

Unfortunately, long-range sales forecasting systems do not provide the answer. This kind of extrapolative approach fails to solve the problem of identifying precisely what has to be done today to ensure success in the future. Exactly the same problem exists in both large diversified companies and in small undiversified companies, except that in the former the problem is magnified and multiplied by the complexities of distance, hierarchical levels of management, and diversity of operations. Nevertheless, the problem is fundamentally the same.

Events that affect economic performance in a business come from so many directions, and in so many forms, that it is impossible for any manager to be precise about how they interact in the form of problems to be overcome, and opportunities to be exploited. The best a manager can do is to form a reasoned view about how they have affected the past, and how they will develop in the future, and what action needs to be taken over a period of time to enable the company to prepare itself for the expected changes. The problem is *how* to get managers to formulate their thoughts about these things, for until they have, it is unlikely that any objectives that are set will have much relevance or meaning.

Einstein wrote: 'The formulation of a problem is far more essential than its solution, which may be merely a matter of mathematical or experimental skill. To raise new questions, new possibilities, to regard old problems from a new angle, requires creative imagination.'

Unfortunately, such creativity is rare, especially when most managers are totally absorbed in managing today's business. Accordingly, they need some system which will help them to think in a structured way about problem formulation.

It is the provision of such a rational framework to help them to make explicit their intuitive economic models of the business that is almost totally lacking from the forecasting and budgeting systems of most companies.

Where companies have provided a framework for problem formulation, the level of management frustration is lower and motivation is higher.

It is apparent that in the absence of any such synthesized and simplified views of the business, setting meaningful objectives for the future seems like an insurmountable problem, and this in turn encourages the perpetuation of systems involving merely the extrapolation of numbers.

There is also substantial evidence that those companies that provide procedures for this process, in the form of standardized methods of presentation, have gone some considerable way to overcoming this problem. Although the possible number of analyses of business situations is infinite, procedural approaches help managers throughout an organization at least to consider the essential elements of problem definition in a structured way. This applies even to difficult foreign markets, where data and information are hard to come by, and even to markets which are being managed by agents, who find that these structured approaches, properly managed, help *their* businesses as well as those of their principals.

However, there are two further major advantages enjoyed by these companies. Firstly, the level of management frustration is lower and motivation is higher because the system provides a method of reaching agreement on such difficult matters as an assessment of the company's distinctive competence and the nature of the competitive environment. The internecine disputes and frustration which we all experience so often in our business lives is largely the result of an almost total absence of the means of discussing these issues and of reaching agreement on them. If a manager's boss does not understand what the environmental problems are, what his or her strengths and weaknesses are, nor what he or she is trying to achieve, and in the absence of any structured procedures and common terminology that can be used and understood by everybody, communications will be bad and the incidence of frustration will be higher.

Secondly, some form of standardized approach which is understood by all considerably improves the ability of headquarters management not only to understand the problems of individual operating units, but also to react to them in a constructive and helpful way.

This is because they receive information in a way which enables them to form a meaningful overview of total company activities and this provides a rational basis for resource allocation.

To summarize, a structured approach to situation analysis is necessary, irrespective of the size or complexity of the organization. Such a system should:

1 Ensure that comprehensive consideration is given to the definition of strengths and weaknesses and to problems and opportunities.
2 Ensure that a logical framework is used for the presentation of the key issues arising from this analysis.

Very few companies have planning systems which possess these characteristics. Those that do, manage to cope with their environment more effectively than those that do not. They find it easier to set meaningful marketing objectives, are more confident about the future, enjoy greater control over the business, and react less on a piecemeal basis to ongoing events. In short, they suffer fewer operational problems and are as a result more effective organizations.

What is marketing planning?

Let us begin by reminding ourselves of what we said in Chapter 2. It is a logical sequence of activities leading to the setting of marketing objectives and the formulation of plans for achieving them. It is a management *process*.

Conceptually, the process is very simple and, in summary, comprises the steps outlined in Figure 2.1. This process is universally agreed by the experts.

> Formalized marketing planning by means of a planning system is, *per se*, little more than a structured way of identifying a range of options for the company, of making them explicit in writing, of formulating marketing objectives which are consistent with the company's overall objectives and of scheduling and costing out the specific activities most likely to bring about the achievement of the objectives.

It is the systematization of this process which is distinctive and was found to lie at the heart of the theory of marketing planning.

Naivety about marketing planning

We have just rehearsed with you the notions that any textbook would offer should you care to re-read it. We have long been bemused, however, by the fact that many meticulous marketing planning companies fare badly while the sloppy or inarticulate in marketing terms do well. Is there any real relationship between marketing planning and commercial success? And, if so, how does that relationship work its way through?

There are, of course, many studies which identify a number of benefits to be obtained from marketing planning. But there is little explanation for the commercial success of those companies, that do *not* engage in formalized planning. Nor is there much exploration of the circumstances of those commercially unsuccessful companies that also have formalized marketing planning systems; and where the dysfunctional consequences are recognized, there is a failure to link this back to any kind of theory.

'Success' is, of course, influenced by many factors apart from just planning procedures. For example:

1 Financial performance at any one point in time is not necessarily a reflection of the adequacy or otherwise of planning procedures (cf the hotel industry, location, tourism etc.).

2 Some companies just happen to be in the right place at the right time(s).
3 Companies have many and varied objectives, such as, for example, stylistic objectives.
4 There is a proven relationship between management style and commercial success.

The process of marketing planning is conceptually simple, but the contextual issues can be very complex. For this reason, at most, 25 per cent of companies are getting marketing planning right.

In other words, marketing planning procedures *alone* are not enough for success.

We have said that the process of marketing planning is conceptually very simple and universally applicable. However, it is this very simplicity and universality that make it extremely complex once a number of contextual issues are added such as (a) company size; (b) degree of internationalization; (c) management style; (d) degree of business environmental turbulence and competitive hostility; (e) marketing growth rate; (f) market share; (g) technological changes; and so on.

It is very clear that the simplistic theories do not adequately address such contextual issues in relation to marketing planning, which may well account for the fact that so few companies actually do it.

In fact, 90 per cent of industrial goods companies in the author's study did not, by their own admission, produce anything approximating to an integrated, co-ordinated and internally consistent plan for their marketing activities.

This included a substantial number of companies that had highly formalized procedures for marketing planning. In six other recent studies in British universities, the highest estimate of companies getting marketing planning right was 25 per cent.

Certainly, few of these companies enjoyed the claimed benefits of formalized marketing planning, which in summary are as follows:

1 Co-ordination of the activities of many individuals whose actions are inter-related over time.
2 Identification of expected developments.
3 Preparedness to meet changes when they occur.
4 Minimization of non-rational responses to the unexpected.
5 Better communication among executives.
6 Minimization of conflicts among individuals which would result in a subordination of the goals of the company to those of the individual.

Indeed, many companies have a lot of the trappings of sophisticated marketing planning systems but suffer as many dysfunctional consequences as those companies that have only forecasting and budgeting systems. It is clear that for any marketing planning system to be effective, certain conditions have to be satisfied, which we shall deal with in detail shortly.

It should be pointed out, however, that it is by no means essential for any company not suffering from hostile and unstable competitive and environmental conditions to have an effective marketing planning system.

> Without exception, all those companies in the author's study which did not have an effective marketing planning system, and which were profitable, were also operating in buoyant or high-growth markets. Such companies, though, were less successful than comparable companies with effective marketing planning systems.

Success was considered to be not only a company's financial performance over a number of years, but also the way it coped with its environment.

What this means is that, apart from profitability, a company with an effective marketing planning system is likely to have:

○ Widely understood objectives
○ Highly motivated employees
○ High levels of actionable market information
○ Greater interfunctional co-ordination
○ Minimum waste and duplication of resources
○ Acceptance of the need for continuous change and a clear understanding of priorities
○ Greater control over the business and less vulnerability from the unexpected

In the case of companies without effective marketing planning systems, while it is possible to be profitable over a number of years, especially in high-growth markets, such companies will tend to be less profitable over time and to suffer problems which are the very opposite of the benefits referred to above.

> Furthermore, companies without effective marketing planning systems tend to suffer more serious commercial organization consequences when environmental and competitive conditions become hostile and unstable.

None of these points are new, in the sense that most of these benefits and problems are discernible to the careful observer. They are, however, actionable propositions for marketers.

Marketing planning systems: design and implementation problems

Many companies currently under siege have recognized the need for a more structured approach to planning their marketing and have opted for the kind of standardized, formalized procedures written about so much in textbooks. These rarely bring the claimed benefits and often bring marketing planning itself into disrepute.

> It is clear that any attempt at the introduction of formalized marketing planning systems has serious organizational and behavioural implications for a company, as it requires a change in its approach to managing its business.

It is also clear that unless a company recognizes these implications, and plans to seek ways of coping with them, formalized marketing planning will be ineffective.

Marketing planning is in practice a complex process, proceeding as it does from reviews to objectives, strategies, programmes, budgets and back again, until some kind of acceptable compromise is reached between what is desirable and what is practicable, given all the constraints that any company has.

It has been stated that the literature underestimates the operational difficulties of designing and implementing systems and procedures for marketing planning, and that the task becomes progressively more complex as the size and diversity of a company increases. Also, the literature is inadequate in the extent to which it provides practical guidance on design and implementation.

The author's research included a number of examples of companies that had been forced by market pressures to initiate procedures to help top management gain better control over the business. In all such cases, those responsible for designing the system found very little of practical help, either in the literature or in management courses. Enormous difficulties in system design and implementation were encountered in every instance.

The purpose of this section is to discuss these design and implementation problems. The most frequently encountered problems are summarized in Table 3.2.

Table 3.2 Marketing planning systems: design and implementation problems

1 Weak support from chief executive and top management
2 Lack of a plan for planning
3 Lack of line management support
   - hostility
   - lack of skills
   - lack of information
   - lack of resources
   - inadequate organization structure
4 Confusion over planning terms
5 Numbers in lieu of written objectives and strategies
6 Too much detail, too far ahead
7 Once-a-year ritual
8 Separation of operational planning from strategic planning
9 Failure to integrate marketing planning into a total corporate planning system
10 Delegation of planning to a planner

Weak support from chief executive and top management

There can be no doubt that unless the chief executive sees the need for a formalized marketing planning system, understands it, and shows an active interest in it, it is virtually impossible for a senior functional marketing executive to initiate procedures that will be used in a meaningful way.

This is particularly so in companies that are organized on the basis of divisional management, for which the marketing executive has no profit responsibility and in which he has no line management authority. In such cases, it is comparatively easy for senior operational managers to create 'political' difficulties, the most serious of which is just to ignore the new procedures entirely. Usually, however, the reasons for not participating in procedures, or for only partially following instructions, centre around the issues summarized in Table 3.2.

The vital role that the chief executive and top management *must* play in marketing planning underlines one of the key points in this section.

The active interest of the chief executive and top management is vital if a formalized marketing planning system is to be successful.

> That is, that it is *people* who make systems work, and that system design and implementation have to take account of the 'personality' of both the organization and the people involved, and that these are different in all organizations.

One of the most striking features we have observed is the difference in 'personalities' between companies, and the fact that within any one company there is a marked similarity between the attitudes of executives. These attitudes vary from the impersonal, autocratic kind at one extreme to the highly personal, participative kind at the other. This is discussed further in Chapter 12.

Any system, therefore, has to be designed around the people who have to make it work, and has to take account of the prevailing traditions, attitudes, skills, resource availability and organizational constraints. Since the chief executive and top management are the key influencers of these factors, without their active support and participation any formalized marketing planning system is unlikely to work. This fact emerged very clearly from the author's research, the worst possible manifestation of which was the way in which chief executives and top managers ignored plans which emerged from the planning system and continued to make key decisions which appeared illogical to those who had participated in the production of the plans. This very quickly destroyed any credibility that the emerging plans might have had, and led to the demise of the procedures and to serious levels of frustration throughout the organization.

Indeed, there is some evidence leading to the belief that chief executives who fail, firstly, to understand the essential role of marketing in generating profitable revenue in a business, and, secondly, to understand how marketing can be integrated into the other functional areas of the business through marketing planning procedures, are a key contributory factor in poor economic performance.

> There is a depressing preponderance of accountants who live by the rule of 'the bottom line' and who apply universal financial criteria indiscriminately to all products and markets, irrespective of the long-term consequences.

There is a similar preponderance of engineers who see marketing as an unworthy activity that is something to do with activities such as television advertising; and who think of their products only in terms of their technical features and functional characteristics, in spite of the overwhelming body of evidence that exists that these are only a part of what a customer buys. Not surprisingly, in companies headed by people like this, marketing planning is either non-existent, or where it is tried, it fails. This is the most frequently encountered barrier to effective marketing planning.

Lack of a plan for planning

The next most common cause of the failure or partial failure of marketing planning systems is the belief that, once a system is designed, it can be implemented immediately.

> One company achieved virtually no improvement in the quality of the plans coming into headquarters from the operating companies over a year after the introduction of a very sophisticated system.

The evidence indicates that a period of around three years is required in a major company before a complete marketing planning system can be implemented according to its design.

Failure, or partial failure, then, is often the result of not developing a timetable for introducing a new system, to take account of the following:

1 The need to communicate why a marketing planning system is necessary.
2 The need to recruit top management support and participation.
3 The need to test the system out on a limited basis to demonstrate its effectiveness and value.
4 The need for training programmes, or workshops, to train line management in its use.
5 Lack of data and information in some parts of the world.
6 Shortage of resources in some parts of the world.

Above all, a resolute sense of purpose and dedication is required, tempered by patience and a willingness to appreciate the inevitable problems which will be encountered in its implementation.

This problem is closely linked with the third major reason for planning system failure, which is lack of line management support.

Lack of line management support

Hostility, lack of skills, lack of data and information, lack of resources, and an inadequate organizational structure, all add up to a failure to obtain the willing participation of operational managers.

> Hostility on the part of line managers is by far the most common reaction to the introduction of new marketing planning systems. The reasons for this are not hard to find, and are related to the system initiators' lack of a plan for planning.

New systems inevitably require considerable explanation of the procedures involved and are usually accompanied by proformae, flow charts and the like. Often these devices are most conveniently presented in the form of a manual. When such a document arrives on the desk of a busy line manager, unheralded by previous explanation or discussion, the immediate reaction often appears to be fear of his possible inability to understand it and to comply with it, followed by anger, and finally rejection. They begin to picture headquarters as a remote 'ivory tower', totally divorced from the reality of the market place.

This is often exacerbated by their absorption in the current operating and reward system, which is geared to the achievement of *current* results, while the new system is geared to the future. Also, because of the trend in recent years towards the frequent movement of executives around organizations, there is less interest in planning for future business gains from which someone else is likely to benefit.

Allied to this is the fact that many line managers are ignorant of basic marketing principles, have never been used to breaking up their markets into strategically relevant segments, nor of collecting meaningful information about them.

This lack of skill is compounded by the fact that there are many countries in the world which cannot match the wealth of useful information and data available in the USA and Europe. This applies particularly to rapidly-growing economies, where the limited aggregate statistics are not only unreliable and incomplete, but also quickly out of date. The seriousness of this problem is highlighted by the often rigid list of home office informational requirements, which is based totally on the home market.

The solution to this particular problem requires a good deal of patience, common sense, ingenuity and flexibility on the part of both headquarters and operating management. This is closely connected with the need to consider resource availability and the prevailing organization structure. The problem of lack of reliable data and information can only be solved by devoting time and money to its solution, and where available resources are scarce it is unlikely that the information demands of headquarters can be met.

Lack of a suitable organizational structure for an integrated marketing function, compounded by lack of meaningful information about market segments, means that marketing planning is unlikely to be successful.

It is for this reason that some kind of appropriate headquarters organization has to be found for the collection and dissemination of valuable information, and that training has to be provided on ways of solving this problem.

Again, these issues are complicated by the varying degrees of size and complexity of companies. It is surprising to see the extent to which organizational structures cater inadequately for marketing as a function. In small companies, there is often no one other than the sales manager, who spends all his time engaged either in personal selling or in managing the sales force. Unless the chief executive is marketing-oriented, marketing planning is just not done.

In medium sized and large companies, particularly those that are divisionalized, there is rarely any provision at board level for marketing as a discipline. Sometimes there is a commercial director, with line management responsibility for the operating divisions, but apart from sales managers at divisional level, or a marketing manager at head office level, marketing as a function is not particularly well catered for. Where there is a marketing manager, he tends to be somewhat isolated from the mainstream activities.

> The most successful organizations are those with a fully integrated marketing function, whether it is line management responsible for sales, or a staff function, with operating units being a microcosm of the head office organization.

However, it is clear that without a suitable organizational structure, any attempt to implement a marketing planning system which requires the collection, analysis and synthesis of market-related information is unlikely to be successful.

> A classic example of this was a large diversified multinational, where no provision was made at headquarters for marketing, other than through the divisional directors, and where divisions also generally had no marketing function other than sales management. Their first attempt at writing a strategic plan as a result of market pressures was a complete failure.

The problem of organizing for marketing planning is discussed further in Chapter 11.

Confusion over planning terms

Confusion over planning terms is another reason for the failure of marketing planning systems. The initiators of these systems, often highly qualified, frequently use a form of planning terminology that is perceived by operational managers as meaningless jargon. One company even referred to the Ansoff matrix, and made frequent references to other forms of matrices, missions, dimensions, quadrants, and so on.

> Those companies with successful planning systems try to use terminology which will be familiar to operational management, and, where terms such as 'objectives' and 'strategies' are used, these are clearly defined, with examples given of their practical use.

Following Chapter 13 there is a glossary of terms.

Numbers in lieu of written objectives and strategies

Most managers in operating units are accustomed to completing sales forecasts, together with the associated financial implications. They are not accustomed to considering underlying causal factors for past performance or expected results, nor of highlighting opportunities, emphasizing key issues, and so on. Their outlook is essentially parochial and short-term, with a marked tendency to extrapolate numbers and to project the current business unchanged into the next fiscal year.

Thus, when a marketing planning system suddenly requires that they should make explicit their implicit economic model of the business, they cannot do it. So, instead of finding words to express the logic of their objectives and strategies, they repeat their past behaviour and fill in the data sheets provided without any narrative.

It is the provision of data sheets, and the emphasis which the system places on the physical counting of things, that encourages the questionnaire-completion mentality and hinders the development of the creative analysis so essential to effective strategic planning.

> Those companies with successful marketing planning systems ask only for essential data and place greater emphasis on narrative to explain the underlying thinking behind the objectives and strategies.

Too much detail, too far ahead

Connected with this is the problem of over-planning, usually caused by elaborate systems that demand information and data that head-quarters do not need and can never use. Systems that generate vast quantities of paper are generally demotivating for all concerned.

The biggest problem in this connection is undoubtedly the insistence on a detailed and thorough marketing audit. In itself this is not a bad discipline to impose on managers, but to do so without also providing some guidance on how it should be summarized to point up the key issues merely leads to the production of vast quantities of useless information. Its uselessness stems from the fact that it robs the ensuing plans of focus and confuses those who read it by the amount of detail provided.

In an over detailed and institutionalized planning system, the key strategic issues may be buried so deep in the detail that they get overlooked until it is too late.

The trouble is that few managers have the creative or analytical ability to isolate the really key issues, with the result that far more problems and opportunities are identified than the company can ever cope with. Consequently, the truly key strategic issues are buried deep in the detail and do not receive the attention they deserve until it is too late.

> In a number of companies with highly detailed and institutionalized marketing planning systems, the resulting plans contain so much detail that it is impossible to identify what the major objectives and strategies are.

Also, the managers in these companies are rarely able to express a simplified view of the business or of the essential things that have to be done today to ensure success. Such companies are often over-extended, trying to do too many things at once. Over-diversity, and being extended in too many directions, makes control over a confusingly heterogeneous portfolio of products and markets extremely difficult.

In companies with successful planning systems, there is at all levels a widespread understanding of the key objectives that have to be achieved, and of the means of achieving them.

In such companies, the rationale of each layer of the business is clear, and actions and decisions are disciplined by clear objectives that hang logically together as part of a rational, overall purpose.

The clarity and cohesiveness is achieved by means of a system of 'layering'. At each successive level of management throughout the organization, lower-level analyses are synthesized into a form that ensures that only the essential information needed for decision-making and control purpose reaches the next level of management. Thus, there are hierarchies of audits, SWOT analyses, assumptions, objectives, strategies and plans. This means, for example, that at conglomerate headquarters, top management have a clear understanding of the really key macro issues of company-wide significance, while at the lower level of profit responsibility, management also have a clear understanding of the really key micro issues of significance to the unit.

It can be concluded that a good measure of the effectiveness of a company's marketing planning system is the extent to which different managers in the organization can make a clear, lucid and logical statement about the major problems and opportunities they face, how they intend to deal with these, and how what they are doing fits in with some greater overall purpose.

Once-a-year ritual

One of the commonest weaknesses in the marketing planning systems of those companies whose planning systems fail to bring the expected benefits is the ritualistic nature of the activity. In such cases, operating managers treat the writing of the marketing plan as a thoroughly irksome and unpleasant duty.

The proformae are completed, not always very diligently, and the resulting plans are quickly filed away, never to be referred to again. They are seen as something which is required by headquarters rather than as an essential tool of management.

In other words, the production of the marketing plan is seen as a once-a-year ritual, a sort of game of management bluff. It is not surprising that the resulting plans are not used.

While this is obviously closely related to the explanations already given as to why some planning systems are ineffective, a common feature of companies that treat marketing planning as a once-a-year ritual is the short lead time given for the completion of the process. The problem with this approach is that, in the minds of managers, it tends to be relegated to a position of secondary importance.

In companies with effective systems, the planning cycle will start in month three or four and run through to month nine or ten, with the total twelve-month period being used to evaluate the on-going progress of existing plans by means of the company's marketing intelligence system. Thus, by spreading the planning activity over a longer period, and by means of the active participation of all levels of management at the appropriate moment, planning becomes an accepted and integral part of management behaviour rather than an addition to it which calls for unusual behaviour. There is a much better chance that plans resulting from such a system will be formulated in the sort of form that can be converted into things that people are actually going to do.

Separation of operational planning from strategic planning

This sub-section must be seen against the background of the difficulty which the majority of companies experience in carrying out any meaningful strategic planning. In the majority of cases, the figures that appear in the long-term corporate plan are little more than statistical extrapolations that satisfy boards of directors. If they are not satisfactory, the numbers are just altered, and frequently the gap between where a company gets to, compared with where it had planned to be in real terms, grows wider over time.

> Nevertheless most companies make long-term projections. Unfortunately, in the majority of cases these are totally separate from the short-term planning activity that takes place largely in the form of forecasting and budgeting.

The view that they should be separate is supported by many of the writers in this field, who describe strategic planning as very different, and therefore divorced, from operational planning. Indeed, many stress that failure to understand the essential difference between the two leads to confusion and prevents planning from becoming an integrated part of the company's overall management system. Yet it is precisely this separation between short- and long-term plans which the author's research revealed as being the major cause of the problems experienced today by many of the respondents.

> It is the failure of long-term plans to determine the difficult choices between the emphasis to be placed on current operations and the development of new business that leads to the failure of operating management to consider any alternatives to what they are currently doing.

The almost total separation of operational planning is a feature of many companies with ineffective systems.

The almost total separation of operational or short-term planning from strategic or long-term planning is a feature of many companies whose systems are not very effective.

More often than not, the long-term strategic plans tend to be straight-line extrapolations of past trends, and because different people are often involved, such as corporate planners, to the exclusion of some levels of operating management, the resulting plans bear virtually no relationship to the more detailed and immediate short-term plans.

This separation positively discourages operational managers from thinking strategically, with the result that detailed operational plans are completed in a vacuum. The so-called strategic plans do not provide the much-needed cohesion and logic, because they are seen as an ivory tower exercise which contains figures in which no one really believes.

> Unless strategic plans are built up from sound strategic analysis at grass-roots level by successive layers of operational management, they have little realism as a basis for corporate decisions.

At the same time, operational plans will become increasingly parochial in their outlook and will fail to incorporate the decisions that have to be taken today to safeguard the future.

Operational planning, then, should very much be part of the strategic planning process, and vice versa. Indeed, wherever possible, they should be completed at the same time, using the same managers and the same informational inputs.

The detailed operational plan should be the first year of the long-term plan, and operational managers should be encouraged to complete their long-term projections at the same time as their short-term projections. The advantage is that it encourages managers to think about what decisions have to be made in the current planning year, in order to achieve the long-term projections.

Failure to integrate marketing planning into a total corporate planning system

It is difficult to initiate an effective marketing planning system in the absence of a parallel corporate planning system. This is yet another facet of the separation of operational planning from strategic planning. For, unless similar processes and time scales to those being used in the marketing planning system are also being used by other major functions such as distribution, production, finance and personnel, the sort of trade-offs and compromises that have to be made in any company between what is wanted and what is practicable and affordable will not take place in a rational way. These trade offs have to be made on the basis of the fullest possible understanding of the reality of the company's multifunctional strengths and weaknesses, and opportunities and threats.

One of the problems of systems in which there is either a separation of the strategic corporate planning process, or in which marketing planning is the only formalized system, is the lack of participation of key functions of the company, such as engineering or production. Where these are key determinants of success, as in capital goods companies, a separate marketing planning system is virtually ineffective.

Where marketing, however, is a major activity, as in fast-moving industrial goods companies, it is possible to initiate a separate marketing planning system. The indications are that when this happens successfully, similar systems for other functional areas of the business quickly follow suit because of the benefits which are observed by the chief executive.

Delegation of planning to a planner

The incidence of this is higher with corporate planning than with marketing planning, although where there is some kind of corporate planning function at headquarters, and no organizational function for marketing, whatever strategic marketing planning takes place is done by the corporate planners as part of a system which is divorced from the operational planning mechanism. Not surprisingly, this exacerbates the separation of operational planning from strategic planning and encourages short-term thinking in the operational units.

Very often, corporate planners are young, highly qualified people, attached to the office of the chairman or group chief executive. They appear to be widely resented and are largely ignored by the mainstream of the business. There is not much evidence that they succeed in clarifying the company's overall strategy and there appears to be very little account taken of such strategies in the planning and thinking of operational units.

Without the co-operation of operational management, a planner becomes little more than a headquarters administrative assistant.

The literature sees the planner basically as a co-ordinator of the planning, not as an initiator of goals and strategies. It is clear that without the ability and the willingness of operational management to co-operate, a planner becomes little more than a kind of headquarters administrative assistant. In many large companies, where there is a person at headquarters with the specific title of marketing planning manager, he or she has usually been appointed as a result of the difficulty of controlling businesses that have grown rapidly in size and diversity, and which present a baffling array of new problems to deal with.

The marketing planning manager's tasks are essentially those of system design and co-ordination of inputs, although he or she is also expected to formulate overall objectives and strategies for the board.

> In all cases, it is lack of line management skills and inadequate organizational structures that frustrates the company's marketing efforts, rather than inadequacies on the part of the planner. This puts the onus on the planner alone to do a lot of the planning, which is, not surprisingly, largely ineffective.

Two particularly interesting facts emerged from the author's research. Firstly, the marketing planning manager, as the designer and initiator of systems for marketing planning, is often in an impossibly delicate political position *vis à vis* both superior line managers and more junior operational managers. It is clear that not too many chief executives understand the role of planning and have unrealistic expectations of the planner, whereas the planner cannot operate effectively without the full understanding, co-operation and participation of top management, and this rarely happens. Often, the appointment of a marketing planning manager, and sometimes of a senior marketing executive, seems to be an easier step for the chief

The inevitable consequence of employing a marketing planning manager is the need for change in management behaviour, the implications of which may be far-reaching.

executive and the board to take than giving serious consideration themselves to the implications of the new forces affecting the business and reformulating an overall strategy.

This leads on naturally to a second point. For the inevitable consequence of employing a marketing planning manager is that he or she will need to initiate changes in management behaviour in order to become effective. Usually these are far-reaching in their implications, affecting training, resource allocation, and organizational structures. As the catalyst for such changes, the planner, not surprisingly, comes up against enormous political barriers, the result of which is that he or she often becomes frustrated and, eventually, ineffective. This is without doubt a major problem, particularly for big companies. The problems which are raised by a marketing planning manager occur directly as a result of the failure of top management to give thought to the formulation of overall strategies. They have not done this in the past because they have not felt the need. However, when market pressures force the emerging problems of diversity and control to the surface, without a total willingness on their part to participate in far-reaching changes, there really is not much that a planner can do.

This raises the question again of the key role of the chief executive in the whole business of marketing planning. Without both his or her support and understanding of the very serious implications of initiating effective marketing planning procedures, whatever efforts are made, whether by a planner or a line manager, they will be largely ineffective.

Requisite marketing planning systems

The implications of all this are principally as follows:

1 Any closed loop marketing planning system (but especially one that is essentially a forecasting and budgeting system) will lead to a gradual decline of marketing and creativity. Therefore, there has to be some mechanism for preventing inertia from setting in through the over-bureaucratization of the system.

2 Marketing planning undertaken at the functional level of marketing, in the absence of a means of integration with other functional areas of the business at general management level, will be largely ineffective.

3 The separation of responsibility for operational and strategic marketing planning will lead to a divergence of the short-term thrust of a business at the operational level from the long-term objectives of the enterprise as a whole. This will encourage a preoccupation with short-term results at operational level, which normally makes the firm less effective in the long term.

4 Unless the chief executive understands and takes an active role in marketing planning, it will never be an effective system.

5 A period of up to three years is necessary (especially in large firms), for the successful introduction of an effective marketing planning system.

In Chapter 12 of this book we will explore in detail what is meant by the term 'requisite marketing planning' when we explain how to design and implement an effective marketing planning system.

For now, we believe we have given sufficient background information about the *process* of marketing planning, and why this apparently simple process requires much more perception and attention than is typically accorded it. We can now go on to explore in more detail each of the elements of this process before putting all the pieces together again in the final chapter.

Application question 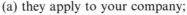 Taking each of the issues listed in Tables 3.1 and 3.2, say in what ways:

(a) they apply to your company;
(b) you deal successfully with them.

Review of Chapter 3

Ignorance

Most companies plan, using a combination of forecasting and budgeting systems. These tend to project current business into the future, which can work if the future is going to be the same as the present or the past. As a result of using such systems, the following problems often occur:

1 Lost opportunities for profit.
2 Meaningless numbers in long-term plans.
3 Unrealistic objectives.
4 Lack of actionable market information.
5 Interfunctional strife.
6 Management frustration.
7 Proliferation of products and markets.
8 Wasted promotional expenditure.
9 Confusion over pricing.
10 Growing vulnerability to changes in the business environment.
11 Loss of control over the business.   *Try Exercise 3.1*

Common implementation problems

1 Weak support from the chief executive and top management.
2 Lack of a plan for planning.
3 Lack of line management support due to:

  ○ Hostility.
  ○ Lack of skills.
  ○ Lack of resources.
  ○ Lack of information.
  ○ Inadequate organization structure.

4 Confusion over planning terms.
5 Numbers in lieu of written objectives and strategies.
6 Too much detail, too far ahead.
7 Once-a-year ritual.
8 Separation of operational marketing planning from strategic marketing planning.

9 Failure to integrate marketing planning into the total corporate planning system.

10 Delegation of planning to a planner. *Try Exercise 3.2*

Questions raised for the company

1 If we introduce marketing planning, will we automatically become more successful?

No. Many other factors come into play.

2 What are these factors?

Here are three common factors:

(a) Companies who by chance are in high growth markets often don't plan. They are just dragged along by the general momentum.

(b) If the company's culture and management style are not really supportive of marketing planning (i.e. there is no real belief in it), no improvements will occur.

(c) If the business is highly competitive, no improvement will necessarily be seen. *But* the company might fare much worse without a marketing plan.

3 Is all the time and effort put into marketing planning going to be worthwhile?

Only you can say. Weigh up the costs of planning against the costs of not planning.

Introduction to Chapter 3 exercises

The first exercise focuses on the types of problem that your company might be experiencing because of inefficiencies in the marketing planning system. In this sense it is providing an additional diagnosis about whether or not you need to improve your system. At the same time it helps to uncover some of the areas on which any new planning process needs to make an impact.

The second exercise attempts to be quite specific in pinpointing which aspects of the company need to be addressed in order to bring about the biggest improvements in marketing planning.

Exercise 3.1 Symptoms of a lack of marketing planning

Put an 'X' at the point you feel is appropriate as being descriptive of your company against each of the statements below:

	Mainly true	Mainly untrue
1 We seem to be missing opportunities for making profit.		
2 Our long-term planning seems to be nothing more than lots of meaningless numbers.		
3 Looked at rationally, our marketing objectives are unreasonable.		
4 We lack actionable marketing information.		
5 Managers are frustrated by the interfunctional strife and rivalry which seem to exist.		
6 There seems to be a steady proliferation of products and/or markets.		

	Mainly true	Mainly untrue
7 Much of our promotional expenditure is wasted.		
8 There is confusion over pricing.		
9 We are becoming increasingly vulnerable to changes in our business environment.		
10 There is a feeling that we are not running the business, but instead, it and outside forces are running us.		

If you find it difficult to put an 'X' against any statement, you should confer with some colleagues rather than making guesses.

Join the 'X' for statement 1 to the 'X' of statement 2 with a straight line. Then join 2 to 3, 3 to 4, etc. in a similar way down to 10.

Interpretation of Exercise 3.1

You have just drawn a 'profile' of 'marketing planning' in your company.

○ If your 'profile line' tends to be positioned to the right-hand side of the spectrum, then it appears that you are not experiencing many of the problems which stem from a lack of marketing planning. In other words, you appear to be doing things fairly well.

○ If, on the other hand, your profile line tends towards the left-hand side, you are much less fortunate, and should consider reviewing your current marketing planning process, paying particular attention to the problems you wish to overcome.

Exercise 3.2 Marketing planning questionnaire – organizational issues

You are asked to answer a series of statements about your organization's approach to marketing planning. Since this quest is for useful and genuine data, please try to be as accurate and objective as you can as you complete this document.

You score the questionnaire by entering a number, 1–5, *only in the position indicated by the line next to each statement*. Choose your scores, using these criteria:

1 If you strongly disagree with statement.
2 If you tend to disagree with statement.
3 If you don't know if you agree or disagree.
4 If you tend to agree with statement.
5 If you strongly agree with statement.

	A	B	C	D	E
1 The chief executive directors show an active interest in marketing planning.					–
2 The chief executive directors demonstrate their understanding of marketing planning.	–				
3 The chief executive directors use the marketing plan as the basis for making key marketing decisions.				–	
4 The chief executive directors allocate adequate resources to ensure the marketing plan is completed satisfactorily.		–			

	A	B	C	D	E
5 The need for a marketing plan is clearly explained to all managers.	–				
6 There is adequate information/data upon which to base a marketing plan.		–			
7 Our marketing plan has a good balance between short-term and long-term objectives.			–		
8 People are clear about their role in the marketing planning process.					–
9 Line managers are trained to understand how the marketing planning process operates.	–				
10 Line operational managers believe the marketing plan is a useful document.				–	
11 Enough time is allowed for the planning process.		–			
12 It is made easy for line managers to understand the plan.	–				
13 Marketing planning is never starved for lack of resources.			–		
14 It is reasonable for a company like ours to have a well-thought-out marketing plan.				–	
15 Reasons for past successes or failures are analysed.			–		
16 In our organization we don't leave planning just to the planners; other managers have a valuable contribution to make.					–
17 Our organizational style encourages a sound marketing planning process.				–	
18 There is a clear understanding of the marketing terminology we use in our organization.	–				
19 Market opportunities are highlighted by the planning process.			–		
20 Functional specialists contribute to the marketing planning process.					–
21 We limit our activities so that we are not faced with trying to do too many things at one time.		–			
22 Taking part in marketing planning in our organization holds a high prospect of being rewarded, either financially or in career terms.				–	
23 Only essential data appear in our plans.			–		
24 Marketing does not operate in an 'ivory tower'.				–	
25 From the wealth of information available to use, we are good at picking out the key issues.	–				
26 There is a balance between narrative explanation and numerical data in our plans.			–		

	A	B	C	D	E
27 Our field salesforce operates in a way which is supportive to our marketing plan.					–
28 Our plan demonstrates a high level of awareness of the 'macro' issues facing us.	–				
29 Inputs to the planning process are on the whole as accurate as we can make them.		–			
30 Marketing planning is always tackled in a meaningful and serious way.			–		
31 Our plan doesn't duck the major problems and opportunities faced by the organization.				–	
32 There is a high awareness of 'micro' issues in our plan.	–				
33 Our plans recognize that in the short term we have to match our current capabilities to the market opportunities.		–			
34 Inputs to the marketing planning process are an integral part of the job of all line managers.					–
35 Marketing planning is a priority issue in our organization.				–	
36 Our planning inputs are not 'massaged' to satisfy senior executives.		–			
37 People understand and are reasonably happy that our marketing planning process is logical and appropriate.	–				
38 We use the same time-scale for our marketing plans as we do for finance, distribution, production and personnel.		–			
39 We view our operational plan as the first year of our long-term plan, not as a separate entity.			–		
40 Senior executives do not see themselves as operating beyond the confines of the marketing plan.				–	
41 The advocates of 'correct' marketing planning are senior enough in the company to make sure it happens.			–		
42 People are always given clear instructions about the nature of their expected contribution to the marketing plan.		–			
43 We try to make data collection and retrieval as simple as possible.	–				
44 Our marketing plans do not go into great detail, but usually give enough information to make any necessary point.			–		
45 The role of specialists is made quite clear in our planning process.					–
46 We are always prepared to learn any new techniques that will make our marketing planning process more effective.	–				

	A	B	C	D	E
47 The role of marketing planning is clearly understood in the organization.					–
48 Marketing research studies (by internal staff or agencies) are often used as inputs to our marketing planning process.		–			
49 Our marketing planning is regularly evaluated in an attempt to improve the process.			–		
50 The chief executive directors receive information which enables them to assess whether or not the marketing plan is coming to fruition as expected.					–
TOTAL SCORES					

The rationale behind the questionnaire

There are many ways of looking at organizations and establishing 'models' of how they operate. One very common model is the organization chart, which attempts to show how responsibility is distributed throughout the company and to clarify the chains of command.

Other models are derived from the inputs and outputs of the company. For example, a financial model is built up by analysing all the necessary financial inputs required to conduct the business and monitoring the efficiency by which these are converted into sales revenue.

The questionnaire in Exercise 3.2 is based on a particularly useful model, one which helps us to understand the relation between different facets of the organization. By understanding the nature of these relations, we are better placed to introduce organizational change – in this case, an improved marketing planning system.

There are three main assumptions behind this model:

1 *That the organization today is to some extent, often very strongly, conditioned by its historical background.* For example, if historically there has never been a pressing need for a comprehensive marketing planning system because of favourable trading conditions, then this will be reflected in the current planning system and the attitudes of the company's staff.
2 *That the organization today is to some extent, sometimes strongly, conditioned and directed by its future goals.* For example, the company that senses its marketing planning processes need to improve will take steps to introduce changes. That these changes will make an impact on organizational life is self-evident. Furthermore, much of the resistance to be overcome will stem from the 'historical' forces mentioned above.
3 *What actually happens in an organization is determined by the skills, knowledge, experience and beliefs of the organization's personnel.* Thus at the heart of any organization is the collective expertise or 'education' at its disposal. This will ultimately determine the success it has in any work it undertakes, whether it is making goods or providing services.

Clearly, then, the level of 'education' will also be a determining factor in the quality and scope of the company's marketing planning process. These assumptions provide the 'skeleton' of our organizational model (Figure 3.1).

There are still important elements missing from this model. Irrespective of the company's corporate sum of available skills and knowledge, nothing can be produced without physical *resources* being made available. The key

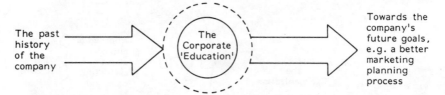

Figure 3.1   Education and marketing planning

resources required for marketing planning will be accurate data, means of storing and retrieving the data, adequate staff and time to analyse the data.

But having the right resources isn't the whole solution; the company must also develop the best systems or *routines* to optimize the use of these resources. In marketing planning terms, concern is likely to focus on routines associated with collecting data, evaluating past performance, spotting marketing opportunities, sifting essential information from non-essential information, etc.

Routines, however, do not necessarily look after themselves. As soon as any system is set up, *roles and relationships* need to be defined. Who is going to do what to ensure that things happen?

Again, in marketing planning terms this will call into question the role of various members of staff from the chief executive downwards. How clear are people about their role in the planning process? Should planning just be left to the planning department. What is the role of functional specialists? Who actually collects marketing data? Whom do they present it to? Many questions have to be answered if the subsequent routines are going to function smoothly.

Even this isn't the end of the story, because once roles are defined, there is still the problem of setting up the right *organizational structure and climate*, one that will enable people to fulfil their roles in a productive way.

From a marketing-planning viewpoint, structure and climate issues surface in several ways. For example, the level of commitment to the planning process, the degree to which functional specialists are integrated into the planning process, the degree to which long- and short-term issues are accommodated, the extent to which the company is prepared to tackle the real and important issues it faces, the openness of communications, etc.

It is now possible to see how the completed model looks (Figure 3.2).

From the foregoing explanation, it is possible to see how the different facets of the organization all interrelate.

(a) the 'corporate education', about marketing planning;
(b) the resources allocated to planning;
(c) the routines or systems that are used;
(d) the roles and relationships of those engaged in marketing planning;
(e) the organizational structure and climate, and the extent to which it supports marketing planning;

Thus to introduce an improved marketing planning system might call for changes in all these areas. Some personnel might need training, more or different resources might be required, routines or systems might need

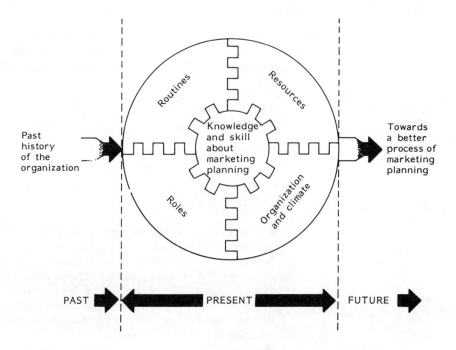

Figure 3.2 Marketing planning model

improving, roles and relationships perhaps need to be reappraised, and the structure and climate of the organization re-examined.

Conversely, only one or two of these areas might need tackling.

The questionnaire is designed to provide a 'snapshot' of the company and to help you identify which areas might be the starting point for introducing improvements.

Interpretation of Exercise 3.2
Add up the scores for columns **A**, **B**, **C**, **D** and **E** and write them in the boxes provided. Each of the letters represents a potential barrier to marketing planning, namely:

A = Cognitive barrier, i.e. knowledge and skills.
B = Resource barrier, i.e. lack of time, people, data.
C = Systems/routine barrier, i.e. lack of procedures.
D = Organizational climate barrier, i.e. belief and interest in marketing planning.
E = Behaviour barrier, i.e. the roles people play.

The maximum score for each of these areas is 50 points. The higher the score, the less that potential barrier to marketing is likely to be making an impact. In other words, the areas with low scores (below 30) will probably be the areas worth investigating initially in the search for improvement.

Personal notes
List what actions need to be taken.

4 Completing the marketing audit: 1 The customer and market audit

Summary

This chapter focuses specifically on whom we sell to, and the next chapter on what we sell to them. The other elements of marketing are covered in Chapters 7–11. Chapter 4 begins by defining the difference between customers and consumers, the meaning of market share and the meaning of Pareto analysis. It then describes market segmentation and the several methods of segmenting markets, including customer behaviour, benefit analysis and customer attitudes. Some examples of market segmentation are provided and the chapter closes by stressing why market segmentation is vital to marketing planning.

Introduction

Now we understand the process of marketing planning, we can begin to look in more detail at its principal components. We have, as it were, seen the picture on the front of the jigsaw puzzle; we can now examine the individual pieces with a better understanding of where they fit.

The next two chapters are designed to help us to carry out a meaningful marketing audit. We have already looked at the issues that need to be considered; what we need now are the means to help us to undertake such an analysis.

It should be stressed that, while the following two chapters deal specifically with how to carry out a customer, market, and product audit, it should not be assumed that, in carrying out a marketing audit, price, promotion, and place, information and organization are unimportant. Indeed, Chapters 7–11 are devoted to these important determinants of commercial success and will provide the marketing auditor with the necessary confidence to carry out these specific parts of the audit.

It is also important to stress that we are still dealing with steps in the marketing planning process, rather than with the all-important output of the process, the strategic marketing plan itself.

It will be recalled that the contents of the strategic marketing plan, outlined in Chapter 2, represent the summarized conclusions emanating from the marketing audit and will only be as good as the audit allows. The marketing audit itself should be a separate step in the process and under no circumstances should voluminous data and analysis appear in the plan itself. All of this rightly belongs in the marketing audit document.

Thus, the marketing audit is a crucial stage in the marketing planning process. Do not, however, confuse it with the marketing plan itself, the actual contents of which are set out in detail in Chapter 13.

The difference between customers and consumers

We now turn our attention to one of the key determinants of successful marketing planning – *market segmentation*. This is fundamental to the matching process described in Chapter 1. But, in order to understand market segmentation, it is first necessary to appreciate the difference between *customers* and *consumers*, the meaning of *market share* and the phenomenon known as the *Pareto effect*.

Let us start with the difference between customers and consumers. The term 'consumer' is interpreted by most to mean the final consumer, who is not necessarily the customer. Take the example of a mother or father who is buying breakfast cereals. The chances are that they are intermediate customers, acting as agents on behalf of the eventual consumers (their family) and, in order to market cereals effectively, it is clearly necessary to understand what the end-consumer wants, as well as what the parents want.

This is only relevant in that it is always necessary to be aware of the needs of eventual consumers down the buying chain.

Consider the case of the industrial purchasing officer buying raw materials such as wool tops for conversion into semi-finished cloths, which are then sold to other companies for incorporation into the final product, say a suit, or a dress, for sale in consumer markets. Here, we can see that the requirements of those various intermediaries and the end-user are eventually translated into the specifications of the purchasing officer to the raw materials manufacturer. Consequently, the market needs that this manufacturing company is attempting to satisfy must in the last analysis be defined in terms of the requirements of the ultimate users – the consumer – even though our direct customer is quite clearly the purchasing officer.

Given that we can appreciate the distinction between customers and consumers and the need constantly to be alert to any changes in the ultimate consumption patterns of the products to which our own contributes, the next question to be faced is: who are our customers?

Direct customers are those people or organizations who actually buy direct from us. They could, therefore, be distributors, retailers and the like. However, as intimated in the previous paragraph, there is a tendency for organizations to confine their interest, hence their marketing, only to those who actually place orders. This can be a major mistake, as can be seen from the following case history.

> A fertilizer company that had grown and prospered during the 1970s and 1980s, because of the superior nature of its products, reached its farmer consumers via merchants (wholesalers). However, as other companies copied the technology, the merchants began to stock competitive products and drove prices and margins down. Had the fertilizer company paid more attention to the needs of its different farmer groups and developed products especially for them, based on farmer segmentation, it would have continued to create demand pull through differentiation.
>
> As it was, their products became commodities and the power shifted almost entirely to the merchants. This company is no longer in business.

There are countless other examples of companies which, because they did not pay sufficient attention to the needs of users further down the value chain, eventually ceased to provide any real value to their direct customers and eventually went out of business.

Closely related to the question of the difference between customers and consumers is the question of what our market share is.

Market share

Most businesspeople already understand that there is a direct relationship between relatively high share of any market and high returns on investment, as shown in Figure 4.1.

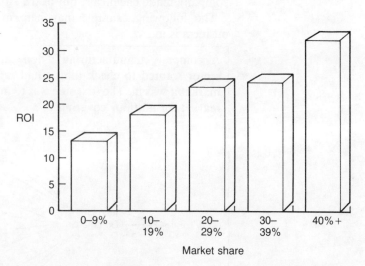

Source: PIMS database.

Figure 4.1 The relationship between market share and return on investment

Clearly, however, since, for example, BMW are not in the same market as Ford, it is important to be most careful about how 'Market' is defined. Correct market definition is crucial for: measuring market share and market growth; the specification of target customers; reconfirmation of relevant competitors; and, most importantly of all, the formulation of marketing strategy, for it is this, above all else, that delivers differential advantage.

The general rule for the definition of 'market' definition is that it is the aggregation of all the products that appear to satisfy the same need. For example, we would regard the in-company caterer as only one option when it came to satisfying lunch-time hunger. This particular need could also be satisfied at external restaurants, public houses, fast food specialists and sandwich bars. The emphasis in the definition, therefore, is clearly on the word 'need'.

Aggregating currently available products/services is, however, simply an aid to arriving at the definition, as it is important to recognize that new products, yet to be developed, could better satisfy the users' need. For example, the button manufacturer who believed their market was the 'button market' would have been very disappointed when zips and Velcro began to satisfy the need for fastenings! A needs-based definition for this company would have enabled the management to recognize the fickleness of current products, and to accept that one of their principal tasks was to seek out better ways of satisfying their market's needs and to evolve their product offer accordingly. The founder of Revlon, Charles Revlon, is credited with one of the more famous needs-based definitions of a market. When he drew the distinction between products and needs for his company, he captured it by describing the factory as being the place where the company made chemicals, but in the store he sold 'hope'.

The following example may help in defining the market your business is in.

A company manufacturing nylon carpet for the commercial sector wanted to check that it had a realistic definition of the market it was in. The first step was to map out the total available market for all floor covering:

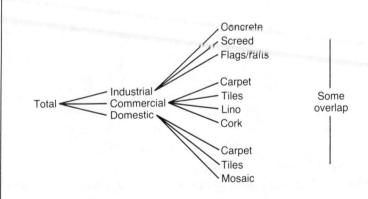

Clearly, it would be wrong to include the three types of floor covering used in the industrial sector in the company's market definition. The qualities required from such flooring cannot hope to be matched in a carpet made from any currently known type of fibre. Similarly, in both the commercial and domestic sectors, nylon carpet is not a competitor for the luxury end of the market. This luxury part of the market buys carpet made from natural fibres, particularly wool.

This leaves the non-luxury commercial and domestic sectors which, in total, represented the company's potential available market. It was potentially available because the company could, for example, produce nylon carpet for the domestic sector and extend its market this way. Similarly, the company could move into manufacturing nylon carpet tiles and extend its operation into this product for both the domestic and commercial sectors. There was also no reason why the company should not look at replacing lino, cork or mosaic flooring with nylon carpet.

It is necessary to arrive at a meaningful balance between a broad market definition and a manageable market definition.

Many of the opportunities in the potentially available market, however, represent possible strategies for the future. They would be considered during the marketing planning process when the future plans for the current business activity did not achieve the required financial targets. The question now, therefore is, what is the company's realistically available market?

To assist the company in this final stage of arriving at a market definition, the 'needs' being met by the current products, as highlighted by the current customers, were first listed. This revealed that the company's nylon carpet was bought because:

○ It fell into a particular price range
○ It was quiet underfoot
○ It had a life expectancy of 15 years
○ It was available in pleasant colours and textures
○ The manufacturing plant was within a 60 mile radius.

In addition to the obvious, this list removed lino, cork and mosaic from the company's available market.

Finally, the company looked at the applicability of its current distribution and selling methods to the potentially available market, ruling out those sections of the market which required different selling and distribution approaches. This meant that it was unrealistic to include the domestic sector in the market definition.

Products and manufacturers which met all the criteria were then listed, along with their end users. The company had now arrived at both a market definition and a current market size.

This example also illustrates the need to arrive at a meaningful balance between a broad market definition and a manageable market definition. Too narrow a definition has the pitfall of restricting the range of new opportunities segmentation could open up for your business. On the other hand, too broad a definition may make marketing planning meaningless. For example, the television broadcasting companies are in the 'entertainment' market, which also consists of theatres, cinemas and theme parks, to name but a few. This is a fairly broad definition. It may, therefore, be more manageable for the television broadcasters, when looking at segmenting their market, to define their market as being the 'home entertainment' market. This could then be further refined into the pre-school, child, teenager, family, or adult home entertainment market.

To help with calculating market share, the following definitions are useful:

o Product class, e.g. cigarettes, computers, fertilizers, carpets
o Product subclass, e.g. filter, personal computers, nitrogen, carpet tiles
o Product brand, e.g. Silk Cut, IBM, Nitram, Heuga

Silk Cut as a brand, for the purpose of measuring market share, is only concerned with *the aggregate of all other brands that satisfy the same group of customer wants*. Nevertheless, the manufacturer of Silk Cut also needs to be aware of the sales trends of filter cigarettes and the cigarette market in total.

One of the most frequent mistakes that is made by people who do not understand what market share really means is to assume that their company has only a small share of some market, whereas, if the company is commercially successful, it probably has a much larger share of a smaller market.

Whilst is it tempting to think that the examples given above amount to 'rigging' the definition of market and that there is the danger of fooling ourselves, we must never lose sight of the purpose of market segmentation, which is to enable us to create competitive advantage for ourselves by creating greater value for our customers. Thus, for the carpet manufacturer, or for a London orchestra that defines its market as the aggregation of all London classical orchestras rather than as all entertainment, as long as its market definition enables it to outperform its competitors and grow profitably, this is the key. Obviously, however, the definition needs to be kept under review and revised, if necessary.

To summarize, correct market definition is crucial for the purpose of:

o Share measurement
o Growth measurement
o The specification of target customers
o The recognition of relevant competitors
o The formulation of marketing objectives and strategies

This brings us to another useful and fascinating observation about markets.

Pareto effect

It is a phenomenon commonly observed by most companies that a small proportion of their customers account for a large proportion of their business. This is often referred to as the 80/20 rule, or the

Pareto effect, whereby about 20 per cent of customers account for about 80 per cent of business.

If we graph the proportion of customers that account for a certain proportion of sales, then we might expect to find a relationship similar to that shown in Figure 4.2. Here, customers have been categorized simply as A, B or C according to the proportion of sales they account for. The A customers, perhaps 25 per cent of the total, account for about 70 per cent of sales; B customers, say 55 per cent of the total, account for 20 per cent of total sales; and C customers, 20 per cent of the total, account for the remaining 10 per cent of sales.

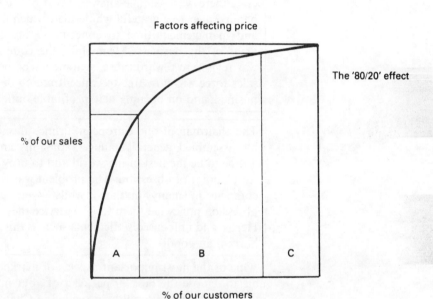

Figure 4.2

The Pareto effect is found in almost all markets, from capital industrial goods to banking and consumer goods. What is the significance of this?

What is certain is that it does not mean that a company should drop 80 per cent of its customers! For one thing, the sales volume bought by these customers makes a valuable contribution to over-heads. For another, it is almost certain that the 80/20 rule would still apply to the remaining 20 per cent. One could go on forever, until there was only a single customer left! However, in carrying out this kind of analysis, it should become obvious where the company should be placing its greatest effort, since most of a company's costs are incurred by the 80 per cent which accounts for only 20 per cent of sales.

There is, however, a serious danger. This form of analysis is static. In other words, the best potential customers may well be in the 80 per cent, or even in the larger group of non-customers.

It is obvious, then, that while such analysis is vital, great care is necessary over how it is used. This is something we can now begin to discuss.

> One manufacturer in the soft drinks industry did an analysis of its trade in the south-east of England and found that almost 85 per cent of its trade was coming from 20 per cent of its customers. Yet exactly the same service was being given to them all. All were receiving fortnightly calls from the sales force, all received a fortnightly delivery, and all paid the same price for the product. Not surprisingly, this led to an enormous investment in depots and vehicles, while the associated operating expenses were out of all proportion to the margins enjoyed by the company. In this case, there was a simple answer. Most of the small accounts were handed over to a grateful wholesaler, which freed valuable capital and management time to concentrate on the really important areas of the business. Meanwhile, the company's pricing policy was revised to reward those customers who bought more, and the sales force was now free to concentrate on developing its existing business and on opening new profitable outlets.

> The chairman of one European airline, alas, now bankrupt, told his assembled general managers that his ambition was for his airline to be the best in the world and to provide customer service to the point of obsession. The problem was that his airline didn't compete in many markets, whilst their unfocused customer obsession policy led them to give service they just couldn't afford. Heroic and unfocused settlements such as this chairman's do more harm than good!

One of the most important aspects of marketing planning is being able to choose the best 20 per cent of your market to focus on. A method of doing this will be provided in Chapter 6.

Market segmentation

We can now begin to concentrate on a methodology for making market segmentation a reality, market segmentation being the means by which any company seeks to gain a differential advantage over its competitors.

Markets usually fall into natural groups, or segments, which contain customers who exhibit the same broad characteristics. These segments form separate markets in themselves and can often be of considerable size. Taken to its extreme, each individual consumer is a unique market segment, for all people are different in their requirements.

However, it is clearly uneconomical to make unique products for the needs of individuals, except in the most unusual circumstances. Consequently, products are made to appeal to groups of customers who share approximately the same needs.

It is not surprising, then, to hear that there are certain universally accepted criteria concerning what constitutes a viable market segment:

○ Segments should be of an adequate size to provide the company with the desired return for its effort.
○ Members of each segment should have a high degree of similarity, yet be distinct from the rest of the market.
○ Criteria for describing segments must be relevant to the purchase situation.
○ Segments must be reachable.

Unless we succeed in identifying a viable market segment for our product we will fail to achieve differential advantage and will become just another company selling 'me too' products.

While many of these criteria are obvious when we consider them, in practice market segmentation is one of the most difficult of marketing concepts to turn into a reality. Yet we must succeed, otherwise we become just another company selling what are called 'me too' products. In other words, what we offer the potential customer is very much the same as what any other company offers and, in such circumstances, it is likely to be the lowest priced article that is bought. This can be ruinous to our profits, unless we happen to have lower costs, hence higher margins, than our competitors. There is more about this important aspect of marketing in Chapter 5.

There are basically three steps to market segmentation, all of which have to be completed.

The first is essentially a manifestation of the way customers actually behave in the market place and consists of answering the question, *who* is buying *what*? The second answers the question *why* are they buying what they buy? The third step involves searching for market segments.

Market mapping

A useful way of tackling the complex issue of market segmentation is to start by drawing a 'market map' as a precursor to a more detailed examination of who buys what.

A market map defines the value chain between supplier and final user, which takes into account the various buying mechanisms found in a market, including the part played by 'influencers'.

In general, if an organization's products or services go through the same channels to similar end users, one composite market map can be drawn. If, however, some products or services go through totally different channels and/or to totally different markets, there will be a need for more than one market map.

It is probably sensible to treat different business units individually because such structures usually exist because the volume or value of business justifies such a specific focus. For example, in the case of a farming co-operative supplying seeds, fertilizer, crop protection, insurance and banking to farmers, it would be sensible to start, initially, by drawing a separate market map for each of these product groups, even though they all appear to go through similar channels to the same end users. In the organization concerned, each one is treated as a separate SBU.

In other words, it is recommended that you start the mapping (and subsequent segmentation) process at the lowest level of disaggregation within the organization's current structure.

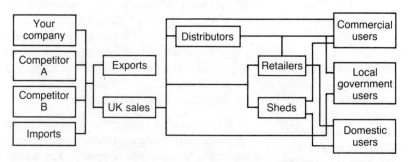

Note: This market map combines domestic and business-to-business end users. Some of the distribution channels are common to both of them.

Figure 4.3 A simple market map

An example of a very basic market map is shown in Figure 4.3.

It is very important that your market map tracks your products/services, along with those of your competitors, all the way through to the final user, even though you may not actually sell to them direct.

In some markets, the direct customer/purchaser will not always be the final user. For example, a company (or household) may commission a third party contractor to carry out some redecoration, or an advertising agency to develop and conduct a promotional campaign, or a bank/accountant/financial adviser to produce and implement a financial programme. For all of us, the doctor we visit when seeking treatment is, in many respects, a contractor when it comes to prescribing medicine. Although the contractor is strictly the direct buyer, they are not the final user. The distinction is important because, to win the commission, the contractor would have needed to understand the requirements of the customer and, in carrying out the commission, would have carried out those requirements on behalf of the customer. To miss out the final user from the market map would, therefore, have ignored an array of different needs which the supplier would need to be aware of (and have included in their product offer) if the supplier were to ensure their company name appeared on the contractor's 'preferred supplier list'. The inclusion of a contractor on a market map is illustrated in Figure 4.4.

Ensuring that your market map continues right the way through to the final user is also appropriate in those situations where final users have their products/services purchased for them by their company's Purchasing Department. In such instances, the market map would track your products/services down the corridors of your business client and continue beyond the Purchasing Department to the department(s) in which the final user(s) were found, each of which either utilized your product/service differently, or utilized it to achieve a different objective. Each of these final user departments

It is important to track your products/services right through to the end user even if you do not actually sell to them direct.

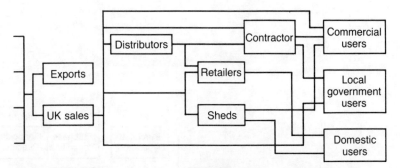

Note: In this particular market map the introduction of contractors has now reduced the similarity between the domestic and business-to-business end users quite notably. Sheds continue to be shared with a proportion of the commercial users, but this new contractor stage only operates in the business-to-business field.

Figure 4.4 Market map with contractor

would be listed separately on your market map. (Where a single final user department, or individual, puts your product/service to a number of different end-user applications, they should only appear on the market map once. Where appropriate, include in your market map the purchasing procedures, such as committees, authorizers, sealed bids, etc., encountered on the way as shown in Figure 4.5.

The map in Figure 4.5 also illustrates a particular purchasing procedure which involves a Purchasing Committee and then the Financial Director. This has therefore been combined into one box.

As the figures have illustrated, most market maps will have at least two principal components:

o The channel (distribution channel)
o Consumers (purchasers/final users)

Be sure to draw a total market map rather than just the part you currently deal with. The purpose of this is to ensure that you understand your market dynamics properly. For example, beware of writing in only the word 'Distributor' if there are, in fact, different kinds of distributors that behave in different ways and that supply different customers. This is explained in more detail below under the heading, 'Leverage points'.

With quantification playing an important part later on in the process, it is useful to mark along each 'route' the volumes and/or values which go down that route (guestimate if necessary). Also, note your market share, if known, as illustrated in Figure 4.6.

Along the market map, ensure you include all the stages which play a part in the flow of products between suppliers and final users.

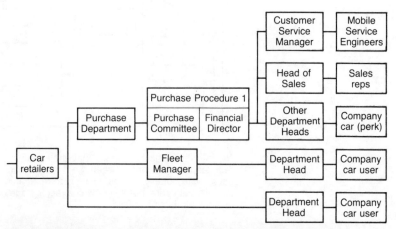

Note: In this market map, the physical delivery of the product to the final user (car retailer to car user) is insufficient in representing the sales route and purchasing routines encountered. The market map also assumes all the final users who appear beyond 'Purchase Procedure 1' are subject to the same purchasing routine. If this is not the case, ensure your market map reflects this. For example all the departments in a company may use mail, but the advertising department may 'purchase' its mail through their direct mail agency and therefore bypass the normal purchase procedures.

Figure 4.5 Market map with business purchasing procedures

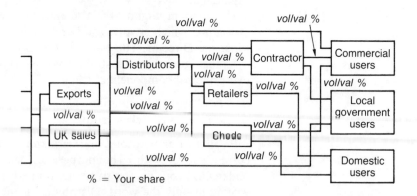

Figure 4.6 Market map with volumes and/or values on each route

These stages will, therefore, include points at which a transaction takes place and/or where influence/advice/decisions occur (not necessarily a transaction) about which products to use. These influencers should also appear on the market map, as shown in Figure 4.7, just as if they were a transaction stage.

These transaction stages are referred to as 'junctions', with each junction on a market map positioned hierarchically, according to

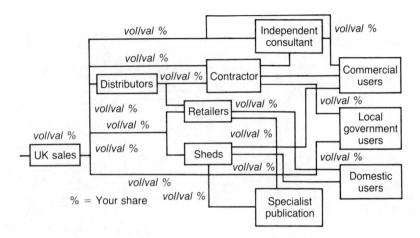

Figure 4.7 Market map with influencers

how close it is to the final user. The last junction along the market map would, therefore, be the final user. The stages in the purchasing procedure found in business-to-business markets are regarded as a single junction (hence their enclosure in one box on the earlier example of a market map).

For most market maps, the decision on which junction a particular activity should be placed will be very clear. However, there will be instances where the decision is not immediately apparent. For example, a co-operative may simply replace a retail outlet or a wholesaler, in which case it could just as easily be placed in the same junction as the retailer or wholesaler, as appropriate. Alternatively, a co-operative may source its products from either a wholesaler, or direct from the manufacturer – here, it is clear to position the co-operative on the market map at a stage which is nearest to the final user. Following the same guidelines, the consultant would be placed in a junction one stage below the membership.

Note at each junction, if applicable, all the currently understood different types of companies/customers which occur there, along with the number as suggested in Figure 4.8.

Allocate to these different company/customer types the volumes and/or values they deal with (guestimate if necessary). Also, note your market share, if known.

The market mapping routine may already be challenging the traditional lists of company/customer types at the various junctions, around which you currently conduct your marketing effort. In such instances replace what now appears to be the out-of-date list with the new list. The segmentation process you are now progressing through does, however, test the validity of your list during later steps.

Leverage points   Now, note those junctions where decisions are made about which of the competing products/services should be purchased by outlining them in **bold**. Attach to each type the approximate number of

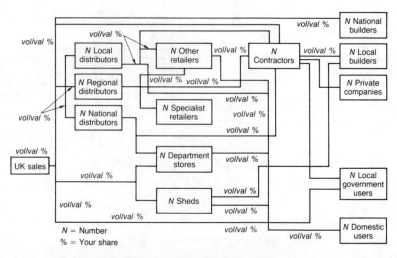

Figure 4.8 Market map with different company/customer types, their volumes and/or values, number of each type and your market share

business units/individual purchasers found in it. Clearly, in those instances where one type has been split into two in order to distinguish between a leverage point and a non-leverage point, for example CB1 and CB2, only a total number for the CB type as a whole can be entered.

The inclusion of leverage points is illustrated in Figure 4.9.

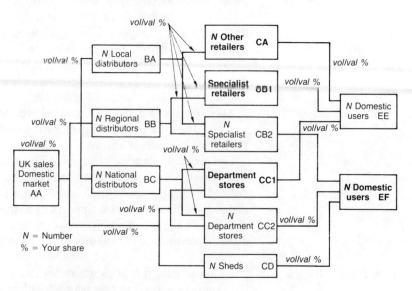

Figure 4.9 Leverage points on a market map for two junctions

So far, we have mapped out the different transactions that take place in your market all the way through to the final user, and seen how the transactions relate to each other. By quantifying these various 'routes' and determining your company's share along them, we have identified the most important routes and seen your company's position along each of them.

By then looking at where decisions are made between the producers/services of competing suppliers, we have identified a number of stages (junctions) where segmentation could occur. For most companies, it is recommended that segmentation should first take place at the junction furthest away from the supplier/manufacturer, where decisions are made.

Most importantly, however, is the fact that we now have a clearer understanding of the structure of our market and how it works.

Who buys and what they buy

Who buys

A useful method for dealing with this stage of market segmentation is to refer to the market map and, at each point at which there is a critical purchase influence, attempt to describe the characteristics of the customers who belong to it. The descriptions can consist of a single characteristic, or a combination, whichever is appropriate to the market being looked at.

The analysis of customer attributes is important in helping us to design our communication programme.

This is when analysis of customer attributes becomes important. It seeks to find some way of describing the customer groups located in our previous analysis for the purpose of communicating with them. For, clearly, however clever we might be in isolating segments, unless we can find some way of describing them such that we can address them through our communication programme, our efforts will have been to no avail.

Demographic descriptors have been found to be the most useful method for this purpose. For consumer markets, this is age, sex, education, stage in the family life cycle, and socio-economic groupings (A, B, C1, C2, D, E). A full list of UK groupings is provided in Table 4.1. This is based on the British census and, although this example is peculiar to the UK, it will be found that there are similar groupings and percentages for most of the advanced economies. This latter method describes people by their social status in life as represented by their jobs. Not surprisingly, A, B and C categories, which include most of the professions and senior managers, are light television viewers; consequently, if they are your target market, it does not make much sense to advertise your product or service on television. However, they can be effectively reached by means of certain newspapers and magazines, where they comprise the principal readership.

From this, it will be gathered that there is a very useful correlation between readership and viewing patterns and these socio-economic groupings, and this can be most useful in helping us to communicate cost-effectively with our target market by means of advertising.

Obviously, however, if we have no real idea of who our target market is, then we are unlikely to be able to take advantage of this convenient method.

Table 4.1 Socio-economic groups

Social grade	Social status	Occupation of household head	Percentage of adults
A	Upper middle class	Higher managerial Administrative Professional	3
B	Middle class	Middle managerial Administrative Professional	10
C1	Lower middle class	Supervisory Clerical Junior managerial Administrative Professional	23
C2	Skilled working class	Skilled manual workers	33
D	Working class	Semi and unskilled manual workers	22
E	Subsistence level	Pensioners Widows Casual Lowest paid workers	9

It is obvious that, at different stages in the family cycle, we have different needs, and this can be another most useful way of describing our market. Banks and insurance companies have been particularly adept at developing products specially for certain age categories. In this respect, because of the gradually reducing relevance of socio-economic group as a predictor of behaviour, there is an emerging concept of 'contexts', such as 'wellness', 'awareness', 'Euroness', 'traditionalism', 'expectism' and 'homecentredness', each one being related to life stages such as 'singles', 'nesters', 'developers' and 'olders'. Thus, Laura Ashley would clearly be in the 'traditionalism' context, while Body Shop would probably be in the 'wellness' context.

Additionally, ACORN (A Classification of Regional Neighbourhood groups), which classifies all households according to thirty-eight different neighbourhood types and is also based on census data, is particularly useful for the retailing business because, when used in conjunction with market research, it can accurately predict consumption patterns in specific geographical locations.

For industrial markets, SIC (Standard Industrial Classification) categories, number of employees, turnover and production processes have been found to be useful demographic descriptors.

What is bought

In respect of what is bought, the value of the market map should now become apparent. We are really talking about the actual structure of markets in the form of volume, value, the physical characteristics of products, place of purchase, frequency of purchase, price paid, and so on. This tells us, firstly, if there are any groups of products (or outlets, or price categories, etc.) which are growing, static, or declining, i.e. where the opportunities are and where the problems are.

> For example, one carpet company whose sales were declining discovered, on analysis, that although the market in total was rising, the particular outlets to which they had traditionally sold were accounting for a declining proportion of total market sales. Furthermore, demand for higher priced products was falling, as was demand for the particular fibre types manufactured by this company. All this added up to a decline in sales and profitability, and led the company to change its emphasis towards some of the growing sectors of the market.

This is market segmentation at its most elementary level, yet it is surprising to find even today how many companies run apparently sophisticated budgeting systems which are based on little more than crude extrapolations of past sales trends and which leave the marketing strategies implicit. Such systems are usually the ones which cause serious commercial problems when market structures change, as in the case of the carpet company. In this case, the company changed direction too late and went bankrupt.

> The same fate befell a shoe manufacturer who doggedly stuck to manufacturing the same products, in the same material, for the same kind of outlets, irrespective of the rapid changes that were taking place in the market.

Secondly, however, apart from telling us how our market works, it also gives us a good understanding of the market structure.

The next task is to list *all* relevant competitive products/services, whether or not you manufacture them, ensuring to unbundle all the components of a purchase so that you arrive at a comprehensive list of 'what is bought'.

Features to take into account when drawing up your list include:

○ Type of product – cleaners, galvanizers, installed, flat pack, made up, resident engineers, on-call engineers, bundled with a service package, etc.
○ Specification – 100 per cent purity, 98 per cent purity, tolerance levels, percentage failure rate, etc.
○ Colour – red, white, blue, pastel, garish, etc.
○ Size of package – single, multiple family pack, 5 litre, 20 kg, bulk, etc.
○ Volume used – small, medium, large, very large, etc.
○ Level/intensity of use – high, medium, low, etc.
○ Type of service – testing service, technical advice (which is sometimes, unintentionally, provided by the sales force), evaluation analysis.

o End-use application – where a single final user department or individual utilizes your product/service for a number of different end-use applications, these should be listed here. For example, the Office Services department may require cleaning services, but the cleaning requirements of the public areas, general office areas and the manufacturing plant (particularly if the manufacturing process involves precision instruments) could all be different. Another example has been identified in the domestic paint market, where the selection process for paint differs according to the type of room it is being bought for – the buying criteria for gloss in the lounge being different from the buying criteria for gloss in the bedroom.

o Brand – manufacturer's, own label, single brand only, any major brand, only local brands, high profile brand.

o Country of origin – UK, German, French, EEC, Scandinavian, Western European, Eastern European, Japanese, etc.

o Independent influencers, advisers, consultants (complementing or competing with the technical/advisory services provided by the manufacturers/suppliers) – specialist publications, consumer publications, accountants, financial advisers, consultants, etc., if they appear at junctions used by buyers at the junction being segmented.

o Type of delivery – next day (or a listing of the competing products which provide this, e.g. courier, first class), within four hours, collected, automatically triggered via links with inventory control systems, etc.

o Volume of purchase – large, medium, small (or by a more precise breakdown if appropriate).

o Value of purchase – high, medium, low (or by a more precise breakdown if appropriate).

o Range of products – all, single, across the range, those at the top/middle/bottom of the range, etc.

The resulting list could be as follows:

Lawnmowers	–	Hover, cylinder, rotary, petrol driven, manual, electrically driven, 12" cut, 16" cut, any mower with a branded engine, extended warranty, with after-sales service, etc.
Paints	–	Emulsion, gloss, non-drip coat, 5 litre cans, 2 litre cans, environmentally friendly, bulk, etc.
Petrol stations	–	Self-service, forecourt service, with loyalty programme, etc.

As part of this step, and without attempting at this stage to link this step with the earlier step, list all the channels (if appropriate) where the listed range of products/services are bought. Note that this only refers to the products/services supplied/manufactured by you and your competitors: it therefore excludes the sourcing details for independent influencers, advisers, consultants, etc.

The channel list could include:

Direct/mail order, distributor, department store, national chain, regional chain, local independent retailer, tied retailer, supermarket, wholesalers, shed, specialist supplier, street stall, through a buying group, through a buying club, door-to-door, local/high-street/out-of-town shop, etc.

Also, draw up a list which covers the different frequencies of purchase experienced for your own, and your competitors', products/services.

The purchase frequency list could include:

Daily, weekly, monthly, seasonally, every two years, at 50,000 miles, occasionally, as needs, only in emergencies, degrees of urgency, infrequency, rarely, special events, only during sales, at the bottom of the market, etc.

Next, draw up a further separate list covering the different methods of purchase and, if applicable, the different purchasing organizations and procedures observed in your market.

Examples which may help in drawing up your list include:

○ Methods of purchase – credit card, charge card, cash, direct debit, standing order, credit terms, Switch, outright purchase, lease-hire, lease-purchase, negotiated price, sealed bid, etc.
○ Purchasing organization – centralized or decentralized; structure and distribution of power in the decision-making unit (DMU), which could be as equally applicable in a household as in a business, e.g. decision to purchase made at one level, with the choice of suitable suppliers able to meet the specification/price, etc. made at a technical level, negotiating of price left to the purchasing department and the final decision left to senior management.

Next, attempt to identify for each active 'who', all the unique combinations of 'what is bought' observed on their particular buying activity. The resulting cascade produces a large number of micro segments, each of which should have a volume or value figure attached. These can be reduced in number by determining the important from the unimportant and by removing anything that is obviously superfluous.

Some preliminary screening at this stage is vital in order to cut this long list down to manageable proportions. This will also act as a preliminary form of market segmentation.

Why they buy

The second part of analysing customer behaviour is trying to understand why customers behave the way they do, for, surely, if we can explain the behaviour of our customers, we are in a better position to sell to them.

Basically, there are two principal theories of customer behaviour. One theory refers to the rational customer, who seeks to maximize satisfaction or utility. This customer's behaviour is determined by the utility derived from a purchase at the margin compared with the financial outlay and other opportunities foregone. While such a view of customers provides some important insights into behaviour, it must be remembered that many markets do not work this way at all, there being many examples of a growth in demand with every rise in price.

Another view of customer behaviour which helps to explain this phenomenon is that which describes the psycho-socio customer, whose attitudes and behaviour are affected by family, work, prevailing cultural patterns, reference groups, perceptions, aspirations, and life style.

While such theories also provide useful insights, they rarely explain the totality of customer behaviour. For example, it is interesting to know that opinion leaders are often the first to adopt new ideas and new products, but unless these people can be successfully identified and communicated with, this information is of little practical use to us.

The most useful and practical way of explaining customer behaviour has been found to be benefit segmentation.

The most useful and practical way of explaining customer behaviour has been found to be benefit segmentation, i.e. the benefits sought by customers when they buy a product. For example, some customers buy products for their functional characteristics (product), for economy (price), for convenience and availability (place), for emotional reasons (promotion), or for a combination of these reasons (a trade-off). Otherwise, how else can the success of firms like Rolls-Royce, Harrods, and many others be explained? Understanding the benefits sought by customers helps us to organize our marketing mix in the way most likely to appeal to our target market. The importance of product benefits will become clearer in Chapter 5 in our discussion of product management.

'*Customers don't buy products; they seek to acquire benefits*'. This is the guiding principle of the marketing director of one of America's more innovative companies in the hair-care business. Behind that statement lies a basic principle of successful marketing. When people purchase products, they are not motivated in the first instance by physical features, or objective attributes of the product, but by the benefit that those attributes bring with them.

> To take an example from industrial marketing, a purchaser of industrial cutting oil is not buying the particular blend of chemicals sold by leading manufacturers of industrial lubricants; rather, he is buying a bundle of benefits which includes the solving of a specific lubrication problem.

The difference between benefits and products is not just a question of semantics. It is crucial to the company seeking success. Every product has its features: size, shape, performance, weight, the material from which it is made, and so on. Many companies fall into the trap of talking to customers about these features, rather than about what those features mean to the customer. This is not surprising. For example, if, when asked a question about the product, the salesperson could not provide an accurate answer, the customer might lose confidence and, doubting the salesperson, will soon doubt his product. Most salespeople are, therefore, very knowledgeable about the technical features of the products they sell. They have to have these details at their fingertips when they talk to buyers, designers and technical experts.

However, being expert in technical detail is not enough. The customer may not be able to work out the benefits which particular features bring and it is therefore up to the salesperson to explain the benefits which accrue from every feature mentioned.

A simple formula to ensure that this customer-oriented approach is adopted is always to use the phrase 'which means that' to link a feature to the benefit it brings:

'Maintenance time has been reduced from 4 to 3 hours, *which means that* most costs are reduced by . . .'

'The engine casing is made of aluminium, *which means that* six more units can be carried on a standard truck load, *which means that* transport costs are reduced by . . .'

'The size of the quench tank has been increased by 25 per cent, *which means that* on oil purchases alone you will save £2,000 in a year.'

'The new special bearing has self-aligning symmetrical rollers, *which means that* the rollers find their own equilibrium, with the load always symmetrically distributed along the length of the roller, *which means* an extended life capacity of a year on average.'

Benefit analysis

A company must undertake a detailed analysis to determine the full range of benefits they have to offer their customers. This can be done by listing the features of major products, together with what they mean to the customer. The analysis will produce various classes of benefit, outlined below.

Standard benefits

These are the basic benefits which arise from the features of the company and its products.

Every benefit must be listed. Care is needed to produce a comprehensive list. Because marketing staff are very familiar with the company and its products, they may take some features for granted. They must not fall into this trap when understanding benefit analysis.

Buyers are rarely as knowledgeable as they appear and the company must make sure they include benefits which are neither unique nor overtly special; some of these benefits may even be offered by competitors.

Double benefits

A company will often be able to identify double benefits. For example, they may be selling a product which will bring benefits to their customer and, through an improvement in the customer's product, to the end-user:

'Our microcomputer has a range of software options to suit a wide variety of business uses, *which means that*:

○ the product will appeal to a wide variety of customers;
○ customers will be able to purchase software which meets their particular needs.'

In the above example, the first benefit applies to the customer because it widens their potential market and the second benefit applies to the potential end-user.

Company benefits

The customer rarely simply buys a product; he buys a relationship with his supplier. Factors such as delivery, credit, after-sales service, the location of depots and offices, reputation, and so on are all relevant to the customer. The benefit analysis should therefore examine the company and back-up services it offers. Typical company benefits include:

'We can offer a 24 hour delivery service because we have a national network of depots, *which means that* you will never lose production due to delivery delays.'

'We are a large international corporation, *which means that* you can rely on a comprehensive service throughout the world.'

'You can be sure of individual attention from us because we are a small family business.'

Differential benefits

Without doubt, however, whilst it is important for the salesperson to go through this process of benefit analysis most thoroughly, it is vital that, in doing it, differential benefits compared with those of major competitors are identified. If a company cannot identify any differential benefits, then either what they are offering is identical to their competitors' offerings (which is unlikely) or they have not done the benefit analysis properly. It is important to make a particular note of differential benefits, for it is in these that the greatest chance of success lies.

Bringing it all together

Our segmentation is now almost complete. The second step involved taking each significant cluster identified earlier (of who buys and what they buy) and listing why they buy. In other words, what benefits are they seeking by buying what they buy?

The third and final step is to look for *clusters* of segments that share the same, or similar, needs and to apply to the resulting clusters the organization's minimum volume/value criteria to determine their viability.* Whilst this final step can be difficult and time-consuming, any care lavished on this part of the market segmentation process will pay handsome dividends at later stages of the marketing planning process.

Table 4.2 provides a useful summary of all these issues relating to market segmentation. However, a comprehensive list of all standard

*A computer program, called 'Market Segment Master' is available for this task. For details, write to Professor Malcolm McDonald, Cranfield School of Management, Cranfield, Bedford, England, MK43 0AL.

approaches to business and consumer market segmentation is given in the Review at the end of this chapter.

Table 4.2 Summary of bases for market segmentation

What is bought	Price
	Outlets
	Physical characteristics
	Geography
Who buys	Demographic
	Socio-economic
	Brand loyalty
	Heavy/light users
	Personality, traits, life styles
Why	Benefits
	Attitudes
	Perceptions
	Preferences

Segmentation case histories

This chapter concludes with three case histories to illustrate how superior profitability results from successful market segmentation.

Case 1 – A national off-licence chain

In the mid-1980s, a national off-licence chain, with retail units in major shopping centres and local shopping parades, was experiencing both a decline in customer numbers and a decline in average spend. The original formula for success of design, product range and merchandising, meticulously copied in each outlet, no longer appeared to be working.

The chain had become a classic example of a business comfortably sat in the middle ground, attempting to be all things to all people, but managing to satisfy very few of them.

Rather than sit back in the belief that the business was just passing through a difficult patch, and what worked yesterday was bound to work again, the company embarked on a project designed to understand both their actual and potential customer base.

The first stage of this study turned to one of the more sophisticated geodemographic packages (CCN's MOSAIC) to understand the residential profiles of each shop's catchment area. Not unexpectedly, many geodemographic differences were found, and the business quickly accepted that it was unlikely the same retail formula would appeal to the different target markets found in them.

Instead of looking at each shop separately, the company subjected catchment area profiles for each shop to a clustering routine in order to place similar catchment areas together. This resulted in 21 different groupings, each of which was then profiled in terms of its potential to buy different off-licence products using purchasing data from national surveys. (The company's own in-house retailing data would, of course, only reflect the purchasing pattern of their existing customers, or, at worst, only a proportion of their requirements if this was limited by the company's current product range.)

However, stocking the requisite range of products in their correct geographical location would not necessarily attract their respective target markets. The chain was already associated with one type of offer which, in addition to including a particular range of drinks, also included the basic design of the shops and overall merchandising.

The project, therefore, moved into a second stage, in which the market's attitudes and motivations to drinking were explored and relative values attached to the various dimensions uncovered. This was achieved through an independently commissioned piece of market research and resulted in the market being categorized into a number of psychographic groups. This included, amongst others, 'happy and impulsive' shoppers, 'anxious and muddled' shoppers, 'reluctant but organized' shoppers, and the 'disorganized, extravagant' shopper.

By ensuring that this stage of the project linked the attitude and motivational findings to demographic data, the two stages could be brought together. This enabled the original 21 clusters to be reduced to give distinct segments, each of which required a different offer.

The company now had to decide between two alternative strategies:

1 To focus into one segment using one brand and re-locate its retail outlets accordingly through a closure and opening programme; or
2 To develop a manageable portfolio of retailing brands, leave the estate relatively intact, and re-brand, re-fit and re-stock as necessary.

They decided to pursue the second strategy.

Realizing that demographic profiles in geographic areas can change over time, and that customer needs and attitudes can also evolve, the company now monitors their market quite carefully and are quite prepared to modify their brand portfolio to suit changing circumstances. For the time being, however, their five retail brands of 'Bottoms Up', 'Wine Rack', 'Threshers Wine Shop', 'Drinks Store from Threshers' and 'Food and Drinks Store' sit comfortably within the five segments. They also sit comfortably together in the same shopping centre, enabling the group to meet effectively the different requirements of the segments found within that centre's catchment area.

Perhaps more importantly, this strategy sits comfortably alongside the financial targets for the business.

Source: Based on 'Market segmentation from Bottoms Up', John Thornton, Market Planning Manager, Threshers (*Research Plus*, December, 1993).

Case 2 – Sodium Tri-Poly Phosphate!

Sodium Tri-Poly Phosphate (STPP) was once a simple, unexciting, white chemical cleaning agent. Today, one of its uses is as the major ingredient of a sophisticated and profitable operation, appearing under many different brand names, all competing for a share of what has become a cleverly segmented market.

Have you ever wondered how the toothpaste marketers classify you in their segmentation of the market? The following chart, adapted from R. Haley's 'Benefit Segmentation: a decision-oriented research tool' (*Journal of Marketing*, Vol. 32, July 1968), which presents the main segments, may assist you:

		Worrier	Sociable	Sensory	Independent
Who buys	Socio-economic	C1 C2	B C1 C2	C1 C2 D	A B
	Demographics	Large families 25–40	Teens Young Smokers	Children	Males 35–50
	Psychographics	conservative: hypochondriosis	high sociability: active	high self involvement: hedonists	high autonomy value oriented
What is bought	% of total market	50%	30%	15%	5%
	Product examples	Crest	McLeans Ultra Bright	Colgate (stripe)	Own label
	Product physics	large canisters	large tubes	medium tubes	small tubes
	Price paid	low	high	medium	low
	Outlet	supermarket	supermarket	supermarket	independent
	Purchase frequency	weekly	monthly	monthly	quarterly
Why	Benefits sought	stop decay	attract attention	flavour	price
Potential for growth		nil	high	medium	nil

Case 3 – Amber nectar

A privately owned brewery in the UK was enjoying exceptional profitability for its industrial sector. In terms of output, it was by no means the largest brewery in the UK, and in terms of geographic cover, it only operated within a particular metropolitan area.

At one of the regular meetings of the Board, it was agreed that the company had clearly developed a very successful range of beers and it was time to expand into new geographic areas.

The expansion programme met with aggressive opposition from other brewers, particularly the very large brewers. This came as no great surprise to the Board who, before setting on the expansion path, had built up a large 'war chest', largely made up of past profits, to finance the plan. The Board knew the competition would react in this way, because they were being challenged by a very successful range of beers, a 'success' that would ensure product trial, then customer loyalty, in the new areas.

As with all good marketing-focused companies, the progress of the marketing plan was regularly monitored against its target by a specially appointed task force headed by the Chief Executive. In addition, the Sales and Marketing Director, a key member of the task force, held regular meetings with his own key staff to ensure continuous evaluation of the sales and marketing strategies being followed.

The plan badly under-performed and was eventually abandoned.

In the post-mortem that followed, the brewery discovered why it had been so successful in the past, and why this success could not be extended to other areas of the UK. To its loyal customers, a key attraction of the beers manufactured by this brewery was the 'local' flavour. The market for this company was the metropolitan area it already operated in, its competitors being other local brewers in the same area. Exporting this success was clearly, therefore, not going to work. Expansion could only be achieved by setting up new local breweries in other areas, or by acquiring already established local breweries.

Without this brewery realizing it, the UK beer drinking market had already segmented itself. This brewer's segment was the 'Regional Chauvinist', and in the particular region it operated in, the company already had an overwhelming market share. Hence its profitability.

With an earlier understanding of this segmentation structure, the company would have spent its war chest more effectively and achieved its growth objectives.

Case history conclusion

These three case histories illustrate the importance of intelligent segmentation in guiding companies towards successful marketing strategies. However, it is easy to understand this success after the event, as occurred in one of the cases! The problem for most of us is how to arrive at a definition of 'market' (market segmentation) that will enable us to create differential advantage.

This has been the purpose of this chapter.

Why market segmentation is vital in marketing planning

In today's highly competitive world, few companies can afford to compete only on price, for the product has not yet been sold that someone, somewhere, cannot sell cheaper – apart from which, in many markets it is rarely the cheapest product that succeeds anyway. This is an issue we will return to in the chapter dealing with the pricing plan. What this means is that we have to find some way of differentiating ourselves from the competition, and the answer lies in market segmentation.

The truth is that very few companies can afford to be 'all things to all people'. The main aim of market segmentation as part of the planning process is to enable a firm to target its effort on the most promising opportunities. But what is an opportunity for firm A is not necessarily an opportunity for firm B. So a firm needs to develop a *typology* of the customer or segment it prefers, for this can be an instrument of great productivity in the market place.

The typology of the customer or the segment have to be related to a firm's distinctive competence.

The typology of the customer or the segment can be based on a myriad of criteria, as we have seen, such as:

○ Size of the firm
○ Its consumption level
○ Nature of its products/production/processes
○ Motivations of the decision-makers (e.g. desire to deal with big firms)
○ Geographical location

The whole point of segmentation is that a company must either:

○ Define its markets broadly enough to ensure that its costs for key activities are competitive; or
○ Define its markets in such a way that it can develop specialized skills in serving them to overcome a relative cost disadvantage.

Both have to be related to a firm's *distinctive competence* and to that of its competitors.

All of this should come to the fore as a result of the marketing audit referred to previously and should be summarized in the SWOT analysis. In particular, the differential benefits of a firm's product or service should be beyond doubt to all key members of the company.

Even more important than this, however, is the issue of marketing planning and all that follows in this book. It is worth repeating why market segmentation is so important. Correct market definition is crucial for:

○ Share measurement
○ Growth measurement
○ The specification of target customers
○ The recognition of relevant competitors
○ The formulation of marketing objectives and strategies

To summarize, the objectives of market segmentation are:

○ To help determine marketing direction through the analysis and understanding of trends and buyer behaviour.
○ To help determine realistic and obtainable marketing and sales objectives.
○ To help improve decision-making by forcing managers to consider in depth the options ahead.

**Application
questions**

1 Choose a major product or service. Identify its features. Identify the benefits (to the customer) of each feature. Identify which of these are differential benefits.
2 If you cannot identify any differential benefits, in what ways could you develop some?
3 For those you have identified, how can they be improved on?
4 Identify your key market segments. How do you describe them?
5 If you cannot identify any distinct segments, how can you begin to identify one or more?

Review of Chapter 4

Customers or consumers?
Customers are people who buy from you. *Consumers* are the users of your products or services, e.g. husband (customer) buys perfume for wife (consumer). Sometimes the customer is also the consumer. Marketers need to know about the characteristics of both if they are to develop the best 'package' to meet their needs.

Market share
Market share is a key concept in marketing. It is the proportion of *actual* sales (either volume or value) within a defined market. How the company defines its market is extremely critical.   *Try Exercise 4.1*

Research shows that there is a direct correlation between market share and profitability.

Critical success factors
Within any given market segment there are critical success factors (CSFs) for winning the business, e.g. reliable delivery, acceptable design, low running costs, and so on. It will be essential for the company to establish what these are *and* how well it compares with its closest competitors, when measured against these factors.   *Try Exercise 4.2*

Market segmentation
A market segment is a group of customers with similar characteristics who share similar needs. A company generally cannot deal successfully with a large number of segments – it would lead to fragmentation of effort. Therefore it should deal with a limited number of segments which meet these criteria:

○ Each segment is sufficiently large to give the company a return for its effort.
○ Members of each segment have a high degree of similarity.
○ The criteria for describing the segment must relate to the buying situation.
○ The segment must be reachable.

Segmentation can be based on a combination of:

1 Analysis of customer behaviour:
   (a) What do they buy and why?

   ○ value/volume
   ○ price

○ frequency
○ where they buy/outlet
○ products/services, etc.

Try Exercise 4.3

(b) Why do they buy?

○ benefits
○ lifestyle
○ fashion/novelty
○ personality types
○ peer-group pressure
○ preferences, etc.

Try Exercise 4.4

2 Analysis of customer characteristics (who they are):

○ Customer size
○ Socio-economic groups
○ Demographic considerations
○ Industrial classification
○ Cultural/geographic factors

Try Exercise 4.5

Questions raised for the company

1 Why is market segmentation so important?

Few companies can be 'all things to all people'. Segmentation allows the firm to target its effort on the most promising opportunities.

2 How can we be expected to know our market share?

The more accurately you can define your market segments, the more accurately you will find you can measure your market share. Correct market definition is also critical for:

○ Growth measurement
○ Specifying target customers
○ Recognizing relevant competitors
○ Setting marketing objectives and strategies

3 How can we keep tabs on all our competitors?

You don't have to – just concentrate on your closest competitors and try to ensure that you maintain some differential advantage over them.

Introduction to Chapter 4 exercises

Exercise 4.1 looks at the most crucial and complex issue in marketing, i.e. how a market is defined. Until this is clearly understood, issues such as market share, the identification of target customers and their needs, and even the recognition of competitors, will continuously cause difficulty.

Exercise 4.2 examines critical success factors.

Exercise 4.3 provides a technique for auditing industrial goods and services.

Exercise 4.4 introduces another technique, benefit analysis, and this is extended and put into practice in Exercise 4.5, which provides a case study for analysis.

Exercise 4.1 Market definition

Often there is confusion regarding what constitutes a market. Unless such confusion is dispelled from the outset, the whole marketing edifice will be built on sand. However, as, so often is the case, what on the surface appears to be a relatively simple task can prove to be extremely testing. Take this example, which vastly simplifies the problem.

XYZ Ltd has five major products, A, B, C, D and E, which are sold to five different markets, as represented in Figure 4.10. Virtually all sales are achieved in the shaded areas.

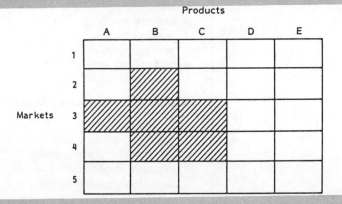

Figure 4.10 Example of market definition

Is this company's market:

(a) The shaded areas?
(b) The intersection of products A, B and C and markets 2, 3 and 4?
(c) Products A, B and C for all markets?
(d) Markets 2, 3 and 4 for all products?
(e) The entire matrix?

Interpretation and scoring for Exercise 4.1

1 It would be possible to define our market as the shaded areas ((a) in the exercise), i.e. the product/market area currently served. The problem with this is that it might tend to close our eyes to other potential opportunities for profitable growth and expansion, especially if there is a danger that our current markets may become mature.

2 It is also possible to define our market as the intersection of products A, B and C and markets 2, 3 and 4 ((b) in the exercise). The problem with this is that while we now have a broader vision, there may be developments in product areas D and E and markets 1 and 5 that we should be aware of.

3 To a large extent, this problem would be overcome by defining our market as products A, B and C for *all* markets ((c) in the exercise). The problem here is that markets 1 and 5 may not require products A, B and C, so perhaps we need to consider product development (products D and E).

4 It is certainly possible to consider our market as all products for markets 2, 3 and 4 ((d) in the exercise). The potential problem here is that we still do not have any interest in markets 1 and 3.

5 Finally, it is clearly possible to call the entire matrix our market ((e) in the exercise), with markets 1 to 5 on the vertical axis and each of

products A to E on the horizontal axis. The problem with this is that we would almost certainly have too many markets, or segments, and this could lead to a costly dissipation of effort.

The answer to the conundrum therefore is that it is purely a matter of management judgement. Any combinations of (a) – (e) above could be used as long as there is a sensible rationale to justify the choice. In addition, remember the following useful definition of market segmentation: 'An identifiable group of customers with requirements in common that are, or may become, significant in terms of developing a separate strategy'.

Often, the way a market was selected in the first instance can provide clues regarding how it can be defined. Generally, either consciously or intuitively, a screening process is used to eliminate unsuitable markets and to arrive at those with potential. This screening process often works something like that shown in Figure 4.11.

Consider one of your current markets and explain:

1 How it came to be chosen.
2 How you would define it, so that it is clearly distinct from any other market.

Remember that the crude method outlined above, while working at a very general level, rarely leads to the development of differential advantage, and it is suggested that the other exercises in this chapter should be completed in order to get a better understanding of the central significance of market segmentation in marketing success.

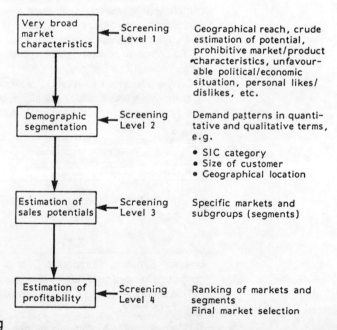

Figure 4.11 Market screening

Exercise 4.2
Critical success factors (CSFs)

Critical success factors can vary from one type of business to another, or indeed from one market segment to another. Therefore it is impossible to be prescriptive about your CSFs, and you will have to draw on the expertise you have about your business and establish which ones are correct for you.

Remember, a CSF is something which helps you to clinch the business. Thus, by definition, if it were absent, your success rate would plummet.

Normally, there would only be a few CSFs, probably not more than five, although there might be many other factors which contribute to success.

Table 4.3 is an example of the way a firm of quantity surveyors analysed their business.

Table 4.3

CSF	Weighting	Score out of 10 (10 = very high standard)	Adjusted score*
1 Reputation for on-time completion	0.5	6	30
2 Track record of quality	0.3	6	18
3 Quality of sales staff	0.2	8	16
	1.0		64%

*Adjusted score = score out of 10 × weighing factor

Weighing factors are distributed to each CSF according to their relative importance. In Table 4.3, CSF1 is the most important, but the company only scores 6, just over average. In contrast, on CSF3, the company scores high, but this factor is the least critical of those listed and so the net result is diminished.

The company now repeats this process (Table 4.4), this time focusing on its nearest competitors.

On the evidence in Table 4.4, our company can see that Competitor A, even with a lower quality salesforce and a slightly poorer track record has a competitive advantage because of its ability to complete contracts

Table 4.4

CSF	Weighing	Comp. A score		Comp. B score		Comp. C score	
		Raw	Adjusted	Raw	Adjusted	Raw	Adjusted
1	0.5	9	45	5	25	7	35
2	0.3	5	15	5	15	7	21
3	0.2	6	12	5	10	5	10
			72%		50%		66%

on-time. Similarly, Competitor C is a force to be reckoned with. In contrast, Competitor B has a lot of ground to make up in all areas.

This technique can be applied to all companies and provides three useful outcomes:

1 It forces people to think about their critical success factors.
2 It provides an overview of relative competitiveness when measured against their main competitors.
3 It highlights the areas where the most effective improvements might be made.

Now try it on your company. See Tables 4.5 and 4.6.

Table 4.5

CSF		Weighting	Score out of 10 (10 = very high standard)	Adjusted score
CSF1				
CSF2				
CSF3				
CSF4				
CSF5				

Table 4.6

CSF	Weighting	Comp. A score Raw	Adjusted	Comp. B score Raw	Adjusted	Comp. C score Raw	Adjusted
CSF1							
CSF2							
CSF3							
CSF4							
CSF5							

Exercise 4.3 Market audit – industrial goods and services

Using your own company as the study vehicle, complete the market audit form (Table 4.7) by following these instructions:

Step 1 In column 1 list all those industries that are consumers of your goods or services. Note that there is no need to structure this list, just write them down as they occur to you.

Step 2 In column 2 write the actual turnover figure.

Step 3 In column 3 write down the percentage value of turnover that results from each of the industries.

Step 4 In column 4 indicate whether or not this, when considered from the point of view of profitability, is high or low, by scoring 10 for high, 5 for good, and 1 for low. (Here, 'profitability' means whatever your company considers it to mean.)

Step 5 Using column 5, consider what capacity and skills you have at your disposal to continue supplying each industry. A score of 10 would show that you have considerable capacity, with minimal interference to other products or services; 1 would indicate severe limitations.

Step 6 Using a similar scoring procedure, complete column 6. Ask yourself how confident is your company that it can supply each industry with the right quality and design of goods/services, delivered on time. Are you more confident about some than others?

Step 7 Now consider the market potential (demand) for your output in each of the listed industries. Using column 7, score 10 for high potential and 1 for low.

Step 8 Add the scores you have allocated in columns 4, 5, 6 and 7, and enter them in column 8.

Step 9 Using the information you have put together, identify your key market segments. They ought to be those industries which collected the highest aggregate scores, but for your type of business you might identify other factors that would influence your choice of market. Make a note of these in column 9. In addition, use column 9 to record any particular opportunities or threats presented in each market.

Step 10 Balancing the notes you made in column 9 against the arithmetic calculations (column 8), study the information you have assembled, and select what you regard as the best industrial market. Enter 1 against this in column 10. Continue ranking each industry, using 2 for the next best, 3 for the third, etc., until column 10 is filled.

Information from this market audit could be used at a later stage, when marketing objectives and strategies are examined (Exercises 6.6 and 6.7).

Table 4.7 Market audit industrial goods and services

1	2	3	4	5	6	7	8	9	10
Industry	*Actual T/O*	*% T/O*	*Profitability* $L_1 \quad _{10}H$	*Capacity* $L_1 \quad _{10}H$	*Confidence* $L_1 \quad _{10}H$	*Potential* $L_1 \quad _{10}H$	*Total (Cols 4, 5, 6, 7)*	*Additional factors, opportunities/ threats*	*Rank*

Exercise 4.4
Benefit analysis

Customers buy products and services because they seek to acquire a range of benefits which go with them. In this sense, all products and services are problem-solvers. Thus, customers buy aspirin to solve the problem of headaches, they buy drills because they need holes, they buy convenience foods because they solve the problem of there not being enough hours in the day.

It is essential for providers of products or services to be aware that their output is only saleable for as long as it provides the benefits the customer requires, and for as long as it is seen by the customer to be good value when compared with other possible methods of solving their problems. Once there is a better, cheaper, quicker, tidier, more enjoyable way of putting holes in walls, the drill manufacturer will go the way of the buggy-whip maker. Therefore it is vitally important to know just as much about the benefits they supply as it is to know about the products or services themselves.

Standard benefits

These are provided by the product but are not in any way unique, e.g. 'the propellant in our aerosol does not damage the ozone layer'.

Although in this respect your product might be like all others, not to make customers aware of this standard benefit could imply that you still use environmentally unfriendly materials. Clearly this would be to your disadvantage.

Company benefits

The business transaction links the customer to the company. In turn, this means that there ought to be some benefits to that customer for making that choice. Customers will prefer to deal with companies that provide better customer service, inspire confidence, have a reputation for fair trading policies, and so on. Company benefits are a means of differentiating your products or services from competing ones, if to all intents and purposes they are similar. For example, some banks are trying to establish specific identities to the benefits they supply. Hence there is 'the listening bank' and 'the bank that likes to say yes'. Perhaps eventually there will be 'the bank that is open when its customers want it to be'!

Differential benefits

These are the benefits that only your products or services provide. It is these that give the company its competitive advantage. It is these that must be identified, developed and exploited if the company is to win success. Here are some examples:

o 'We are the only company that provides a genuine 24-hour breakdown service. Therefore, any time you need us, we are there to get you moving again.'
o 'This is the only product on the market with this self-cleaning facility, so you can install it and have no maintenance worries.'

Not every benefit will have equal appeal to all customers, or groups of customers. However, by talking to them, or carrying out research, it ought to be possible to establish which are the important benefits in their eyes.

It is now possible to prepare a systematic benefit analysis along the lines shown in these examples. See Table 4.8.

Note

1 To get from a feature to an advantage, and then to a benefit, the phrase 'which means that' can be helpful, e.g. 'It's coated in new formula paint (feature), which means that the colour will never fade (advantage)'. If you *know* this is what the customer *needs*, then you have also arrived at a *benefit*.
2 To check if you have arrived at a benefit and not just an advantage, apply the 'so what?' test. Ask this question after the benefit. If the 'so what?' prompts you to go further, the chances are you have not yet reached the real benefit, e.g. 'Our products are handmade (feature), which means they are better quality than machine-made ones (benefit?)' – 'so what?' – 'which means they last longer (the real benefit)'.

Now try producing a benefit analysis for one of your own products or services, as it impacts on a specific customer or customer group. Use Table 4.9.

Table 4.8

Customer(s) . . . .
Service/product . . . .

Customer appeal	Features	Advantages	Benefits	Proof
What issues are of particular concern to the customer, e.g. cost, reliability, safety, simplicity, etc.?	What features of the product/service best illustrate these issues? How do they work?	What advantages do these features provide, i.e. what do they do for the customer?	How can tangible benefits be expressed to give maximum customer appeal, i.e. what does the customer get that he/she *needs*?	What evidence can be provided to back up the benefit and show it can be attained?

Example – saucepans

Ease of use, ease of washing-up	Teflon-coated	This is a non-stick material	Troublefree cooking, quicker washing-up	Results of tests

Example – office services bureau

Accuracy and speedy turn-round of work	We use the latest equipment and very skilled staff	We are extremely versatile	Minimum of errors, cost-saving	What customers say

Table 4.9

Customer(s) . . . .
Service/product . . . .

Customer appeal	Features	Advantages	Benefits	Proof

The customer audit applied to your own company
Working alone, and using your own company as the study vehicle:

1 Choose a major product or service, and identify
   (a) The main customers
   (b) The features with maximum customer appeal
   (c) The benefits to the customer of each feature
   (d) Which of these benefits are differential benefits, i.e. are benefits not recognized or stressed by your major competitors

2 If you cannot identify any differential benefits, in what ways could you develop them?
3 For those you have identified, how could they be improved upon?
4 Identify your key market segments. How do you describe them?
5 If you cannot readily identify any distinct segments, what would be a sensible way to segment your markets?

Notes

Exercise 4.5 The customer audit – Car Mart Ltd

As a prerequisite to establishing marketing objectives for your company, it will be important to analyse the customers of your products or services. For some businesses, it is adequate to focus on the needs of groups of individual customers; for others, it is more important to look at customers as being whole industries. In this exercise, we will concentrate on the former type of customer base.

The information you assemble by completing this exercise can be used at a later stage of the marketing planning process.

Types of customer audit

There are many different ways of auditing customers. Most of them work on the premise that customer needs will, to a large extent, be influenced by personal circumstances such as age, personality, occupation, lifestyle and financial situation.

The following exercise will give you an opportunity to explore the practical implications of using one such approach.

Car Mart objective

Car Mart produces a record of a series of sales transactions from which you have to identify the key market segment(s) and useful customer audit material.

Materials for Car Mart

1 *Twelve customer cards* (to be cut out from the back of the book), consisting of:

o A lift attendant
o A bricklayer
o A self-employed plumber
o A bank manager (local branch)
o A computer programmer
o A sales manager
o A school teacher
o A chairman of an industrial group
o A senior partner in a firm of solicitors
o A tool-maker
o A factory machine operator
o An elderly granny

2 *Six product cards – the showroom* (to be cut out from the back of the book), consisting of:
o Economy car
o Family saloon

    o Executive transport

    o Estate car

    o Second car

    o Sports car

3 *Car Mart sales record sheet* (see later in this exercise)

4 *Two dice*

Assumptions

This simulation does not attempt to portray real life in accurate detail, but merely to be the vehicle for learning, and thereby provide an opportunity for experimentation. To this end, the following assumptions are made:

1 Anyone tackling this exercise will have completed Exercise 4.4 or have a clear understanding about the difference between features and benefits.

2 The 'customers' in Car Mart have the financial resources to make their purchases.

3 The 'customer needs' expressed are a genuine attempt to reflect the likely views of that particular 'customer'.

4 The car 'chosen' is in an acceptable condition for the customer, i.e. it is new if the customer wants new, or second-hand if that is what the customer is looking for.

Generating the data for Car Mart

There are two methods of developing the necessary data for this exercise:

1 Procedure for a group of four 'players'

(a) A group of four players is seated at a suitable table.

(b) The twelve customer cards are shuffled by Player 1 and then laid face up on the table in a vertical column by one of the players. The six product cards are also placed on the table in a separate group, face upwards, to represent the Car Mart showroom.

(c) Player 2, on the left of Player 1, shakes the two dice and uses the aggregate score to designate a customer card, e.g. if the dice showed 8 as a total score, Player 2 counts down the column of customer cards to the *eighth* card.

(d) Player 2 then becomes this customer and improvises a realistic buying need of that person by saying 'I'm looking for a car that (own words)', e.g. 'I'm looking for a car that will always start in the mornings'.

(e) Player 3 responds to this by selecting one of the product cards from the table (showroom), and explains a feature of this particular car by saying 'This one has (own words)', e.g. 'This car has been on the market for many years'.

(f) Player 4 then has to add a benefit statement to the feature raised by Player 3, by saying 'Which means that (own words)', e.g. 'Which means that it is now a very reliable vehicle'.

(g) One of the players (probably the neatest writer) then fills in the first transaction row of the 'sales record sheet', at this stage ignoring columns 2, 4 and 9, the narrow ones.

(h) This whole procedure is repeated, this time Player 3 shaking the dice and being the customer.

(i) This rotation of starter continues until twenty sales transactions have been completed, i.e. the sales record sheet is filled.

2 Procedure for individual study

If it is not possible to work in a group of four as described, an individual can work through the Car Mart exercise alone. He or she will of course have to play the role of each player described above. Nevertheless, this process will produce the completed sales record sheet, which is an essential prerequisite for the rest of this exercise.

If it is possible, procedure 1 is recommended, because, with other people, the exercise becomes much more creative and stimulating.

Once the sales record sheet is completed, answer the questions in the next sections.

The customer audit (socio-economic groups and buying motives)

Imagine that the sales record sheet you have just completed was multiplied tenfold. In other words, it is a record of 200 sales transactions, which represents Car Mart's trading for the last year.

CAR MART SALES RECORD SHEET

1	2	3	4	5	6	7	8	9
Customer		Needs		Product	New or S/H	Feature	Benefit	

S/H = second-hand

Working in the same group as that which generated the data for the sales record sheet, proceed as follows:

1 Decide into which socio-economic category each customer falls. Enter your decisions in Column 2 of the sales record sheet.
2 Look at customer needs (Column 3) and decide which are *R*ational and which are more *P*sychological. Enter R or P in Column 4.
3 Similarly, look at benefits (Column 8) and enter R or P in Column 9, depending on whether or not the benefit is likely to appeal to the 'rational customer' or to his/her psychological needs.
4 Tick all those benefits where the R or P in Column 9 matches up with an R or P in Column 4.
5 Consider the ease/difficulty of completing 1 to 4 above, and reconcile any differences that occurred between Columns 4 and 9.
6 If time permits, you can discuss any interesting points which came out of the Car Mart sales record sheet.
7 When you have completed these tasks, proceed to the next section.

The customer audit (segmentation)

Staying in the same group as before, use the information you have collected on the completed sales record sheet and answer the following:

1 What is the key market segment(s) for Car Mart?
2 List the particular features of this or these segment(s).
3 Describe which products and benefits best meet the needs of this segment(s).
4 Suggest ways that Car Mart could exploit this information to become a more successful business.
5 Is Car Mart the best name for this company? How might it be changed to communicate more accurately its type of business or the customers it serves?
6 Consider the main learning points from Car Mart and decide how you could apply them to your own company.

You might find it useful to make notes of any interesting issues that come out of this analysis in the following space, or on a separate sheet of paper. Once you have completed those questions, proceed to the next section.

Notes

Interpretation of Exercise 4.5 – rationale behind Car Mart

1 The twelve customers represent two of each of the socio-economic groups:

Grade A	Chairman of industrial group
	Senior partner in firm of solicitors
Grade B	Bank manager
	Sales manager
Grade C1	Teacher
	Computer programmer
Grade C2	Tool-maker
	Plumber
Grade D	Bricklayer
	Machine operator
Grade E	Lift attendant (often a reserved occupation for the disabled)
	Elderly granny

2 The mechanism of using two dice in the way described means that, over about twenty transactions, something approaching Pareto's Law comes into play, i.e. that 20 per cent of customers account for 80 per cent of sales. This is because card 1 is never chosen and cards in positions 6, 7 and 8 should be prominent. But since the layout of the cards is random, there can be no preconceived notions about customers – it must all be interpreted from the sales analysis.

3 There are some hidden learning objectives, because, by playing the game, people become aware of, and can distinguish:

(a) Socio-economic groupings.
(b) Differences between features and benefits.
(c) Differences between rational and psychological buying motives.

4 Car Mart provides enough data for anyone to bring to life the main points about customer analysis and segmentation.

5 Those who need to apply this learning to their own company situation will be able to proceed with more confidence.

6 Car Mart demands that there is a high level of focus on customers and ensures that there is high awareness of customer needs.

Standard approaches to business market segmentation

1. Demographic characteristics

o Standard Industrial Classification (SIC) – The latest details are available from the Central Statistical Office. A summary appears below.

Agriculture, Forestry and Fishing (0)	**Construction (5)**
Agriculture and Horticulture (01) Forestry (02) Fishing (03)	Construction (50)
Energy and Water Supply Industries (1)	**Distribution, Hotels and Catering; Repairs (6)**
Coal extraction and manufacture of solid fuels (11)	Wholesale distribution – except dealing in scrap and waste

Coke ovens (12) Extraction of mineral oil and natural gas (13) Mineral oil processing (14) Nuclear fuel production (15) Production and distribution of electricity, gas, and other forms of energy (16) Water supply industry (17)	material (61) Dealing in scrap and waste material (62) Commission agents (63) Retailing – food, CTN, leather, chemists, clothing, footwear (64) Other retailing – cars, fuel, books, mixed retailers, etc. (65) Hotels and catering (66) Repairs of consumer goods and vehicles (67)
Extraction of Minerals and Ores Other Than Fuels; Manufacture of Metals, Mineral Products and Chemicals (2)	**Transport and Communications (7)**
Extraction and preparation of metalliferous ores (21) Metal manufacturing (22) Extraction of minerals not elsewhere specified (23) Manufacture of non-metallic mineral products (24) Chemical industry (25) Production of man-made fibres (26)	Railways (71) Other inland transport (72) Sea transport (73) Air transport (74) Supporting services to transport (75) Miscellaneous transport services and storage not elsewhere specified (76) Postal and telecom services (77)
Metal Goods, Engineering and Vehicle Industries (3)	**Banking, Finance, Insurance, Business Services, Leasing (8)**
Manufacture of metal goods not elsewhere specified (31) Mechanical engineering (32) Manufacture of office machinery and data processing equipment (33) Electrical and electronic engineering (34) Manufacture of motor vehicles and parts thereof (35) Manufacture of other transport equipment (36) Instrument engineering (37)	Banking and finance (81) Insurance, except for compulsory social security (82) Business services (83) Renting moveables (84) Owning and dealing in real estate (85)
Other Manufacturing Industries (4)	**Other Services (9)**
Food manufacturing industries (41) Drink and tobacco manufacturing industries (42) Textile industry (43) Manufacture of leather and leather goods (44)	Public administration, national defence and compulsory social security (91) Sanitary services (92) Education (93) Research and development (94) Medical and other health

Footwear and clothing industries (45)	services; veterinary services (95)
Timber and wooden furniture industries (46)	Other services provided to the general public (96)
Manufacture of paper and paper products; printing and publishing (47)	Recreational services and other cultural services (97)
Processing of rubber and plastics (48)	Personal services (98) Domestic services (99)
Other manufacturing industries (49)	Diplomatic representation, international organizations and allied armed forces (00)

o Size of Company

Very small	Small	Small-Med.	Medium
Med.-Large	Large	Very Large	Very Large+

o Department/Section

Manufacturing	Distribution	Customer Service
Sales	Marketing	Commercial
Financial	Bought Ledger	Sales Ledger
Personnel	Estates	Office Services
Planning	Contracts	IT

2. Geographic

o Postcode
o City, town, village, rural
o County
o Region – frequently defined in the UK by TV region (see Consumers)
o Country
o Economic/Political Union or Association (e.g. ASEAN)
o Continent

3. Psychographics – buyer characteristics
o Personality – stage in its business life cycle (start-up, growth, maturity, decline, turn-round); style/age of staff (formal, authoritarian, bureaucratic, disorganized, positive, indifferent, negative, cautious, conservative, old fashioned, youthful).
o Attitude – risk takers or risk avoiders; innovative or cautious, and many of the adjectives used to describe different types of personality can also express a company's attitude towards your product line (as opposed to their distinctive personal character).
o Life Style – environmentally concerned; involved with the community; sponsor of sports/arts.

Standard approaches to consumer market segmentation
1. Demographic characteristics

o Age

< 3	3–5	6–11	12–19
20–34	35–49	50–64	65 +

o Sex – male, female

o Family life cycle – Bachelor (young, single), split into dependants (living at home or full time student) and those with their own household; Newly married (no children); Full nest (graded according to the number and age of children); Single parent; Empty nesters (children left home or a childless couple); Elderly single.
o Family size

| 1–2 | 3–4 | 5 + |

o Type of residence – Flat/house; terraced/semi-detached/detached; private/rented/council; number of rooms/bedrooms.
o Income (£k)

| < 10 | 10–15 | 16–20 | 21–30 | 31–50 | > 50 |

o Occupation – Operatives; craftsman, foreman; managers, officials, proprietors; professional, technical; clerical, sales; farmers; retired, students; housewife; unemployed. White-collar (professional, managerial, supervisory, clerical); Blue-collar (manual).
o Education (highest level) – Secondary, no qualifications; GCSE; graduate; postgraduate.
o Religion – Christian: Jewish; Muslim; Buddhist; Other.
o Ethnic origin – African; Asian; Caribbean; UK, Irish; Other European.
o Nationality
o Socio-economic. The following definitions are those agreed between Research Services Ltd, and National Readership Survey (NRS Ltd).

A	Upper middle class (higher managerial, administrative, professional)
B	Middle class (middle managerial, administrative, professional)
C1	Lower middle class (supervisory, clerical, junior management, administrative, professional)
C2	Skilled working class (skilled manual workers)
D	Working class (semi and unskilled manual workers)
E	Subsistence level (state pensioners, widows with no other earner, casual or lowest-grade workers)

o Multi-demographic – Combining a selection of demographic criteria. For example, Research Services Ltd have combined each of four life cycle stages (Dependent, Pre-family, Family and Late) with the two occupation groupings of White-collar (A, B, C1) and Blue-collar (C2, D, E) producing eight segments. They have then further split out 'Family' and 'Late' into 'Better Off' and 'Worse Off' producing a total of twelve segments in their 'Sagacity' model. The basic thesis of the model is that people have different aspirations and behaviour patterns as they go through their life cycle. Their definition of these life cycle stages is as follows:

Dependent	Mainly under 24s, living at home or full-time student.
Pre-family	Under 35s, who have established their own household but have no children.
Family	Housewives and heads of household, under 65, with one or more children in the household.
Late	Includes all adults whose children have left home or who are over 35 and childless.

2. Geographic

o Postcode
o City, town, village, rural
o Coastal, inland
o County
o Region (frequently defined in the UK by 15 ITV Regions – Carlton, Meridian, Central Television, HTV Wales, Anglia, Scottish Television, Grampian Television, Granada Television, Yorkshire, Tyne Tees, Westcountry, LWT, Border Television, Ulster Television, and Group in the Channel Islands).
o Country
o Economic/Political Union or Association (e.g. NAFTA)
o Continent
o Population density
o Climate

3. Geodemographics

o ACORN (A Classification of Residential Neighbourhoods) produced by CACI Information Services Ltd is one of the longer established geodemographic classifications, updated in 1993 using the 1991 Census data. It consists of 54 types summarized into 17 basic groups which in turn are condensed into 6 broad categories. These six broad categories act as a simplified reference to the overall household classification structure. The categories are:

Category 'A' – 'Thriving'	Accounts for 19.8% of all households in the UK
Category 'B' – 'Expanding'	Accounts for 11.6%
Category 'C' – 'Rising'	7.5%
Category 'D' – 'Settling'	24.1%
Category 'E' – 'Aspiring'	13.7%
Category 'F' – 'Striving'	22.8%
Unclassified	0.5%

○ PIN from Pinpoint, which combines geodemographics and financial data.

Other, more recent, classifications have been developed by some of the larger database companies which, as well as linking residential areas with selected demographics, also add psychographic factors (see 'Multi-dimensional' in 4).

4. Psychographic characteristics

○ Personality – compulsive, extrovert, gregarious, adventurous, formal, authoritarian, ambitious, enthusiastic, positive, indifferent, negative, hostile. Specific ones by sex have also been developed, e.g. Wells eight male psychographic segments:

Quiet Family Man	Self-sufficient, shy, loner, lives for his family, practical shopper, low education, low income
Traditionalist	Conventional, secure, has self-esteem, concerned for others, conservative shopper, likes well known brands and manufacturers, low education, low/middle income
Discontented	Nearly everything (job, money, life) could be better, distrustful, socially aloof, price conscious, lowest educational and socio-economic group
Ethical Highbrow	Content with life and work, sensitive to others, concerned, cultured, religious, social reformer, driven by quality, well educated, middle/upper socio-economic group
Pleasure Oriented	Macho, self-centred, views himself as a leader, dislikes his work, impulsive buyer, low education and socio-economic group
Achiever	Status conscious, seeks success (power, money and socially), adventurous in leisure time pursuits, stylish (good food, music, clothes), discriminating buyer, good education, high socio-economic group
He-Man	Action, excitement, drama, views himself as capable and dominant, well educated, middle socio-economic group
Sophisticated	Attracted to intellectual and artistic achievements, broad interests, cosmopolitan, socially concerned, wants to be dominant and a leader, attracted to the unique and fashionable, best educated, higher socio-economic groups

Attitude – degree of loyalty (none, total, moderate), risk takers or risk avoiders, likelihood of purchasing a new product (innovator, early adopter, early majority, late majority, laggard), and many of the adjectives used to describe different types of personality can also express an individual's attitude towards your product line (as opposed to their distinctive personal character). Some companies have

o also developed specific behavioural groups, such as 'Monitor' from Taylor Nelson Ltd which has seven social value groups, each with a distinct pattern of behaviour.

o Customer status – purchase stage (aware, interested, desirous, ready for sale), user classification (non-user, lapsed user, first time, potential).

o Lifestyle – consists of three main dimensions;

Activities	Work, hobbies, social events, vacation, entertainment, club membership, community, shopping, sports
Interests	Family, home, job, community, recreation, fashion, food, media, achievements
Opinions	Selves, social issues, politics, business, economics, education, products, future, culture

In the UK, the three main providers of Lifestyle data are NDL (National Demographics and Lifestyles), CMT (Computerized Marketing Technologies) and ICD (International Communications and Data). Each obtains its information from consumer questionnaires. NDL's 'questionnaires' are product registration guarantee forms containing questions on household demographics, income and leisure interests, and distributed with durable goods such as electrical equipment. This has enabled NDL to collect over 10 million deduplicated 'questionnaires' which can be matched up to census data in order to produce accurate (for the census data) geographic profiles.

o Multi-dimensional – combining psychographic profiles with selected demographic data and identifying geographic areas where the resulting segments are to be found. For example, CCN Marketing have developed 20 Persona behavioural types using CMT's National Shoppers Survey database. These types range from so called 'Bon Viveurs' to 'New Teachers' and 'Craftsmen and Homemakers'. CCN's MOSAIC system now also extends into certain mainland European markets, classifying neighbourhoods into ten lifestyle types:

Elite Suburbs	Well-established suburban neighbourhoods in large and medium-sized cities, consisting of residential properties in large grounds. Wealthy but living in restrained luxury.
Average Areas	Average in age, income and family composition. Usually found in small market towns and local centres. Low poverty level.

Luxury Flats	Found in the centre of large conurbations, whose occupants set the country's fashion style and cultural agenda. Stylish accommodation for the political, artistic and media elite.
Low Income Inner City	Poor quality older housing, mixed with bars, cinemas, take-aways and football clubs, in the industrial and commercial inner city areas of large towns and cities.
High Rise Social Housing	Many social problems with a reliance on welfare caused by unemployment, divorce and illness.
Industrial Communities	Older terrace housing occupied by blue-collar workers in the traditional heavy industries.
Dynamic Families	Higher income families living in modern, privately-owned housing. Materialistic and up-to-date with the latest gadgets.
Lower Income Families	Living in both private and social housing in regional centres and average-sized towns. A good market for strongly branded packaged goods.
Rural/ Agricultural Areas	Occupied by older, conservative, traditional people, not commuters, very dependent on agriculture, keen supporters of the independent retailer.
Vacation/ Retirement	Mix of tourists, second homers and the retired. Both seasonal and week day changes in population.

5 Completing the marketing audit:
2 The product audit

Summary

Chapter 5 defines what a product is, product life cycle analysis, and the Boston matrix. It outlines certain weaknesses in the Boston matrix approach, and goes on to discuss in detail the use of the directional policy matrix as a tool of analysis.

Once again, it must be stressed that the purpose of this chapter is to outline what types of information are needed about products as part of the marketing audit. As such, it includes details of a number of fundamental marketing diagnostic tools.

What is a product?

The central role that the product plays in marketing management makes it such an important subject that mismanagement in this area is unlikely to be compensated for by good management in other areas.

The vital aspects of product management we shall discuss in this chapter are concerned with the nature of products, product life cycles, how products make profits, the concept of the product portfolio, and new product development. The purpose of this discussion is to help us to carry out a product audit in order that we can set meaningful marketing objectives. But before we can begin a proper discussion about product management, it is necessary first to understand what a product is, since this is the root of whatever misunderstanding there is about product management.

We have already looked at customers; now we begin to look at what we sell to them. Let us begin by explaining that a product is a problem solver, in the sense that it solves the customer's problems, and is also the means by which the company achieves its objectives. And since it is what the customer actually gets for what they pay, it is clearly a subject of great importance.

The clue to what constitutes a product can be found in an examination of what it is that customers appear to buy. For instance, Theodore Levitt, the famous management writer, illustrates that what customers want when they buy $\frac{1}{4}$ inch drills is $\frac{1}{4}$ inch holes. In other words the drill itself is only a means to an end. The lesson here for the drill manufacturer is that if they really believe their business is the manufacture of drills rather than, say, the manufacture of the means of making holes in materials, they are in grave danger of going out of business as soon as a better means of making holes is invented – such as, say, a pocket laser.

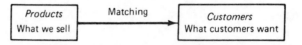

Figure 5.1

> The important point about this is that a company which fails to think of its business in terms of customer benefits rather than in terms of physical products or services is in danger of losing its competitive position in the market.

This is why so much attention was paid to the subject of benefit analysis in Chapter 4.

But while this is important at the highest level of a company, it is also extremely relevant even at the level of the salesperson. A salesperson announcing that the quench tank on his or her furnace is three times bigger than a competitor's quench tank must not be surprised if this news is met with complete indifference, especially if this feature requires a hole to be dug in the ground three times bigger than the one the customer currently has! Much more relevant would be the fact that this larger quench tank would enable the customer to save £10,000 a year on operating costs, which is a benefit and which is the main aspect the customer is interested in.

So far, we have not said much about service products, such as consulting, banking, insurance, and so on. The reason for this is simply that, as we said in Chapter 1, the marketing of services is not very different from the marketing of goods. The greatest difference is that a service product has benefits that cannot be stored. Thus, an airline seat, for example, if not utilized at the time of the flight, is gone forever, whereas a physical product may be stored and used at a later date.

The marketing of services is not very different from the marketing of goods.

In practice, this disadvantage makes very little difference in marketing terms. The major problem seems to lie in the difficulty many service product companies have in actually perceiving and presenting their offerings as 'products'. Consider the example of the consultant. This country is full of a constantly changing army of people who set themselves up as consultants, and it is not unusual to see people presenting themselves, for example, as general marketing consultants. It would be difficult for any prospective client to glean from such a description exactly what benefits this person is offering. Yet the market for consulting is no different from any other market, and it is a simple matter to segment the market and develop 'products' which will deliver the particular package of benefits desired.

We can now begin to see that, when a customer buys a product, even as an industrial buyer purchasing a piece of equipment for a company, he or she is still buying a particular bundle of benefits perceived as satisfying their own particular needs and wants.

We can now begin to appreciate the danger of leaving product decisions entirely to engineers or R and D people. If we do, engineers will often assume that the only point in product management is the actual technical performance, or the functional features of the product itself. These ideas are incorporated in Figure 5.2.

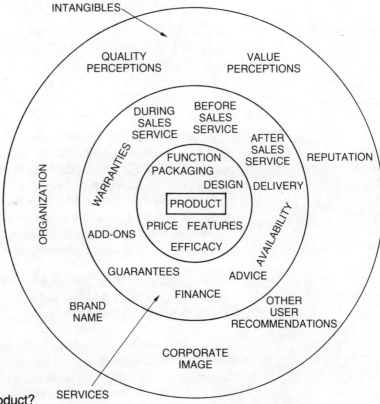

Figure 5.2 What is a product?

We can go even further than this and depict the two outer circles as 'product surround'. Figure 5.3 shows that this product surround can account for as much as 80 per cent of the added values and impact of a product. Often, these only account for about 20 per cent of costs, whereas the reverse is often true of the core product.

The importance of the brand

It will be clear that here we are talking about not just a physical product, but a *relationship* with the customer, a relationship that is personified either by the company's name or by the brand name on the product itself. ICI, IBM, BMW and Cadburys are excellent examples of company brand names. Persil, Coca Cola, Fosters Lager, Dulux Paint and Castrol are excellent examples of product brand names.

Most people are aware of the Coca Cola/Pepsi Cola blind taste tests, in which little difference was perceived when the colas were drunk 'blind'. On revealing the labels, however, 65 per cent of

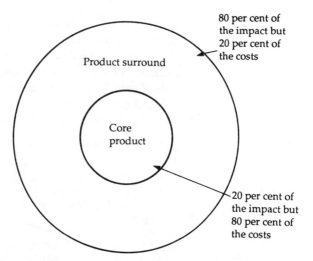

80 per cent of the impact but 20 per cent of the costs

Product surround

Core product

20 per cent of the impact but 80 per cent of the costs

Figure 5.3

consumers claimed to prefer Coca Cola. This is one of the best indications of the value of what we have referred to as the 'product surround'. That it is a major determinant of commercial success there can be little doubt. When one company buys another, as in the case of Nestlé and Rowntrees, it is abundantly clear that the purpose of the acquisition is not to buy the tangible assets which appear on the balance sheet, such as factories, plant, vehicles and so on, but the *brand names* owned by the company to be acquired.

> This is because it is not factories which make profits, but relationships with customers, and it is company and brand names which secure these relationships.

It is also a fact that, whenever brand names are neglected, what is known as 'the commodity slide' begins. This is because the physical characteristics of products are becoming increasingly difficult to differentiate and easy to emulate. In situations like these, one finds that purchasing decisions tend to be made on the basis of price or availability.

Business history is replete with examples of strong brand names which have been allowed to decay through lack of attention, often because of a lack of both promotion and continuous product improvement programmes.

> The fruit squash drink market in the UK is typical of this. The reverse can be seen in the case of Perrier water in the UK, which is a fantastic branding success story.

Figure 5.4 depicts the process of decay from brand to commodity as the distinctive values of the brand are eroded over time, with a consequent reduction in the ability to command a premium price.

The difference between a brand and a commodity can be summed up in the term 'added values', which are the additional attributes, or intangibles, that the consumer perceives as being embodied in the product. Thus, a product with a strong brand name is more than just

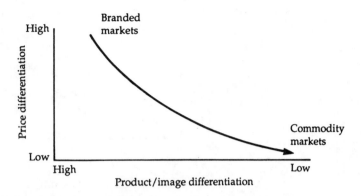

Figure 5.4

the sum of its component parts. The Coca Cola example is only one of thousands of examples of the phenomenon.

> In the same way, ICI's Nitram in the fertilizer market communicates an aura of quality and reliability that enables it to protect its advantage over lesser known brands.

Research has shown that perceived product quality, as explained above, is a major determinant of profitability. This issue is further discussed in Chapter 6 under the heading 'Competitive strategies'.*

Product life cycle

Having discussed the vital factor of benefits as a part of product management, we must now ask ourselves whether one product is enough.

There are many examples of entrepreneurs who set themselves up in business to manufacture, say, toys such as clackers, who make their fortune and who then just as quickly lose it when this fashion-conscious market changes to its latest fad. Such examples are merely the extreme manifestation of what is known as the *product life cycle*. This, too, is such a vital and fundamental concept that it is worth devoting some time to a discussion of the subject.

Historians of technology have observed that all technical functions grow exponentially until they come up against some natural limiting factor which causes growth to slow down and, eventually, to decline as one technology is replaced by another. There is universal agreement that the same phenomenon applies to products, so giving rise to the concept of the product life cycle, much written about in marketing literature during the past four decades.

The product life cycle postulates that if a new product is successful at the introductory stage (and many fail at this point), then gradually repeat purchase grows and spreads and the rate of sales growth increases. At this stage, competitors often enter the market and their additional promotional expenditures further expand the market. But no market is infinitely expandable, and eventually the *rate* of growth

*For further detailed discussion of branding, see *Creating Powerful Brands*, Leslie de Chernatony and Malcolm H. B. McDonald, Butterworth-Heinemann, 1992.

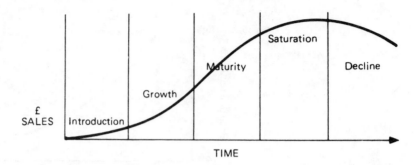

Figure 5.5

slows as the product moves into its maturity stage. Eventually, a point is reached where there are too many firms in the market, price wars break out, and some firms drop out of the market, until finally the market itself falls into decline. Figure 5.5 illustrates these apparently universal phenomena.

Nevertheless, while the product life cycle may well be a useful practical generalization, it can also be argued that particular product life cycles are determined more by the activities of the company than by any underlying 'law'.

> For example, a particular brand of cigarettes, while exhibiting all the characteristics of the classic product life cycle, went on to new record sales heights following the appointment of a new brand manager. Had this appointment not been made, the brand would probably have been withdrawn.

Nevertheless, while this example illustrates the dangers inherent in incorrect interpretation of life cycle analysis, even in this case sales will eventually mature.

From a management point of view, the product life cycle concept is useful in that it focuses our attention on the likely future sales pattern if we take no corrective action. There are several courses of action open to us in our attempts to maintain the profitable sales of a product over its life cycle.

> Figure 5.6 illustrates the actual courses taken by a British company in the management of one of its leading industrial market products. As sales growth began to slow down, the company initiated a programme of product range extensions and market development which successfully took the brand into additional stages of growth. At the same time the company was aggressively seeking new products and even considering potential areas for diversification.

Even more important are the implications of the product life cycle concept on every element of the marketing mix. The same diagram gives some guide as to how the product has to change over its life cycle. In addition to this, however, every other element also has to change. For example, if a company rigidly adhered to a premium pricing policy at the mature stage of the product life cycle, when markets are often overcrowded and price wars begin, it could well

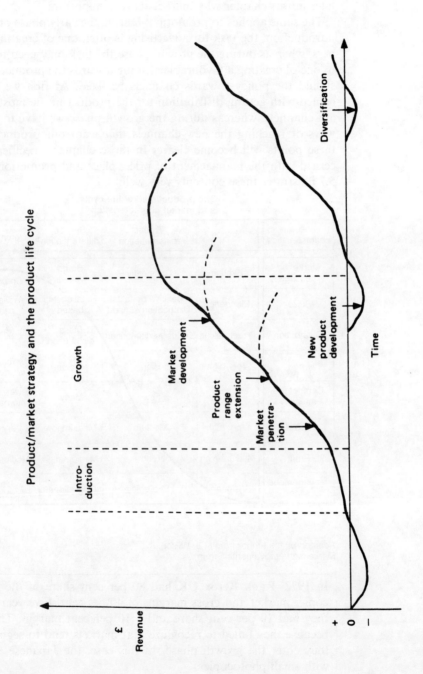

Product/market strategy and the product life cycle

Revenue £

+
0
–

Introduction

Growth

Market penetration

Product range extension

Market development

New product development

Diversification

Time

Figure 5.6

lose market share. It could be regretted later on when the market has settled down, for it is often at this stage that products provide extremely profitable revenue for the company. It will become clearer later in this chapter why market share is important.

The same applies to promotion. During the early phase of product introduction, the task for advertising is often one of creating awareness, whereas during the growth phase the task may need to change to one of creating a favourable attitude towards the product. Neither should the policy towards channels be fixed. At first we are concerned with getting distribution for the product in the most important channels, whereas during the growth phase we have to consider ways of reaching the new channels that want our product. All of these points will become clearer in those chapters specifically concerned with the management of price, place and promotion. Figure 5.7 illustrates these concepts very well.

The product/market life cycle and market characteristics

Key characteristics	Unique	Product differentiation	Service differentiation	'Commodity'
Marketing message	Explain	Competitive	Brand values	Corporate
Sales	Pioneering	Relative benefits Distribution support	Relationship based	Availability based
Distribution	Direct selling	Exclusive distribution	Mass distribution	80:20
Price	Very high	High	Medium	Low (consumer controlled)
Competitive intensity	None	Few	Many	Fewer, bigger, international
Costs	Very high	Medium	Medium/low	Very low
Profit	Medium/high	High	Medium/high	Medium/low
Management style	Visionary	Strategic	Operational	Cost management

Time

Figure 5.7

Adapted by the author from M.L. Wilson, Marketing Improvements Group

> In 1972, Rank Xerox UK had 80 per cent share of the photocopier market and gross margins of 40 per cent. Five years later, they had 10 per cent share and a 10 per cent margin. This was because they failed to recognize that markets tend to segment as they enter the growth phase. In this case, the Japanese entered with small photocopiers.

Drawing a product life cycle, however, can be extremely difficult, even given the availability of some form of time series analysis. This is connected with the complex question of market share measurement.

Firstly, let us remind ourselves that a firm needs to be concerned with its share (or its proportion of volume or value) of an *actual* market, rather than with a *potential* market. The example of the carpet manufacturer given in Chapter 4 emphasized the importance of measuring the right things when determining what a company's market is.

For the purpose of helping us to draw life cycles, it is worth repeating the definitions given in Chapter 4:

○ Product class, e.g. carpets
○ Product subclass, e.g. nylon rolls
○ Product brand, e.g. 'X'

'X' as a brand, for the purpose of measuring market share, is *concerned only with the aggregate of all other brands that satisfy the same group of customer wants.*

Nevertheless, the manufacturer of 'X' also needs to be aware of the sales trends of other kinds of carpets and floor covering in the institutional market, as well as of carpet sales overall.

One of the most frequent mistakes made by companies that do not understand what market share really means, is to assume that their company has only a small share of some market, whereas if the company is commercially successful, it probably has a much larger share of a smaller market segment.

The important point to remember at this stage is that the concept of the product life cycle is not an academic figment of the imagination, but a hard reality which is ignored at great risk.

It is interesting to see how many commercial failures can be traced back to a naive assumption on the part of managements that what was successful as a policy at one time will continue to be successful in the future.

A reference back to Figure 5.7 will immediately explain the demise of many companies, particularly in the Information Technology industry, who continued to pursue policies more appropriate to the second column, when, in reality, the markets for some of their products had moved to the fourth column.

Table 5.1 shows a checklist used by one major company to help it determine where its markets are on the life cycle.

Table 5.1 Guide to market maturity

Maturity stage factor	Embryonic	Growth	Mature	Declining
1 *Growth rate*	Normally much greater than GNP (on small base).	Sustained growth above GNP. New customers. New suppliers. Rate decelerates toward end of stage.	Approximately equals GNP.	Declining demand. Market shrinks as users' needs change.

Table 5.1 *cont.*

Maturity stage factor	Embryonic	Growth	Mature	Declining
2 *Predictability of growth potential*	Hard to define accurately. Small portion of demand being satisfied. Market forecasts differ widely.	Greater percentage of demand is met and upper limits of demand becoming clearer. Discontinuities, such as price reductions based on economies of scale, may occur.	Potential well defined. Competition specialized to satisfy needs of specific segments.	Known and limited.
3 *Product line proliferation*	Specialized lines to meet needs of early customers.	Rapid expansion.	Proliferation slows or ceases.	Lines narrow as unprofitable products dropped.
4 *Number of competitors*	Unpredictable.	Reaches maximum. New entrants attracted by growth and high margins. Some consolidation begins toward end of stage.	Entrenched positions established. Further shakeout of marginal competitors.	New entrants unlikely. Competitors continue to decline.
5 *Market share distribution*	Unstable. Shares react unpredictably to entrepreneurial insights and timing.	Increasing stability. Typically, a few competitors emerging as strong.	Stable with a few companies often controlling much of industry.	Highly concentrated or fragmented as industry segments and/or is localized.
6 *Customer stability*	Trial usage with little customer loyalty.	Some loyalty. Repeat usage with many seeking alternative suppliers	Well-developed buying patterns with customer loyalty. Competitors understand purchase dynamics and it is difficult for a new supplier to win over accounts.	Extremely stable. Suppliers dwindle and customers less motivated to seek alternatives.
7 *Ease of entry*	Normally easy. No one dominates. Customers' expectations uncertain. If barriers exist, they are usually technology, capital or fear of the unknown.	More difficult. Market franchises and/or economies of scale may exist, yet new business is still available without directly confronting competition	Difficult. Market leaders established. New business must be 'won' from others.	Little or no incentive to enter.
8 *Technology*	Plays an important role in matching product characteristics to market needs. Frequent product changes.	Product technology vital early, while process technology more important later in this stage.	Process and material substitution focus. Product requirements well known and relatively undemanding. May be a thrust to renew the industry via new technology.	Technological content is known, stable and accessible.

Diffusion of innovation

An interesting and useful extension of the product life cycle is what is known as the 'diffusion of innovation'. This will be referred to again in Chapter 6.

Diffusion is:

1 The adoption
2 of new products or services
3 over time
4 by consumers
5 within social systems
6 as encouraged by marketing

Diffusion refers to the cumulative percentage of potential adopters of a new product or service over time. Everett Rogers examined some of the social forces that explain the product life cycle. The body of knowledge often referred to as 'reference theory' (which incorporates work on group norms, group pressures etc.) helps explain the snowball effect of diffusion. Rogers found that the actual rate of diffusion is a function of a product's:

1 Relative advantage (over existing products)
2 Compatibility (with life styles, values, etc.)
3 Communicability (is it easy to communicate?)
4 Complexity (is it complicated?)
5 Divisibility (can it be tried out on a small scale before commitment?)

Diffusion is also a function of the newness of the product itself, which can be classified broadly under three headings:

○ Continuous innovation (e.g. the new miracle ingredient)
○ Dynamically continuous innovation (e.g. disposable lighter)
○ Discontinuous (e.g. microwave oven)

However, Rogers found that, for all new products, not everyone adopts new products at the same time, and that a universal pattern emerges as shown in Figure 5.8.

In general, the innovators think for themselves and try new things (where relevant); the early adopters, who have status in society, are

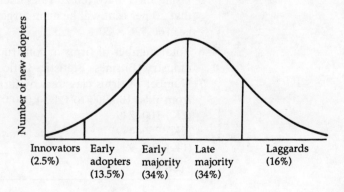

Figure 5.8

opinion leaders and they adopt successful products, making them acceptable and respectable; the early majority, who are more conservative and who have slightly above-average status, are more deliberate and only adopt products that have social approbation; the late majority, who are below average status and sceptical, adopt products much later; the laggards, with low status, income, etc., view life through the rear mirror and are the last to adopt products.

This particular piece of research can be very useful, particularly for advertising and personal selling. For example, if we can develop a typology for opinion leaders, we can target our early advertising and sales effort specifically at them. Once the first 7–8 per cent of opinion leaders have adopted our product, there is a good chance that the early majority will try it. Hence, once the 10–12 per cent point is reached, the champagne can be opened, because there is a good chance that the rest will adopt our product.

We know, for example, that the general characteristics of opinion leaders are that they are: venturesome; socially integrated; cosmopolitan; socially mobile; and privileged. So we need to ask ourselves what the specific characteristics of these customers are in our particular industry. We can then tailor our advertising and selling message specifically for them.

It can, however, also be both a practical diagnostic and forecasting tool.

There follows a worked example of how forecasts, and eventually strategic marketing plans, were developed from the intelligent use of the diffusion of innovation curve in respect of computerized business systems for the construction industry in the UK.

1	Number of contracting firms (Department of Environment Housing and Construction)	160,596	
2	Number of firms employing 4–79 direct employees	43,400	
3	Exclude painters, plasterers, etc.	6,100	
4	Conservative estimate of main target area	37,300	(1)
		or 23% of total	
5	Using the Pareto (80/20 rule) likelihood that 20 per cent will be main target area, i.e. 160,596 × 20%	32,000	(2)
6	Total number of firms in construction industry (Business Statistics Office)	217,785	
7	Number of firms classified by turnover from Pds. 100,000 to Pds. 1,000,000		
	(£K) 100–249	26,698	
	(£K) 250–499	10,651	
	(£K) 500–999	5,872	
	(£K)	43,221	(3)

8 Company's best estimate of size of target   37,300
   market
9 Company's estimate of the number of   3,500   (9.4%)
   micro installations in this segment
10 Plotting this on the diffusion of
    innovation curve shows:
11 Penetration of innovators and early adopters has taken four
    years. Adoption rate will now accelerate. It will probably be
    complete within one year.
12 *One year* balance of early adopters = 6.6 per cent = 2.462
    firms = installed base of 5968.
    Sales objective = 360 installations plus present base of 400 =
    760 = 12.7 per cent market share

It will be seen from this that three independent estimates were
made of the market size in order to establish the current position
on the diffusion of innovation curve.

In contrast, a Dutch computer supplier attempted to launch
hardware and software into the motor trade using an
undifferentiated product at a high sales price. An elementary
study would have indicated that this market is already well into
the late majority phase, when price and product features become
more important. Not surprisingly, the product launch failed.

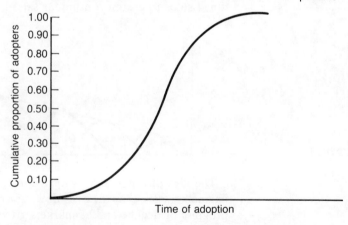

Generalized cumulative and non-cumulative diffusion patterns

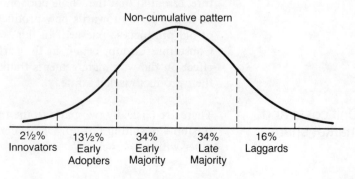

Non-cumulative pattern

Figure 5.9

The diffusion of innovation curve, when seen in conjunction with the product life cycle, helps to explain the dynamics of markets. Figure 5.9 illustrates this relationship. It shows that, when all potential users of a product are using it, the market is a replacement market.

Product portfolio

We might well imagine that, at any point in time, a review of a company's different products would reveal different stages of growth, maturity and decline.

In Figure 5.10, the dotted line represents the time of our analysis, and this shows one product in severe decline, one product in its introductory stage, and one in the saturation stage.

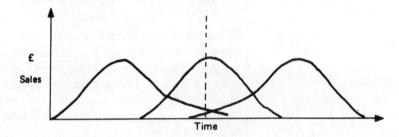

Figure 5.10

If our objective is to grow in profitability over a long period of time, our analysis of our product portfolio should reveal a situation like the one in Figure 5.11, in which new product introductions are timed so as to ensure continuous sales growth.

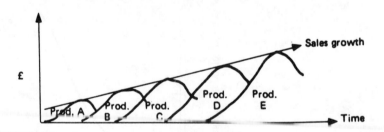

Figure 5.11

The idea of a portfolio is for a company to meet its objectives by balancing sales growth, cash flow and risk. As individual products progress or decline and as markets grow or shrink, then the overall nature of the company's product portfolio will change. It is, therefore, essential that the whole portfolio is reviewed regularly and that an active policy towards new product development and divestment of old products is pursued. In this respect, the work of the Boston Consulting Group, begun in the early 1960s, has had a profound effect on the way managements think about this subject and about their product/market strategy.

Unit costs and market share

There are basically two parts to the thinking behind the work of the Boston Consulting Group. One is concerned with *market share*; the other with *market growth*.

It is a well-known fact that we become better at doing things the more we do them. This phenomenon is known as the *learning curve*. It manifests itself especially with items such as labour efficiency, work specialization and methods improvement.

Such benefits are themselves a part of what we can call the *experience effect*, which includes such items as process innovations, better productivity from plant and equipment, product design improvements, and so on. In addition to the experience effect, and not necessarily mutually exclusive, are *economies of scale* that come with growth. For example, capital costs do not increase in direct proportion to capacity, which results in lower depreciation charges per unit of output, lower operating costs in the form of the number of operatives, lower marketing, sales, administration, and research and development costs, and lower raw materials and shipping costs. It is generally recognized, however, that cost decline applies more to value-added elements of cost than to bought-in supplies. In fact, the Boston Consulting Group discovered that costs decline by up to 30 per cent for every cumulative doubling of output. This phenomenon is shown in Figure 5.12. While there are many implications from this for marketing strategy, particularly in relation to pricing policy, we will confine ourselves here to a discussion of the product/market implications.

Cost decline applies more to the value-added elements of cost than to bought-in supplies.

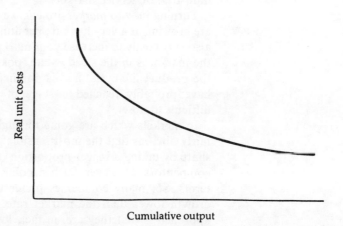

Real unit costs

Cumulative output

Figure 5.12

There is an overwhelming body of evidence to show that this real cost reduction actually occurs, in which case it follows that the greater your volume, the lower your unit costs should be. Thus, irrespective of what happens to the price of your product, providing you have the highest market share (hence the biggest volume), you should always be relatively more profitable than your competitors. This is illustrated in Figure 5.13.

Thus, as a general rule, it can be said that market share *per se* is a desirable goal.

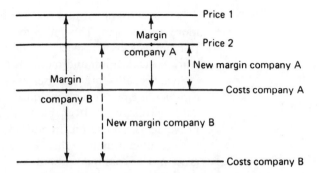

Figure 5.13

Indeed, research has confirmed that market share and profitability are linearly related. However, as we made clear in Chapter 4, we have to be certain that we have carefully defined our market, or segment. This explains why it is apparently possible for many small firms to be profitable in large markets. The reason is, of course, that, in reality, they have a large share of a smaller market segment. This is another reason why understanding market segmentation is the key to successful marketing. It would be unusual if there were not many caveats to the above 'law', and, although what these might be are fairly obvious, nevertheless it should be noted that the evidence provided by the Boston Consulting Group shows overwhelmingly that, in general, these 'laws' apply universally, whether for consumer, industrial or service markets.

Turning now to *market growth*, we observe that, in markets which are growing at a very low rate per annum, it is extremely difficult and also very costly to increase your market share. This is usually because the market is in the steady state (possibly in the saturation phase of the product life cycle) and is dominated by a few major firms who have probably reached a stage of equilibrium, which it is very difficult to upset.

In markets which are going through a period of high growth, it is fairly obvious that the most sensible policy would be to gain market share by taking a bigger proportion of the market growth than your competitors. However, such a policy is very costly in promotional terms. So, many companies prefer to sit tight and enjoy rates of growth lower than the market rate. The major problem with this approach is that they are, in fact, losing market share, which gives cost advantages (hence margin advantages) to competitors.

Since we know from previous experience of product life cycles that the market growth rate will fall, when this stage is reached and the market inevitably becomes price sensitive, the product will begin to lose money and we will probably be forced out of the market. Indeed, seen in this light, it becomes easier to understand the reasons for the demise of many industries in those countries of the world where the Japanese have entered the market.

Typical of this is the motor-cycle industry in the UK in which the output of the Japanese increased from thousands of units to

> millions of units during a period of market growth, while the output of the British remained steady during the same period. When the market growth rate started to decline, the inevitable happened. Even worse, it is virtually impossible to recover from such a situation, while the Japanese, with their advantageous cost position, have now dominated practically every market segment, including big bikes.

The Boston matrix

The Boston Consulting Group combined these ideas in the form of a simple matrix, which has profound implications for the firm, especially in respect of *cash flow*. Profits are not always an appropriate indicator of portfolio performance, as they will often reflect changes in the liquid assets of the company, such as inventories, capital equipment, or receivables, and thus do not indicate the true scope for future development. Cash flow, on the other hand, is a key determinant of a company's ability to develop its product portfolio.

The Boston matrix classifies a firm's products according to their cash usage and their cash generation along the two dimensions described above, i.e. relative market share and market growth rate. Market share is used because it is an indicator of the product's ability to generate cash; market growth is used because it is an indicator of the product's cash requirements. The measure of market share used is the product's share *relative* to the firm's largest competitor. This is important because it reflects the degree of dominance enjoyed by the product in the market. For example, if company A has 20 per cent market share and its biggest competitor also has 20 per cent market share, this position is usually less favourable than if company A had 20 per cent market share and its biggest competitor had only 10 per cent market share. The relative ratios would be 1:1 compared with 2:1. It is this ratio, or measure of market dominance, that the horizontal axis measures. This is summarized in Figure 5.14.

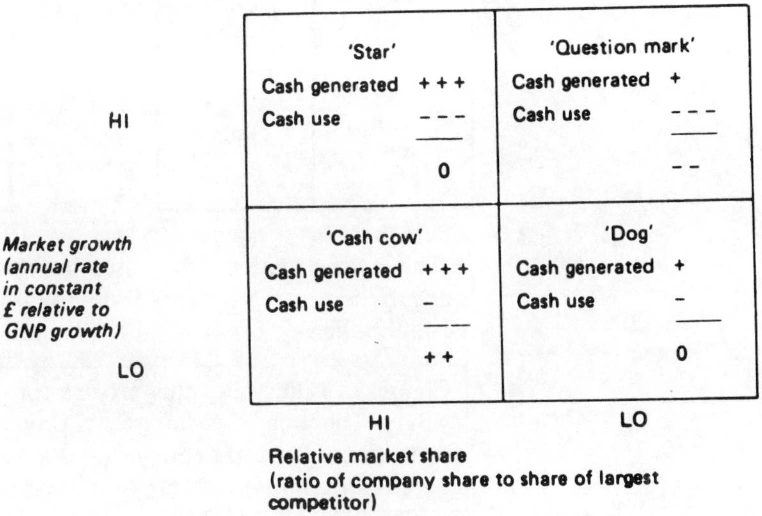

	'Star'	'Question mark'
	Cash generated + + +	Cash generated +
HI	Cash use – – –	Cash use – – –
	_____	_____
	0	– –
Market growth (annual rate in constant £ relative to GNP growth)	'Cash cow'	'Dog'
	Cash generated + + +	Cash generated +
	Cash use –	Cash use –
	_____	_____
LO	+ +	0
	HI	LO

Relative market share
(ratio of company share to share of largest competitor)

Figure 5.14

The definition of high relative market share is taken to be a ratio of one or greater than one. The cut-off point for high, as opposed to low, market growth should be defined according to the prevailing circumstances in the industry, but this is often taken as 10 per cent. There is, however, no reason why the dividing line on the vertical axis cannot be zero, or even a minus figure. It depends entirely on the industry, or segment, growth or decline. Sometimes, in very general markets, gross domestic product (GDP) can be used.

The picturesque labels given to the four categories in the Boston matrix gives some indication of the prospects for products in each quadrant.

The somewhat picturesque labels attached to each of the four categories of products give some indication of the prospects for products in each quadrant. Thus, the 'question mark' is a product which has not yet achieved a dominant market position and thus a high cash flow, or perhaps it once had such a position but has slipped back. It will be a high user of cash because it is in a growth market. This is also sometimes referred to as a 'wildcat'.

The 'star' is probably a newish product that has achieved a high market share and which is probably more or less self-financing in cash terms.

The 'cash cows' are leaders in markets where there is little additional growth, but a lot of stability. These are excellent generators of cash and tend to use little because of the state of the market.

'Dogs' often have little future and can be a cash drain on the company. They are probably candidates for divestment, although often such products fall into a category aptly described by Peter Drucker as 'investments in managerial ego'.

The art of product portfolio management now becomes a lot clearer. What we should be seeking to do is to use the surplus cash generated by the 'cash cows' to invest in our 'stars' and to invest in a selected number of 'question marks'. This is indicated in Figure 5.15.

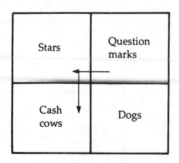 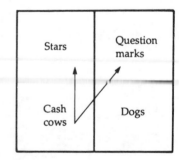

Figure 5.15

The Boston matrix can be used to forecast the market position of our products, say, five years from now, if we continue to pursue our current policies.

Figure 5.16 illustrates this process for a manufacturer of plastic valves. The area of each circle is proportional to each product's contribution to total company sales volume. In the case of this particular company, it can be seen that they are following what

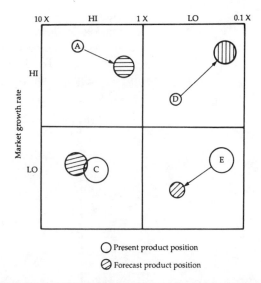

Figure 5.16

> could well prove to be disastrous policies in respect of their principal products. Product A, although growing, is losing market share in a high-growth market. Product D is also losing market share in a high-growth market. Products E and C are gaining market share in declining markets.

Such a framework also easily helps to explain the impracticability of marketing objectives such as 'to achieve a 10 per cent growth and a 20 per cent return on investment'. Such an objective, while fine as an *overall* policy, if applied to individual products in the portfolio, clearly becomes a nonsense and totally self-defeating. For example, to accept a 10 per cent growth rate in a market which is growing at, say, 15 per cent per annum, is likely to prove disastrous in the long run. Likewise, to go for a much higher than market growth rate in a low-growth market is certain to lead to unnecessary price wars and market disruption.

This type of framework is particularly useful to demonstrate to senior management the implications of different product/market strategies. It is also useful in formulating policies towards new product development.

Weaknesses in the Boston matrix approach

Unfortunately, many companies started using the Boston matrix indiscriminately during the 1970s and, as a result, it gradually lost its universal appeal. The reason, however, had more to do with lack of real understanding on the part of management than with any major defects in the methodology.*

Nonetheless, there are circumstances where great caution is required in its use. Imagine for a moment a company with 80 per cent

*For readers who would like to experiment with computer software for the BCG matrix, a computer-based training pack, by the author of this book, is available on request from Butterworth-Heinemann, Oxford.

of its products in low growth markets, and only 20 per cent of its products market leaders. Their matrix would look as depicted in Figure 5.17. As can be seen, almost 65 per cent of the company's products are 'dogs'. To divest these may well be tantamount to throwing the baby out with the bath water!

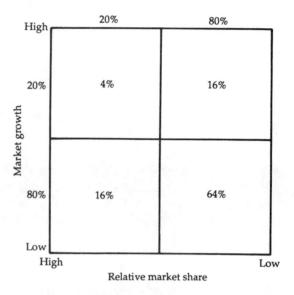

Figure 5.17

Consider, also, those industries in which market share for any single product in the range has little to do with its 'profitability'. Often a low market share product enjoys the same production, distribution and marketing economies of scale as other products in the portfolio, as, for example, in the case of beers and chemical products.

> Let us take the case of a product which is manufactured using basically the same components as other large market share products, is manufactured in the same plant as part of a similar process, and is distributed on the same vehicles and via the same outlets. In such a case it is easy to see how this low market share product can indeed be extremely profitable.

None of this, however, invalidates the work of the Boston Consulting Group, the principles of which can be applied to companies, divisions, subsidiaries, strategic business units, product groups, products, and so on. Providing great care is taken over the 'market share' axis, it is an extremely valuable planning tool.

Further developments of the Boston matrix

It is complications such as those outlined above that make the Boston matrix less relevant to certain situations. While it is impossible to give absolute rules on what these situations are, suffice it to say that great caution is necessary when dealing with such matters. In any case, two principles should always be adhered to.

> Firstly, a business should define its markets in such a way that it can ensure that its costs for key activities will be competitive. Or, it should define the markets it serves in such a way that it can develop specialized skills in servicing those markets and hence overcome a relative cost disadvantage. Both, of course, have to be related to a company's *distinctive competence*.

However, the approach of the Boston Consulting Group is fairly criticized in such circumstances as those described above as relying on two single factors, i.e. relative market share and market growth. To overcome this difficulty, and to provide a more flexible approach, General Electric and McKinsey jointly developed a multi-factor approach using the same fundamental ideas as the Boston Consulting Group. They used *industry attractiveness* and *business strengths* as the two main axes and built up these dimensions from a number of variables. Using these variables, and some scheme for weighting them according to their importance, products (or businesses) are classified into one of nine cells in a 3 × 3 matrix. Thus, the same purpose is served as in the Boston matrix (i.e. comparing investment opportunities among products or businesses) but with the difference that multiple criteria are used. These criteria vary according to circumstances, but often include those shown in Figure 5.18.

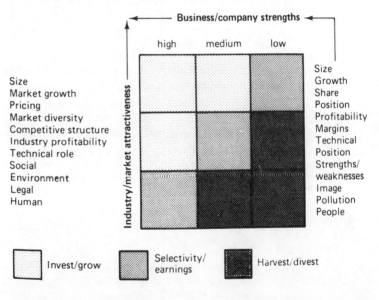

Figure 5.18

It is not necessary, however, to use a nine-box matrix, and many managers prefer to use a four-box matrix similar to the Boston box. Indeed this is the author's preferred methodology, as it seems to be more easily understood by, and useful to, practising managers.

The four-box directional policy matrix is shown in Figure 5.19. Here, the circles represent sales into an industry, market or segment and in the same way as in the Boston matrix, each is proportional to that segment's contribution to turnover.

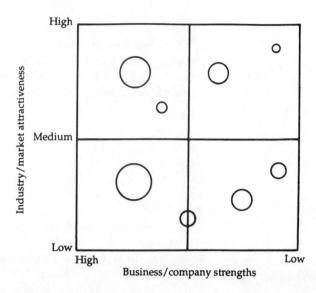

Figure 5.19

The difference in this case is that, rather than using only two variables, the criteria which are used for each axis are totally relevant and specific to each company using the matrix. It shows:

○ Markets categorized on a scale of attractiveness to the firm.
○ The firm's relative strengths in each of these markets.
○ The relative importance of each market.

The specific criteria to be used should be decided by key executives using the device, but a generalized list for the vertical axis is given in Table 5.2. It is advisable to use no more than five or six factors, otherwise the exercise becomes too complex and loses its focus. Read on, however, before selecting these factors, as essential methodological instructions on the construction of a portfolio matrix follow.

Table 5.2 Factors contributing to market attractiveness

Market factors	Financial and economic factors
Size (money units or both)	Contribution margins
Size of key segments	Leveraging factors, such as
Growth rate per year:	economies of scale and experience
total	Barriers to entry or exit (both
segments	financial and non-financial)
Diversity of market	Capacity utilization
Sensitivity to price, service features	
and external factors	**Technological factors**
Cyclicality	Maturity and volatility
Seasonality	Complexity
Bargaining power of upstream	Differentiation
suppliers	Patents and copyrights
Bargaining power of downstream	Manufacturing process technology
suppliers	required
Competition	**Socio-political factors in your**
Types of competitors	**environment**

Table 5.2 (*cont.*)

Degree of concentration	Social attitudes and trends
Changes in type and mix	Laws and government agency regulations
Entries and exits	Influence with pressure groups and government representatives
Changes in share	
Substitution by new technology	Human factors, such as unionization
Degrees and types of integration	and community acceptance

Advanced portfolio analysis in marketing

The strategic business unit (SBU)

Although the DPM, like other models of 'portfolio analysis', attempts to define a firm's strategic position and strategy alternatives, this objective cannot be met without considering what is meant by the term 'firm'. The accepted level at which a firm can be analysed using the DPM is that of the 'strategic business unit'.

The most common definition of an SBU is as follows:

1 It will have common segments and competitors for most of the products.
2 It will be a competitor in an external market.
3 It is a discrete, separate and identifiable 'unit'.
4 Its manager will have control over most of the areas critical to success.

The process of defining an SBU can be applied all the way down to product or department level.

It is possible, however, to use the DPM for any unit that has in it a number of different variables that could be usefully plotted using a two-dimensional matrix.

What should be plotted on the matrix?

This is also comparatively simple to deal with, but confusion can arise because the options are rarely spelled out.

Exercise 4.1, from the previous chapter, is repeated here in order to clarify what should be plotted on the matrix.

Let us take a hypothetical two-dimensional 'market' into which a number of products are sold (Figure 5.20). Each square might be considered as a segment, and various combinations could be considered to be the 'market', as follows:

(a) the actual product/customer cells served
(b) the intersection of product functions A, B, C and customer groups 2, 3, 4
(c) product functions A, B, C for *all* customer groups
(d) customer groups 2, 3, 4 for *all* product functions
(e) the entire matrix.

The DPM is useful where there is more than one (at least three, and a maximum of ten are suggested) 'markets' or segments between

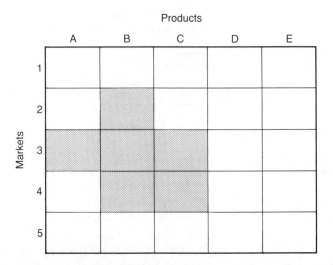

Figure 5.20

which the planner wishes to distinguish. These can be either existing or potential markets.

In order to implement the DPM, the following definition of 'market' and 'market segment' is offered:

> 'An identifiable group of customers with requirements in common that are, or may become, *significant* in determining a separate strategy.'

The answer is, clearly, a matter of management judgement and, at the beginning of any exercise using the DPM, the most important priority must be to define correctly the unit of analysis in terms of the combinations of product and markets. For example, it is clearly possible to put 25 circles (or crosses, where there is no turnover) on a portfolio matrix, with markets 1–5 on the vertical axis and each of products A–E on the horizontal axis (i.e. (e) above), but that would result in a very confusing array of circles and crosses.

It would also be possible to put six circles on a matrix (i.e. the actual product/customer cells served, (a) above, with markets 2, 3 and 4 on the vertical axis and products A, B and C as appropriate for each of these served markets on the horizontal axis).

Alternatively, instead of products A, B and C being individually plotted, an aggregate value or volume could be plotted for all products in any served market. Or, indeed, any of the combinations listed in the example above could be used. The user has to decide early on exactly what will be the unit of analysis for the purpose of determining the size of each circle that will appear in the matrix.

To summarize, the principal unit of analysis for the purpose of entering data will be the user's definition of 'product for market'.

Preparation

Prior to commencing analysis, the following preparation is recommended:

(i)   Product profiles should be available for all products/services to be scored.

(ii) The markets in which the products/services compete should be clearly defined.

(iii) Define the time period being scored. Three years are recommended.

(iv) Define the competitors against which the products/services will be scored.

(v)   Ensure sufficient data is available to score the factors (where no data is available, this is no problem as long as. a sensible approximation can be made for the factors).

(vi) Ensure up-to-date sales forecasts are available for all products/services, plus any new products/services.

Analysis team

In order to improve the quality of scoring, it is recommended that a group of people from a number of different functions score, as this encourages the challenging of traditional views through discussion. It is recommended that there should be no more than six people involved in the analysis.

Ten steps to producing the DPM

Step 1   Should define the products/services for markets that are to be used during the analysis.

Step 2   Should define the criteria for market attractiveness.

Step 3   Should score the relevant product/services for market.

Step 4   Should define the organization's relative strengths for each product/service for market.

Step 5   Should analyse and draw conclusions from the relative position of each product/service for market.

Step 6   Should draw conclusions from the analysis with a view to generating objectives and strategies.

Step 7   (Optional) Should position the circles on the box assuming no change to current policies. That is to say, a *forecast* should be made of the future position of the circles.

Step 8   Should redraw the portfolio to position the circles where the organization wants them to be. That is to say, the *objectives* they wish to achieve for each product/service for market.

Step 9   Should detail the strategies to be implemented to achieve the objectives.

Step 10 Should detail the appropriate financial consequences in terms of growth rate by product/service for market and return on sales.

Two key definitions

Market attractiveness is a measure of the *potential* of the market place to yield growth in sales and profits. It is important to stress that this should be an objective assessment of market attractiveness using data *external* to the organization. The criteria themselves will, of course, be determined by the organization carrying out the exercise and will be relevant to the objectives the organization is trying to achieve, but it should be independent of the organization's position in its markets.

Business strengths/position is a measure of an organization's *actual* strengths in the market place (i.e. the degree to which it can take advantage of a market opportunity). Thus, it is an objective assessment of an organization's ability to satisfy market needs relative to competitors.

The process

Step 1 *List the population of products/services for markets that you intend to include in the matrix*

The list can consist of: countries; companies; subsidiaries; regions; products; markets; segments; customers; distributors; or any other unit of analysis that is important.

The DPM can be used at any level in an organization and for any kind of SBU.

Step 2 *Define market attractiveness factors*

In this step, you should list the factors you wish to consider in comparing the attractiveness of your markets.

It is also important to list the markets that you intend to apply the criteria to before deciding on the criteria themselves, since the purpose of the vertical axis is to discriminate between more and less attractive markets. The criteria themselves must be specific to the population and must not be changed for different markets in the same population.

Factors	*Example weight*
Growth rate	40
Accessible market size	20
Profit potential	40
Total	**100**

Note: As profit = market size × margin × growth, it would be reasonable to expect a *weighting* against each of these to be at *least* as shown, although an even higher weight on *growth* would be understandable in some circumstances (in which case, the corresponding weight for the others should be reduced).

This is a combination of a number of factors. These factors, however, can usually be summarized under three headings.

(a) *Growth rate* Average annual growth rate of revenue spent by that segment (% growth '94 over '93, *plus* % growth '95 over '94, *plus* % growth '96 over '95, divided by 3). If preferred, compound average growth rate could be used.

(b) *Accessible market size* An attractive market is not only large – it can also be accessed. One way of calculating this is to estimate the *total* revenue of the segment in $t + 3$, *less* revenue impossible to access, *regardless of investment made*. Alternatively, total market size can be used, which is the most frequent method, as it does not involve any managerial judgement to be made that could distort the truth. *This latter method is the preferred method.* A market size factor score is simply the score multiplied by the weight (20 as in the example above).

(c) *Profit potential* This is much more difficult to deal with and will vary considerably, according to industry. For example, Porter's Five Forces model could be used to estimate the profit potential of a segment, as in the following example:

Sub-factors	*10 = Low × Weight* *0 = High*	*Weighted* *factor* *score*
1 Intensity of competition	50	
2 Threat of substitute	5	
3 Threat of new entrants	5	
4 Power of suppliers	10	
5 Power of customer	30	
	Profit potential factor score	

Alternatively, a combination of these and industry-specific factors could be used. In the case of the pharmaceutical industry, for example, the factors could be:

Sub-factors	*High Medium Low × Weight*	*Weighted* *factor* *score*
o Unmet medical needs (efficacy)	30	
o Unmet medical needs (safety)	25	

o Unmet medical
    needs
    (convenience)
	15	

o Price potential	10	
o Competitive intensity	10	
o Cost of market entry	10	
	Profit potential factor score	

These are clearly a proxy for profit potential. Each is weighted according to its importance. The weights add up to 100 in order to give a *profit potential factor score*, as in the Porter's Five Forces example above.

Note that, following this calculation, the *profit potential factor score* is simply multiplied by the weight (40 as in the example above).

Variations

Naturally, growth, size and profit will not encapsulate the requirements of all organizations. For example, in the case of an orchestra, artistic satisfaction may be an important consideration. In another case, social considerations could be important. In yet another, cyclicality may be a factor.

It is possible, then, to add another heading, such as 'Risk' or 'Other' to the three factors listed at the beginning of Step 2. In general, however, it should be possible to reduce it to just the three main ones, with sub-factors incorporated into these, as shown.

Step 3   *Score the relevant products/services for markets*

In this step you should score the products/services for markets against the criteria defined in Step 1.

Can market attractiveness factors change whilst constructing the DPM?

The answer to this is no. Once agreed, under no circumstances should market attractiveness factors be changed, otherwise the attractiveness of our markets is not being evaluated against common criteria and the matrix becomes meaningless. Scores, however, will be specific to each market.

Can the circles move vertically?

No is the obvious answer, although yes is also possible, providing the matrix shows the current level of attractiveness at the present time. This implies carrying out one set of calculations for the present time according to market attractiveness factors, in order to locate markets on the vertical axis, then carrying our another set of calculations for a future period (say, in three years' time), based on our forecasts according to the same factors. In practice, it is easier to carry out only the latter calculation, in which case the circles can only move horizontally.

Step 4   *Define business strengths/position*

(i)   This is a measure of an organization's *actual* strengths in the market place and will differ by market/segment opportunity.

These factors will usually be a combination of an organization's relative strengths versus competitors in connection with *customer-facing* needs, i.e. those things that are required by the customer.

These can often be summarized under:

○ Product requirements
○ Price requirements
○ Service requirements
○ Promotion requirements

The weightings given to each should be specific to each market/segment. In the same way that 'profit' on the market attractiveness axis can be broken down into sub-headings, so can each of the above be broken down further and analysed. Indeed, this is to be strongly recommended. These sub-factors should be dealt with in the same way as the sub-factors described under 'market attractiveness'.

For example, in the case of pharmaceuticals, product strengths could be represented by:

- ○ Relative product strengths
- ○ Relative product safety
- ○ Relative product convenience
- ○ Relative cost effectiveness

(ii) *Broadening the analysis*

It will be clear that an organization's relative strengths in meeting customer-facing needs will be a function of its *capabilities* in connection with *industry-wide success factors*. For example, if a depot is necessary in each major town/city for any organization to succeed in an industry and the organization carrying out the analysis doesn't have this, then it is likely that this will account for its poor performance under 'customer service', which is, of course, a customer requirement. Likewise, if it is necessary to have low feedstock costs for any organization to succeed in an industry and the organization carrying out the analysis doesn't have this, then it is likely that this will account for its poor performance under 'price', which is, of course, a customer requirement.

Thus, in the same way that sub-factors should be estimated in order to arrive at 'market attractiveness' factors, so an assessment of an organization's capabilities in respect of *industry-wide success factors* could be made in order to understand what needs to be done in the organization in order to satisfy customer needs better. This assessment, however, is quite separate from the quantification of the business strengths/position axis and its purpose is to translate the analysis into actionable propositions for other functions within the organization, such as purchasing, production, distribution and so on.

In the case of pharmaceuticals, for example, factors such as 'patent life' are simply an indication of an organization's capability to provide product differentiation. They are irrelevant to the doctor, but need to be taken account of by the organization carrying out the analysis.

(iii) *How to deal with business strengths/position*

The first of these concerns the quantification of business strengths within a 'market'.

Many books for the manager are not particularly useful when used to construct a marketing plan. Few of the factors they mention take account of the need for a company to make an 'offer' to a particular 'market' that has a sustainable competitive advantage over the 'offers' of relevant competitors.

The only way a company can do this is to understand the real needs and wants of the chosen customer group, find out by means of market research how well these needs are being met by the products on offer, and then seek to satisfy these needs better than their competitors.

The following is a typical calculation to assess the strength of a company in a market. The information has been gathered by means of a self-assessment questionnaire, where the following three questions are used to plot the firm's (SBU's) position on the horizontal axis (competitive position/business strengths):

1 What are the few key things that any competitor has to do right to succeed (i.e. what are the critical success factors, also known as CSFs, in this industry sector)?
2 How important is each of these critical success factors (measured comparatively using a score out of 100)?
3 How do you and each of your competitors score (out of 10) on each of the critical success factors?

These questions yield the information necessary to make an overall assessment of an SBU's competitive strengths:

Critical success factors (What are the few key things that any competition has to do right to succeed?)	*Weighting (How important is each of these CSFs? Score out of 100)*		*Strengths/weaknesses analysis (Score yourself and each of your main competitors out of 10 on each of the CSFs, then multiply the score by the weight)*		
				Competition	
			You	*Comp A*	*Comp B* *Comp C*
1 Product	20		9 = 1.8	6 = 1.2	5 = 1.0 4 = 0.8
2 Price	10		8 = 0.8	5 = 0.5	6 = 0.6 10 = 0.1
3 Service	50		5 = 2.5	9 = 4.5	7 = 3.5 6 = 3.0
4 Image	20		8 = 1.6	8 = 1.6	5 = 1.0 3 = 0.6
These should normally be viewed from the customer's point of view	**Total 100**	**Total score × weight**	**6.7**	**7.8**	**6.1** **5.4**

From this it will be seen that:

○ This organization is not market leader
○ All competitors score more than 5.0

The problem with this and many similar calculations is that rarely will this method discriminate sufficiently well to indicate the relative strengths of a number of products in a particular company's product/market portfolio, and many of the SBU's products would appear on the left of the matrix.

Some method is required to prevent all products appearing on the left of the matrix. This can be achieved by using a ratio, as in the Boston matrix. This will indicate a company's position relative to the best in the market.

In the example provided, Competitor A has most strengths in the market, so our organization needs to make some improvements. To reflect this, our weighted score should be compared with that of Competitor A (the highest weighted score). Thus 6.7:7.8 = 0.86:1.

If we were to plot this on a logarithmic scale on the horizontal axis, this would place our organization to the right of the dividing line as follows:

$$3\times \qquad\qquad 1 \qquad\qquad 0.3$$

(We should make the left hand extreme point $3\times$ and start the scale on the right at 0.3).

A scale of $3\times$ to 0.3 has been chosen because such a band is likely to encapsulate most extremes of competitive advantage. If it doesn't, just change it to suit your own circumstances.

Step 5   *Producing the DPM*
Finally, circles should be drawn on a four-box matrix, using market size (as defined in Step 2 above) to determine the area of the circle. An organization's market share can be put in as a 'cheese' in each circle. Alternatively, an organization's own sales into each market can be used.

In practice, however, it is advisable to do both and compare them in order to see how closely actual sales match the opportunities.

Step 6   *Analysis and generation of marketing objectives and strategies*
The objective of producing the DPM is to see the portfolio of products/services for markets relative to each other in the context of the criteria used. This analysis should indicate whether the portfolio is well balanced or not and should give a clear indication of any problems. As an option, it is sometimes advisable to move to Step 7 at this point.

Step 7   (Optional) Forecasting

The forecast position of the circles should now be made. This is simply done by re-scoring the products/services for markets in three years' time, assuming the organization doesn't change its strategies (see Step 3). This will indicate whether the position is getting worse or better.

It is not absolutely necessary to change the scores on the vertical axis (see Step 3).

Step 8   Setting marketing objectives

This involves changing the volumes/values and/or market share (marketing objectives) and the scores on the horizontal axis (relative strength in market) in order to achieve the desired volumes/values. Conceptually, one is picking up the circle and moving it/revising it without specifying how this is to be achieved. Strategies are then defined, which involve words and changes to individual CSF scores (Step 9).

Step 9   Spell out strategies

This involves making specific statements about the marketing strategies to be employed to achieve the desired volumes/values.

Step 10 Sales and profit forecasts

Once this is done, organizations should be asked to do the following:

1 Plot average % growth in sales revenue by segment ($t - 3$ to $t0$)
   Plot average % ROS by segment ($t - 3$ to $t0$)
2 Plot *forecast* average % growth in sales revenue by segment ($t0$ to $t + 3$)
   Plot *forecast* average % ROS by segment ($t0$ to $t + 3$)

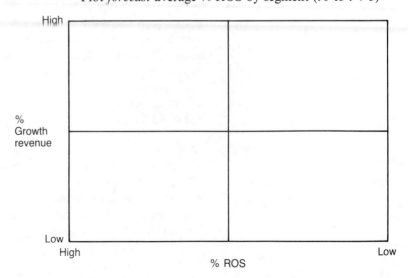

This will show clearly whether past performance *and*, more importantly, forecasts match the market rating exercise above. *This should preferably be done by someone else (e.g. accountants).*

One major chemical company used the directional policy matrix to select fifty distributors out of the 450 they were dealing with. They needed to do this because the market was in decline and the distributors began *buying* for customers rather than *selling* for the supplier. This led to a dramatic fall in prices. The only way the chemical company could begin to tackle the problem was by appointing a number of exclusive distributorships. The issue of which distributorships to choose was tackled using the directional policy matrix, as clearly some were more attractive than others, while the company had varying strengths in their dealings with each distributor.

Case histories

This selection concludes with some case histories showing the use and misuse of the DPM.

Case 1

The first concerns a senior marketing manager of a blue-chip company who dismissed the DPM as irrelevant because he had only four principal products, each one of which was sold to the same customer (or market). Clearly we are talking about major capital sales in this instance.

The manager had plotted products A, B, C and D on the horizontal axis with only 1 'market' on the vertical axis. The resulting matrix obviously had 4 circles in a straight line. Since the purpose of a matrix is to develop a relationship between two or more variables judged by the planner to be of significance in a given planning context, this matrix was clearly absurd and served no useful purpose whatever.

If this manager really wished to use the DPM, he would have to put products A, B, C and D on the vertical axis and look at their respective size and strengths on the horizontal axis. In such a case, all we have done is to change the nomenclature, making a product equivalent to a market, which is clearly acceptable. The main point is that the purpose of the DPM is to display clearly and visibly the relationship between product/market variables.

Case 2

This is certainly the case for a School of Management portfolio completed by the author in 1984. Here, the 'product' (for example the MBA programme) equals 'market'. This is shown in Figure 5.21. (By astute management, some of these circles have since been moved to the left of the matrix, surely the purpose of using the DPM in the first place!)

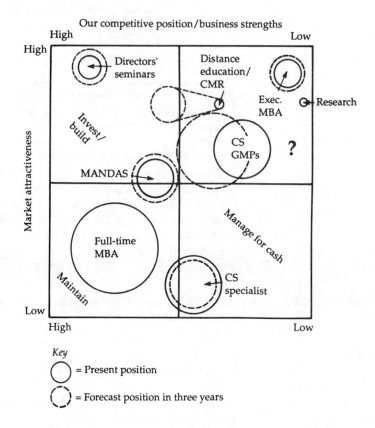

Figure 5.21

Let us now look at two companies whose revenue and profits were static for two consecutive years, and both of which kept their shareholders at bay by selling off part of their assets. The boards of both companies attempted to use the DPM to help clarify the options. In both cases, the resulting matrix was not a reflection of the reality.

Case 3: An International engineering company

Here, the Shipping, Food, Thermal and Separation Divisions were all operating in no-growth markets, only the Biotechnology Division was in a growth market. Using market growth as a factor obviously caused all Divisions to appear in the bottom half of the matrix, except the Biotechnology Division. The other factor used, however, was profitability, which in the case of Shipping and Separation was high. The weighting of 60% on the profit factor pulled both of these Divisions into the upper part of the matrix. Strengths in each case were different, and the resulting matrix looked as shown in Figure 5.22.

However, since both the Shipping and Separation Divisions had little (if any) potential to increase their volume and profitability in mature markets, and since the Food and Biotechnology Divisions did, the circles were clearly in the wrong place. The reality facing the company was as shown in Figure 5.23.

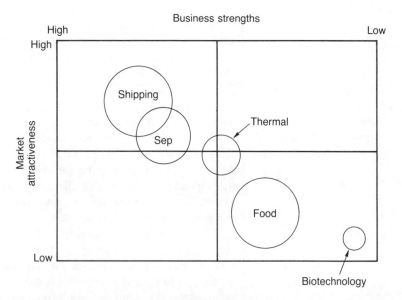

Figure 5.22

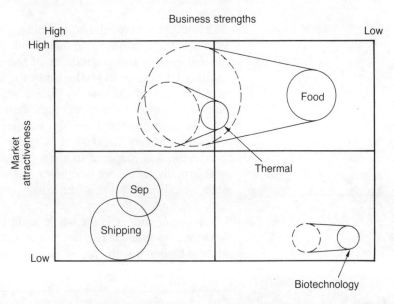

Figure 5.23

The opportunity was clearly there for this company to invest in the Food Division, where it was comparatively weak, and also in the Thermal Division. Both of these markets provided ample opportunity for the company to improve its market share and strengths (especially if it also used productivity measures at the same time), in spite of the fact that both markets were relatively mature.

In other words, all we are really interested in is the potential for us to increase our volume and profits, and, in some instances, externally derived factors of market growth and profitability, however accurate, are not particularly useful.

> Having reached the conclusion above, obviously this company then took each Division in turn and completed the DPM for each of their component parts in order to decide how best to allocate resources.

Case 4: A conglomerate with 12 separate companies

This group, although enjoying very high return on capital employed (ROCE), was also under extreme pressure from the financial institutions because its turnover and profits were static. At a directors' meeting, the DPM was used as one of the basic tools of analysis. ROCE of the companies varied between 500% and 5%, with seven about 50% and five below 15%.

Again, using market growth and industry return-on-sales (ROS) as the factors, weighted 30 and 70, not surprisingly all the high-profit companies appeared in the top left of the matrix and all the low-profit companies appeared in the bottom half of the matrix. All this did was to confirm the group's existing position, but was of little value when considering the future.

The directors were advised to change the factors to encapsulate potential for growth in volume and profits rather than the inherent growth and profitability of the markets themselves. The resulting DPM then showed most of the high-profit companies in the lower half of the matrix, since few of them were in growth markets and most already had high market shares.

It also demonstrated clearly another point of policy. One company enjoying a 500% ROCE could grow, providing the chairperson was prepared to allow them to redefine their market more broadly and move into lower ROS segments. Such a policy move would have put this particular company back into the top part of the matrix!

But this, of course, is the whole point of using the DPM in the first place. It should raise key issues and force senior executives into thinking about the future in a structured way.

Case 5

This Australian division of an international agrochemical company was under extreme pressure to grow the revenue and profits in a declining market. At first glance, the marketing plans looked to be extremely sophisticated. The plans themselves were also well presented.

The problem was that they did not succeed in spelling out a clear strategy to achieve the corporate objectives, the individual product/market objectives appearing to be little more than 'wish lists'. On closer examination, it became clear that the underlying diagnosis was at fault.

The SWOT analysis shown in Table 5.3 is a typical example of the format used.

Table 5.3

Critical success factors	Success factor scores			
	Weight	*Us*	*Comp A*	*Comp B*
Product efficacy	30	9	8	8
Product price	25	9	9	9
Product image	20	9	8	9
Profitability	20	8	9	6
Formulation	5	8	8	7
		8.8	**8.4**	**8.0**

Even a cursory glance at this shows that none of these factors are discriminators in the choice of supply. On discovering, however, that the SWOT had been done on the merchants (or channel) and that merchants were motivated mainly by price, it was easy to conclude that the three main brands were really commodities in the eyes of the merchant, albeit they were major brand names.

The real bottom line on all of this was that the merchants were calling the shots, a situation that was bound to get worse and that would continue to drive the price down.

The next obvious conclusion was that this company needed to go down the value chain to the farmer and to segment them according to need in order to enable the company to create demand pull, thus reducing the power of the channel. SWOTing at the next link in the chain quickly revealed two things:

(i) There was ample opportunity for this company to create value for the farmer
(ii) Not enough was known about farm needs to enable proper SWOTs to be done on them

The marketing plan of this company contained what looked to be quite sophisticated DPMs. Again, however, on closer examination of the underlying data, one circle that appeared at the top of the 'market attractiveness' axis was clearly in the wrong place, as the data in Table 5.4 illustrates.

Table 5.4

Product 1		Product 2	
Sales in 1993	$10 million	Sales in 1993	$5 million
Profits in 1993	$1 million	Profit in 1993	$0.5 million
Projected sales in 1996	$10 million	Projected sales in 1996	$7 million
Projected profit in 1996	$1 million	Projected profit in 1996	$0.7 million

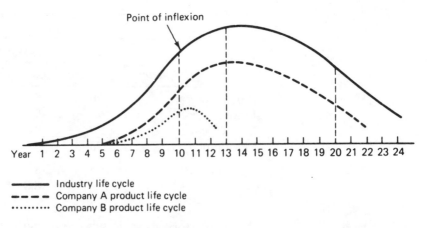

Point of inflexion

Year 1 2 3 4 5 6 7 8 9 10 11 12 13 14 15 16 17 18 19 20 21 22 23 24

——— Industry life cycle
— — — Company A product life cycle
··········· Company B product life cycle

Figure 5.24 Short-term profit maximization versus market share and long-term profit maximization

> From this, it can be seen that the product manager doing the analysis believed that Product 1 was more attractive than Product 2 because, even in 1996, the absolute dollar profits were going to be greater. Clearly, however, positioning Product 1 near the top of the vertical axis of the DPM implied an *invest* strategy, while the implied strategy for Product 2 was a *maintain* (or manage for sustained earnings) strategy. Both strategies would have been wholly inappropriate, thus reducing the value of the DPM as an analytical tool.
>
> Even worse, since we have already seen that the CSF calculation (to derive the position on the horizontal axis of the DPM) was also wrong, the resulting DPM merely served to *confuse*, rather than to clarify and to provide valuable insights about competitive strategy.

Since then, having had the DPM properly explained to them, all of these organizations were able to develop objectives and strategies designed to grow the business and all are now thriving and prospering.

Finally, it may be useful to conclude this section with a definition of a portfolio matrix: 'The use of graphic models to develop a relationship between two or more variables judged by the planner to be of significance in the planning context.'

Whichever approach is used, it can be seen that obvious consideration should be given to marketing objectives and strategies which are appropriate to the attractiveness of a market (market growth in Boston matrix) and the extent to which such opportunities match our capabilities (market share in Boston matrix). What these objectives should be will be discussed in Chapter 6.

Combining product life cycles and portfolio management

Figure 5.24 illustrates the consequences of failing to appreciate the implications of both the product life cycle concept and the dual combination of market share and market growth.

Companies A and B both start out with question marks (wildcats) in years 5 and 6 in a growing market. Company A invests in building market share and quickly turns into a star. Company B, meanwhile, manages its product for profit over a four-year period so that, while still growing, it steadily loses market share (i.e. it remains a question mark or wildcat). In year 10, when the market becomes saturated (when typically competitive pressures intensify), Company B with its low market share (hence typically higher costs and lower margins) cannot compete and quickly drops out of the market. Company A, on the other hand, aggressively defends its market share and goes on to enjoy a period of approximately ten years with a product which has become a cash cow. Thus, company B, by pursuing a policy of short-term profit maximization, lost at least ten years profit potential.

Relevance of life-cycle analysis and portfolio management to the marketing audit

It will be recalled that this discussion took place against the background of the need to complete a full and detailed marketing audit prior to setting marketing objectives. Such analyses as those described in this chapter should be an integral part of the marketing audit.

The audit should contain a product life cycle for each major product and an attempt should be made (using other audit information) to predict the future shape of the life cycle. It should also contain a product portfolio matrix showing the present position of the products.

Application questions

1 Select a major product and draw a life cycle of:

o the product itself;
o the market (segment) in which it competes.

2 Explain why it is the shape it is.
3 Predict the shape and length of the life cycle in the future.
4 Say *why* you are making these predictions.
5 Plot your products on a Boston matrix.
6 Explain their relative positions.
7 Forecast where they will be (and why), say, five years from now.
8 List your main markets or segments.
9 List criteria for attractiveness (to you).
10 List criteria for business strengths (you *vis-à-vis* competitors).
11 Devise a scoring and weighting system for each axis.
12 Put the markets or segments through the criteria.
13 Draw circles around the co-ordinates. The diameter of each circle should be proportional to that segment's contribution to turnover.
14 Is this where you want the circles to be?

Review of Chapter 5

What is a product?
A product (or service) is a problem-solver, in the sense that it provides what the customer needs or wants. A product consists of:

1 A core (functional performance).
2 A surround (a bundle of features and benefits).

Usually the core product has 20 per cent of the impact, yet leads to 80 per cent of the cost. The surround is the reverse of this.   *Try Exercise 5.1*

The product life cycle

All products or services have a life cycle which follows this pattern:

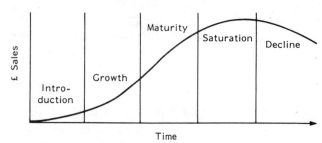

The phases of the life cycle are:

A Introduction.
B Growth.
C Maturity.
D Saturation.
E Decline.

The total life cycle depends on the type of product or service, e.g. fashion products have short life cycles.

There is a trend for life cycles of most products to get shorter as changes in technology and customer expectations make greater impact. Each phase of the life cycle calls for different management responses.

Try Exercise 5.2

Diffusion of innovation

Some people/companies are always prepared to buy new products, while others wait until things are tried and tested. All products and services have customers which fall into these categories.

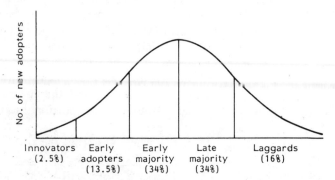

A Innovators (2.5 per cent of total).
B Early adopters (13.5 per cent of total).
C Early majority (34 per cent of total).
D Late majority (34 per cent of total).
E Laggards (16 per cent of total).

Discovering a typology for innovators and early adopters can help in the promotion of new products.

Product portfolio
Ideally, a company should have a portfolio of products whose life cycles overlap. This guarantees continuity of income and growth potential.

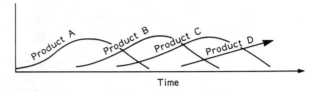

Boston matrix
The product portfolio can be analysed in terms of revenue- producing potential, using this technique.

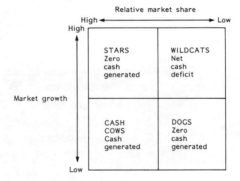

Cash cows need to generate sufficient funds to sustain stars and wildcats, and make a profit. *Try Exercise 5.3*

Directional policy matrix
Not all companies possess the data required by the Boston matrix (above). Similar results can be obtained using this technique. The axes become:

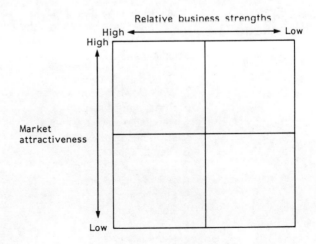

Try Exercises 5.4 and 5.5

Questions raised for the company

1 How useful is a brand name?

Well-known brands have successfully differentiated themselves from competing products by conveying something extra. Such differentiation enables them to command a higher price than unbranded, 'commodity' products.

2 How does market share relate to cash generation, as in the Boston matrix?

The higher the market share, the higher the output, and the lower the unit costs through economies of scale and the learning curve. Thus a company can command higher margins and generate more revenue.

3 Should 'dogs' always be killed off?

It is a question of timing. It is possible sometimes to squeeze extra earnings from a 'dog'. Sometimes a 'dog' is supportive of another product. Sometimes a 'dog' product can be profitable because it shares in the economies of scale of another product in the range.

Introduction to Chapter 5 exercises

The exercises are designed to help you to look at your product or service range in three different ways:

1 As a 'package' of benefits (Exercise 5.1).

2 From the point of view of their life cycles (Exercise 5.2).

3 As a total portfolio to be developed and managed in the best possible way. There are two approaches to this idea of a portfolio:

(a) One uses the approach developed by the Boston Consulting Group, the Boston matrix (Exercise 5.3).

(b) The other uses the approach developed by General Electric and McKinsey, the directional policy matrix (Exercise 5.4).

The final exercise in this section invites you to construct and interpret a directional policy matrix for your own company (Exercise 5.5).

Exercise 5.1 Benefit package analysis

It has been shown that customers buy products and services for many reasons. Different people look for different types of benefits from the product to satisfy their needs. Here are some typical sources of customer benefits:

1 Good comparative price
2 Well-known product/service
3 Good after-sales service
4 Reputable company image
5 Low after-sales costs
6 Prompt delivery
7 Efficient performance
8 Well-designed product
9 Fashionable
10 Ease of purchase
11 Good quality
12 Reliability
13 Safety factors

Obviously, the better one's products/services provide benefits to customers and match their needs, the more competitive they are going to be in the marketplace. The following process is designed to help you complete a benefit analysis on your products or services.

By doing this you will discover or confirm which items of your range are the strongest on the market when compared to your competitors. It should also provide you with insights about where attention might be paid to your products or services, either to improve existing customer benefits or to put emphasis on new ones.

Proceed as follows:

1 Study the customer benefits list above. Are these typical of the reasons that people buy your products or services? If you can think of others that are more pertinent to your particular business, write them down in the spaces provided.

2 Taking into account the market segments with which you do business, look at the customer benefits list and decide which are the three most important benefits demanded by your most important segment(s). Make a note of these.

3 Now identify the next three most important benefits demanded by these customers, and also make a note of these.

4 Finally, tick any other benefits on the list that are relevant to these customers.

5 Repeat this exercise for other important segments.

6 You are now asked to transpose this information on to Worksheet 1 (an example of a completed sheet is provided in Worksheet 2). Proceed as follows:

Step 1　In column 1 list the products or services you supply. No particular order is required.

Step 2　Take the three most important benefits that you selected above and use them as headings for columns 2, 3 and 4 on the work sheet, so that column 2 represents one benefit, column 3 another and column 4 the third.

Step 3　Fill in columns 2, 3 and 4 as follows. Starting with column 2, look at the benefit heading and work down your list of products or services scoring each one on a *1 to 10 point scale*: 1 will show that the product barely supplies this particular benefit to the customer and compares badly with competitors' performance, whereas a 10 score would demonstrate very high meeting of customer needs, superior to that provided by competitors. For example, if the benefit heading was 'Delivery' and, working down the list of products, the first product had a good delivery record, as good as any in the trade, then it could be allocated 9 or 10 points. If the next product on the list had a very patchy record on meeting delivery, and we knew several competitors were better, then we might only allocate 4 or 5 points, and so on. Follow the same procedure for columns 3 and 4. Note that the 1–10 scoring scale is only used on columns 2, 3 and 4 because these represent the major benefits to your customers and thus need to be weighted accordingly.

Step 4　Now take the second three most important benefits and use these as headings for columns 5, 6 and 7.

Step 5 As before rate each of your products or services against each heading, in comparison with competitor performance, but this time only *use a scoring scale of 1–6*, where again 1 point represents low provision of the benefit and 6 high. The 1–6 scoring scale is in recognition of the reduced importance these benefits have for customers.

Step 6 Finally take any other benefits you ticked above and use these as headings for column 8 and onwards as far as required.

Step 7 Again work through your list of products or services comparing them against how well they meet the benefit heading of each column, but this time only *use a 1–3 points scoring scale*. The reduced scale reflects the reduced level of importance of the customer benefits in this last group.

Step 8 Aggregate the scores you have allocated to each product or service and enter the result in the Total column.

Step 9 The product or service with the highest points score is clearly that which provides most benefits to your customers and competes favourably with the competition. Therefore allocate this product with the ranking of 1 in the Ranking column. Find the next highest total score and mark that 2 and so on. You might find some total scores so close to each other that it would be helpful to rank your products or services by groups of similar scores, rather than individually, e.g. have a first 'division', second 'division', etc., of product groupings.

Step 10 On either Worksheet 1 or a separate sheet of paper, make notes about any relevant points. For example, should some scores be qualified because of recent design improvements, are some products under threat from new competition, does the ranking reflect particular strengths or weaknesses, are there any surprises?

What are the main lessons to be learned from this type of benefit analysis for your company's products/services? What steps can you recommend to improve future product development? Use the space in 'Personal notes' to record your thoughts.

Note: This analysis shows that 'containers' provide the best 'benefits package' when compared to the rest of the product range. In contrast, 'water butts' provide least benefits, falling down on price, delivery and design. This analysis enables a company to see where it needs to work at the 'product surround' to become more effective.

Personal notes

Worksheet 1 Benefit package analysis (Exercise 5.1)

	Major benefits		Medium benefits			Lesser benefits														
	Low High score 1 — 10		Low High score 1 — 6			Low High score 1 — 3														
Col. nos. (1)	(2)	(3)	(4)	(5)	(6)	(7)	8	9	10	11	12	13	14	15	16	17	18	Total	Ranking	Notes, Observations, Qualifying comments, Strengths, etc.
Customer benefits Prods or servicess																				

Worksheet 2 Benefit package analysis (Exercise 5.1)

	Major benefits		Medium benefits			Lesser benefits														
	Low High score 1 — 10		Low High score 1 — 6			Low High score 1 — 3														
Col. nos. (1)	(2) Price	(3) Quality	(4) Delivery	(5) Design	(6) Safety	(7) Reliability	8 Our image	9 After-sales service	10 Packaging	11 Comprehensive range	12	13	14	15	16	17	18	Total	Ranking	Notes, Observations, Qualifying comments, Strengths, etc.
Water butts	5	8	5	3	6	6	1	1	2	2								39	4	Check costing and deliveries
Containers	8	8	7	5	6	3	3	2	3	2								47	1	Again business difficult to improve except on delivery and reliability
Toy (compts)	3	8	9	5	6	5	1	1	2	2								42	2	Doesn't always mix with other work
Cones for road works, etc.	7	8	6	4	6	5	1	1	3	1								42	2	Work at price and delivery. Also need to improve designs and range

Exercise 5.2
Life-cycle analysis

It is universally accepted that all products or services go through a life cycle of five stages – introduction, growth, maturity, saturation and, ultimately, decline.

Depending upon the nature of the particular product and its market, the life cycle can be of short or long duration. Similarly, different products will have different levels of sales. Nevertheless, allowing for these differences in 'width' and 'height', product life-cycle curves all have a remarkably similar and consistent shape. It is because of consistency of the life-cycle curve that this aspect of the product audit becomes such a powerful analytical tool.

The following exercise is designed to help you construct a life-cycle analysis for your company's products or services. By doing this it will help to focus on information that will be used in setting marketing objectives and strategies.

1 Using Worksheet 1, invent a suitable scale for the sales volume axis, i.e. one that will encompass the sales peaks you have had or are likely to experience in your business.

2 At the position marked Current sales, record the levels of sales volume for your products or services. You will have to select the time-scale you use. If your products are short-lived, perhaps you might have to calculate sales figures in terms of days or weeks. For longer-lived products, perhaps annual sales figures will be more appropriate.

3 Taking each product in turn, plot a life-cycle curve based upon the historical data at your disposal, e.g. if in 2 above you decided that a monthly sales analysis would be necessary to capture the movement on the life-cycle curves, then check back through your sales records and plot the sales volume for each product at monthly intervals.

4 From the life-cycle curves you have drawn, extend those into the future where extrapolation looks feasible, i.e. where a distinct pattern exists. You should finish up with a worksheet looking something like Worksheet 2.

5 Make notes about your key findings from this exercise in the space below.

6 So far you have only looked at your products in isolation. Now on a separate piece of paper (or on the same worksheet if it doesn't cause too much confusion), compare each life-cycle pattern of your major products or services with the *total market* life cycle for each one. Do your product patterns mirror the market life cycle? Are your sales falling, while the total market sales are steady or increasing? Is the reverse happening? Many outcomes will be possible, but whatever they are, you are asked to explain them and to write in the space below what these comparisons between the total market and your sales tell you about your product/service range and its future prospects. If you find it difficult to establish total market life cycles then refer to the 'Guide to market maturity', later in this exercise.

7 Finally, and to demonstrate that this examination of product life cycles is not just an intellectual exercise, prepare a short presentation for one of your senior colleagues, or, better still, your boss, following the instructions given on the 'Special project brief', at the end of this exercise.

Personal notes

Worksheet 1 Life-cycle analysis (Exercise 5.2)

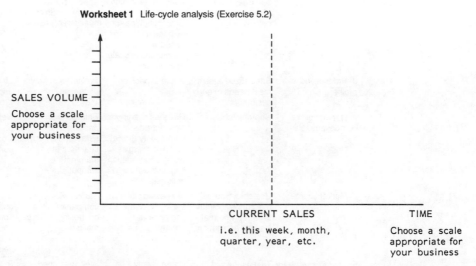

SALES VOLUME

Choose a scale
appropriate for
your business

CURRENT SALES

i.e. this week, month,
quarter, year, etc.

TIME

Choose a scale
appropriate for
your business

Worksheet 2 Life-cycle analysis (Exercise 5.2) – a plastics processing company

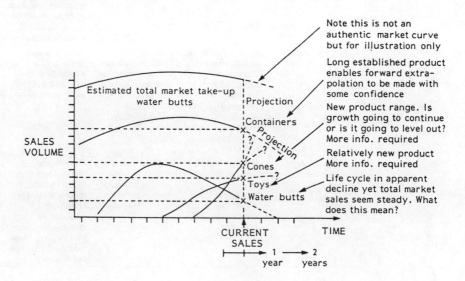

Guide to market maturity

The following checklist is used by one major company to help it determine where its markets are on the life cycle.

Maturity stage Factor	Embryonic	Growth	Mature saturation	Declining
1 Growth rate	Normally much greater than GNP (on small base)	Sustained growth above GNP. New customers. New suppliers. Rate decelerates towards end of stage	Approximately equals GNP	Declining demand. Market shrinks as users' needs change
2 Predictability of growth potential	Hard to define accurately. Small portion of demand being satisfied. Market forecasts differ widely	Greater percentage of demand is met and upper limits of demand becoming clearer. Discontinuities such as price reductions based on economies of scale may occur	Potential well defined. Competiton specialized to satisfy needs of specific segments	Known and limited
3 Product line proliferation	Specialized lines to meet needs of early customers	Rapid expansion	Proliferation slows or ceases	Lines narrow as unprofitable products dropped
4 Number of competitors	Unpredictable	Reaches maximum. New entrants attracted by growth and high margins. Some consolidation begins toward end of stage	Entrenched positions established. Further shakeout of marginal competitors	New entrants unlikely. Competitors continue to decline
5 Market share	Unstable. Shares react unpredictably to entrepreneurial insights and timing	Increasing stability. Typically, a few competitors emerging as strong	Stable, with a few companies often controlling much of the industry	Highly concentrated, sometimes fragmented if market becomes segmented
6 Customer stability	Trial usage with little customer loyalty	Some loyalty. Repeat usage with many seeking alternative suppliers	Well developed buying patterns, with customer loyalty. Competitors understand purchase dynamics and it is difficult for a new supplior to win over accounts	Extremely stable. Suppliers dwindle and customers less motivated to seek alternatives
7 Ease of entry	Normally easy. No one dominates. Customers' expectations uncertain. If barriers exist they are usually technology, capital or fear of the unknown	More difficult. Market franchises and/or economies of scale may exist, yet new business is still available without directly confronting competition	Difficult. Market leaders established. New business must be 'won' from others	Little or no incentive to enter
8 Technology	Plays an important role in matching product characteristics to market needs. Frequent product changes	Product technology vital early, while process technology more important later in this stage	Process and material substitution focus. Product requirements well known and relatively undemanding. May be a thrust to renew the industry via new technology	Technological content is known, stable and accessible

Special project brief
Product life cycles
Take any product you know well and prepare a short presentation (say 10 minutes) which covers the following areas/questions:

1 Brief product description – your definition of the market it serves.
2 Your estimates of the product's current point in the life-cycle curve.
3 Your reasons for believing it is at this point.
4 Your estimate of the length and shape of this life cycle.
5 Your reasons for this estimate.
6 Your predictions of the prospects for this product over the next 3 years.
7 Your reasons for these predictions.

Exercise 5.3 Case study: International Bearings Ltd (IBL)

The objectives of this case study are as follows:

1 To demonstrate a useful method of reviewing, at any point in time, the commercial implications of decision-making for a company with a number of different products, in different markets, at different stages of growth, maturity or decline. This is known as a product portfolio. This method was introduced by the Boston Consulting Group and is known as the Boston matrix.
2 To demonstrate the application of the Boston matrix by using a case study in which an industrial company competes with a number of competitors in a number of different market segments.
3 To give the user practical experience by working through the situation analysis and decision-making process illustrated in the case study.
4 To encourage the user to apply the principles learned in the case study to his/her own commercial situation.

You are asked to write down your answers to the questions on the worksheet provided. The correct answers are given in Appendix 1.

International Bearings Limited (IBL) sells a number of fast moving industrial products in a market with about sixty competitors, most of whom are relatively small. Eight companies, including IBL, are significant in terms of size. IBL has seven major product groups.

The situation of IBL is shown in Table 5.5.

Table 5.5

Product	Sales volume (units)	Relative market share	Current market growth (year 1, %)	Forecast market growth (year 3, %)
1	1,500	*	20	25
2	1,300	2:1	9	6
3	1,000	0.9:1	12	25
4	1,000	0.6:1	10	2
5	900	0.5:1	5	3
6	800	0.2:1	3	0
7	500	0.1:1	22	25
Total	7,000			

*This ratio has been omitted, as it forms part of the exercise later in this case study.

Definitions of headings in Table 5.5

Relative market share is the ratio of your market share to the share of the largest competitor in your market. Thus, if you have 10 per cent market share and your biggest competitor has 40 per cent market share, then the ratio (or relative market share) is 1:4. This is usually expressed as 0.25:1. If you have a market share of 20 per cent and your biggest competitor has a market share of 10 per cent, then the ratio would be 2:1.

Current market growth is the percentage growth in sales of a product in a market over the previous year's sales. Thus, if a market was 100 last year and 120 this year, then the growth would be 20 per cent.

Forecast market growth is the annual rate at which you believe the market will grow in the future. For example, you may forecast that the market will grow by 10 per cent in Year 2 and 20 per cent in Year 3. So 10 per cent forecast market growth for Year 2 is Year 1 figure of 120 × 10 per cent: answer: 132. For Year 3 it is Year 2 figure of 132 × 20: answer: 158.4.

Table 5.6

	IBL	B	C	D	E	F	G	H	Companies Others (about 50)
Absolute market share (%)	15	10	8	8	8	7	5	5	34

IBL has 15 per cent absolute market share. Table 5.5 states that figure represents 1,500, so:

$$\frac{1500}{1} \times \frac{100}{15} = 10,000$$

which is the current year total market size for product 1.

Definitions of headings in Table 5.6

Absolute market share is the percentage of a total market that your product enjoys. For example, total market size = 100 units per annum. Your sales are 25 per annum. Therefore you have 25 per cent absolute market share. Absolute market share is expressed as a percentage of the total market.

As defined above, relative market share is expressed as a ratio, e.g. 2:1. This compares your market share and degree of dominance to one other competitor.

The market forecast for IBL's product 1 is as shown in Table 5.7.

Table 5.7

	Current year (%)	Year 2 (%)	Year 3 (%)
Actual production	20		
Forecast growth		22	25

IBL's own forecast for product 1 is shown in Table 5.8.

Table 5.8

	Current year	Year 2	Year 3
Actual sales	1,500 units		
Sales forecast		1,650 units	1,815 units

Please note that the forecast market growth for product 1 in Table 5.7 is different from IBL's own forecast of product 1 in Table 5.8.

A senior executive from company B has recently joined IBL, as a result of which IBL has received some accurate market intelligence about company B's product 1, which competes with IBL's own product 1. This is shown in Table 5.9.

Table 5.9

	Current year	*Year 2*	*Year 3*
Actual sales	1,000 units		
Sales forecast		1,500 units	1,562 units

Please answer the following questions:

Question 1

What is IBL's relative market share for product 1? Remember that relative market share is a ratio, e.g. 3.5:1.

Write your answer to this question and all others on the answer sheet provided in Appendix 1.

Question 2

What will IBL's relative market share be for product 1 in year 3? Limit your answer to two decimal places.

For this question you may need to refer to Tables 5.8 and 5.9.

Question 3

What is the annual growth of the market for product 1?

Question 4

What will be the total market volume for product 1 in year 3?

Question 5

What is the absolute market share of IBL's product 1 in year 3?

Round up your answer to the nearest whole number.

Question 6

Is the market growth in the current year, high or low, relative to the industry average of 10%?

Question 7

Relative market share and market growth are important factors a company should consider when appraising its product portfolio. Rather than looking at masses of figures, which are hard to interpret individually, the Boston Consulting Group (BCG), devised a matrix to show these two factors as a graphic drawing.

The matrix is square and the relative market share (RMS) is placed on the horizontal axis. The imaginary lines are vertical. Market growth is measured on the vertical axis. See Figure 5.25.

The lowest figure (usually zero) is at the bottom, and, depending on the industry, up to 20 per cent. (This upper figure may vary, e.g. an established product may be under 10 per cent or a new product may be in excess of 100 per cent.)

The decision on what constitutes 'high' or 'low' growth is thus dependent on the industry. The decision is yours. In this case we have chosen to use 10 per cent as the dividing line between high growth, i.e. greater than 10 per cent, and low growth, i.e. less than 10 per cent.

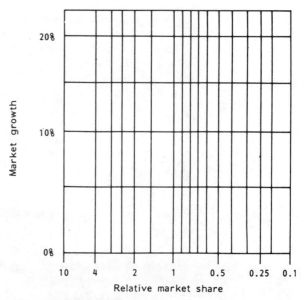

Figure 5.25 Boston matrix

In the example, we are using a scale ending at approximately 20 per cent. The imaginary lines run horizontally across the matrix.

Take the products numbered 1 to 7 and, using Table 5.5 data, place them at the correct coordinates for relative market share and market growth. For this purpose, a matrix is provided on the answer sheet later *in this exercise*.

Question 8

The next stage is to make these co-ordinates into circles. This is necessary so that the executive completing the matrix can understand the relative importance to the company of the products which appear in the matrix. Some circles will be bigger than others, indicating a greater contribution to turnover.

It is also important because the executive can forecast the size of each circle and its likely position on the matrix in, say, 3 years' time. He or she could, for example, show the position and size of the circles if the company continued with its current policies, or where they will be if different policies are pursued.

In this case the diameter of each circle represents the relative contribution of each product to the total volume of IBL. The scale adopted is your decision. It generally depends on the size of paper you are using. For example, you may choose 1 mm = 10,000 units, so a product selling 50,000 units will measure 5 mm and so on for each product. (To be technically correct, we should take the square root of each of the sales volumes to detemine the proportionate area of each circle. However, for the sake of simplicity, we have used the method described above.)

On Figure 5.25 the next task is to convert the coordinates marked 1–7 into circles representing the relative contribution of each product. First, however, using a scale of 1 mm = 100 units of sales volume, calculate the correct diameter for each of the seven products and write your answers

answers in the answer sheet provided. Next, draw circles on the matrix provided, using the answers given above for the diameters.

A short explanation of the principles behind the Boston matrix is given in Appendix 2. Understanding the matrix will enable you to answer the questions which follow.

Question 9
Do you think IBL currently have a well-balanced product portfolio? Give reasons for your answer.

Question 10
State the forecast position of IBL's Product 1 in Year 3.

Write in figures the RMS (including a decimal point and colon, e.g. 5.2:1). Write in figures the RMG (e.g. 50%).

Question 11
Using a scale of 1 mm = 100 units of sales volume, what will the diameter of the circle for IBL's product 1 be in year 3?

State your answer in figures to the nearest whole number.

Question 12
Are the signs ahead good, comparing the forecast position of IBL's product 1 with the current situation? Give reasons for your answer.

Question 13
What is happening to IBL's main product in the current situation? Choose from the options A–D listed below:

A Losing market share in a declining market.
B Gaining market share in a growing market.
C Losing market share in a growing market.
D Losing profitability in a stable market.

Question 14
What policy should IBL pursue for product 1? Choose from the options listed below:

A Increase price, reduce promotion.
B Reduce price, reduce promotion.
C Hold price, reduce promotion.
D Hold price, increase promotion.
E Reduce price, increase promotion.
F Increase price, increase promotion.

Question 15
In this situation it was decided to maintain product 1's market share by investing in it, to grow at the same rate of forecast market growth of 20, 22, 25 per cent. Which other products from the list below would you invest in? Choose from the combinations A, B, C or D below:

A Products 2 and 5.
B Products 3 and 7.
C Products 3 and 6.
D Products 4 and 7.

Question 16
Select one product's position you should maintain from the options of products 2 to 7.

Select product 2, 3, 4, 5, 6 or 7.

Question 17

Which combinations of products might it be appropriate to manage for cash from the options below?

A Products 5, 6 and 7.
B Products 3, 4 and 5.
C Products 4, 5 and 6.
D Products 4, 5 and 7.

Having completed this case study, you should by now fully understand the principles and the methodology of the Boston matrix.

There are, of course, other approaches to portfolio management. However, before considering these, using the methodology explained in this case study, produce a Boston matrix for your own company's products.

Some practical suggestions for producing your own Boston matrix now follow:

1 Try not to use more than ten products. If in doubt, choose the 20 per cent of your products that account for the majority of your turnover.
2 If this still proves to be too many, then find some way of grouping your products until you have a manageable number.
3 Directors and senior managers doing this additional exercise may prefer to use companies, divisions, countries, markets, or strategic business units instead of products. They all work just as well.
4 Great care is needed in defining 'market' share. Remember, a 'market consists of all other brands that satisfy the same needs as your brand.
5 Forecast the size and position of your products in say, 3 years' time. Ask yourself:

   (a) Is it a well-balanced portfolio?
   (b) Are you pursuing appropriate policies for each of your products or business areas?

Worksheet for Answers – Case Study IBL
See page 185

Appendix 1   Answers to the IBL Case Study

1 1.5:1 (1500 ÷ 1000)
2 1.16:1 (1815 ÷ 1562)
3 20%, 22%, 25% (from Table 5.7)
4 Table 5.5 gave product 1 sales as 1,500. Table 5.6 gave absolute market share of 15% for IBL. Market size in year 1 is

$$\frac{1,500}{1} \times \frac{100}{15} = 10,000$$

Thus, market size for year 3 is found from the % figures in Table 5.7. Thus, $10,000 \times 22\% \times 25\% = 15,250$
5 12% from Table 5.7, year 3 (1815), divide that by the answer to question 4 (15,250) = 11.9
6 High. In each of the three years the market is forecast to grow at a higher rate than 10% (20%, 22%, 25%)
7
	RMS	RMG
1	1.5:1	20%
2	2:1	9%
3	0.9:1	12%

<u>Case study IBL</u>

Last name

First name

*Question
number*

Answer

1

2

3

4   Yr 1.... Yr 2.... Yr 3....

5

6

7

Product	RMS	RMG
1		
2		
3		
4		
5		
6		
7		

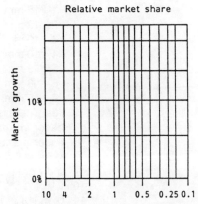

8   1

      2

      3

      4

      5

      6

      7

9

10

11

12

13

14

15

16

17

185

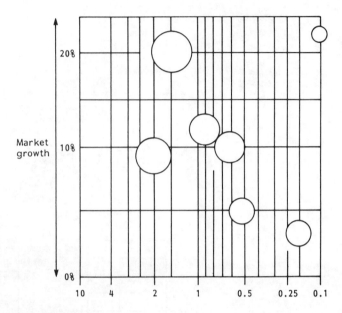

Figure 5.26   Coordinates for RMS and RMG

4	0.6:1	10%
5	0.5:1	5%
6	0.2:1	3%
7	0.1:1	22%

8
1	15 mm
2	13 mm
3	10 mm
4	10 mm
5	9 mm
6	8 mm
7	5 mm

9 Yes. There is one significant cash cow. 'Cash cow' product 1 is market leader in a fast-growing market (a 'star'). Product 3 is almost market leader in a fast-growing market. Product 7 is a 'question mark'. Products 4, 5 and 6 are 'dogs', but this is not a problem as long as products 2, 3 and 7 are managed appropriately.

10 1.16:1, 25%

11 1815, 18

12 No. IBL's main product is losing market share in a growing market.

13 C is the best answer, but not the only one. You may wish to consider other factors, including company policy, e.g. improving the product.

14 D

15 B

16 2

17 C

Appendix 2   *The principles of the Boston matrix*
The principles of the Boston matrix can be applied to practical commercial situations for improving business planning and assisting decision-taking where a company has a number of products.

What is the Boston matrix?

The Boston matrix is used for what is known as product portfolio planning. It uses graphic models to develop a relationship between two or more variables known to be of significance in the corporate context.

The two main variables are relative market share and market growth. Both have been shown to be strongly related to profitability. In general, the bigger a firm's relative market share is, the lower its costs are, and the bigger its return on investment. The rate of market growth also has a significant impact on a company's performance.

The Boston Consulting Group combined these two variables in the form of a simple matrix, which has been shown to have profound implications for the firm, especially in respect of cashflow.

The Boston matrix classifies a firm's products according to their cash usage and their cash generation along the two dimensions, relative market share and market growth.

Why use a matrix rather than a sheet of figures?

The Boston matrix shows graphically the positions in terms of relative market share and market growth of a number of products at a glance. Presented in a matrix, it is easier for an executive to see the relationship between a number of different products. It is also a very powerful presentation device for planning purposes.

How is the Boston matrix used?

Different products have to be managed in ways appropriate to their different business environments and according to their different strengths and weaknesses. There is a need to maintain strong and profitable products. There is a need to invest in new products as existing products mature and die.

The Boston matrix provides a powerful vehicle for assessing a firm's position as represented by its portfolio or products. Finally, it enables appropriate policies to be developed for each product to ensure continuing growth in sales and profits.

Some examples of the use of the Boston matrix

The Boston Consulting Group chose picturesque labels to attach to each of the four categories of products to give some indication of the prospects for products in each quadrant:

o Star
o Cash cow
o Question mark
o Dog

'Cash cows' are leaders in markets where there is little additional growth. They are excellent generators of cash and tend to use little. 'Stars' are leaders in high growth markets. They tend to generate a lot of cash, but also use a lot because of growth market conditions. 'Question marks' have not yet achieved a dominant market position, and so do not generate much cash. They can, however, use a lot of cash because of growth market conditions. Sometimes these are referred to as 'wildcats'. 'Dogs' have little future and are often a cash drain on the company.

The art of portfolio management now becomes clearer. We should be seeking to use surplus cash generated by 'cash cows' to invest in 'stars' and a selected number of 'question marks'.

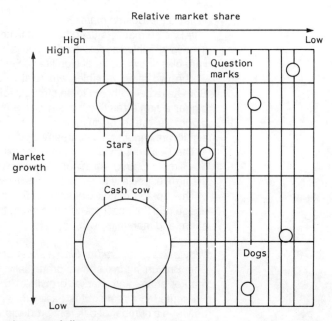

Figure 5.27 Well-balanced product portfolio

Figure 5.27 shows a well-balanced product portfolio. There is one large 'cash cow', two sizeable 'stars', and three emerging products in high growth markets. There are only two small 'dogs'.

Figure 5.28 shows a poorly balanced product portfolio. The company has no 'cash cows'. There is only one small 'star'. It has three 'question marks' and three 'dogs', one of which is a sizeable product. This company probably has cashflow problems.

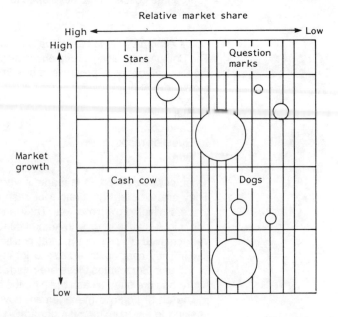

Figure 5.28 Poorly balanced product portfolio

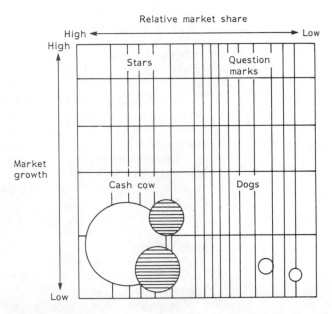

Figure 5.29   Poorly balanced product portfolio

Figure 5.29 also shows a poorly balanced product portfolio. This company is probably cash-rich, with three sizeable 'cash cows'. However, all the danger signs are evident. There are no new products coming along to replace the 'cash cows', which may well decline in the future.

Exercise 5.4 International Bearings Ltd – directional policy case study

The main business of IBL is the sale of a portfolio of bearings and assemblies based on bearings to a variety of end-use markets in Europe, in which IBL is a very significant and well-established player. IBL manufactures products in five different locations, each making only part of the product range to achieve maximum production cost benefits.

Each country has its own sales organization marketing the whole range. These national organizations have two salesforces, one dealing with original equipment manufacturers (OEMs), the other selling via independent distributors to the replacement market, except for large customers, who are handled direct.

There is a European marketing organization responsible for strategy in terms of product range development, pricing structures, corporate promotion, etc. Under the European Marketing Director, it is split into market sector managers (e.g. automotive, electrical machinery, etc.) who develop strategies for their own segments. The European marketing organization reports to the Director-Europe, as do the country general managers, to whom the country sales organizations report.

In the mid-1980s a new European marketing director was appointed. His first task was to develop a long-term strategic marketing plan. From a detailed study of past and present performance, he noted that, though historically successful, European market share was hovering at around 28 per cent and that profits, although satisfactory, were mainly stagnant. These results were being caused by lack of growth in some key markets, e.g. automotive, and intensified competition, notably from Japan.

One of the key effects of these market and competitive pressures that he noted as he travelled around Europe was a lack of vision and motivation in the national sales organizations. During the late 1970s/early 1980s, under a policy of decentralization, they had been left largely alone to do the best they could in what were difficult recessionary times.

He concluded that performance could be significantly improved, especially as there were signs that some key segments were becoming buoyant, and he obtained top management approval to develop a long-term plan, 'Going for growth'. The key objective agreed by the board was 'To increase European market share to 35 per cent by the end of the planning period in 3 years'.

In order to achieve this, the European marketing director knew that he would have to look at the product/market portfolio in a different way and to establish realistic strategies in the areas most likely to produce dividends. To help him do this, he decided to construct a directional policy matrix.

As you work through this case study you will observe how the task was tackled. You will appreciate the calculations and the reasons behind decision-making.

The marketing director first set his market research manager the task of selecting SIC (Standard Industrial Classification) categories, based on his current bearing business in order to select those segments best suited for investment. (The governments of most countries keep records of industrial activity under SIC listings. The SIC listings in most countries of the world are comparable for the purpose of comparisons and cross-references.)

His market research manager came up with the information in Table 5.10

Table 5.10

SIC category	Market size (£ million)	Growth (%)	Competitive intensity	Profitability (%)	Vulnerability
1 Meat-processing	20	12	Low	17	Low
2 Automotive	200	2	High	<10	High
3 Local govt	20	4	High	<10	High
4 Food-processing	40	10	Medium	18	Medium
5 Forestry	20	11	Low	20	Medium
6 Electrical	100	0	High	<10	High
7 Agricultural	40	2	Medium	<10	High
8 Chemical	15	15	Low	16	Low

The first stage is to apply the information in Table 5.10, and to establish positions on the vertical scale labelled 'market attractiveness' on the directional policy matrix (DPM). However, before that can be done, some criteria about what constitutes an attractive market for International Bearings have to be established and weighted in terms of their relative importance.

Precisely how this is done is a matter of management judgement, but it is important to follow three golden rules:

1 Never do this in isolation.
2 Make sure your key colleagues are in agreement over the criteria and weightings to be used.
3 Whenever quantitative information, or techniques such as market research, is available, it should be used in preference to opinions, no matter how well founded these opinions might be.

Being aware of these rules, the European marketing director got his marketing team together and they came up with the information in Table 5.11. With this new information available to him, the marketing director was able to begin calculating the market attractiveness 'scores' for different industries.

Table 5.11

Factor	Scoring criteria*			Weighting (%)**
	10–7	*6–3*	*2–1*	
1 Market size (m)	>100	33–100	<33	15
2 Volume growth (units)	>10%	5–9%	<5%	25
3 Competitive intensity	Low	Medium	High	15
4 Profitability	>5%	10–15%	<10%	30
5 Vulnerability	Low	Medium	High	15

* The precise score given is a matter of management judgement.
** The weightings given to each factor are also a matter of management judgement.

From Table 5.10, it will be seen that the market size is £20m. From Table 5.11, you will see that any category £<33m is scored in the range 1–2 points, with a weighting of 15, so in this case a score of 1 can be given. It is then multiplied by the weighting of 15 per cent to give a result of 0.15. You will observe from this that you must use your judgement in deciding whether the score should be 1 or 2 (or something in between).

This inevitably means that there will be a range of possible answers. In this case the range could be 0.15 to 0.3.

Bearing this in mind, see if you can complete the market attractiveness scoring for meat-processing in Table 5.12. You can check if your answer is correct by looking at Table 5.13 and comparing your result with that produced by the company.

You will note that the remaining criteria of attractiveness were all high, and, because of that, each carried a score of between 7 and 10. Depending on the actual scores given, the total, after being multiplied by the weighting factor, could fall within the range given in Table 5.13 shown in brackets.

Table 5.12 Meat-processing

	Scoring criteria	*Weighting (%)*	*Total*
Market size	1	× 15	= 0.15
Growth	–	× 25	= _____
Competitive intensity	–	× 15	= _____
Profitability	–	× 30	= _____
Vulnerability	–	× 15	= _____
		Total	_____

Table 5.13 Meat-processing

	Scoring criteria	Weighting (%)	Total
Market size	1	× 15	= 0.15
Growth	– (7–10)	× 25	= ___ (1.75–2.5)
Competitive intensity	– (7–10)	× 15	= ___ (2.1–3.0)
Profitability	– (7–10)	× 30	= ___ (1.05–1.5)
Vulnerability	– (7–10)	× 15	= ___ (1.05–1.5)
		Total	___ (6.10–8.65)

It is important that you are clear about how the total market attractiveness score is calculated. If you feel that you would like another opportunity to work at this, see if you can arrive at a score for the automotive industry. All the information you require is in Tables 5.14 and 5.15.

Table 5.14 Automotive

	Scoring criteria	Weighting (%)	Total
Market size	–	× 15	= ___
Growth	–	× 25	= ___
Competitive intensity	–	× 15	= ___
Profitability	–	× 30	= ___
Vulnerability	–	× 15	= ___
		Total	___

The answer to Table 5.14 is shown in Table 5.15. Again, you will note that there has to be an element of judgement in the scoring.

Table 5.15 Automotive

	Scoring criteria	Weighting (%)	Total
Market size	– (7–10)	× 15	= ___ (1.05–1.5)
Growth	– (1–2)	× 25	= ___ (0.25–0.5)
Competitive intensity	– (1–2)	× 15	= ___ (0.15–0.3)
Profitability	– (1–2)	× 30	= ___ (0.3–0.6)
Vulnerability	– (1–2)	× 15	= ___ (0.15–0.3)
		Total	___ (2.35–3.2)

From these two examples you can see the idea of how the figures are arrived at for *market attractiveness*. As you will see, the final figures are within a minimum and maximum range for each category. For the purpose of this case study, the figures are stated as below:

1 Meat-processing   0.65
2 Automotive   2.35
3 Local government   1.25
4 Food-processing   7.45
5 Forestry   8.05
6 Electrical   2.35
7 Agriculture   2.4
8 Chemical   0.65

Now we will look at how the calculations are made for establishing the relative positions of these markets on the horizontal axis, or *business strengths*, of the DPM.

Two tables, similar to Tables 5.10 and 5.11, are given. The first, Table 5.16, shows factor, scoring criteria, and weighting; and the next, Table 5.17, the marketing team's assessment of the firm's competitive strengths in each of the SIC categories.

Table 5.16

| Factor | Scoring criteria* | | | Weighting |
	10–7	6–3	2–1	(%)**
1 Product advantage	High	Medium	Low	25
2 Image with market	Excellent	Average	Poor	50
3 Ability to supply engineering support	High	Medium	Low	25

* The precise score given is a matter of management judgement.
** The weightings given to each factor are also a matter of management judgement.
Remember the three golden rules still apply:

1 Key colleagues should be in agreement.
2 Do not do this in isolation.
3 Use quantitative techniques to determine criteria whenever available.

There are, of course, a whole range of possible factors which could be viewed as business strengths. However, from International Bearing's point of view, in order to assess the business strengths in each of the eight markets, the marketing director was only concerned with the three key factors given in Table 5.17.

Table 5.17 Marketing team's assessment

SIC category	Product advantage	Image	Engineering support
1 Meat-processing	High	Excellent	High
2 Automotive	Low	Excellent	High
3 Local government	Low	Poor	Medium
4 Food-processing	High	Excellent	High
5 Forestry	Low	Poor	Low
6 Electrical	Low	Poor	Low
7 Agricultural	High	Excellent	Medium
8 Chemical	Low	Poor	Medium

Table 5.17 uses the criteria to assess the firm's competitive strengths. The process to transfer the information from Tables 5.18 and 5.19 is similar to the previous exercise done with Tables 5.10 and 5.11.

Take meat-processing as an example. The product advantage is high in Table 5.17. In Table 5.16 a high assessment may be scored between 7 and 10. The weighting is 25 per cent. You may choose 9 for product advantage, so this, multiplied by the weighting of 25 per cent, gives 2.25 as the score. Table 5.18 shows how the scoring could be completed and the possible range of the end result.

Table 5.18 Meat-processing

	Scoring criteria	Weighting (%)	Total
Product advantage	9	× 25	= 2.25
Image	– (7–10)	× 50	= (3.5–5.0)
Engineering support	– (7–10)	× 25	= (1.75–2.5)
		Total	(7.0–10)

If you would like the practice, work out the score for automotive (Table 5.19). The answer is given in Table 5.20.

Table 5.19 Automotive

	Scoring criteria	Weighting (%)	Total
Product advantage	–	× 25	=
Image	–	× 50	=
Engineering support	–	× 25	=
		Total	

Table 5.20 Automotive

	Scoring criteria	Weighting (%)	Total
Product advantage	– (1–2)	× 25	= (0.25–0.50)
Image	– (7–10)	× 50	= (3.5–5.0)
Engineering support	– (7–10)	× 25	= (1.75–8.0)
		Total	(5.5–2.5)

Using this technique, the marketing director made the following assessment of the business strengths for the eight product areas:

1	Meat-processing	8.75
2	Automotive	7.75
3	Local government	2.0
4	Food-processing	10.0
5	Forestry	1.0
6	Electrical	1.0
7	Agriculture	9.0
8	Chemical	2.25

He was now in a position to start plotting the various markets on the directional policy matrix. You will note that, because of the way the scoring and weighting were established, i.e. a maximum of 10 points and the highest weighting being 100 per cent, the highest possible total is ten. Therefore the matrix can be designed with each side being of 10 units length. Equally, because of this scoring system, 5 represents a genuine mid-point, in the sense that scores above this figure are tending towards the 'more attractive' or 'higher business strengths', whereas those below 5 are, relatively speaking, the poor relations.

The numbers at the intersections refer to the markets as listed above. Thus 1 is meat-processing, 2 automotive and so on.

The DPM is almost complete. What remains to be done is to indicate the sales volume for each of the markets. This is achieved by drawing a circle proportional to the sales volume at each of the market location points that have just been plotted.

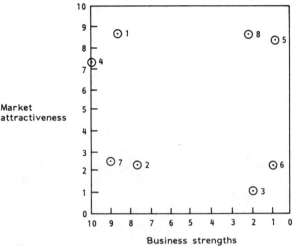

Figure 5.30

It is often a matter of trial and error to establish the correct basis for drawing these circles. If, for example, the largest sales volume was 1,500 and the smallest was 300, you may decide that every 100 units = 3 mm of diameter. So, 1,500 is shown as 15 units × 3 = 45 mm, and 300 as 3 units × 3 = 9 mm. If this scale is too small or large, then change it to suit the diagram.

This is the sales volume for each category:

SIC	Sales volume
1 Meat-processing	1,500
2 Automotive	1,300
3 Local government	1,000
4 Food-processing	900
5 Forestry	800
6 Electrical	700
7 Agricultural	500
8 Chemical	300

Continuing with the example of 100 units = 3 mm of diameter, we get this representative sales volume for each category:

SIC	Sales volume	Diameter
1 Meat-processing	1,500	45
2 Automotive	1,300	39
3 Local government	1,000	30
4 Food-processing	900	27
5 Forestry	800	24
6 Electrical	700	21
7 Agricultural	500	15
8 Chemical	300	9

Figure 5.31 shows the points representing the sales volume of each category in the correct locations on the matrix.

This form of presentation is superior in terms of the impact and clarity given to the data presentation shown in Tables 5.10, 5.11, 5.16, 5.17. It clearly shows at a glance:

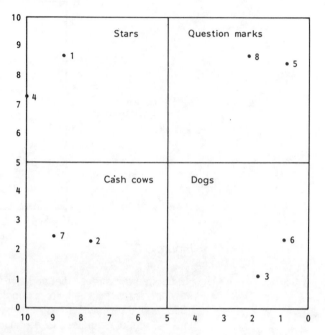

Figure 5.31

○ The relative importance of each market to the business
○ The relative attractiveness of each market
○ The company's relative strengths in each market

The same names can be given to each quadrant as are used in the Boston matrix, although you should note that it is not necessary to give any names at all to each of the boxes. The Boston matrix names are used here only because you are by now familiar with them.

Faced with the above information, if you were in the marketing director's position, what would be your objectives and strategies for each of the markets?

Write your proposals on a separate piece of paper. When you have completed this task, you can check your answers with those of the marketing director below.

Here is how the marketing director of International Bearings used the DPM to arrive at objectives and strategies for each market:

1 In the event, he concentrated much effort on growing the very attractive meat-process and food processing segments, because he was well placed to do this and because he was able to add value in so doing. In the next 3 years, he added a further 2,000 units of very profitable volume to these two segments.
2 Automotive and agriculture were maintained by aggressive pricing whenever he had to in order to keep the business, but he cut down dramatically on costs. In these businesses he succeeded in increasing volume sales from 1,000 to 2,000 units during the next 3 years. Margins were down, but so were costs.
3 He invested some resources to improve his position in the chemical segment, paying for it by taking money out of the forestry segment. Here he grew his volume from 300 to 700 units.

4 Finally, he did not invest in either local government or electrical, but while he lost market share, with volume dropping from 1,700 to 1,300, he was able to invest some of this revenue in developing a range of bearings for the emerging freezing industry, which promised high margins for the future, i.e. an investment in R and D.

The cumulative result of these strategies was that in year 3 he had a volume of 9,400 units, i.e. an increase of over 30 per cent, and a well-balanced portfolio of products. There was also the prospect of new business in Europe from the freezing industry.

This case study demonstrates how the DPM can be constructed and used to good effect. Any organization should be able to follow a similar process to that used by International Bearings. The only contentious point is that a company must be clear about how it defines its markets. Any woolly thinking about these will undermine the value of the DPM and will probably generate some downright misleading information.

Anyone with any doubts about market definition would be well advised to look back at Exercise 4.1.

Exercise 5.5
Applying the directional policy matrix to your own organization

Follow these instructions:

1 Choose a product (or group of products) that is bought by many different markets (or segments).
2 List no more than eight of these markets (or segments).
3 Develop a set of criteria for judging:

   o Market attractiveness
   o Your strength in these markets.

4 Develop a scoring and weighting system for these criteria.
5 Evaluate the markets you have chosen, using these criteria.
6 Locate the point of each of these markets on a four-box directional policy matrix.
7 Using an approximate scale of your own choice, make the circle diameter proportional to your current turnover.
8 Comment on the current portfolio.
9 Indicate approximately the size and position of each circle in 3 years' time.
10 Outline (briefly) the strategies you would pursue to achieve these objectives.

6 Setting marketing objectives and strategies

Summary

Chapter 6 defines what marketing objectives are and how they relate to corporate objectives, and shows how to set them. There is a section on competitive strategies. Where and how to start the process of marketing planning is described, using the method known as 'gap analysis', and new product development is discussed as a growth strategy. Finally, there is an explanation of what marketing strategies are and how to set them. Without doubt, this is the key step in the marketing planning process, for it will by now be clear that, following the analysis that takes place as part of the marketing audit, realistic and achievable objectives should be set for the company's major products in each of its major markets. Unless this step is carried out well, everything that follows will lack focus and cohesion. It is really a question of deciding on the right target. After all, it is no good scoring a bulls-eye on the wrong target!

Once again, we remind you that the actual contents of a strategic marketing plan are set out in Chapter 13. It is important, however, to read the present chapter most carefully before trying to complete this crucial step in the process.

Marketing objectives: what they are and how they relate to corporate objectives

There are no works on marketing which do not include at least one paragraph on the need for setting objectives. Setting objectives is a mandatory step in the planning process. The literature on the subject, though, is not very explicit, which is surprising when it is considered how vital the setting of marketing objectives is.

An objective will ensure that a company knows what its strategies are expected to accomplish and when a particular strategy has accomplished its purpose. In other words, without objectives, strategy decisions and all that follows will take place in a vacuum.

Following the identification of opportunities and the explicit statement of assumptions about conditions affecting the business, the process of setting objectives should, in theory, be comparatively easy, the actual objectives themselves being a realistic statement of what

198

the company desires to achieve as a result of a market-centred analysis, rather than generalized statements borne of top management's desire to 'do better next year'.

However, objective setting is more complex than at first it would appear to be.

The logical approach to the difficult task of setting objectives is to proceed from the broad to the specific.

Most experts agree that the logical approach to the difficult task of setting marketing objectives is to proceed from the broad to the specific. Thus, the starting point would be a statement of the nature of the business (the mission statement), from which would flow the broad company objectives. Next, the broad company objectives would be translated into key result areas, which would be those areas in which success is vital to the firm. Market penetration and growth rate of sales are examples of key result areas. The third step would be creation of the sub-objectives necessary to accomplish the broad objectives, such as product sales volume goals, geographical expansion, product line extension, and so on.

The end result of this process should be objectives which are consistent with the strategic plan, attainable within budget limitations, and compatible with the strengths, limitations, and economics of other functions within the organization.

At the top level, management is concerned with long-run profitability; at the next level in the management hierarchy, the concern is for objectives which are defined more specifically and in greater detail, such as increasing sales and market share, obtaining new markets, and so on. These objectives are merely a part of the hierarchy of objectives, in that corporate objectives will only be accomplished if these and other objectives are achieved. At the next level, management is concerned with objectives which are defined even more tightly, such as: to create awareness among a specific target market about a new product; to change a particular customer attitude; and so on. Again, the general marketing objectives will only be accomplished if these and other sub-objectives are achieved.

It is clear that sub-objectives *per se*, unless they are an integral part of a broader framework of objectives, are likely to lead to a wasteful misdirection of resources.

For example, a sales increase in itself may be possible, but only at an undue cost, so that such a marketing objective is only appropriate within the framework of corporate objectives. In such a case, it may well be that an increase in sales in a particular market sector will entail additional capital expenditure ahead of the time for which it is planned. If this were the case, it may make more sense to allocate available production capacity to more profitable market sectors in the short term, allowing sales to decline in another sector. Decisions such as this are likely to be more easily made against a backcloth of explicitly stated broad company objectives relating to all the major disciplines.

Likewise, objectives should be set for advertising, for example, which are wholly consistent with wider objectives. Objectives set in this way integrate the advertising effort with the other elements in the marketing mix and this leads to a consistent, logical marketing plan.

So what is a corporate objective and what is a marketing objective?

A business starts at some time with resources and wants to use those resources to achieve something. What the business wants to achieve is a corporate objective, which describes a desired destination, or result. How it is to be achieved is a strategy. In a sense, this means that the only true objective of a company is, by definition, what is stated in the corporate plan as being the principal purpose of its existence.

> Most often this is expressed in terms of profit, since profit is the means of satisfying shareholders or owners, and because it is the one universally accepted criterion by which efficiency can be evaluated, which will, in turn, lead to efficient resource allocation, economic and technological progressiveness and stability.

The only true objective of a company is, by definition, what is stated in the corporate plan as being the principal purpose of its existence.

This means that stated desires, such as to expand market share, to create a new image, to achieve an *x* per cent increase in sales, and so on, are in fact strategies at the corporate level, since they are the means by which a company will achieve its profit objectives. In practice, however, companies tend to operate by means of functional divisions, each with a separate identity, so that what is a strategy in the corporate plan becomes an objective within each department.

> For example, marketing strategies within the corporate plan become operating objectives within the marketing department and strategies at the general level within the marketing department themselves become operating objectives at the next level down, so that an intricate web of inter-related objectives and strategies is built up at all levels within the framework of the overall company plan.

The really important point, however, apart from clarifying the difference between objectives and strategies, is that the further down the hierarchical chain one goes, the less likely it is that a stated objective will make a cost-effective contribution to company profits, unless it derives logically and directly from an objective at a higher level.

Corporate objectives and strategies can be simplified in the following way:

Corporate objective ○ desired level of profitability
Corporate strategies ○ which products and which markets (marketing)
  ○ what kind of facilities (production and distribution)

○ size and character of the staff/labour force (personnel)
○ funding (finance)
○ other corporate strategies such as social responsibility, corporate image, stock market image, employee image, etc.

It is now clear that at the next level down in the organization, i.e. at the functional level, what products are to be sold into what markets become *marketing objectives*, while the means of achieving these objectives using the marketing mix are *marketing strategies*. At the next level down, there would be, say, *advertising objectives* and *advertising strategies*, with the subsequent *programmes* and *budgets* for achieving the objectives. In this way, a hierarchy of objectives and strategies can be traced back to the initial corporate objective. Figure 6.1 illustrates this point.

How to set marketing objectives

The Ansoff matrix can be introduced here as a useful tool for thinking about marketing objectives.

A firm's competitive situation can be simplified to two dimensions only – products and markets. To put it even more simply, Ansoff's framework is about what is sold (the 'product'), and who it is sold to (the 'market'). Within this framework Ansoff identifies four possible courses of action for the firm:

○ Selling existing products to existing markets
○ Extending existing products to new markets
○ Developing new products for existing markets
○ Developing new products for new markets

The matrix in Figure 6.2 depicts these concepts.

It is clear that the range of possible marketing objectives is very wide, since there will be degrees of technological newness and degrees of market newness. Nevertheless, Ansoff's matrix provides a logical framework in which marketing objectives can be developed under each of the four main headings above.

> In other words, marketing objectives are about products and markets only.

Common sense will confirm that it is only by selling something to someone that the company's financial goals can be achieved, and that advertising, pricing, service levels, and so on, are the means (or strategies) by which it might succeed in doing this. Thus, pricing objectives, sales promotion objectives, advertising objectives, and the like, should not be confused with marketing objectives.

Marketing objectives are generally accepted as being selected qualitative and quantitative commitments, usually stated either in standards of performance for a given operating period, or conditions to be achieved by given dates. Performance standards are usually

**Marketing planning in a
corporate framework**

Corporate mission
Define the business and its boundaries
using considerations such as:
– distinctive competence
– environmental trends
– consumption market trends
– resource market trends
– stakeholder expectations

Corporate objectives
e.g. ROI, ROSHF, image (with stock market, public and employees), social responsibility, etc.

Corporate strategies
e.g. involve corporate resources, and must be within corporate business boundaries

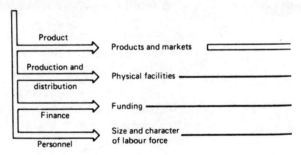

Product → Products and markets

Production and distribution → Physical facilities

Finance → Funding

Personnel → Size and character of labour force

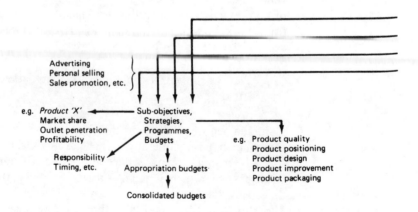

Advertising
Personal selling
Sales promotion, etc.

e.g. *Product 'X'* ← Sub-objectives,
Market share   Strategies,
Outlet penetration   Programmes,
Profitability   Budgets

Responsibility
Timing, etc.

Appropriation budgets

Consolidated budgets

e.g. Product quality
Product positioning
Product design
Product improvement
Product packaging

Figure 6.1

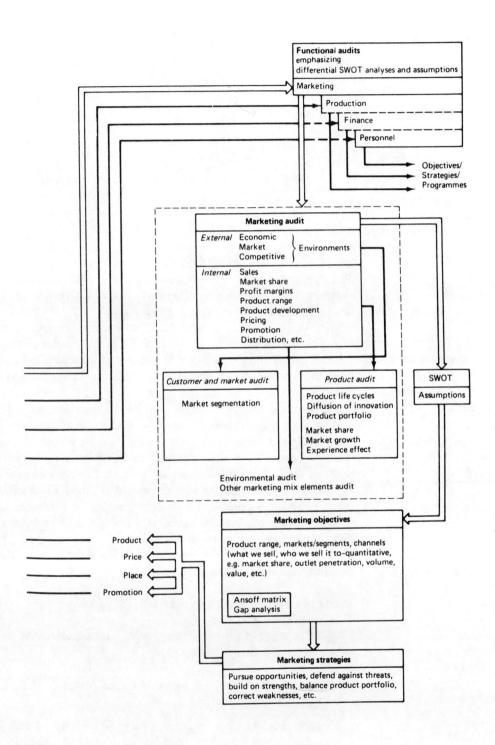

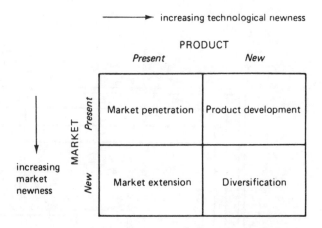

Figure 6.2 Ansoff matrix

stated in terms of sales volume and various measures of profitability. The conditions to be attained are usually a percentage of market share and various other commitments, such as a percentage of the total number of a given type of retail outlet.

There is also broad agreement that objectives must be specific enough to enable subordinates to derive from them the general character of action required and the yardstick by which performance is to be judged. Objectives are the core of managerial action, providing direction to the plans. By asking where the operation should be at some future date, objectives are determined. Vague objectives, however emotionally appealing, are counter-productive to sensible planning, and are usually the result of the human propensity for wishful thinking which often smacks more of cheerleading than serious marketing leadership. What this really means is that while it is arguable whether directional terms such as 'decrease', 'optimize', 'minimize' should be used as objectives, it seems logical that unless there is some measure, or yardstick, against which to measure a sense of locomotion towards achieving them, then they do not serve any useful purpose.

Ansoff defines an objective as 'a measure of the efficiency of the resource-conversion process.

Objectives are the core of managerial action, providing direction to the plans.

> 'An objective contains three elements: the particular attribute that is chosen as a measure of efficiency; the yardstick or scale by which the attribute is measured; and the particular value on the scale which the firm seeks to attain'.

Marketing objectives then are about each of the four main categories of the Ansoff matrix:

1 *Existing products in existing markets.* These may be many and varied and will certainly need to be set for all existing major products and customer groups (segments).
2 *New products in existing markets.*

3 *Existing products in new markets.*
4 *New products in new markets.*

Thus, in the long run, it is only by selling something (a 'product') to someone (a 'market') that any firm can succeed in staying in business profitably. Simply defined, product/market strategy means the route chosen to achieve company goals through the range of products it offers to its chosen market segments. Thus the product/market strategy represents a commitment to a future direction for the firm. Marketing objectives, then, are concerned solely with products and markets.

The general marketing *directions* which lead to the above objectives flow, of course, from the life cycle and portfolio analysis conducted in the audit and revolve around the following logical decisions:

1 *Maintain*. This usually refers to the 'cash cow' type of product/market and reflects the desire to maintain competitive positions.
2 *Improve*. This usually refers to the 'star' type of products/market and reflects the desire to improve the competitive position in attractive markets.
3 *Harvest*. This usually refers to the 'dog' type of product/market and reflects the desire to relinquish competitive position in favour of short-term profit and cash flow.
4 *Exit*. This also usually refers to the 'dog' type of product/market, also sometimes the 'question mark', and reflects a desire to divest because of a weak competitive position or because the cost of staying in it is prohibitive and the risk associated with improving its position is too high.
5 *Enter*. This usually refers to a new business area.

As already stated, however, great care should be taken not to follow slavishly any set of 'rules' or guidelines related to the above. Also, the use of pejorative labels like 'dog', 'cash cow', and so on should be avoided if possible.

A full list of marketing guidelines as a precursor to objective setting is given in Table 6.1. Figure 6.3 sets out a fuller list which includes guidelines for functions other than marketing. One word of warning, however. Such general guidelines should not be followed unquestioningly. They are included more as checklists of questions that should be asked about each major product in each major market *before* setting marketing objectives and strategies.

It is at this stage that the circles in the directional policy matrix can be moved to show their relative size and position in three years' time. You can do this to show, first, where they will be if the company takes no action, and second, where you would ideally prefer them to be. These latter positions will, of course, become the marketing objectives. Precisely how this is done is shown in Chapter 13. It is, however, the key stage in the marketing planning process.

Competitive strategies

At this stage of the planning process, it would be helpful to explain recent developments in the field of competitive strategies, since an understanding of the subject is an essential prerequisite to setting appropriate marketing objectives.

> One of the principal purposes of marketing strategy is for you to be able to choose the customers, and hence the markets, you wish to deal with.

If we are to succeed we need to work hard at developing a sustainable competitive advantage.

In this respect, the directional policy matrix discussed in Chapter 5 is particularly useful. The main components of the strategy are:

○ The company
○ Customers
○ Competitors

So far, we have said very little about customers, although, clearly, if we are to succeed, we need to work hard at developing a sustainable competitive advantage. The important word here is 'sustainable', as temporary advantages can be gained in numerous ways, such as, for example, a price reduction or a clever sales promotion.

Most business people would agree that, as markets mature, the only way to grow the business without diversifying is at the expense of competitors, which implies the need to understand in depth the characteristics of the market and of the main competitors in it. The leading thinker in this field is Michael Porter of the Harvard Business School, and any reader wishing to explore this vital subject in more depth should refer to his book.

Perhaps the best way to summarize this complex subject would be to tell a story.

Imagine three tribes on a small island fighting each other because resources are scarce. One tribe decides to move to a larger adjacent island, sets up camp, and is followed eventually by the other two, who also set up their own separate camps. At first it is a struggle to establish themselves, but eventually they begin to occupy increasing parts of the island, until many years later, they begin to fight again over adjacent land. The more innovative tribal chief, i.e. the one who was first to move the new island, sits down with his senior warriors and ponders what to do, since none are very keen to move to yet another island. They decide that the only two options are:

1 Attack and go relentlessly for the enemy's territory.

2 Settle for a smaller part of the island and build in it an impregnable fortress.

Table 6.1 Strategies suggested by portfolio matrix analysis

	Business strengths High	**Low**	
High	*Invest for growth* Defend leadership, gain if possible Accept moderate short-term profits and negative cash flow Consider geographic expansion, product line expansion, product differentiation Upgrade production introduction effort Aggressive marketing posture, viz. selling, advertising, pricing, sales promotion service levels, as appropriate	*Opportunistic* The options are: (i) Move it to the left if resources are available to invest in it (ii) Keep a low profile until funds are available (iii) Divest to a buyer able to exploit the opportunity	
Market 10 **attractiveness** **Low**	*Maintain market position, manage for sustained earnings* Maintain market position in most successful product lines Prune less successful product lines Differentiate products to maintain share of key segments Limit discretionary marketing expenditure Stabilize prices, except where a temporary aggressive stance is necessary to maintain market share	*Selective** Acknowledge low growth Do not view as a 'marketing' problem Identify and exploit growth segments Emphasize product quality to avoid 'commodity' competition Systematically improve productivity Assign talented managers	*Manage for profit* Prune product line aggressively Maximize cash flow Minimize marketing expenditure Maintain or raise prices at the expense of volume
0			
	3.0	1.0	0.3

*Selective refers to those products or markets which fall on or near the vertical dividing line in a directional policy matrix.

These two options, i.e. terrain or impregnable fortress (or both) are in fact the same options that face business people as they contemplate competitive strategy. Let's look in turn at each of these options,

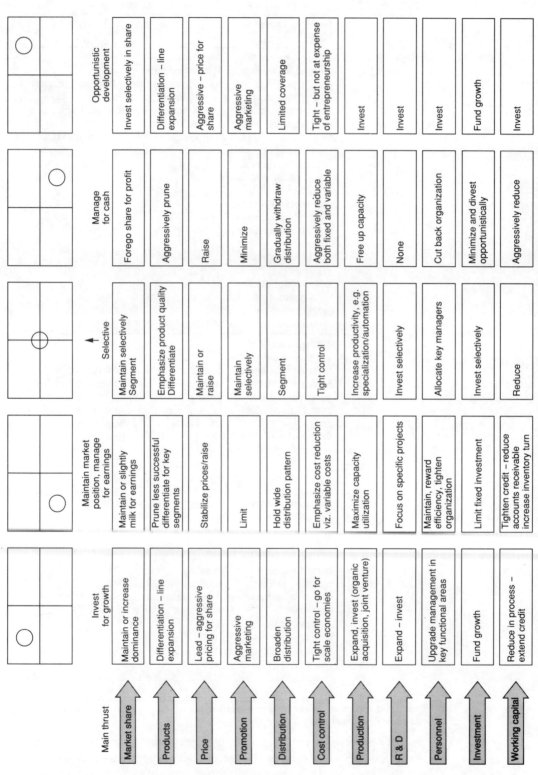

Figure 6.3 Programme guidelines suggested for different positioning on the directional policy matrix

continuing for a moment longer with the military analogy, and starting with terrain.

Imagine two armies facing each other on a field of battle (depicted by circles). One army has fifteen soldiers in it, the other twelve. Imagine also that they face each other with rifles and all fire one shot at the other at the same time, also that they don't all aim at the same soldier! Figure 6.4 depicts the progress of each side in disposing of the other. It will be seen that after only three volleys, the army on the right has only one soldier remaining, while the army on the left, with eight soldiers remaining, is still a viable fighting unit.

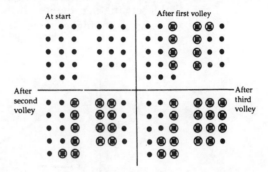

Figure 6.4 The importance of market share

One interesting fact about this story is that the effect observed here is *geometric* rather than *arithmetic*, and is a perfect demonstration of the effect of size and what happens when all things are equal except size. The parallel in industry, of course, is market share.

Just look at what happened in the computer industry when General Electric, Rank Xerox, RCA, ICL and others attacked the giant IBM. The larger competitor was able to win the battle. So, all things being equal, a company with a larger market share than another should win over a smaller competitor. Or *should* they? Clearly, this is not inevitable, providing the smaller companies take evasive action. Staying with the computer industry, just look at how successful AT&T Global Information Systems have been with their 'global fortress' strategy (e.g. ATMs for the financial market), Control Data with their scientific controls, and, more recently, Dell Computers.

In 1992 and 1993, IBM got caught unawares, with disastrous financial results, by quicker-moving, smarter, smaller competitors. No doubt they will recover by regrouping and re-segmenting their market, just as Rank Xerox did in the 1970s to recover from the successful entry of the Japanese with small photocopiers.

In the banking market in the UK, First Direct is beginning to take a commanding position by means of a differentiated product, dispensing with all the paraphernalia of expensive branches.

> In the insurance market, Direct Line have completely changed the rules of warfare by dispensing with brokers, with a consequent saving in premiums for customers.

Put yet another way, look for a moment at the economists' model of supply and demand shown in Figure 6.5. Here we see that when supply is greater than demand, price will fall, and that when demand exceeds supply, the price will tend to rise. The equilibrium point is when supply matches demand. The only way a competitor can avoid the worst effects of such a situation is by taking one of the following actions:

1 Being the lowest cost supplier.
2 Differentiating the product in some way so as to be able to command a higher price.

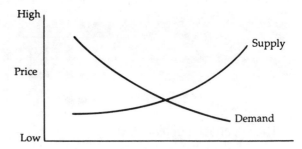

Figure 6.5

Michael Porter combined these two options into a simple matrix, as shown in Figure 6.6. It can be seen that Box 1 represents a sound strategy, particularly in commodity-type markets such as bulk chemicals, where differentiation is harder to achieve because of the identical nature of the chemical make-up of the product. In such cases, it is wise to recognize the reality and pursue a productivity drive with the aim

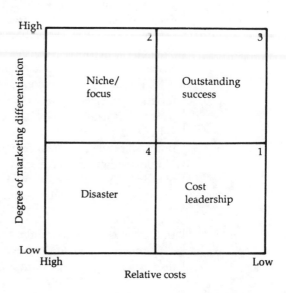

Figure 6.6

of becoming the lowest cost producer. It is here that the experience effect described in Chapter 5 becomes especially important.

> Many companies, however, such as Jaguar and BMW, could not hope to be low cost producers. Consequently, their whole corporate philosophy is geared to differentiation and what we have called added value. Clearly, this represents a sensible strategy for any company that cannot hope to be a world cost beater and indeed many of the world's great companies succeed by means of such a focus. Many of these companies also succeed in pushing themselves into Box 3, the outstanding success box, by occupying what can be called 'global fortresses'. A good example of this is AT&T Global Information Systems, who dominate the world's banking and retail markets with their focused technological and marketing approach.

> Companies like IBM, McDonalds and General Electric, however, typify Box 3, where low costs, differentiation and world leadership are combined in their corporate strategies.

Only Box 4 remains. Here we can see that a combination of commodity-type markets and high relative costs will result in disaster sooner or later. A position here is tenable only while demand exceeds supply. When, however, these markets mature, there is little hope for companies who find themselves in this unenviable position.

An important point to remember when thinking about differentiation as a strategy is that you must still be *cost effective*. It is a myth to assume that sloppy management and high costs are acceptable as long as the product has a good image and lots of added values. Also, in thinking about differentiation, please refer back to the section on benefit analysis in Chapter 4, for it is here that the route to differentiation will be found. It is also clear that there is not much point in offering benefits that are costly for you to provide but which are not highly regarded by customers. So consider using a matrix like the one given in Figure 6.7 to classify your benefits. Clearly, you will succeed best by providing as many benefits as possible that fall into the top right-hand box.

> ICI is a good example of a company that is proactively attempting to change its global strategy by systematically moving away from bulk chemicals in Box 1 (in Figure 6.6) towards speciality chemicals in Box 2 and then going on to occupy a 'global fortress' position in these specialities (Box 3).

The main point here, however, is that when setting marketing objectives, it is essential for you to have a sound grasp of the position in your markets of yourself and your competitors and to adopt appropriate postures for the several elements of your business, all of

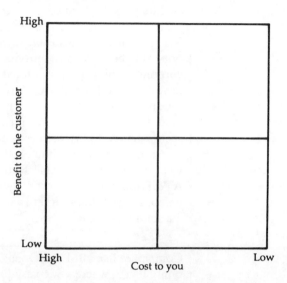

Figure 6.7

which *may* be different. It may be necessary, for example, to accept that part of your portfolio is in the 'Disaster' box (Box 4). You may well be forced to have some products here, for example, to complete your product range to enable you to offer your more profitable products. The point is that you must adopt an appropriate stance towards these products and set your marketing objectives accordingly, using, where appropriate, the guidelines given in Table 6.1 and Figure 6.3.

Finally, here are some very general guidelines to help you think about competitive strategies.

1   Know the terrain on which you are fighting (the market).
2   Know the resources of your enemies (competitive analysis).
3   Do something with determination that the enemy isn't expecting.

In respect of this last one, the great historian of military strategy, Lanchester, put forward the following equation when applying his findings to industry:

Fighting strength = weapon efficiency × (number of men)^2

Let us simplify and summarize this. 'Weapon efficiency' can be elements such as advertising, the sales force, the quality of your products, and so on. '(number of men)^2' is more difficult to explain, but is similar in concept to Einstein's theory of critical mass:

Energy = mass × (velocity of light)^2
$E = mc^2$

Let us take as an example the use of the sales force. If your competitor's sales person calls on an outlet, say, four times a month for six months, he or she will have called twenty-four times. If your salesperson calls eight times a month for six months, he or she will have called forty-eight times.

What Lanchester's Square Law says, however, is that the *effect* is considerably more than twice that of your competitor.

> An example of this was the Canada Dry attack on the British mixer market during the 1970s. By training the sales force to a high peak of effectiveness (weapon efficiency), and by focusing on specific market segments and out-calling their much larger rival, they were gradually able to occupy particular parts of the market and then move on to the next, until eventually they gained a significant market share. What would have been foolhardy would have been to tackle the market leader head on in a major battle. The result would have been similar to the fate of the troops in the Charge of the Light Brigade!

Where to start (gap analysis)

Figure 6.8 illustrates what is commonly referred to as 'gap analysis'. Essentially, what it says is that if the corporate sales and financial objectives are greater than the current long-range forecasts, there is a gap which has to be filled.

The 'operations gap' can be filled in two ways:

1 Improved productivity, e.g. reduce costs, improve the sales mix, increase prices, reduce discounts, improve the productivity of the salesforce, and so on.
2 Market penetration, e.g. increase usage, increase market share.

The 'new strategies gap' can be filled in three ways:

1 Market extension, e.g. find new user groups, enter new segments, geographical expansion.
2 Product development
3 Diversification, e.g. selling new products to new markets.

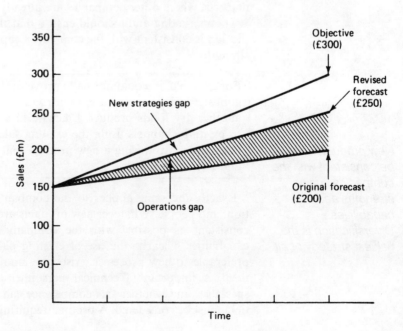

Figure 6.8

A fourth option, of course, is to reduce the objectives!

Gap analysis is best done in two separate steps. Step 1 should be done for sales revenue only, so, under the operations gap, above, reducing costs is not relevant, as we are only interested in revenue growth. Step 2 should then go through the same stages, but this time looking at the profit and costs implications of achieving the sales growth.

A detailed, step-by-step methodology for completing both steps is given in Chapter 13.

If improved productivity is one method by which the profit gap is to be filled, care must be taken not to take measures such as to reduce marketing costs by 20 per cent overall. The portfolio analysis undertaken during the marketing audit stage will indicate that this would be totally inappropriate to some product/market areas, for which increased marketing expenditure may be needed, while for others 20 per cent reduction in marketing costs may not be sufficient.

As for sales growth options, it is clear that market penetration should always be a company's first option, since it makes far more sense to attempt to increase profits and cash flow from *existing* products and markets initially, because this is usually the least costly and the least risky. This is so because, for its present products and markets, a company has developed knowledge and skills which it can use competitively.

For the same reason, it makes more sense in many cases to move along the horizontal axis for further growth before attempting to find new markets. The reason for this is that it normally takes many years for a company to get to know its customers and markets and to build up a reputation. That reputation and trust, embodied in either the company's name or in its brands, is rarely transferable to new markets, where other companies are already entrenched.

The marketing audit should ensure that the method chosen to fill the gap is consistent with the company's capabilities and build on its strengths.

> For example, it would normally prove far less profitable for a dry goods grocery manufacturer to introduce frozen foods than to add another dry foods product. Likewise, if a product could be sold to existing channels using the existing sales force, this is far less risky than introducing a new product that requires new channels and new selling skills.

New products should be consistent with the company's known strengths and capabilities. Diversification is the riskiest strategy of all.

Exactly the same applies to the company's production, distribution, and people. Whatever new products are developed should be as consistent as possible with the company's known strengths and capabilities. Clearly, the use of existing plant capacity is generally preferable to new processes. Also, the amount of additional investment is important. Technical personnel are highly trained and specialist, and whether this competence can be transferred to a new field must be considered. A product requiring new raw materials may also require new handling and storage techniques which may prove expensive.

> It can now be appreciated why going into new markets with new products (diversification) is the riskiest strategy of all, because *new* resources and *new* management skills have to be developed. This is why the history of commerce is replete with examples of companies which went bankrupt through moving into areas where they had little or no distinctive competence.

This is also why many companies that diversified through acquisition during periods of high economic growth have since divested themselves of businesses that were not basically compatible with their own distinctive competence.

The Ansoff matrix, of course, is not a simple four-box matrix, for it will be obvious that there are degrees of technological newness as well as degrees of market newness. Figure 6.9 illustrates the point. It also demonstrates more easily why any movement should generally aim to keep a company as close as possible to its present position, rather than moving it to a totally unrelated position, except in the most unusual circumstances.

Nevertheless, the product life cycle phenomenon will inevitably *force* companies to move along one or more of the Ansoff matrix axes if they are to continue to increase their sales and profits. A key question to be asked, then, is *how* this important decision is to be taken, given the risks involved.

A full list of the possible methods involved in the process of gap analysis is given in Figure 6.10. From this it will be seen that there is nothing an executive can do to fill the gap that is not included in

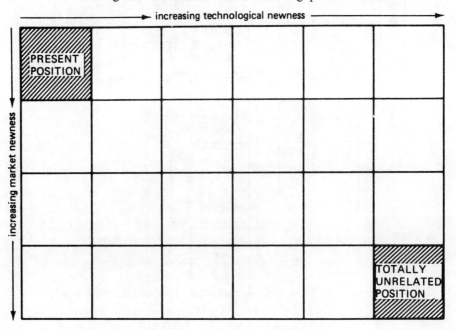

Figure 6.9

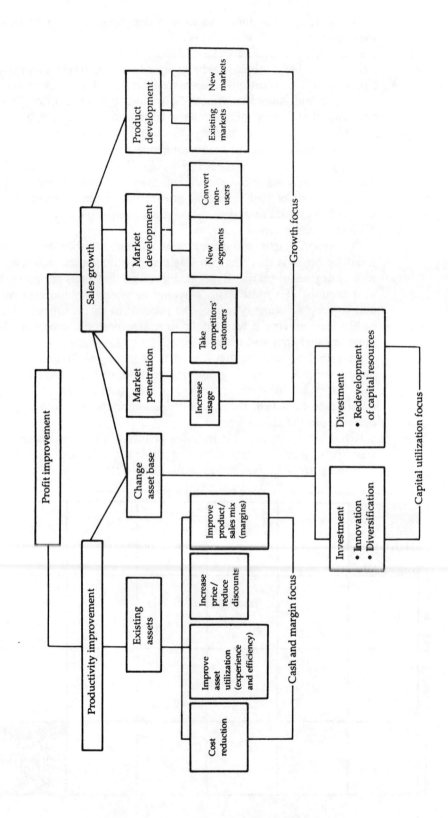

Figure 6.10 Profit/division profit improvement options (after John Saunders, Loughborough University, used with his kind permission)

the list. It is worth mentioning again that the precise methodology to implement this concept is given in the final chapter of this book, which provides a marketing planning system.

> At this point, it is important to stress that the 'objectives' point in gap analysis should *not* be an extrapolation, but your own view of what revenue would make this into an excellent business.

The word 'excellent' must, of course, be relative only to comparable businesses. If all the executives in a company responsible for SBUs were to do this, then work out what needed to be done to fill any gaps, it is easy to understand why this would result in an excellent overall business performance. Instead, what often happens is that executives wait until there is a crisis before doing any strategic planning. For many such organizations, alas, during the late 1980s and early 1990s, it was all left too late and many went bankrupt.

One final point to make about gap analysis based on the Ansoff matrix is that, when completed, the details of exactly *how* to achieve the objectives still need to be worked out. This is the purpose of the strategic marketing plan. So, gap analysis represents a very useful starting point in mapping out the general route, which is why we suggest you start here, rather than going to all the trouble of preparing a strategic marketing plan only to have to change it later.

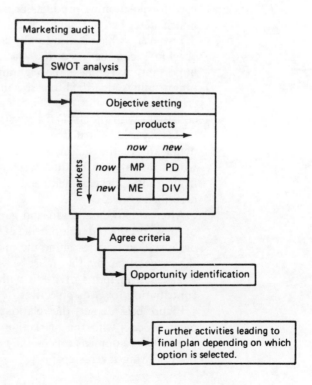

Figure 6.11

New product development/ market extension/ diversification

As stated earlier in this chapter, sooner or later all organizations will need to move along one or both axes of the Ansoff matrix. How to do this should be comparatively simple if the marketing audit has been completed thoroughly.

It is not the purpose here to explore in detail sub-sets of marketing, such as market research, market selection, new product development, and diversification. What is important, however, in a book on marketing planning is to communicate an understanding of the framework in which these activities should take place.

What we are aiming to do is to maximize *synergy*, which could be described as the 2 + 2 = 5 effect. The starting point is the marketing audit, leading to the SWOT (strengths, weaknesses, opportunities and threats) analysis. This is so that development of any kind will be firmly based on a company's basic *strengths* and *weaknesses*. External factors are the opportunities and threats facing the company.

Once this important analytical stage is successfully completed, the more technical process of opportunity identification, screening, business analysis, and, finally, activities such as product development, testing and entry planning can take place, depending on which option is selected. The important point to remember is that no matter how thoroughly these subsequent activities are carried out, unless the objectives of product development/market extension are based firmly on an analysis of the company's capabilities, they are unlikely to be successful in the long term. Figure 6.11 illustrates the process.

The criteria selected will generally be consistent with the criteria used for positioning products or businesses in the nine-cell portfolio matrix described in Chapter 5. The list shown in Table 5.2 in Chapter 5, however, (which is also totally consistent with the marketing audit checklist) can be used to select those criteria which are most important. A rating and weighting system can then be applied to opportunities identified to assess their suitability or otherwise. Those criteria selected and the weighting system used will, of course, be consistent with the SWOT analysis.

Having said that it is not the purpose of this book to explore in detail any of the subsets of marketing such as market research, it would nonetheless be quite useful briefly to outline the process of new product development and its relationship to the gap analysis described above.

After a marketing audit and gap analysis have clarified the place of new product development in a broad company context, the organization must examine the micro considerations. These involve the range of factors that must be taken into account when a product is assessed in terms of its fit within the product portfolio and its contribution towards objectives.

Figure 6.12 depicts the relationship of the new product development process with the marketing audit and SWOT analysis. New product development can usefully be seen as a process consisting of the following seven steps:

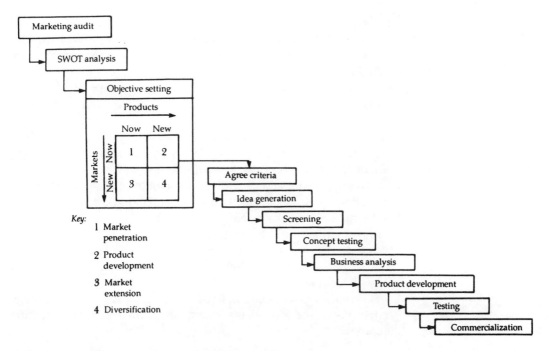

Figure 6.12 The new product development process

1 *Idea generation* – the search for product ideas to meet company objectives.
2 *Screening* – a quick analysis of the ideas to establish those which are relevant.
3 *Concept testing* – checking with the market that the new product ideas are acceptable.
4 *Business analysis* – the idea is examined in detail in terms of its commercial fit in the business.
5 *Product development* – making the idea into hardware.
6 *Testing* – market tests necessary to verify early business assessments.
7 *Commercialization* – full-scale product launch, committing the company's reputation and resources.

Marketing strategies

What a company wants to accomplish, then, in terms of such things as market share and volume, is a marketing objective. How the company intends to go about achieving its objectives is strategy. Strategy is the overall route to the achievement of specific objectives and should describe the means by which objectives are to be reached, the time programme and the allocation of resources. It does not delineate the individual courses the resulting activity will follow.

There is a clear distinction between strategy, and detailed implementation, or tactics.

Strategy is the route to achievement of specific objectives and describes how objectives will be reached.

Marketing strategy reflects the company's best opinion as to how it can most profitably apply its skills and resources to the market place. It is inevitably broad in scope.

219

The plan which stems from it will spell out action and timings and will contain the detailed contribution expected from each department.

There is a similarity between strategy in business and strategic military development. One looks at the enemy, the terrain, the resources under command, and then decides whether to attack the whole front, an area of enemy weakness, to feint in one direction while attacking in another, or to attempt an encirclement of the enemy's position. The policy and mix, the general direction in which to go, and the criteria for judging success, all come under the heading of strategy. The action steps are tactics.

Similarly, in marketing, the same commitment, mix and type of resources as well as guidelines and criteria that must be met, all come under the heading of strategy.

For example, the decision to use distributors in all but the three largest market areas, in which company salespeople will be used, is a strategic decision. The selection of particular distributors is a tactical decision.

The following headings indicate the general content of strategy statements in the area of marketing which emerge from marketing literature:

1 Policies and procedures relating to the products to be offered, such as number, quality, design, branding, packaging and labelling, etc.
2 Pricing levels to be adopted, margins and discount policies.
3 Advertising and sales promotion. The creative approach, the type of media, type of displays, the amount to spend, etc.
4 What emphasis is to be placed on personal selling, the sales approach, sales training, etc.
5 The distributive channels to be used and the relative importance of each.
6 Warehousing, transportation, inventories, service levels, etc. in relation to distribution.

> Thus, marketing strategies are the means by which marketing objectives will be achieved and are generally concerned with the four major elements of the marketing mix.

These are:

Product	The general policies for product branding, positioning, deletions, modifications, additions, design, packaging, etc.
Price	The general pricing policies to be followed for product groups in market segments.
Place	The general policies for channels and customer service levels.
Promotion	The general policies for communicating with customers under the relevant headings, such as: advertising, sales force, sales promotion, public relations, exhibitions, direct mail, etc.

The following list of marketing strategies (in summary form), covers the majority of options open under the headings of the four Ps:

1 *Product*
   o expand the line
   o change performance, quality or features
   o consolidate the line
   o standardize design
   o positioning
   o change the mix
   o branding
2 *Price*
   o change price, terms or conditions
   o skimming policies
   o penetration policies
3 *Promotion*
   o change advertising or promotion
   o change selling
4 *Place*
   o change delivery or distribution
   o change service
   o change channels
   o change the degree of forward integration

Chapters 7–10 are devoted to a much more detailed consideration of promotion, pricing and distribution. These chapters describe what should appear in advertising, sales, pricing and place plans. This detail is intended for those whose principal concern is the preparation of a detailed one-year operational or tactical plan. The relationship of these chapters to the strategic plan is in the provision of information to enable the planner to delineate broad strategies under the headings outlined above. There is no chapter specifically on product management because all the product options have been covered already, particularly in Chapter 5 in the discussion on the product audit.

Formulating marketing strategies is one of the most critical and difficult parts of the entire marketing process.

There are further steps in the marketing planning process before detailed programmes are put together. These are estimating in broad terms the cost of the strategies, and delineating alternative plans. Both of these steps will be covered in more detail in Chapter 11.

Formulating marketing strategies is one of the most critical and difficult parts of the entire marketing process. It sets the limit of success. Communicated to all management levels, it indicates what strengths are to be developed, what weaknesses are to be remedied, and in what manner.

> Marketing strategies enable operating decisions to bring the company into the right relationship with the emerging pattern of market opportunities which previous analysis has shown to offer the highest prospect of success.

Before proceeding to describe the next stage of marketing planning, i.e. the construction of actual working plans, it should be stressed that the vital phase of setting objectives and strategies is a highly complex process which, if done badly, will probably result in considerable misdirection of resources.

This chapter has confirmed the need for setting clear, definitive objectives for all aspects of marketing, and that marketing objectives themselves have to derive logically from corporate objectives. The advantages of this practice are that it allows all concerned with marketing activities to concentrate their particular contribution on achieving the overall marketing objectives, as well as facilitating meaningful and constructive evaluation of all marketing activity.

For the practical purpose of marketing planning, it will be apparent from the observations above concerning what was referred to as a hierarchy of objectives, that overall marketing objectives have to be broken down into sub-objectives which, taken all together, will achieve the overall objectives. By breaking down the overall objectives, the problem of strategy development becomes more manageable, hence easier.

> A two-year study of 35 top industrial companies by McKinsey and Company revealed that leader companies agreed that product/market strategy is the key to the task of keeping shareholders' equity rising. Clearly, then, setting objectives and strategies in relation to products and markets is a most important step in the marketing planning process.

Once agreement has been reached on the broad marketing objectives and strategies, those responsible for programmes can now proceed to the detailed planning stage, developing the appropriate overall strategy statements into sub-objectives.

Plans constitute the vehicle for getting to the destination along the chosen route, or the detailed execution of the strategy. The term 'plan' is often used synonymously in marketing literature with the terms 'programme' and 'schedule'. A plan containing detailed lists of tasks to be completed, together with responsibilities, timing and cost, is sometimes referred to as an appropriation budget, which is merely a detailing of the actions to be carried out and of the expected financial results in carrying them out. More about this in Chapters 7 to 10.

Application questions

1 Critically analyse your company's corporate objectives.
2 Critically analyse your company's corporate strategies.
3 Critically analyse your company's marketing objectives.
4 Critically analyse your company's marketing strategies.
5 Has there been any product/market extension during the past ten years which has not been compatible with your company's distinctive competence? If so, state why.
6 Draw up criteria for product/market extension which *are* compatible with your company's distinctive competences.

Review of Chapter 6

Corporate objective

This is the desired level of profit the organization seeks to achieve. The *corporate strategy* for doing this covers:

1 Which products and which markets (marketing).
2 What facilities are required (e.g. production, distribution).
3 The number and character of employees (personnel).
4 What funding is required and how (finance).
5 Social responsibility, corporate image etc. (other corporate strategies).

Gap analysis

Gap analysis explores the shortfall between the corporate objective and what can be achieved by various strategies.

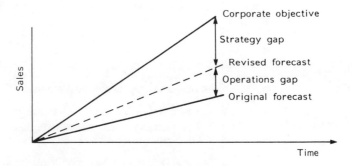

The *operations gap* can be filled by reducing costs, improving the sales mix, increasing market share.

The *strategy gap* can be filled by finding new user groups, entering new segments, geographical expansion, diversification, new product development. *Try Exercise 6.1*

The marketing audit

This is the systematic collection of data and information about the external environment and about your own company's operations.
Try Exercise 6.2

The SWOT analysis

This is the summary of the marketing audit, which lists:

Internally
The company's strengths and weaknesses.

Externally
The opportunities and threats facing the company.

The SWOT analysis should provide strong evidence about what the company should and should not try to set as marketing objectives. It should use strengths to exploit opportunities, while minimizing threats and weaknesses. *Try Exercises 6.3, 6.4 and 6.5*

Marketing objectives

These are concerned with what is sold (products) and to whom it is sold (markets). There are four possible combinations of products and markets (Ansoff matrix).

'An objective contains three elements:

1 The attribute chosen for measurement, e.g. sales, market share.
2 The particular value selected, e.g. 25 per cent market share.
3 For a given operating period, e.g. by the end of year 3.

The matrix suggests four main categories of objectives:

A = market penetration
B = product development
C = market extension
D = diversification

Try Exercise 6.6

Marketing strategies

There are four broad strategies:

1 To invest and grow.
2 To extract earnings selectively.
3 To harvest.
4 To divest.

There are also more specific marketing strategies concerning the four Ps:

1 *Product*
   o Expand range.
   o Improve quality or features.
   o Consolidate range.
   o Standardize design.
   o Reposition product.
   o Change the mix.
   o Branding.
2 *Price*
   o Change price.
   o Change terms and conditions.

- o Penetration policy.
- o Skimming policy.
3 *Promotion*
  - o Change advertising.
  - o Change promotion.
  - o Change selling.
  - o Change communication mix.
4 *Place*
  - o Change channels.
  - o Change delivery or distribution.
  - o Change service levels.
  - o Forward or backward integration.

Try Exercise 6.7

Questions raised for the company

1 Q: Who should set the marketing objectives and strategies?
  A: Usually they would be formulated by the marketing Director, but they must be agreed at the highest level in the company so that there is genuine commitment to them.
2 Q: Is diversification really a viable objective, bearing in mind the risk in moving into the unknown?
  A: It depends how strong the *factual* evidence is for this step. Clearly it is not a decision to be taken lightly.
3 Q: How secret should marketing objectives and strengths be? Should staff at lower levels know what they are?
  A: Staff are much more committed to a company which 'knows where it is going'. Ideally subordinates should be given the necessary information to understand their job context.
4 Q: What happens if we get our marketing objectives and strategies wrong?
  A: If the process used for arriving at them was based on facts, the chances are they will not be wrong. Clearly it will be essential to monitor progress and take corrective action when required.

Introduction to Chapter 6 exercises

In these exercises, the most critical part of the marketing planning process will be tackled.

Exercise 6.1 is concerned with carrying out a gap analysis.

Exercise 6.2 is concerned with collecting relevant data about your company and subjecting this to a hard-hitting examination, in summary form, of the opportunities and threats facing your organization.

Exercise 6.3 is concerned with competitor analysis, which clearly is an important part of a marketing audit.

Exercise 6.4 is concerned with carrying out a SWOT analysis.

Exercise 6.5 looks at the assumptions that are made before setting marketing objectives. Clearly, such assumptions should be kept to a minimum, but it is useful to be under no misapprehension regarding what they are, and, just as importantly, the risks attached to making such assumptions.

Exercise 6.6 gets to the heart of the matter and is concerned with setting marketing objectives, while Exercise 6.7 addresses the issue of selecting the most appropriate marketing strategies to match the chosen objectives.

Exercise 6.1 Gap analysis

You are asked to complete this two-part exercise. The first part is concerned with *revenue*, the second with *profit*.

Revenue

Objective
Start by plotting the sales position you wish to achieve at the end of the planning period, point E (Figure 6.13). Next plot the forecast position, point A.

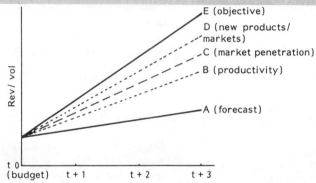

Figure 6.13

Table 6.1

Productivity (NB: not all factors are mutually exclusive)	Revenue
Better product mix (1)	
Better customer mix (2)	
More sales calls (3)	
Better sales calls (4)	
Increase price	
Reduce discounts	
Charge for deliveries	
Total	

Productivity
Are there any actions you can take to close the gaps under the headings in Table 6.1, point B? (These represent cash and margin focus.)

Ansoff product/market (market penetration)
List principal products on the horizontal axis (in Figure 6.14) and principal markets on the vertical axis. In each smaller square write in current sales and achievable sales during the planning period.

Next, plot the market penetration position, point C (Figure 6.13). This point will be the addition of all the values in the right-hand half of the small boxes in the Ansoff matrix. Please note, revenue from (1), (2), (3) and (4) from the productivity box should be deducted from the market penetration total before plotting point C.

Ansoff product/market matrix (new products/new markets)
Next, list the value of any new products you might develop which you might sell to existing markets (Figure 6.15). Alternatively, or as well as, if necessary, list the value of any existing products that you might sell to new markets. Plot the total value of these on Figure 6.13, point D.

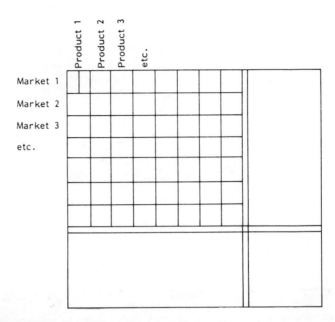

Figure 6.14

Diversification
List the value of any new products you might develop for new markets
until point E is reached. (Steps 3, 4 and 5 represent a sales growth focus.)

Capital utilization
If none of this gives the required return on investment consider changing
the asset base. This could be:

(A) Acquisition
(B) Joint venture

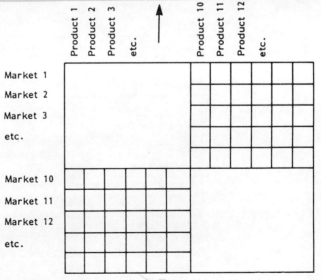

Figure 6.15

Profit

Objective
Start by plotting the profit position you wish to achieve at the end of the planning period, point E (Figure 6.16).
Next plot the forecast profit position, point A.

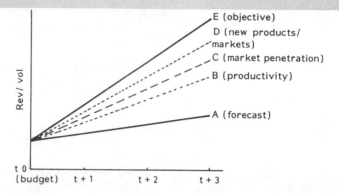

Figure 6.16

Productivity
Are there any actions you can take to close the gap under the headings in Table 6.2? Plot the total profit value of these in Figure 6.16, point B. (These represent cash and margin focus.)

Ansoff product/market (market penetration)
List principal products on the horizontal axis in Figure 6.16 and principal markets on the vertical axis. In each smaller square write in current profit and achievable profit value during the planning period.
Next plot the market penetration position, point C, Figure 6.16. This point will be the addition of all the values in the right-hand half of the small boxes in the Ansoff matrix (Figure 6.17).

Table 6.2

Productivity (NB: not all factors are mutually exclusive)	Profit
Better product mix	
Better customer mix	
More sales calls	
Better sales calls	
Increase price	
Reduce discounts	
Charge for deliveries	
Reduce debtor days	
Cost reduction	
Others (specify)	
Total	

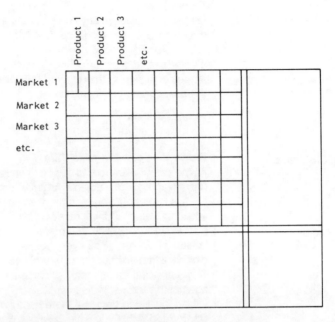

Figure 6.17

Ansoff product/market matrix (new products/new markets)
Next, list the value of any new products you might develop which you might sell to existing markets (Figure 6.18). Alternatively, or as well as, if necessary, list the value of any existing products that you might sell to new markets. Plot the total value of these on Figure 6.15, point D.

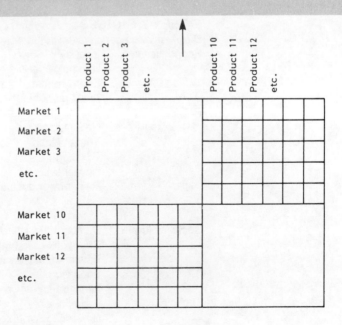

Figure 6.18

**Exercise 6.2
The marketing
audit**

Diversification
List the profit value of any new products you might develop for new markets
until point E is reached. (Steps 3, 4 and 5 represent a sales growth focus.)

Capital utilization
If none of this gives the required return on investment consider changing
the asset base. This could be:

(A) Acquisition
(B) Joint venture

Stage 1   Collecting the data

All the earlier exercises in this book have been designed to improve your
understanding of aspects of marketing planning and to discover
information about your company and/or its key products and markets. If
you completed all the preceding exercises, you should by now be in
possession of a fairly comprehensive marketing audit of your organization. However, since every business is in some ways unique, there is
a chance that an important piece of information might have been missed.
The marketing audit checklist which follows is provided as a safeguard
against this happening.

Use this list to decide if there is any additional information you would
want to add to that you have already collected. When you have completed

assembling as much information as you can, you are in a position to
progress to Stage 2 of this exercise.

THE MARKETING AUDIT CHECKLIST

The following is a list of factors that can affect some businesses. You
should only be interested in those that will affect your particular business.

This list doesn't claim to be exhaustive but it is intended to provide fair
coverage of most areas thereby acting as a guide and stimulus.

EXTERNAL FACTORS
Business and economic environment

Economic	Inflation
	Unemployment
	Energy prices
	Price volatility
Political/	Availability of materials, etc.
fiscal/legal	Nationalization
	Trade unions
	Taxation
	Duties/levies
	Regulatory constraints, e.g. labelling
	quality
	safety etc.
Social/cultural	Demographic issues, e.g. age distribution, etc.
	Changes in consumer lifestyle
	Environmental issues, e.g. pollution
	Education
	Immigration/emigration
Technical	Religion, etc.
	New technology/processes

Intra-company	Energy-saving techniques
	New materials/substitutes
	New equipment
	New products, etc.
	Capital investment
	Closures/start-ups
	Strikes, etc.

The market

Total market	Size (value/volume)
	Growth (value/volume)
	Trends (value/volume)
Characteristics	Developments, etc.
Products	Principal products bought
	How they are used
	Where they are used
	Packaging
	Accessories, etc.
Prices	Price levels/range
	Terms and conditions of sale
	Trade practices
	Special discounts
	Official regulations, etc.
Physical distribution	Principal methods
	Batch sizes
	Mechanical handling
	Protection, etc.
Distribution channels	Principal channels
	Purchasing patterns
	Geographical disposition
	Stocks
	Turnover
	Incentives
	Purchasing ability
	Needs
	Tastes
	Profits
	Prices paid, etc.
Customers and consumers	as for Distribution channels plus
	Demographic considerations, e.g. age, height, etc.
Communications	Principal methods
	Salesforce
	Advertising
	Exhibitions
	Public relations
	Promotions
	New developments, etc.
Industry practices	Inter-firm comparisons
	Trade associations
	Trade regulations/practices
	Links with government
	Historical attitudes
	Image, etc.

Competition

Industry structure	The companies in the Industry
	Their make-up
	Their market standing/reputation
	Their capacity to produce
	market
	distribute
	Their diversification
	Their origins and ownership
	New entrants
	Mergers and acquisitions
	Bankruptcies
	International links
	Strengths/weaknesses, etc.
Industry profitability	Historical data
	Current performance
	Relative performance of competitors
	Structure of operating costs
	Level of investment
	Return on investment
	Pricing/volume
	Sources of funding, etc.

INTERNAL FACTORS (OWN COMPANY)

Sales	Total (value/volume)
	by geographical location
	by industry/market segment
	by customer
	by product, etc.
Market share	
Profit margins	
Marketing procedures	
Organization structure	
Sales/marketing control data	
Marketing mix variables	Market research
	Product development
	Product range
	Product quality
	Unit of sale
	Stock levels
	Distribution
	Dealer support
	Pricing/discounts/credit
	Packaging
	Samples
	Exhibitions
	Selling
	Sales aids
	Point of sale
	Advertising
	Sales promotion

Public relations

After-sales service

Training and development

Systems and
procedures

Marketing planning system, e.g. is it effective?

Marketing objectives, e.g. clear, consistent with
  corporate objectives

Marketing strategy, e.g. appropriate for objectives

Structure, e.g. are duties and responsibilities clear?

Information, e.g. adequacy of marketing
  intelligence, its presentation

Control, e.g. suitable mechanisms

Communications, e.g. effective? in all areas?

Interfunction efficiency, e.g. between
  functions/departments

Profitability, e.g. regular monitoring and analysis

Cost-effectiveness, e.g. are functions/products continually reviewed in attempts to reduce excess costs?

Stage 2 The SWOT analysis

From the above list you will see that the *external factors* are the sources of all opportunities or threats, whereas the *internal factors* reflect the company's strengths or weaknesses.

In respect of *external factors (opportunities and threats)*, try the following exercise:

Step 1 List the principal *opportunities* (we suggest no more than twenty).

Step 2 Allocate a code to each of these (e.g. A, B, C etc.)

Step 3 Allocate a number between 1 and 9 to each of them. The number 1 means that in your view there is little chance of a particular opportunity occurring within the planning time-scale (say 3 years). A 9 would mean that there is a high probability of it occurring within the planning time-scale.

Step 4 Allocate a number between 1 and 9 to indicate the importance of the *impact* each of these opportunities would have on the organization, were it to occur.

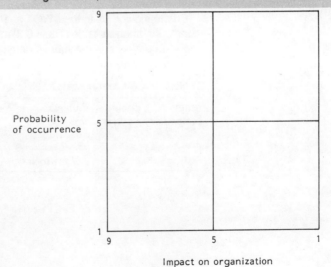

Figure 6.19 Opportunities matrix

Step 5   Now put each of your *opportunities* on the *opportunities matrix* (Figure 6.19).

Step 6   You will now have a number of points of intersection which should correspond to your coding system.

Step 7   All those in the *top left* box should be tackled in your marketing objectives and should appear in your SWOT analysis (Exercise 6.4). All the others, while they should not be ignored, are obviously less urgent. The whole exercise should now be repeated for *threats*, using the matrix in Figure 6.20.

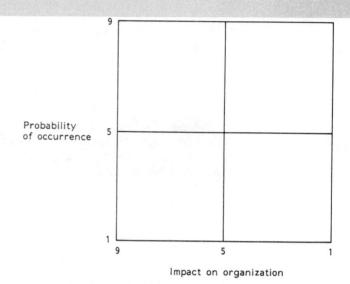

Figure 6.20 Threats matrix

Exercise 6.3 Competitor analysis

Exercise 6.3 is concerned with summarizing the information gathered about your opportunities and threats in your marketing audit in a more usable format, in the SWOT analysis.

Before moving on to the SWOT analysis (Exercise 6.4), complete the competitor analysis table (Table 6.3) in order to help you to rate yourself more accurately against your competitors.

Guidelines for completing Table 6.3 are given below.

Table 6.3 Competitor analysis

Main competitor	Products/ markets	Business direction and current objectives and strategies	Strengths	Weaknesses	Competitive position

Guide to competitive position classifications

Leadership	o Has major influence on performance or behaviour of others.
Strong	o Has a wide choice of strategies.
	o Able to adopt independent strategy without endangering short-term position.
	o Has low vulnerability to competitors' actions.
Favourable	o Exploits specific competitive strength, often in aa product-market niche.
	o Has more than average opportunity to improve position; several strategies available.
Tenable	o Performance justifies continuation in business.
Weak	o Currently unsatisfactory performance; significant competitive weakness.
	o Inherently a short-term condition; must improve or withdraw.

The following list includes five business directions that are appropriate for almost any business. Select those that best summarize the competitor's strategy.

Business directions

1 *Enter* – allocate resources to a new business area. Consideration should include building from prevailing company or unit strengths, exploiting related opportunities and defending against perceived threats. It may mean creating a new industry.

2 *Improve* – to apply strategies that will significantly improve the competitive position of the business. Often requires thoughtful product/market segmentation.

3 *Maintain* – to maintain one's competitive position. Aggressive strategies may be required, although a defensive posture may also be assumed. Product/market position is maintained, often in a niche.

4 *Harvest* – to relinquish intentionally competitive position, emphasizing short-term profit and cashflow but not necessarily at the risk of losing the business in the short term. Often entails consolidating or reducing various aspects of the business to create higher performance for that which remains.

5 *Exit* – to divest oneself of a business because of its weak competitive position or because the cost of staying in it is prohibitive, and the risk associated with improving its position is too high.

Exercise 6.4 The SWOT analysis

Having completed the marketing audit, your task now is to summarize it into a cogent and interesting analysis of your company's particular situation. The SWOT approach (the word SWOT incidentally being derived from the initial letters of Strengths, Weaknesses, Opportunities and Threats) will enable you to list in simple terms:

1 Your company's differential strengths and weaknesses *vis-à-vis* competitors.
2 Where the best opportunities exist, i.e. market segments.

3 The present and future threats to your business in the market segments.

The SWOT analysis should only be a few pages in length and should concern itself with key factors only, supported by relevant data.

Some of the most valuable information for the SWOT analysis will come from the life-cycle analysis and the portfolio matrix you prepared in Chapter 5. The former will give you insights about the prospects for your key products and/or services and this information can then be used on the portfolio matrix, thereby highlighting how the portfolio will change. An example of this is shown in Figure 6.21.

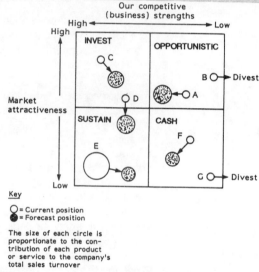

Figure 6.21

In Figure 6.21, clearly the future portfolio is going to be significantly different from the current one. Products/segments B and G will disappear. The sales volume of A, C and D will increase, while that of E will reduce quite dramatically. All this has a tremendous bearing on how funds are generated, and, again, this is where the portfolio matrix can be helpful in letting one understand what is happening. If you recall, the text explained that different quadrants of the matrix had different characteristics when viewed as sources of funds (Figure 6.22).

The significance of this for any company is to have a balanced portfolio, where there are adequate 'sustains' to fund research and development and selected 'opportunistics'.

The effort and costs associated with keeping the market share for 'invests' makes them unreliable sources of funds. The benefits will be reaped later when today's 'invests' sink into the 'sustain' quadrant.

You can now proceed to complete the profoma provided in respect of *all you key market segments*. Thus, if you have six key market segments, you will complete six proformae. In this book, we have provided you with one. If you need more, just repeat the exercise using duplicate forms. See Figure 6.23.

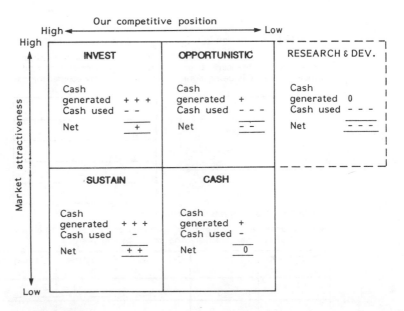

Figure 6.22

Exercise 6.5
Assumptions

Often it is forgotten that in conducting the SWOT analysis we have had to make assumptions, or educated guesses, about some of the factors that will affect the business, e.g. about market- growth rates, about government economic policy, about the activities of our competitors, etc. Most planning assumptions tend to deal with the environment or market trends and as such are critical to the fulfilment of the planned marketing objectives and strategies.

What then are the risks attached to making assumptions? Suppose we get it wrong?

To give some measure of risk assessment, a technique has been developed that looks at the assumption from the negative point of view. It leads one to ask 'What can go wrong with each assumption that would change the outcome?' For example, suppose the product was an oil derivative and was thus extremely sensitive to the price of oil. For planning purposes an assumption about the price of oil would have to be made. Using this 'Downside Risk' technique we would assess to what level the price could rise before increased material costs would make our products too expensive and cause our marketing plans to be completely revised.

Now complete the following 'Downside risk assessment form' (Table 6.4) to evaluate some of the key assumptions you used in your SWOT analysis, and which you are now to use as the basis for setting marketing objectives and strategies.

Exercise 6.6
Setting marketing objectives

Marketing objectives are solely concerned with *which products go to which markets*, and marketing strategies are concerned with *how* that is done. Therefore, because marketing objectives are only concerned about products and markets, an extremely useful planning aid is provided by the Ansoff matrix, depicted in Figure 6.24.

1   *SBU description*

Here, describe the market for which the SWOT is being done

2   *Critical success factors*

What are the few key things from the customer's point of view, that any competitor has to do right to succeed?

1

2

3

4

5

3   *Weighting*

How important is each of these CSFs? Score out of 100

Total 100

4   *Strengths/weaknesses analysis*

Score yourself and each of your main competitors out of 10 on each of the CSFs. Then multiply the score by the weight

CSF / Comp	You	Competitor A	Competitor B	Competitor C	Competitor D
1					
2					
3					
4					
5					
Total (score x weight)					

5 *Opportunities/threats*

What are the few key things outside your direct control that have had, and will continue to have, an impact on your business?

Opportunities   *Threats*

6   *Key issues that need to be addressed*

1

2

3

4

5

Figure 6.23   Strategic planning exercise (SWOT analysis)
Note: This form should be completed for each product/market segment under consideration

7

	Key assumptions for the planning period
1	
2	
3	
4	
5	
6	
7	

8 *Key objectives*

9 *Key strategies*

Financial consequences

Figure 6.23   Continued

Table 6.4 Downside risk assessment form

Key assumption	Basis of assumption	Confidence in assumption high/med/ low	What would have to happen to make outcome unattractive?	What is the risk of this happening? High/med/ low	What would be impact if event occurs?	How far could things be allowed to deviate from plan before action is taken?	What contingency action is planned?

Exercise 6.6
Setting marketing objectives

Marketing objectives are solely concerned with *which products go to which markets*, and marketing strategies are concerned with *how* that is done. Therefore, because marketing objectives are only concerned about products and markets, an extremely useful planning aid is provided by the Ansoff matrix, depicted in Figure 6.24.

This matrix suggests there are four types of marketing objective:

1 Selling established products into established markets (market penetration).
2 Selling established products into new markets (market extension).
3 Selling new products into established markets (product development).
4 Selling new products into new markets (diversification).

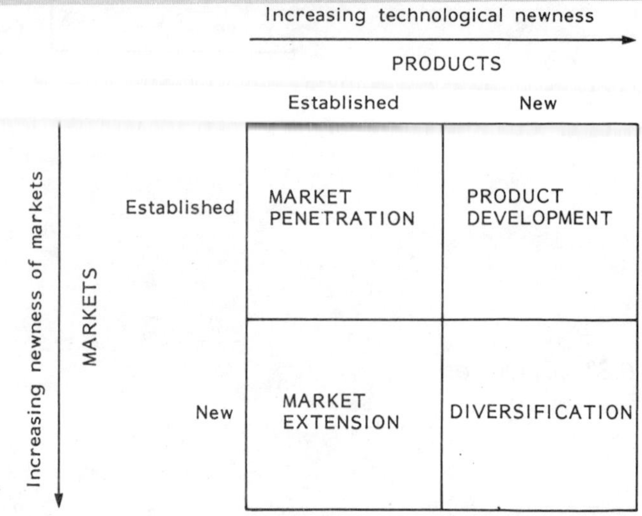

Figure 6.24

Task 1

Using the blank Ansoff matrix (Figure 6.25), or perhaps using a larger sheet of paper, draw the matrix for your company's products and markets.

Please note that when you consider whether or not a market is new or established, the question you must ask yourself is 'How long does it take to get one's distinctive competence known in this market?' If you have been dealing with the market for anything less than your answer to this question, then that is a new market.

Similarly, new products are those probably at the early stages of their life cycles, where the company is still 'learning' how to make them, i.e. it hasn't solved all the tooling, scheduling, quality, design and technical problems in the same way as it has for the established products.

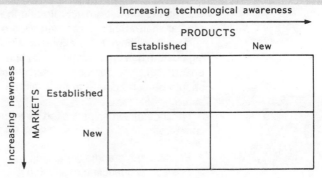

Figure 6.25 The Ansoff matrix

Task 2

Combining the information on the Ansoff matrix with that of your SWOT analysis, pick out those areas of business that offer the best prospects for your company. For each one, summarize your marketing objective for your longer-term planning horizon, i.e. 2, 3, 4 or 5 years. This must be quite explicit in terms of:

(a) The product/service
(b) The customer/market segment
(c) The volume of sales
(d) The market share

Now repeat the exercise, stating the specific objectives for the first year of your planning horizon.

The marketing objectives should be consistent with the information from the product life cycle analysis and portfolio matrix, completed in Chapter 5. Further guidance is provided in the notes which follow.

Guidelines for setting marketing objectives

Contained within your SWOT analysis will be key information gleaned from your marketing audit. You will know the reasons why customers want your products or services. You will know your best market segments. You will know the 'life' of your products or services and, probably most important of all, the portfolio matrix will have shown you how the various items of your range relate to each other in terms of raising funds.

Creative and intelligent interpretation of the portfolio matrix is the secret behind setting the right marketing objectives for your company. For this to happen, it is important to distinguish the essentially different characteristics of products or services falling into the four quadrants of the matrix. Let us take in turn:

Invest

Products or services in this quadrant are by implication aimed at those markets most attractive to your company. These will almost certainly be the markets with the higher growth rates.

Marketing objectives for such products should be calculated to match or exceed the market-growth rate and thereby hold or extend the company's market share. Since these markets are likely to be attractive to others, the company will have to be aggressive to achieve its objectives. This marketing posture has to be supported by tight budgeting and control processes to ensure that all resources are used effectively. Concern for present earnings should be subordinate to the main thrust of keeping or extending market share.

The increase in sales looked for in these products or services is likely to come from:

1 Possible geographic expansion
2 Possible product line expansion
3 Possible product line differentiation

These may be achieved by internal development, acquisition or joint ventures.

Sustain

In these less attractive markets it doesn't make sense to go for aggressive growth as with the invest quadrant – it would prove to be too costly and counter-productive. Instead, the objectives should be aimed at maintaining a profitable position with greater emphasis on present earnings.

The most successful products/services should be maintained, while less successful ones should be pruned. Marketing effort should be aimed at maintaining the market share of key market segments with minimum expenditure. Prices should be stabilized except when a temporary aggressive stance is required to maintain market share.

Sustain products must be managed to be the major source of funding for the company.

Selective

For products/services in this quadrant there are two broad choices:

1 Invest in the products for future earnings i.e. groom them to be tomorrow's invest products and subsequent sustain products; or
2 Manage them for present earnings.

In practice it is only feasible to 'groom' a limited number of question marks and so these have to be carefully chosen for their genuine potential. Investment across the range would be prohibitive.

Cash

In effect there are two kinds of product/service in this quadrant:

1 Genuine cash products (to the right of the quadrant)
2 Select products (to the left of the quadrant, adjacent to the sustain quadrant)

The marketing objectives for *genuine cash products* should be to divest where appropriate or to manage for present earnings. Marketing expenditure should be minimized, product lines pruned and prices stabilized or raised where possible, even at the expense of sales volume.

The marketing objectives for *select products* should acknowledge the low growth/attractiveness of these products and services, but still seek to identify and exploit growth segments, not by flying in the face of reason and trying to restore the product to its previous higher growth rate by costly advertising and promotion, but by emphasizing product quality and looking for improvements in productivity. Judicious marketing expenditure might be reasonable in special circumstances, but the emphasis should be on maximizing present earnings.

Exercise 6.7 Marketing strategies

Now that the marketing objectives have determined *what* the company must achieve, you have to decide how that might be done by your marketing strategy. Whereas there are only four types of marketing objective, there are a whole range of possible marketing strategies which can be used either singly or in combination with others. A choice of possible marketing strategies is shown in the list below.

Using this list, identify the broad marketing strategies most supportive to each of the marketing objectives you set for the company. Having done this, you will probably find it helpful to refer back to Figure 6.3. The left-hand column of this figure lists the marketing variables that need to be considered, such as pricing, distribution, etc. The other columns represent the key positions on the portfolio matrix and are headed accordingly. Thus it becomes a fairly straightforward procedure to identify the best marketing strategies for your chosen objectives.

Chapters 7–10 will provide you with additional information about advertising, sales promotion, selling, pricing and distribution. Only finalize your marketing strategies after completing these later sections of this book.

Possible marketing strategies
1 Change product performance.
2 Change quality or features of product.
3 Change advertising.
4 Change promotion.
5 Change pricing.
6 Change delivery arrangements.
7 Change distribution channels.
8 Change service levels.
9 Improve production efficiency.
10 Improve marketing efficiency.
11 Improve administrative procedures.
12 Change the degree of forward integration.
13 Change the degree of backward integration.

14 Rationalize product range.
15 Withdraw from selected markets.
16 Standardize design.
17 Specialize in certain products/markets.
18 Change sourcing.
19 Buy into new markets.
20 Acquire new/different facilities.
21
22
23
24

Add any other strategies that occur to you in the spaces provided.

7 The communication plan: 1 The advertising and sales promotion plans

Summary

Chapter 7 opens by discussing the difference between personal and impersonal communications and provides a method for deciding on the communications mix. It shows how to prepare the advertising plan, and discusses in some detail what advertising objectives are, and how to set them. There is a brief discussion of the role of the diffusion of innovation curve in advertising. The sales promotion plan is then introduced. There is a section on how it can be used, what different types there are, and its strategic role is discussed. Finally, there is a section on how to prepare a sales promotion plan.

Different forms of communication

Now that we have explored the important area of marketing objectives and strategies, let us turn our attention to the question of how we communicate with customers, both current and potential.

It is a fact that organizations communicate with their customers in a wide variety of ways, but it is still possible to distinguish the following two main categories:

1 *Impersonal communications*, e.g. advertising, point-of-sale displays, promotions, and public relations.
2 *Personal* (or direct person-to-person) *communications*, e.g. the face-to-face meeting between a salesperson and the customer.

So companies have at their disposal an armoury of communication techniques, which may be used either singly or in a combination (the 'communication mix') as the particular situation demands, to achieve maximum effect within given budget constraints.

Companies with acknowledged professionalism in the area of communicating with customers are continually experimenting with the mix of communicating techniques they employ in an attempt to become more cost-effective in this important, sometimes expensive, part of their business.

Deciding on the communications mix

A number of the possible means of communicating with customers will now be examined under the two broad headings given above. This chapter will look in more detail at advertising and sales promotion with the objective of deciding how to go about preparing detailed plans for these important elements of the marketing mix.

In Chapter 8, we will do the same for personal selling and the sales plan.

Advertising is a popular method of impersonal communications using such media as the press, television, radio, billboard posters, and so on. However, there are a number of problems which need to be carefully considered before any decision can be made about whether to spend any money on advertising at all, let alone *how* to spend it. For example, many people believe that advertising is a waste of money and that media expenditure would be better spent on personal selling.

So, the first question that has to be grappled with is the question of how to determine the communications mix. To help with this question, let us consider two separate surveys on how industry buys. These are shown in Tables 7.1 and 7.2.

Even a cursory glance at these will reveal the following information:

1 More than one person has an influence on what is bought.
2 Salespeople do not manage to see all the important 'influencers'.
3 Companies get the information on which they make their decisions from a variety of sources, only one of which is the salesperson.

Table 7.1 Buying influences by company size

Number of employees	Average number of buying influences	Average number of contacts made by salespeople
0–200	3.42	1.72
201–400	4.85	1.75
401–1000	5.81	1.90
1000+	6.50	1.65

Source: McGraw-Hill

Table 7.2 Sources of information

	% Small companies	Large companies
Trade and technical press	28	60
Salesperson – calls	47	19
Exhibitions	8	12
Direct mail	19	9

Source: Maclean Hunter

It can be seen, then, that the buying process, but in particular the *industrial* buying process, is complicated by the fact that it is not just one person who is involved. Industrial buying is a decision-making process which can involve a large number of people and which can take a considerable time. It is possible to split the decision-making process into several distinct steps, as follows:

1 The buyer organization recognizes it has a problem and works out a general solution. For example, the design team of a new plant, or piece of machinery, may decide that they need a specialist component which cannot be provided from within the company or from existing suppliers' stocks.
2 The characteristics and quantity of what is needed are worked out. This is the outline design process specifying performance and particular characteristics such as weight, size, operating conditions, and so on.

The buying process is complicated by the number of people involved and the amount of time taken.

3 A specification is then drawn up.
4 A search is made for possible sources of supply. This may merely involve a search of suppliers' catalogues to buy a component from stock, or a complete new product may have to be designed.
5 Potential suppliers will submit plans and products for evaluation.
6 After the necessary trials, suppliers are selected.
7 An order is placed and the product eventually delivered.
8 The goods supplied are checked against specification.

Not all these phases are followed in every buying decision. When something is being bought for a new project, all the phases would be followed.

Where it is a case of simply re-ordering something which has been bought before, the search and even tender processes may not be necessary. The newness of the decision to the buying organization also determines which types of people and how many are involved at each stage. Newness is a function of:

o The complexity of the product.
o The commercial uncertainty surrounding the outcome of the purchase.

The higher the 'newness' on both these dimensions, the more people are involved and the higher their status. If product complexity is high, but commercial uncertainty low, then the more important role is that of the design engineer and technologist. If newness is low on both dimensions, purchasing officers tend to dominate the process.

When faced with a new buy situation, the salesperson will be involved with a large number of people over a long period, helping, advising and informing, always trying to influence the decision process and to build up a growing commitment towards his product.

A typical example of this process at work can be seen in the following example of the purchase of a telecommunications system:

1 The Managing Director proposes to replace the company's telecommunications system.
2 Corporate purchasing and corporate telecommunications departments analyse the company's needs and recommend likely matches with potential selling organizations.
3 Corporate telecommunications department and data processing managers have an important say about which system and firm the company will deal with. Other company directors also have a key influence on this decision.
4 All employees who use the telecommunications equipment are 'consulted'.
5 The Director of Administration selects, with influence from others, the supplying company and the system.

It is important to identify the people with significant influence on the purchase decision and the specific benefits each influencer wants.

The reason for going into such detail about the industrial buying process is simply to illustrate that it is not possible to determine the precise role of advertising versus, say, personal selling, until a company fully understands how its potential customers buy and who are the important people that have to be contacted at the different stages in the buying process. For, clearly, financial and administrative people will be involved at a different stage from, say, the engineers, and they will also require different kinds of information. For example, price, performance characteristics, delivery, before and after sales service, reputation/reliability, guarantees, payment terms, and so on, are not relevant to all people at all stages in the buying process.

> The first point, then, is that a firm must understand the buying process of the markets to which it addresses itself.

There are many models for helping with this process, but essentially we should use a simple model which answers these questions:

1 Who are the people with a significant influence on the purchase decision?
2 What specific *benefits* does each important influencer want?

Figure 7.1 provides a logical approach to analysing an organization. As can be seen, it can be used equally effectively in either a product or service company. Having done this analysis for our major customers/potential customers, it should be comparatively easy to:

1 Group them in some way (segmentation).
2 Determine the most cost-effective way of communicating these benefits to each group.

Only then can some qualitative judgements be made about the relative cost-effectiveness of, say, advertising versus personal selling, neither of which, incidentally, will be mutually exclusive in anything but unusual circumstances. Table 7.3 lists some communication objectives.

Customer analysis form	Customer _____

Customer analysis form

Salesperson _____

Products _____

Customer _____

Address _____

_____ Telephone number _____

	Buy class	new buy	straight re-buy	modified re-buy

Date of analysis _____

Date of reviews _____

Member of decision-making unit (DMU)	Production	Sales and marketing	Research and development	Finance and accounts	Purchasing	Data processing	Other
Buy phase Name							
1 Recognizes need or problem and works out general solution							
2 Works out characteristics and quantity of what is needed							
3 Prepares detailed specification							
4 Searches for and locates potential sources of supply							
5 Analyses and evaluates tenders, plans, products							
6 Selects supplier							
7 Places order							
8 Checks and tests product							

Factors for consideration	1 Price	4 Back-up service	7 Guarantees and warranties
	2 Performance	5 Reliability of supplier	8 Payment terms, credit, or discount
	3 Availability	6 Other users' experience	9 Other, e.g. past purchases, prestige, image, etc.

Figure 7.1 Customer analysis form
Adapted from P. Robinson, C. W. Farris and G. Wind, *Industrial Buying and Creative Marketing*, Allyn and Bacon, 1967

Table 7.3 Some communication objectives

	To . . .	
Education and information	Create awareness	
	Inform	
	Get enquiries	These objectives
Branding and image building	Get company name in file	contribute
	Create company image	towards a total
	Reach personnel	marketing
	inaccessible to salespeople	programme, the
Affecting attitudes	Ease the selling task	objective of
	Get editorial	which is to
	Overcome prejudice	achieve
	Influence end-users	profitable
Loyalty and reminding	Reduce selling costs	sales
	Achieve sales	

We can now turn our attention specifically to advertising.

Preparing the advertising plan

For many years, people believed that advertising worked in a delightfully simple way, with the advertiser sending a message and the target receiving it and understanding it. Research, however, has

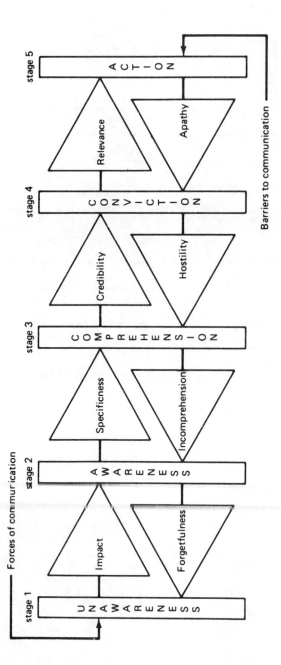

Figure 7.2 Brand loyalty ladder: the five stages of communication

shown that in a grossly over-communicated society, the process is more complex. Figure 7.2 gives some indication of the process involved.

Advertising, then, is not the straightforward activity that many people believe it to be. It is highly unlikely, for example, that any firm will be able simply to put out an advertisement and expect their sales to increase.

This brings us to perhaps the greatest misconception of all about advertising – that objectives for advertising for the purpose of measuring effectiveness should be set in terms of sales increases. Naturally, we hope that advertising will have an important influence on sales levels, but in most circumstances advertising is only one of a whole host of important determinants of sales levels (such as product quality, prices, customer service levels, the competence of the sales force, and so on).

Generally, then, it is absurd to set sales increases as a direct objective for advertising.

So, what objectives should be set for advertising? Well, we can start by agreeing that we need to *set* objectives for advertising, for the following reasons:

1 We need to set the budget for advertising.
2 We need to determine who our target audience is.
3 We need to determine the content of advertisements.
4 We need to decide on what media to use.
5 We need to decide on the frequency of advertising.
6 We need to decide how to measure the effectiveness of our advertising.

These decisions can be summarized as follows:

1 *Why* (objectives)
2 *Who* (target)
3 *What* (copy platform)
4 *Where* (media)
5 *How* (creative platform)
6 *When* (timing)
7 *How much* (budget)
8 *Schedule*
9 *Response*
10 *Evaluation*

The whole edifice, however, depends on the first of these.

Advertising objectives

Research has shown that many companies set objectives for advertising which advertising cannot achieve on its own. Apart from increasing sales, the 'annihilation of the enemy' and other such ridiculously unachievable objectives are set. For example, it is unreasonable to set as an objective 'to convince our target market that our product is best' if it is perfectly clear to the whole world that someone else's product is better. You cannot blame your advertising agency if this objective is not achieved!

> Another example of inadequate thought being given to advertising expenditure was the bus company who spent vast sums advertising the reliability of their bus service, while research showed the real reason sales were deteriorating was that many people thought buses were 'working class'. Again, this is a classic example of scoring a bulls-eye at the wrong target.

One more example should serve to prove the point.

> A machine tool company could not understand why, after an expensive advertising campaign in Germany in which they emphasized the extremely high quality and reliability of their products, they made little headway in the market. Subsequent market research showed that their target customers already believed this company had the best product. What they were concerned about, and why they were not buying, was their dissatisfaction over *delivery* and *customer service*. This is yet another example of advertising wasted because of ignorance about customer beliefs.

The first step, then, is to decide on reasonable objectives for advertising. The question which must be asked is: 'Is it possible to achieve the objective through advertising alone?' If the answer is *yes*, it is an objective for advertising. If the answer is *no*, it is not an objective for advertising. Advertising through media can do the following:

- Convey information
- Alter perceptions/attitudes
- Create desires
- Establish connections (e.g. powdered cream/coffee)
- Direct actions
- Provide reassurance
- Remind
- Give reasons for buying
- Demonstrate
- Generate enquiries

Setting reasonable, achievable objectives, then, is the first and most important step in the advertising plan. All the other steps in the process of putting together the advertising plan flow naturally from this and are summarized briefly below.

Who   . . . are the target audience(s)?
What do they already know, feel, believe about us and our product/service?
What do they know, feel, believe about the competition?
What sort of people are they? How do we describe/identify them?

What   . . . response do we wish to evoke from the target audience(s)?

. . . are these specific communications *objectives*?

. . . do we want to 'say', make them 'feel', 'believe', 'understand', 'know' about buying/using our product/service?

. . . are we offering?

. . . do we *not* want to convey?

. . . are the priorities of importance of our objectives?

. . . are the objectives which are *written* down and *agreed* by the Company and Advertising Agency?

How   . . . are our objectives to be embodied in an appealing form?
What is our creative strategy/platform?
What evidence do we have that this is acceptable and appropriate to our audience(s)?

Where   . . . is the most cost-effective place(s) to expose our communications (in cost terms *vis-à-vis* our audience)?
. . . is the most beneficial place(s) for our communications (in expected response terms *vis-à-vis* the 'quality' of the channels available)?

When   . . . are our communications to be displayed/conveyed to our audience?
What is the reasoning for our scheduling of advertisements/communications over time?
What constraints limit our freedom of choice?
Do we have to fit in with other promotional activity on our products/services supplied by our company?
other products/services supplied by our company?
competitors' products?
seasonal trends?
special events in the market?

Result   What results do we expect?
How would we measure results?
Do we intend to measure results and, if so, do we need to do anything *beforehand*?
If we cannot say how we would measure precise results, then maybe our *objectives* are not sufficiently specific or are not communications objectives?
How are we going to judge the relative success of our communications activities (good-bad-indifferent)?
Should we have action standards?

Budget   How much money do the intended activities need?
How much money is going to be made available?
How are we going to *control* expenditure?

Schedule   Who is to do what and when?
What is being spent on what, where and when?

The usual assumption is that advertising is deployed in an aggressive role and that all that changes over time is the creative content. But the role of advertising usually changes during the life cycle of a product.

> For example, the process of persuasion itself cannot usually start until there is some level of awareness about a product or service in the market place. Creating awareness is, therefore, usually one of the most important objectives early on in a life cycle.

If awareness has been created, interest in learning more will usually follow.

Attitude development now begins in earnest. This might also involve reinforcing an existing attitude, or even changing previously held attitudes, in order to clear the way for a new purchase. This role obviously tends to become more important later in the product life cycle, when competitive products are each trying to establish their own 'niche' in the market.

Diffusion of innovation

Also relevant to this is what is known as the 'diffusion of innovation curve', discussed in Chapter 5. To refresh our memories we will repeat the curve in Figure 7.3.

Research into any product's progress along the diffusion curve can be very useful, particularly for advertising and personal selling. For example, if we can develop a typology for opinion leaders, we can target our early advertising and sales effort specifically at them. Once the first 3 per cent of innovators have adopted our product, there is a good chance that the early adopters, or opinion leaders, will try it, and once the 8–10 per cent point is reached, the champagne can be opened, because there is a good chance that the rest will adopt our product.

We know, for example, that the *general* characteristics of opinion leaders are that they are: venturesome; socially integrated; cosmopolitan; socially mobile; and privileged. So we need to ask ourselves what are the *specific* characteristics of these customers in our particular industry. We can then tailor our advertising message specifically for them.

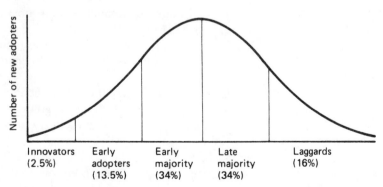

Figure 7.3

Finally, we should remind ourselves that advertising is not directed only at consumers. It can be directed at channels, shareholders, media, employees, suppliers and government, all of whom have an important influence on a firm's commercial success.

Sales promotion

> The term *advertising* (often referred to as 'above-the-line expenditure') can be defined as all non-personal communication in measured media. This includes television, cinema, radio, print, and outdoor media.

Sales promotion, for which the term 'below-the-line expenditure' is often used as a synonym, is not easily defined. For example, the Americans use the term to describe all forms of communication, including advertising and personal selling. In Britain some use the term to describe any non-face-to-face activity concerned with the promotion of sales; some use it to describe any non-media expenditure; while others use it specifically to mean in-store merchandising.

The fact is that none of these definitions is an accurate reflection of how sales promotion works in practice, which is why there is so much confusion about many aspects of this important area of marketing activity.

> In practice, sales promotion is a specific activity, which can be defined as the making of a featured offer to defined customers within a specific time limit.

In other words, to qualify as a sales promotion, someone must be offered something which is featured, rather than just being an aspect of trade. Furthermore, the offer must include benefits not inherent in the product or service, as opposed to the intangible benefits offered in advertising, such as adding value through appeals to imagery.

Seen this way, every other element of the marketing mix, including advertising, personal selling, point-of-sale material, pricing, after-sales service, and so on, can be used as part of a structured activity in order to achieve specified objectives.

Sales promotion in practice

> Sales promotion is essentially a problem-solving activity designed to get customers to behave more in line with the economic interests of the company.

Typical tasks for sales promotion are: slow stock movement; counteracting competitive activity; encouraging repeat purchase; securing marginal buyers; getting bills paid on time; inducing trial purchase; and so on.

From this, it will be seen that sales promotion is not necessarily concerned with volume increases. For example, it is often used to assist production and distribution scheduling by persuading customers to bring forward their peak buying from one period to another. To summarize, sales promotion seeks to influence:

Salespeople to sell
Customers to buy
Customers to sell } more, earlier, faster, etc.
Users to buy
Users to use

In recent years sales promotion activity has increased to such an extent that it now accounts for as much expenditure as above-the-line advertising.

> However, it is important to realize that, on its own, sales promotion will not replace selling, change long-term trends, or build long-term customer loyalty.

Nevertheless, while sales promotion is essentially a tactical device, it also has an important strategic role to play, as we shall see later.

Different kinds of sales promotion

The many and varied types of sales promotions are listed in Table 7.4. Each of these different types is appropriate for different circumstances and each has advantages and disadvantages. For example, with a promotion that consists of a free case bonus, it is possible to measure precisely both the cost of the extra cases and the additional volume resulting from the offer; it is fast and flexible; it is effective where the customer is profit conscious; it can be made to last as long as required; and it is simple to set up, administer and sell. On the other hand, it has no cumulative value to the customer, is unimaginative, and can often be seen as a prelude to a permanent price reduction.

Table 7.4   Types of sales promotions

Target market	Money Direct	Money Indirect	Goods Direct	Goods Indirect	Services Direct	Services Indirect
Consumer	Price reduction	Coupons Vouchers Money equivalent Competitions	Free goods Premium offers (e.g. 13 for 12) Free gifts Trade-in offers	Stamps Coupons Vouchers Money equivalent Competitions	Guarantees Group participation events Special exhibitions and displays	Cooperative advertising Stamps Coupons Vouchers for services Events admission Competitions
Trade	Dealer loaders Loyalty schemes Incentives Full-range buying	Extended credit Delayed invoicing Sale or return Coupons Vouchers Money equivalent	Free gifts Trial offers Trade-in offers	Coupons Vouchers Money equivalent Competitions	Guarantees Group participation events Free services Risk reduction schemes Training Special exhibitions Displays Demonstrations Reciprocal trading schemes	Stamps, coupons Vouchers for services Competitions

Table 7.4 *Continued*

| Target market | Type of promotion | | | | | |
| | Money | | Goods | | Services | |
	Direct	*Indirect*	*Direct*	*Indirect*	*Direct*	*Indirect*
Sales-force	Bonus Commission	Coupons Vouchers Points systems Money equivalent Competitions	Free gifts	Coupons Vouchers Points systems Money equivalent	Free services Group participation events	Coupons Vouchers Points systems for services Event admission Competitions

Points schemes are flexible, have wide appeal, do not involve the company in holding stocks of gifts, customers cannot easily value gifts, and they are easy to administer. On the other hand, they offer no advantages in bulk buying, are difficult to budget, and they lack the immediacy of dealer loaders.

Great care is necessary, therefore, in selecting a scheme appropriate to the objective sought.

The strategic role of sales promotion

Because sales promotion is essentially used as a tactical device, it often amounts to little more than a series of spasmodic gimmicks lacking in any coherence. Yet the same management that organizes sales promotion usually believes that advertising should conform to some overall strategy. Perhaps this is because advertising has always been based on a philosophy of building long-term brand franchise in a consistent manner, whereas the basic rationale of sales promotion is to help the company retain a tactical initiative.

Even so, there is no reason why there should not be a strategy for sales promotion, so that each promotion increases the effectiveness of the next.

In this way a bond between seller and buyer is built up, so that the tactical objectives are linked in with some overall plan, and so that there is generally a better application of resources.

That this is possible can be seen from the sales promotional campaigns involving the Home Pride Flour Graders, who first appeared in the early sixties, from the 20 million enamel brooches given out by Robertsons since the nineteen thirties, from Mighty Ajax, Miss Pears, the Ovaltines, and many other campaigns which have used schemes and devices which have been consistently incorporated into a product's promotional strategy.

More recent schemes, such as the Esso tiger, are proof that it is possible to establish a style of promotion which, if consistently applied, will help to establish the objectives of a product over a long period of time, which are flexible, and which have staying power.

Applying sales promotion to industrial products

Industrial goods are always sold to other organizations and this has the effect of changing the emphasis placed on certain elements of the marketing mix, rather than having any fundamental effect on the relevancy of the marketing concept.

It will not be surprising, then, to learn that, suitably adapted, most consumer goods sales promotional techniques can be applied to industrial goods.

Yet in spite of this, sales promotion is comparatively rare in industrial markets, perhaps partly from a belief born in the engineering discipline that if a firm has to promote its products, there must be something wrong with them.

In recent years, however, industrial goods companies have begun to take note of the enormous success of sales promotion campaigns and are becoming more aware of sales promotion as a flexible and competitive tool of marketing.

One industrial goods company with divisions spanning a range of products from fast-moving industrial goods to high-priced capital goods has developed a range of special promotional schemes which include the following: trade-in allowances; competitions; reciprocal trading schemes; credit arrangements; training schemes; desk-top give-aways; custom-built guarantees – all made as featured offers.

Preparing the sales promotion plan

There is widespread acknowledgement that sales promotion is one of the most mismanaged of all marketing functions. This is mainly because of the confusion about what sales promotion is, which often results in expenditures not being properly recorded. Some companies include it with advertising, others as part of sales force expenditure, others as a general marketing expense, others as a manufacturing expense (as in the case of extra product, or special labels, or packaging), while the loss of revenue from special price reductions is often not recorded at all.

Such failures can be extremely damaging because sales promotion is such an important part of marketing strategy. Also, with increasing global competition, troubled economic conditions, and growing pressures from channels, sales promotion is becoming more widespread and more acceptable.

Sales promotion is an important part of marketing strategy, but it is one of the most mismanaged of all marketing functions.

This means that companies can no longer afford not to set objectives, or to evaluate results after the event, or to fail to have some company guidelines. For example, a 1 ecu case allowance on a product with a contribution rate of 3 ecu per case has to increase sales by 50 per cent just to maintain the same level of contribution.

Failure at least to realize this, or to set alternative objectives for the promotion, can easily result in loss of control and a consequent reduction in profits.

In order to manage a company's sales promotion expenditure more effectively, there is one essential step that must be taken.

> First, an objective for sales promotion must be established in the same way that an objective is developed for advertising, pricing, or distribution.

The objectives for each promotion should be clearly stated, such as trial, repeat purchase, distribution, display, a shift in buying peaks combating competition, and so on. Thereafter, the following process should apply:

○ Select the appropriate technique
○ Pretest
○ Mount the promotion
○ Evaluate in depth

Spending must be analysed and categorized by type of activity (e.g. special packaging, special point-of-sale material, loss of revenue through price reductions, and so on).

> One company manufacturing self-assembly kitchens embarked on a heavy programme of sales promotion after a dramatic reduction in consumer demand. While they managed to maintain turnover, they were worried that their sales promotional activities had been carried out in such a haphazard and piecemeal fashion that they were unable to evaluate the cost-effectiveness of what they had done. They were also very concerned about its effect on company image and their long-term consumer franchise. So, the company made a concentrated study of this area of expenditure, which now represented over half their communication budget. Next time round they had: clear objectives; a clear promotional plan properly integrated into the marketing plan; an established means of assessment.

As for the sales promotional plan itself, the objectives, strategy and brief details of timing and costs should be included. It is important that too much detail should *not* appear in the sales promotional plan. Detailed promotional instructions will follow as the marketing plan unfurls. For example, the following checklist outlines the kind of detail that should eventually be circulated. However, only an outline of this should appear in the marketing plan itself.

Checklist for promotional instruction

Heading	Content
1 *Introduction*	Briefly summarize content – what? where? when?
2 *Objectives*	Marketing and promotional objectives for new product launch.
3 *Background*	Market data. Justification for technique. Other relevant matters.
4 *Promotional offer*	Detail the offer: special pricing structure; describe premium; etc. Be brief, precise and unambiguous.
5 *Eligibility*	Who? Where?

6 *Timing*	When is the offer available? Call, delivery or invoice dates?
7 *Date plan*	Assign dates and responsibilities for all aspects of plan prior to start date.
8 *Support*	Special advertising, point of sale, presenters, leaflets, etc., public relations, samples, etc.
9 *Administration*	Invoicing activity. Free goods invoice lines. Depot stocks. Premium (re)ordering procedure. Cash drawing procedures.
10 *Sales plan*	Targets. Incentives. Effect on routing. Briefing meetings. Telephone sales.
11 *Sales presentation*	Points to be covered in call.
12 *Sales reporting*	Procedure for collection of required data not otherwise available.
13 *Assessment*	How will the promotion be evaluated?

Appendices

Usually designed to be carried by salespeople as an aid to selling the promotion:

- Summary of presentation points
- Price structures/profit margins
- Summary of offer
- Schedules of qualifying orders
- Blank order forms for suggested orders
- Copies of leaflets

Also required by the salesforce may be:

- Samples of (new) product
- Demonstration specimen of premium item
- Special report froms
- Returns of cash/premiums etc. issued

Note: It is assumed that the broad principles of the promotion have already been agreed by the Sales Manager.

Application questions

1 How does your company determine its communications mix (i.e. the relative emphasis given to advertising, sales promotion and personal selling)?
2 Describe the buying process in one of your major customer groups. Who are the key influencers? Critically appraise your strategy for communicating with them.
3 Critically appraise your advertising objectives.
4 Using the checklist given in the text, critically appraise your advertising plan.
5 When you launch a new product/service, do you target your communications specifically at the opinion leaders? Do you know who they are? Can you describe them in terms that are relevant to advertising?

6 Critically evaluate your sales promotional plan.
7 How do you evaluate your sales promotional activities?

Review of Chapter 7

The communications mix

In order to achieve its marketing objectives, the company has to communicate with *existing* and *potential* customers. It can do this *directly*, face to face, generally using a salesforce, or *indirectly*, using advertising, promotion and point of sale displays. The choice of communications mix should be determined on the basis of what is going to be most cost-effective in terms of achieving objectives, i.e. whatever gets the best results per given cost. We will look at direct communication in the next chapter.

Advertising objectives

There are many possible advertising objectives:

o To convey information
o To alter perceptions
o To alter attitudes
o To create desires
o To establish connections, e.g. egg and bacon
o To direct actions
o To provide reassurance
o To remind
o To give reasons for buying
o To demonstrate
o To generate enquiries   *Try Exercises 7.1 and 7.2*

Acid test
Is it possible to achieve this objective by advertising alone?

No – rethink objective and/or the means of achieving it
Yes – go ahead

The advertising plan

The advertising plan has a number of questions to ask:

o Who is the target audience? What do we know about them? What sort of people are they? etc.
o What response do we want to achieve? What do we want to say, convey, make them feel, believe or understand, etc.?
o How are we going to proceed? What is our creative platform? Can we be sure this is appropriate?
o Where is the best place to put our communications? Will it be cost-effective? Does it generate the right image, etc?   *Try Exercise 7.3*
o When will our communications be displayed? Is this the best time? Does it mesh in with other activities, etc.?
o Result – what do we expect to achieve? How will we measure this? Does it mesh in with other activities, etc.?
o Budget – how much is needed? How much is going to be available? How will it be controlled, etc.?

○ Schedule – who is going to do what, where and when? What is being spent on what, where and when?   *Try Exercise 7.4*

Sales promotion objectives
Sales promotion seeks to influence:

○ salespeople to sell
○ customers to buy   more,
○ customers to use   earlier,
○ users to buy   faster,
○ users to use   etc.
○ distributors to stock

It is essentially a short-term tactic. In order to achieve these objectives the promotion can use:

Money   – price reductions, coupons, competitions, etc.
Goods   – free goods, e.g. two for the price of one, trade-ins, free trials, redeemable coupons, etc.
Services – guarantees, training, prizes for events, free services, etc.
                                                    Try Exercise 7.5

The sales promotion plan
The sales-promotion plan covers:

○ The objectives of the promotion
○ Background – why the method was chosen
○ Eligibility – who and where?
○ Timing – opening and closing dates
○ Support in terms of materials
○ Administration required
○ The sales plan – target, incentives
○ Sales presentation – points to cover
○ Monitoring procedure to collect data regarding progress, etc.
○ Assessment – how will it be evaluated?   *Try Exercise 7.6*

Questions raised for the company
1 Q: Who should design the advertising?
  A: There is no golden rule and options might be limited by the available budget. Most companies use outside agencies in order to achieve the required level of professionalism. Advertising objectives, however, should *always* be set by you and *not* by an advertising agency.
2 Q: It's been said that 'half the advertising budget is wasted; the problem is to know which half'. Is this true?
  A: It might be for some companies, but, by following the notes and exercises provided here, you should be able to avoid such a problem.
3 Q: Sales promotions aren't used in our business, so would they be a viable marketing tactic for us?
  A: If, by using a promotion, a company breaks new ground, it could give it a differential advantage over competitors.
4 Q: If a sales promotion is successful, should it be kept running?
  A: Once it has achieved its objectives, there seems little point in continuing. It can always be brought back later, and thereby retain its impact and 'freshness'.

Introduction to Chapter 7 exercises

These exercises look at the topics in the context of a 'communications mix'.

It starts with an examination of what advertising objectives are (Exercise 7.1).

It then goes on to look at how to set advertising objectives for one of your own product/market areas (Exercise 7.2), how to choose the most appropriate advertising media (Exercise 7.3) and how to build up an advertising plan (Exercise 7.4).

Sales promotion is tackled in a slightly different way. The first question that is asked is: 'Is a promotion necessary?' (Exercise 7.5). If the answer to this question is affirmative, then Exercise 7.6 demonstrates how to plan a sales promotion.

Exercise 7.1 What are advertising objectives?

There are two basic questions that advertising objectives should address. 'Who are the people we are trying to influence?' and 'What specific benefits or information are we trying to communicate to them?'

Research has shown that many companies set objectives for advertising which advertising cannot possibly achieve on its own. For example, 'to increase sales' or 'to wipe out the competition'. Equally, it is unrealistic to set for an objective 'to convince the target market that our product is best', when any rational analysis would clearly show this not to be true.

Often there is an element of confusion about what advertising objectives are and what marketing objectives are. Remember, marketing objectives are concerned with what products go to which markets, whereas advertising objectives are measurable targets concerned principally with changing attitudes and creating awareness.

Here is a list of marketing objectives and advertising objectives mixed up together. Read through this list and write against each objective:

A – if you believe it to be an advertising objective, or
M – if you believe it to be a marketing objective.

*Marketing (M) or advertising (A) objectives?**

1 To make attitudes more favourable to a particular product.
2 To build an image for the product.
3 To stop existing users turning to competitive products.
4 To get across the idea of a unique product.
5 To create a brand leader to help the launch of additional products at a future date.
6 To win back previous product users who have defected to a competitive product.
7 To expand the whole market.
8 To reduce existing negative attitudes.
9 To keep building loyalty.
10 To establish the brand and position it in a particular way, e.g. as warm and friendly.
11 To create a brand leader in a particular market.
12 To increase sales among existing users.
13 To improve the frequency of purchase.
14 To keep new entrants out of the market.

*Based on a list provided by Professor David Corkindale (formerly of Cranfield School of Management) and used with his kind permission

15 To convey the idea that the product is 'value for money'.
16 To say how much people like the product.
17 To improve market share compared with competitors.
18 To maintain brand distribution.

The answers to Exercise 7.1 are as follows:

Advertising objectives: numbers 1, 2, 4, 8, 9, 10, 15 and 16.
Marketing objectives: numbers 3, 5, 6, 7, 11, 12, 13, 14, 17 and 18.

If you made some mistakes in identifying the objectives correctly, go back and have another look at them and see if you can work out where you went wrong.

Exercise 7.2
Setting advertising objectives

Behind all effective advertising there lies a lot of careful thought and planning, and much of it goes into ensuring that the advertising objectives are the right ones. If these are wrong, everything else which follows is doomed to failure.

In this exercise you are asked to concentrate on just one key market or market segment. It should be a relatively simple matter to repeat the process for other markets at some later date.

Make a note somewhere about which market or segment you will be addressing. Remember, from the Boston matrix or directional policy matrix, 'stars' will probably be most deserving of the advertising budget.

Now make a note about the marketing objectives which have been set for this market/segment, e.g. what products? what quantities? to whom? etc. Having assembled this information, from the list of 'Possible advertising objectives' below:

1 Select the most appropriate objectives, i.e. those that look the most promising to help the company achieve these marketing objectives (tick in the column).
2 From those you have ticked, eliminate any objectives that you believe can *only* be achieved by personal communication, i.e. by the salesforce
3 List your remaining objectives in rank order, the most important being at the top of the list.
4 Use only the top objective (and perhaps the second) as a basis for your advertising campaign.

Possible advertising objectives

	Tick here		Tick here
o To establish an immediate sale		o To promote the idea of a unique product	
o To bring a prospect closer to a sale		o To back up promotions	
o To change customer perceptions		o To develop favourable attitudes to a particular product	
o To direct customer action		o To counter price competition	

o To support the salesforce	o To remind customers about our product
o To reinforce attitudes of existing customers	o To reinforce the company image
o To open up distribution	o To defend market position
o To improve company image	o To support the launch of a new product/service
o To demonstrate the product capabilities	o To explain new uses for product
o To generate enquiries	o To emphasize range and choice
o To impart information	o To reinforce brand recognition
o To reassure customers	o To inform about product availability
o To 'score points' off competitors' advertising	o To educate customers
o To enter new markets	o To communicate company strengths
o To give reasons for buying	o To build customer loyalty
o To create awareness	o To say how much people like the product
o To support retailers	
o To convey the idea of 'value for money'	
o To reach new geographical areas	

If you think this list omits possible advertising objectives for your company, then extend the list by adding your possibilities to it.

Exercise 7.3 Choosing the advertising media

The previous exercise should have helped to identify the advertising objectives for your chosen market/segment. The next logical step would be to decide exactly what you want to communicate – your creative platform.

However, such a step does not really lend itself to an exercise. Indeed, copywriting is such a specialized form of communication that most companies engage outside specialists to deal with it. Even so, having decided upon the advertising objectives, you must switch your focus of attention now to the target population you hope to influence:

o Who are they?
o What positions do they hold?
o What is their influence on the purchasing decision?
o What personality traits do they exhibit?
o What socioeconomic groupings do they belong to?
o What lifestyles do they have?
o How old are they? What sex are they? Are they married? and so on.

Please note that it is usually easier to determine the most appropriate media in the case of *industrial* customers, although the same logic applies.

You need to assemble as much information as you can about the target population. The more you know about them, the better your chances of selecting the best medium for your advertising platform.

The accompanying worksheet gives a list of possible advertising media. Study this list and select what would be the best choice, taking into account your objectives and the profile of the target audience.

In making your choice, you will need to take four factors into account:

1 *The character of the medium* – the geographical coverage it gives, the types of audience it reaches, its frequency of publication or showing, its physical possibilities (such as colour, sound, movement), its power or potential to reach special groups, etc.

2 *The atmosphere of the medium* – its ability to convey an image consistent with your objectives, e.g. hard and punchy, discreet, elegant, exclusive, etc.

3 *The 'size' of the medium* – the number of people exposed to the medium in terms of being aware of the contents. For example, a newspaper might be read by two or three members of a family, whereas a technical journal might be circulated to a large number of managers within a company. Alternatively, a poster might be passed by tens of thousands of people.

4 *The comparative cost* – how much will it cost to reach a specific audience. The cost per 1,000 viewers is often used as a comparative ratio.

There is space on the accompanying worksheet to make notes about these factors, should you be required to keep a record of what influenced your choice of medium.

Worksheet Advertising media (Exercise 7.3)

	Medium	Characteristics	Atmosphere	Size	Comparative cost
Printed media	Local newspapers National newspapers Trade and technical press Magazines and periodicals Direct mail Leaflets Directories (Yellow Pages, buyers' guides, etc.)				
Others	Television Posters (static) Transport (on trains, buses, vans, etc.) Cinema Radio Other (specify)				

Exercise 7.4 The advertising plan

Having decided what you want to communicate (your advertising objectives, Exercise 7.1), worked out the creative platform of the exact message you wish to convey, and decided on the choice of media (Exercise 7.2), you have assembled the key ingredients of an advertis- ing plan. What remains to be done is to establish when the advertising

will be used, who will be responsible for the various activities in bringing what is still an idea into life, how progress will be monitored and the criteria by which success will be judged.

The accompanying worksheet provides a simple format to record all this information. We would recommend that you try using it, and then adapt it to your particular purposes, so that you finish up with something that is genuinely tailor-made.

Worksheet   Advertising plan (Exercise 7.4)

ADVERTISING PLAN FOR _____ (either product or service/ market or segment)							
ADVERTISING OBJECTIVES TO _____							
Selected media	Brief description of advert	Timing	Responsibility	Budget	Actual cost	Criteria by which success will be judged	Evaluation comments

Note: Now complete advertising plans for other products/services and market segments.

**Exercise 7.5
Is a promotion
necessary?**

Sales promotions should be seen as the logical development of the company's marketing strategy. As such, they should be complementary to all other parts of the communications mix and should not be seen as an alternative, or some disconnected activity.

There are three key questions to be answered.

1   How do we decide whether or not to run a promotion?
2   What form should the promotion take?
3   How do we plan it?

The first two questions are addressed by this exercise. The planning element is covered in Exercise 7.6.

In order to give this exercise a clear focus, please select just one of the product/market areas of your portfolio and work with it. Once you have worked through this process, you will see how it can be used elsewhere, with other products/markets.

Step 1   On a separate piece of paper, write down the problems you see affecting sales of the product or service in the market/market segment you have chosen. If there are no problems, you might question why a sales promotion is being considered in this area. Your efforts might be better spent focusing on another part of your product/service range.

Step 2   Look at the problems you have listed and rank them in order of 'seriousness', 1 being the major problem, 2 the next, and so on.

Step 3   Transfer the information you have just assembled to column 1 of the accompanying Worksheet.

Step 4   Taking the major problem first, work across the page on the worksheet and consider the possible solutions to the problem listed there. You will note that there is space to add solutions of your own.

Clearly, a sales promotion is not always going to be the way to resolve a sales problem. However, the economics or convenience of one type of solution compared with another might well sway the argument. For example, the best solution to the sales problem might be to modify the product, but this might be very costly and take time to achieve. In such circumstances, a sales promotion might work in terms of both costs and immediacy.

Therefore, considered judgement has to be used in weighing up the costs and likely chances of success of each possible solution. *Only* when the sales-promotion option looks favourable should you take matters to the next stage of deciding upon the type of promotion

Step 5   If a sales promotion will not make any impact on the major sales problem, work across the page again for the next problem down. Continue this process for other sales problems until a sales promotion is found which would appear to hold the promise of success.

Ideally, the sales promotion should make impact on a fairly serious sales problem. If it is only going to affect a marginal issue, it raises questions about whether or not it is worth spending the time and effort on the promotion and whether another area might be more deserving of attention.

Worksheet   Deciding if sales promotion will help (Exercise 7.5)

PRODUCT/SERVICE/MARKET SEGMENT UNDER CONSIDERATION _____

Problems affecting sales	POSSIBLE SOLUTIONS													
	More advertising?		More sales effort?		Change price?		Change product?		Sales promotion?		Other ideas (add your own)			
	Cost	Likely success	Cost	Likely success	Cost	Likely success	Cost	Likely success	Cost	Likely success	Cost	Likely success	Cost	Likely success
1														
2														
3														
4														
5														

Major problem

Problems listed in reducing order

Having established that a sales promotion is a suitable way to have an impact on a particular sales problem you must now decide on the nature of the promotion.

In broad terms, a promotion can be aimed at three target groups:

1 Customers or consumers
2 Channels/intermediaries
3 Your own salesforce

The promotion can also take one of three forms:

1 It can involve money
2 It can involve goods
3 It can involve services

You will have to decide first of all which target group needs to be influenced most to make impact on your sales problem. You might even decide it is more than one group.

Having made that decision, you then have to work out what type of promotion will have maximum appeal to that group. Ideally, you will be able to devise something with maximum appeal, at a modest cost. However, when considering the cost element, you must remember that the promotional costs have to be weighed up against the benefits of reducing the specific sales problem.

Table 7.4 provides a number of ideas about sales promotions and enables you to select the most appropriate type for your purposes.

Exercise 7.6 Planning a sales promotion

It is important to ensure that any sales promotion is well coordinated in terms of what happens before, during and after the promotion. At different stages, different people might be participating and special resources might be required. Therefore a plan needs to be prepared in a simple way that most people can follow. In essence, this is all you need in a plan.

Heading	Content
Introduction	Briefly summarize the problem upon which the promotion is designed to make impact
Objectives	Show how the objectives of the promotion are consistent with the marketing objectives
Background	Provide the relevant data or justification for the promotion
Promotional offer	Briefly, but precisely, provide details of the offer
Eligibility	Who is eligible? Where?
Timing	When is the offer available?
Date plan	The dates and responsibilities for all elements of the promotion
Support	Special materials, samples, etc. that are required by the salesforce, retailers, etc.
Administration	Budgets, storage, invoicing, delivery, etc.
Sales plan	Briefing meetings, targets, incentives, etc.
Sales presentation	Points to be covered
Sales reporting	Any special information required
Assessment	How the promotion will be evaluated

Using these guidelines, and the accompanying worksheet, try to extend the information you assembled in Exercise 7.5 into a complete promotional plan.

Worksheet   Promotion plan (Exercise 7.6)

	Heading	Content
1	Introduction	
2	Objectives	

Worksheet Promotion plan (Exercise 7.6)	
3	Background
4	Promotional offer
5	Eligibility
6	Timing
7	Date plan
8	Support
9	Administration
10	Sales plan
11	Sales presentation
12	Sales reporting
13	Assessment

8 The communication plan: 2 The sales plan

Summary

Chapter 8 discusses the importance and role of personal selling in the marketing mix and goes on to outline a method for determining the correct number of salespeople required. Quantitative and qualitative sales force objectives are defined and a method for improving sales force productivity is given. Sales force management is briefly discussed. Finally, the reader is shown how to prepare the sales plan.

Introduction

Personal selling has an important strategic role to play in communicating between a company and its customers. To have a chance of success, management must be able to answer the following kinds of question:

○ How important is personal selling?
○ What is the role of personal selling in the marketing mix?
○ How many salespeople do we need?
○ What do we want them to do?
○ How should they be managed?

These and other questions will be considered in this chapter as important determinants of the sales plan.

How important is personal selling?

Most organizations had an organized sales force long before they introduced a formal marketing activity of the kind described throughout this text. In spite of this fact, sales force management has traditionally been a neglected area of marketing management.

There are several possible reasons. One is that not all marketing and product managers have had experience in a personal selling or sales management role; consequently, these managers often underestimate the importance of efficient personal selling.

Another reason for neglect of sales force management is that sales personnel themselves sometimes encourage an unhelpful distinction between sales and marketing by depicting themselves as 'the sharp end'. After all, isn't there something slightly daring about dealing with real live customers as opposed to sitting in an office surrounded by marketing surveys, charts and plans? Such reasoning is obviously misleading.

> Unless a good deal of careful marketing planning has taken place before the salesperson makes his or her effort to persuade the customer to place an order, the probability of a successful sale is much reduced.

The suggested distinction between marketing 'theory' and sales 'practice' is further invalidated when we consider that profitable sales depend not just on individual customers and individual products but on groups of customers (that is, market segments) and on the supportive relationship of products to each other (that is, a carefully planned product portfolio).

> Another factor to be taken into account in this context is the constant need for the organization to think in terms of where future sales will be coming from, rather than to concentrate solely on present products, customers and problems.

The author of this text has investigated many European sales forces over the last decade and has found an alarming lack of planning and professionalism. Salespeople frequently have little idea of which products and which groups of customers to concentrate on, have too little knowledge about competitive activity, do not plan presentations well, rarely talk to customers in terms of *benefits*, make too little effort to close the sale, and make many calls without any clear objectives. Even worse, marketing management is rarely aware that this important and expensive element of the marketing mix is not being managed effectively.

> The fact that many organizations have separate departments and directors for the marketing and sales activities increases the likelihood of such failures of communication.

Although its importance varies according to circumstances, in many businesses the sales force is the most important element in the marketing mix.

> In industrial goods companies, for example, it is not unusual to find very small amounts being spent on other forms of communication and very large sums being spent on the sales force in the form of salaries, cars and associated costs.

> Personal selling is also used widely in many service industries where customers are looking for very specific benefits. Insurance companies, for example, do use media advertising, but many rely

for most of their sales on personal selling. Customers for insurance policies almost invariably need to discuss which policy would best fit their particular needs and circumstances; it is the task of the salesperson to explain the choices available and to suggest the most appropriate policy.

Recent surveys show that more money is spent by companies on their sales forces than on advertising and sales promotion combined. Personal selling, then, is a vital and expensive element in the marketing mix.

The solution to the problem of poor sales force management can only be found in the recognition that personal selling is, indeed, a crucial part of the marketing process, but that it must be planned and considered as carefully as any other element. Indeed, it is an excellent idea for any manager responsible for marketing to go out into a territory for a few days each year and attempt to persuade customers to place orders. It is a good way of finding out what customers really think of the organization's marketing policies!

The role of personal selling

Personal selling can be seen most usefully as part of the *communications mix*. (Other common elements of the communications mix, it will be remembered, are advertising, sales promotion, public relations, direct mail, exhibitions, and so on.) The surveys set out in Chapter 7 shows that organizations cannot leave the communications task only to the sales force. The same question remains, however, as with advertising. This is how the organization is to define the role of personal selling in its communications mix. Again, the answer lies in a clear understanding of the buying process which operates in the company's markets.

The efficiency of any element of communication depends on achieving a match between information required and information given.

The efficiency of any element of communication depends on achieving a match between information required and information given. To achieve this match, the marketer must be aware of the different requirements of different people at different stages of the buying process. This approach highlights the importance of ensuring that the company's communications reach *all* key points in the buying chain. No company can afford to assume that the actual sale is the only important event.

In order to determine the precise role of personal selling in its communications mix, the company must identify the major influencers in each purchase decision and find out what information they are likely to need at different stages of the buying process.

Most institutional buying decisions consist of many separate phases, from the recognition of a problem through to performance evaluation and feedback on the product or service purchased. Furthermore, the importance of each of these phases varies according to whether the buying situation is a first-time purchase or a routine re-purchase. Clearly, the information needs will differ in each case. (This was discussed in some detail in Chapter 7.)

Personal selling has a number of advantages over other elements of the communications mix:

1 It is a two-way form of communication, giving the prospective purchaser the opportunity to ask questions of the salespeople about the product or service.
2 The sales message itself can be made more flexible and, therefore, can be more closely tailored to the needs of individual customers.
3 The salesperson can use in-depth product knowledge to relate his or her message to the perceived needs of the buyer and to deal with objections as they arise.
4 Most importantly, the salesperson can ask for an order and, perhaps, negotiate on price, delivery or special requirements.

Once an order has been obtained from a customer and there is a high probability of a re-buy occurring, the salesperson's task changes from persuasion to reinforcement. All communications at this stage should contribute to underlining the wisdom of the purchase. The salesperson may also take the opportunity to encourage consideration of other products or services in the company's range.

Clearly, in different markets, different weighting is given to the various forms of communication available. In the grocery business, for example, advertising and sales promotion are extremely important elements in the communications process. However, the food manufacturer must maintain an active sales force which keeps in close contact with the retail buyers. This retail contact ensures vigorous promotional activity in the chain. In the wholesale hardware business frequent and regular face-to-face contact with retail outlets through a sales force is the key determinant of success. In industries where there are few customers (such as capital goods and specialized process materials) an in-depth understanding of the customers' production processes has to be built up; here, again, personal contact is of paramount importance. In contrast, many fast-moving industrial goods are sold into fragmented markets for diverse uses; in this area, forms of communication other than personal selling take on added importance.

Many companies in the electronics business use personal selling to good advantage. Word processors, for example, vary enormously in the range of capabilities they offer. Technical details can be supplied in brochures and other promotional material, but the administrative staff likely to be taking the purchase decision often find it difficult to evaluate the alternatives. A good salesperson can ascertain quickly the requirements of a particular client and identify to what extent these will be fulfilled by their equipment. For their part, the customer can identify quickly whether the company understands their requirements, whether it appears credible, and whether or not it is able to provide the back-up service necessary to install the equipment and establish its use in the organization. Such considerations are likely to be far more influential than the comparison of technical data sheets in a decision to purchase.

Determining the requisite number of salespeople

The organization should begin its consideration of how many sales-people it needs by finding out exactly how work is allocated at present. Start by listing all the things the current sales force actually does. These might include opening new accounts; servicing existing accounts; demonstrating new products; taking repeat orders; and collecting debts. This listing should be followed by an investigation of alternative ways of carrying out these responsibilities. For example, telephone selling has been shown to be a perfectly accept-able alternative to personal visits, particularly in respect of repeat business. The sales force can thus be freed for missionary work, which is not so susceptible to the telephone approach. Can debts be collected by mail or by telephone? Can products be demonstrated at exhibitions or showrooms? It is only by asking these kinds of question that we can be certain we have not fallen into the common trap of committing the company to a decision and then seeking data and reasons to justify the decision. At this stage, the manager should concentrate on collecting relevant, quantified data and then use judgement and experience to help in making a decision.

Basically, all sales force activities can be categorized under three headings. A salesperson:

○ Makes calls
○ Travels
○ Performs administrative functions

These tasks constitute what can be called the *workload*. If we first decide what constitutes a reasonable workload for a salesperson, in hours per month, then we can begin to measure how long their current activities take, hence the exact extent of their current work-load.

This measurement can be performed either by some independent third party or, preferably, by the salespeople themselves. All they have to do for one simple method of measurement is to record distance travelled, time in and out of calls, and the outlet type. This data can then be analysed easily to indicate the average duration of a call by outlet type, the average distance travelled in a month, and the average speed according to the nature of the territory (that is, city, suburbs or country). With the aid of a map, existing customers can be allocated on a trial-and-error basis, together with the con-comitant time values for clerical activities and travel. In this way, equitable workloads can be calculated for the sales force, building in, if necessary, spare capacity for sometimes investigating potential new sales outlets.

This kind of analysis sometimes produces surprising results, as when the company's 'star' salesperson is found to have a smaller workload than the one with the worst results, who may be having to work much longer hours to achieve sales because of the nature of the territory.

There are, of course, other ways of measuring workloads. One major consumer goods company used its Work Study Department to measure sales force effectiveness. The results of this study are summarized in Table 8.1.

The table showed the company how a salesperson's time was spent and approximately how much of their time was actually available for selling. One immediate action taken by the company was to initiate a training programme which enabled more time to be spent on selling as a result of better planning. Another was to improve the quality of the sales performance while face-to-face with the customers.

Table 8.1 Breakdown of a salesperson's total daily activity

		Per cent of day		Minutes per day	
Outside call time	Drive to and from route	15.9		81	
	Drive on route	16.1		83	
	Walk	4.6		24	
	Rest and breaks	6.3		32	
	Pre-call administration	1.4		7	
	Post-call administration	5.3		27	
			49.6		254
Inside call time	Business talks	11.5		60	
	Sell	5.9		30	
	Chat	3.4		17	
	Receipts	1.2		6	
	Miscellaneous	1.1		6	
	Drink	1.7		8	
	Waiting	7.1		36	
			31.9		163
Evening work	Depot work	9.8		50	
	Entering pinks	3.9		20	
	Pre-plan route	4.8		25	
			18.5		95
			100.0		8 hr 32 min

Armed with this kind of quantitative data, it becomes easier to determine how many salespeople are needed and how territories can be equitably allocated.

Determining the role of salespeople

Whatever the method used to organize the salesperson's day, there is always comparatively little time available for selling. In these circumstances, it is vital that a company should know as precisely as possible what it wants its sales force to do. Sales force objectives can be either *quantitative* or *qualitative*.

Quantitative objectives

Principal quantitative objectives are concerned with the following measures:

O How much to sell (the value of unit sales volume)
O What to sell (the mix of product lines to sell)
O Where to sell (the markets and individual customers that will take the company towards its marketing objectives)
O Desired profit contribution (where relevant and where the company is organized to compute this)
O Selling costs (in compensation, expenses, supervision, and so on)

The first three types of objectives are derived directly from the marketing objectives, which are discussed in detail in Chapter 6, and constitute the principal components of the sales plan.

There are, of course, many other kinds of quantitative objectives which can be set for the sales force, including the following:

O Number of point-of-sale displays organized
O Number of letters written to prospects
O Number of telephone calls to prospects
O Number of reports turned or not turned in
O Number of trade meetings held
O Use of sales aids in presentations
O Number of service calls made
O Number of customer complaints
O Safety record
O Collections made
O Training meetings conducted
O Competitive activity reports
O General market condition reports

Salespeople may also be required to fulfil a co-ordinating role between a team of specialists and the client organization.

A company selling mining machinery, for example, employs a number of 'good general salespeople' who establish contacts and identify which ones are likely to lead to sales. Before entering into negotiations with any client organization, the company selling the machinery may feel that it needs to call in a team of highly specialized engineers and financial experts for consultation and advice. It is the task of the salesperson in this company to identify when specialist help is needed and to co-ordinate the people who become involved in the negotiation.

However, most objectives are subservient to the major objectives outlined above which are associated directly with what is sold and to whom.

Qualitative objectives   Qualitative objectives can be a potential source of problems if sales managers try to assess the performance of the sales force along dimensions which include abstract terms such as 'loyalty', 'enthusiasm', 'co-operation', and so on, since such terms are difficult to measure objectively. In seeking qualitative measurements of performance, managers often resort to highly subjective interpretations, which cause resentment and frustration among those being assessed.

However, managers can set and measure qualitative objectives which actually relate to the performance of the sales force on the job. It is possible, for example, to assess the skill with which a person applies their product knowledge on the job, or the skill with which they plan their work, or the skill with which they overcome objections during a sale interview. While still qualitative in nature, these measures relate to standards of performance understood and accepted by the sales force.

Given such standards, it is not too difficult for a competent field sales manager to identify deficiencies, to get agreement on them, to coach in skills and techniques, to build attitudes of professionalism, to show how to self-train, to determine which training requirements cannot be tackled in the field, and to evaluate improvements in performance and the effect of any past training.

> One consumer goods company with thirty field sales managers discovered that most of them were spending much of the day in their offices engaged in administrative work, most of it self-made. The company proceeded to take the offices away and insisted that the sales managers spend most of their time in the field training their salespeople. To assist them in this task, they trained them in how to appraise and improve salespeople's performance in the field. There was a dramatic increase in sales and, consequently, in the sales managers' own earnings. This rapidly overcame their resentment at losing their offices.

Improving sales force productivity

Many salespeople might secretly confess to a proclivity to call more frequently on those large customers who give them a friendly reception and less frequently on those who put business in their way.

If we classify customers according to their friendliness to us, as well as to their size, it is easy to see how a simple matrix can be developed to help us decide where our major effort should be directed. From Figure 8.1, it can be seen that the boxes which offer the greatest potential for increased sales productivity are Boxes 4 and 5, with Boxes 1 and 2 receiving a 'maintenance' call rate. Boxes 7 and 8 should receive an 'alternative strategy' approach to establish whether hostility can be overcome. If these alternative approaches fail, a lower call rate may be appropriate. Box 9 is the 'Don't bother' box, while Boxes 3 and 6 will receive the minimum attention consistent with our goals.

None of this is meant to indicate definitive rules about call frequencies, which will always remain a matter of management judgement. Its sole purpose is to question our assumptions about call frequencies on existing and potential accounts to check that we are not using valuable time which could be more productively used in other directions.

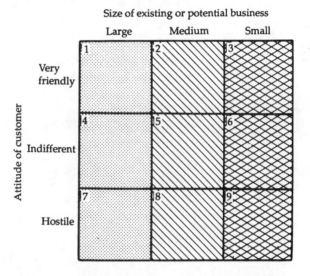

Figure 8.1

Managing the sales force

Sales force motivation has received a great deal of attention in recent times, largely as a result of the work done by psychologists in other fields of management. There is now widespread appreciation of the fact that it is not sufficient merely to give someone a title and an office and expect to get good results.

> Effective leadership, it is acknowledged, is as much 'follower-determined' as it is determined by management.

If performance is a function of incentives minus disincentives, then the more that incentives can be increased and disincentives reduced, the better will be performance.

While for the purposes of this discussion it is not necessary to enter into a detailed discussion of sales force motivation, it is worth mentioning briefly some important factors that contribute to effective sales force management.

If a sales manager's job is to improve the performance of the sales force, and if performance is a function of incentives minus disincentives, then the more that incentives can be increased and disincentives reduced, the better will be performance.

Research has shown that an important element of sales force motivation is a sense of doing a worthwhile job. In other words, desire for praise and recognition, the avoidance of boredom and monotony, the enhancement of self-image, freedom from fear and worry, and the desire to belong to something believed to be worthwhile, all contribute to enhanced performance. One well-known piece of research carried out in the USA examined the reasons for the results of the twenty highest producing sales units in one company compared with the twenty lowest producing sales units. The research showed all the above factors to be major determinants of success.

However, remuneration will always be a most important determinant of motivation. This does not necessarily mean paying the most money, although clearly unless there are significant financial motivations within a company, it is unlikely that people will stay. In drawing up a remuneration plan, which would normally include a basic salary plus some element for special effort, such as bonus or commission, the following objectives should be considered:

○ To attract and keep effective salespeople.
○ To remain competitive.
○ To reward salespeople in accordance with their individual performance.
○ To provide a guaranteed income plus an orderly individual growth rate.
○ To generate individual sales initiative.
○ To encourage teamwork.
○ To encourage the performance of essential non-selling tasks.
○ To ensure that management can fairly administer and adjust compensation levels as a means of achieving sales objectives.

A central concept of sales force motivation is that the individual salespeople will exert more effort if these are led to concentrate on:

1 Their expectations of accomplishing their sales objectives.
2 The personal benefits derived from accomplishing those objectives.

This theory of sales force motivation is known as the path-goal approach because it is based on the particular path the salesperson follows to a particular sales objective and the particular goals associated with successfully travelling down that path. The salesperson estimates the probability of success of travelling down various paths or sales approaches and estimates the probability that their superiors will recognize their goal accomplishments and will reward them accordingly.

> The motivational functions of the sales manager consist of increasing personal pay-offs to salespeople for work-goal attainment, making the path to these pay-offs easier to travel by clarifying it, reducing road blocks and pitfalls, and increasing the opportunities for personal satisfaction *en route*.

Few people would deny that sales force motivation is a difficult and highly emotive subject, and at the end of the day common sense must prevail. The writer once attended a sales conference which opened with girls dancing to the company song. They were followed immediately by a tawdry-looking marketing manager who spent an hour pointing to bar charts on an overhead projector. Not surprisingly, few of the salesmen present remembered much about the central issues of the conference, while the saleswomen present were offended.

Another common feature of sales conferences is the use of bellicose language, such as 'our plan is to wipe out the enemy . . .' and so on. The use of such imagery is often in sharp contrast to the day-to-day circumstances of the average salesperson, who gets up on a rainy Monday morning, gets into their small company car, and is rejected on their first call of the week!

> A bit of excitement at sales conferences is necessary, of course, but most sales directors and managers would be better occupied providing the sales force with information and tools designed to make the selling task easier.

Naked ladies jumping out of giant cans may well have a place somewhere, but not at sales conferences!

Preparing the sales plan

No two sales plans will contain precisely the same headings. However, some general guidelines can be given. Table 8.2 is an example of setting objectives for an individual salesperson. Clearly, these objectives will be the logical result of breaking down the marketing objectives into actual sales targets.

All companies set themselves overall objectives, which in turn imply the development of specific marketing objectives. In this chapter, we have discussed personal selling in the context of the overall marketing activity. This approach leads us to the following hierarchy of objectives: *corporate objectives – marketing objectives – sales objectives*, as outlined in Figure 8.2.

The benefits to sales force management of following this approach can be summarized as follows:

1 Co-ordination of corporate and marketing objectives with actual sales effort.
2 Establishment of a circular relationship between corporate objectives and customer wants.
3 Improvement of sales effectiveness through an understanding of the corporate and marketing implications of sales decisions.

> The following example illustrates the main point that a sales force cannot be managed in isolation from ' broad corporate and marketing objectives. The sales force of a company manufacturing stainless steel containers was selling almost any kind of container to almost anybody who could buy. This caused severe production planning and distribution problems throughout the business, down to the purchase of raw materials. Eventually, the company's

> profitability was seriously affected. The sales force was finally instructed to concentrate on certain kinds of products and on certain kinds of user industries. This decision eventually led to economies of scale throughout the whole organization.

Table 8.2 Objectives for the individual salesperson (based on the original work of Stephen P. Morse when at Urwick Orr and Partners)

Task	The standard	How to set the standard	How to measure performance	What to look for
1 To achieve his personal sales target	Sales target per period of time for individual groups and/or products	Analysis of ○ territory potential ○ individual customers' potential Discussion and agreement between salesperson and manager	Comparison of individual salesperson's product sales against targets	Significant shortfall between target and achievement over a meaningful period
2 To sell the required range and quantity to individual customers	Achievement of specified range and quantity of sales to a particular customer or group of customers within an agreed time period	Analysis of individual customer records of ○ potential ○ present sales Discussion and agreement between manager and salesperson	Scrutiny of ○ individual customer records ○ observation of selling in the field	Failure to achieve agreed objectives. Complacency with range of sales made to individual customers
3 To plan journeys and call frequencies to achieve minimum practicable selling cost	To achieve appropriate call frequency on individual customers. Number of live customer calls during a given time period	Analysis of individual customers' potential. Analysis of order/call ratios. Discussion and agreement between manager and salesperson	Scrutiny of individual customer records Analysis of order/call ratio. Examination of call reports	High ratio of calls to an individual customer relative to that customer's yield. Shortfall on agreed total number of calls made over an agreed time period
4 To acquire new customers	Number of prospect calls during time period. Selling new products to existing customers	Identify total number of potential and actual customers who could produce results. Identify opportunity areas for prospecting	Examination of ○ call reports ○ records of new accounts opened ○ ratio of existing to potential customers	Shortfall in number of prospect calls from agreed standard. Low ratio of existing to potential customers
5 To make a sales approach of the required quality	To exercise the necessary skills and techniques required to achieve the identified objective of each element of the sales approach. Continuous use of sales material	Standard to be agreed in discussion between manager and salesperson related to company standards laid down	Regular observations of field selling using a systematic analysis of performance in each stage of the sales approach	Failure to ○ identify objective of each stage of sales approach ○ specific areas of skill, weakness ○ use of support material

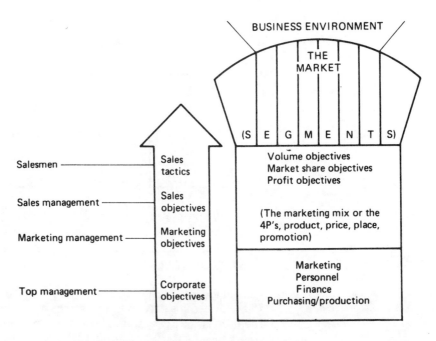

Figure 8.2

To summarize, the sales force is a vital but very expensive element of the marketing mix and as much care should be devoted to its management as to any other area of marketing management. This is most likely to be achieved if intuitive sense, which is associated with experience, can be combined with the kind of logical framework of thinking outlined here (see Figure 8.3).

Application questions

1 What are the key functions of salespeople in your organization? How is their work co-ordinated?

2 How is the sales force deployed: by geographical territory; by product range; by type of customer? Is this deployment optimal? What other patterns of deployment should be considered by your organization?

3 Who is responsible for the sales force in your organization? What is the relationship between this post of responsibility and other marketing responsibilities in the organization? Does this cause any problems? Where problems arise, how could they be solved?

4 Can you make a case to justify the present size and type of sales force used? Could you defend your position if you were requested to cut back the sales force by 30 per cent? How would you make your case? What do you believe would be the consequences of a 30 per cent cutback in the sales force?

5 How is your own organization's sales force used? Is this the best possible use of the sales force? In what ways do activities of the sales force complement other forms of marketing communications used? Identify any other ways in which you feel the activities of the sales force could enhance the total marketing communications effort.

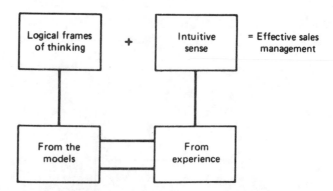

Figure 8.3

6 Critically appraise your company's sales plan. Does it flow naturally from the company's marketing objectives?

Review of Chapter 8

What is the role of personal selling?

This provides the face-to-face element of the communications mix. There are things it can achieve that advertising and promotion can't, e.g. sales people can be flexible in front of the customer and ask for an order. However, personal selling has to be seen in the context of the total communication mix. *Try Exercise 8.1*

How important is personal selling?

Traditionally, companies had salesforces long before marketing was in vogue. Companies still spend more on salesforces than on advertising and promotion combined. Though key parts of the marketing mix, sales departments often act independently of marketing. Thus, in achieving their short-term sales goals, they sometimes fail to achieve the mix of products and markets consistent with the longer-term strategic marketing objectives.

How many sales people should you have?

Basically salespeople have three activities. They:

○ Make calls
○ Travel
○ Administrate

Their workload should be analysed to establish how many calls it is possible to make in a typical working day. Equally, an assessment of existing and potential customers should be made and the annual total number of calls calculated (bear in mind different customer categories need different call rates).

Boxes 1 + 2 = maintenance call rate
Boxes 4 + 5 = increase effort
Boxes 3 + 6 = minimum attention
Boxes 7 + 8 = new strategy
Box 9   = don't bother

Number of salespeople equals:

$$\frac{\text{Annual total calls required}}{\text{Number of working days} \times Cs}$$

Size of business

Customer attitude		Large	Medium	Small
	Friendly	1	2	3
	Average	4	5	6
	Hostile	7	8	9

where Cs = all salespeople's calls per day.

What should they do?

Achieve objectives consistent with the marketing plan in terms of:

o How much to sell (volume)
o What to sell (mix)
o Where to sell (market segments)
o Allowable costs
o Profit margins

There can be many other types of sub- or enabling objectives, e.g.

o Number of telephone contacts
o Number of sales letters written
o Number of calls made
o Use of sales aids
o Number of reports submitted
o Safety record, etc.   *Try Exercise 8.2*

How are they managed?

To maximize performance, get the optimal balance between incentives and disincentives. Incentives are:

o Rewards consistent with performance
o Giving praise and recognition where it is due
o Minimal boredom and monotony
o Freedom from fear and worry
o Feeling of belonging
o Sense of doing a useful job

'There are no bad sales people, only bad sales managers.'

Try Exercise 8.3

Questions raised for the company

1 Q: Should sales or marketing be responsible for the sales plan?

   A: Marketing objectives should be agreed first. Then, if there is a separate salesforce, sales managers can devise a tactical plan to meet the objectives.

2 Q: Salespeople are sometimes described as notoriously reactive and optimistic. Can they be expected to conform to a sales plan?

   A: Salespeople such as the ones described here are perhaps the salespeople you don't need. The sales plan is designed to make best use of a scarce and expensive resource, a wholly admirable objective. It must not be undermined.

3 Q: Suppose the sales plan requires salespeople to play a different role. Can 'old dogs' be taught new tricks?

   A: Whenever change is introduced, there are often some casualties. However, with well-designed training and sensitive management the problem is not insurmountable.

Introduction to Chapter 8 exercises

While it is quite possible that some companies will not use advertising and sales promotion, very few fail to have some element of face-to-face selling in their marketing mix. Often the salesforce was in existence long before the company became concerned about marketing. This sometimes explains why, in many organizations, sales and marketing are regarded as two separate functions.

When the total cost of recruiting, managing and providing salespersons with all the necessary resources and support systems is taken into account, the salesforce is likely to be one of the most costly elements of the company's marketing activities. In order to obtain value for money, it will be important to plan how personal selling will be integrated into the 'communications mix', then organize the logistics to ensure that the right results are achieved.

Exercise 8.1 looks at how the role of the salesforce can be established.

Exercise 8.2 tackles the task of how to set quantifiable objectives for the salesforce.

Exercise 8.3 examines issues about managing the salesforce and, in particular, how to set the right motivational climate.

Exercise 8.1 The role of personal communication in the communications mix

Before attempting to produce a sales plan, we must spend a few minutes getting back to basics and examining exactly what information customers will require from the salesforce.

For different sorts of businesses, the role of the salesperson can be entirely different. In some they will just be order-takers, in others negotiators, in others demonstrators, and in others perhaps a composite of these and still other roles. Clearly, then, to claim that a salesperson 'just sells' is very much an oversimplification of the role, and sometimes can be downright misleading.

Taking your marketing objectives as the starting point, i.e. which products/services go to which markets or segments, select one of your key markets/segments as a study vehicle and focus on the customers. What sort of information do they require from your salesforce?

The next worksheet is designed to help you with this task. There are three steps to be tackled:

1 Establish the communication areas that need to be covered.
2 Because of the costs of having a salesforce, assess if there are less costly feasible alternatives to personal visits to achieve the same results.
3 List what these alternatives are, together with when and how they will be used.

Thus, on completion of the worksheet you will have a complete breakdown of the personal communications necessary to achieve the company's marketing objectives in your study market segment. In addition, you will have other information to show how personal visits can be 'backed up', using other methods of contact.

Worksheet   What information do customers want from sales representatives? (Exercise 8.1)

For study purposes, just consider *one* market segment. You can repeat the same procedure for the others afterwards.

Recognizing that the salesforce plays an important part in the company's communication mix, study the list below and then tick those activities 'demanded' by customers in column A. Now look carefully at the activities you have just ticked, and, taking each in turn, ask yourself if this information/communication could be provided in a more efficient way than by a sales visit. For example, knowing the customer usage of a particular product might make it possible to obtain repeat orders by telephone.

Wherever you see the possibility of an alternative approach, place a tick in column B and make a brief note about the alternative.

Customer info. requirement	A	B	Alternative provision of information
About:			
product range			
product performance			
price			
discounts			
special offers			
promotions			
placing order			
after-sales service			
running cost in use			
guarantees			
spares and accessories			
new developments			
competitor products/performance			
assistance with displays			
assistance with merchandising			
training for own staff			
technical services			
quality assurance			
proof that product/service works			
warehousing/storage			
reordering			
load sizes			
leasing agreement			
delivery arrangements			
franchise agreement			
answers to objections			

(Continued)

Customer info. requirement	A	B	Alternative provision of information
joint ventures demonstration of product long-term contracts financial arrangements Add any other information requirements that are pertinent to your business			

**Exercise 8.2
Quantifiable
objectives**

Having decided what role the salesforce is to play in the communications mix to service your chosen market segment, you can now get down to drawing up some quantifiable objectives. These stem quite logically from the marketing objectives and should cover three main areas:

1 How much to sell (value of unit sales volume)
2 What to sell (the mix of product lines)
3 Where to sell (the markets/segments that take the company towards its marketing objectives)

Please note that in Exercise 8.1, you have already chosen one component, 'where to sell', by selecting an important market or segment.

The sales plan is in effect the translation of these 'ball park' figures into individual targets for each sales representative, taking into account special factors such as their territory size, the size of customers within a particular territory, etc. Thus how much to sell breaks down into individual targets. The mix of the product lines becomes an individual target. Where to sell becomes a specific customer list.

In addition, there can be other quantifiable objectives, typical examples of which are given on the next Worksheet. Using this worksheet, you will be able to devise a set of targets appropriate for each of your sales representatives. The entries towards the end of the worksheet show how the basic targeting can be made somewhat more elaborate if it suits your company to make it so.

If you use one sheet per person, the total will become the sales plan for this particular market segment.

**Exercise 8.3
Managing the
salesforce**

Although some purists might claim this is an oversimplification, the key *management* activities are:

o Setting performance standards (both quantifiable and qualitative)
o Monitoring achievements against these standards
o Helping/training those who are falling behind
o Setting the right motivational climate

The word 'management' has been emphasized because many sales managers perceive themselves to be 'super' salespeople and continue to put most of their energies into selling rather than managing.

Worksheet   Individual sales targets (Exercise 8.2)

Market segment   . . . .

Salesperson   . . . .

Territory   . . . .

Period to which these
targets apply, e.g. year,
month, week, call cycle, etc. . . . .

Target	Number	Qualifying notes (assumptions, special local factors, etc.)
Unit sales volume		
Product A		
Product B		
Product C		
Product D		
Number of calls planned to be made		
Number of interviews to be secured		
Number of enquiries to be raised		
Number of quotations to be submitted		
Number of orders to be taken		
Call/interview ratio*		
Interview/enquiries ratio*		
Enquiries/quotations ratio*		
Quotations/order ratio*		
Cost per visit		
Calls per day planned		
Average length of call		
Average daily mileage		
Number of new accounts planned		
Number of letters to be written		
Number of reports to be written		
Number of point of sale displays to be organized		
Number of meetings to be held, e.g. with trade		
Number of service calls to be made		
Number of customer complaints		
Number of customer training sessions to be run		
Number of competitor activity reports to be submitted		
Number of general market condition reports to be submitted		
Add any others that are relevant to your type of business		

*based on past experience and future expectations.

Setting performance standards

Exercise 8.2 concentrated on the quantifiable standards – *what* has to be achieved. Equally important are the more subjective elements of *how* the tasks are achieved: the quality of the actions.

Some companies have quite deliberately set out to create a style to which salespeople are expected to conform. This can cover appearance (of person and his property), the layout of letters and reports, the way work is planned, the way customers are addressed and various other aspects of the work. You might have to give some consideration to this question of 'the way we do things around here'. But please note that in the examples given above, there is a standard to work against and performance is therefore measurable.

Place less emphasis on non-measurable factors, such as creativity, loyalty, interest, enthusiasm – relying on them too heavily is to plant the seeds of discord. Such subjective judgements can easily be misconstrued as favouritism by some and unfairness by others who have been 'scored' lower. Nonetheless, they can be relevant, so we have included a way of 'measuring' these elements in this exercise.

Monitoring performance

What salespeople are doing can be largely measured by reports, sales figures, internal memos and suchlike. *How* they do things can in most cases only be assessed by being with them and observing their actual performance.

Thus performance will have to be monitored at these two levels, and the frequency for doing so will depend upon the experience of the salesperson, the newness of the operation and the uncertainty of the situation. As a rule of thumb, the higher the uncertainty surrounding the salesperson, the territory, the product range, the customers etc., the more frequently should performance be monitored. The appraisal summary (Worksheet 1) provided will enable you to monitor and 'measure' all the relevant quantitative and qualitative elements of your salesforce.

Helping/training those whose performance is below par

By having measurable standards of performance, it becomes possible to be quite precise about the area and nature of help that salespeople need. After discussing the problem with them, you will be able to decide if it can be best solved by providing the salespeople with:

o More information (about products, prices etc.)
o More support (typing, more joint visits, etc.)
o More training (which generally means improving their skills)

Often training, which can be the most costly solution, is rushed into when other actions would serve the purpose more effectively.

Should training be required, much of it can be carried out on the job by a suitable skilled instructor, who would follow a process like this:

1 Instruction/demonstration by instructor.
2 Practice by the salesperson.
3 Feedback by the instructor.
4 Further practice with feedback until performance is acceptable.

Setting the right motivational climate

Perhaps little of the above will really work unless the motivation of the salesforce is right. While this subject could be the basis of a whole book

Worksheet 1 Individual appraisal summary (Exercise 8.3)

SALESPERSON _____

DIVISION _____

TERRITORY _____ YEAR _____

MANAGER _____

Note:
Score between 5 and 1, when 5 represents excellent and 1 represents poor.

Salesmanship	JAN	FEB	MAR	APR	MAY	JUN	JUL	AUG	SEP	OCT	NOV	DEC
Product knowledge												
Pre-planning												
Objectives												
Introduction												
Participation												
Handling objections												
Use of benefits												
Visual aids												
Third-party proof												
Investment merit												
Closing techniques												
Merchandising												
Range selling												
TOTAL												

Organisation	JAN	FEB	MAR	APR	MAY	JUN	JUL	AUG	SEP	OCT	NOV	DEC
Territory planning												
Use of time												
Reporting												
Records												
Sales statistics												
New account												
Follow-up												
Care of equipment												
TOTAL												

Attributes	JAN	FEB	MAR	APR	MAY	JUN	JUL	AUG	SEP	OCT	NOV	DEC
Enthusiasm and drive												
Training and self-development												
Appearance												
Punctuality												
Cooperation												
Customer relations												
TOTAL												
GRAND TOTAL												

by itself, it is possible to see a fairly straightforward way of cutting through much of the theoretical undergrowth.

By and large, if you can reduce those factors which tend to demotivate your staff and at the same time accentuate those which motivate them, then the motivational climate must improve. In saying this, it is important to recognize the difference between removing a demotivating factor and accentuating a motivating one. Removing a demotivating factor will not of itself bring about motivation. All it will do is to stop the moaning and groaning about the situation. In contrast to this, accentuating or adding to the motivating factors will undoubtedly lead to a higher commitment to the work.

Worksheet 2 enables you to establish exactly what these factors will be for your organization.

Worksheet 2   Motivational climate

Get your salespeople to consider the various things, incidents or situations, that have happened to them in their work over the last, say 6 months. (You can select the time period.) Then ask them to make brief notes under the headings shown on the form.

Those things I found *DISSATISFYING*	Those things which gave me *SATISFACTION*

Find ways to reduce or eliminate as many of these factors as possible.	Find ways to build on or add to these factors. These are the real *motivators*.

9 The pricing plan

Summary

Chapter 9 begins by cautioning against cost-plus pricing approaches. It discusses the pricing decision in the context of portfolio management, product life cycle analysis and product positioning. Costs are explored as an input for pricing policy, as is pricing for channels. There is a section on pricing for competitive advantage through value-in-use pricing. Finally, the reader is shown how to prepare a pricing plan.

Introduction

The first important point to be made about the pricing plan is that very rarely is there a pricing plan in a marketing plan!

The reason is not too hard to find. Promotion, in all its various forms, can be managed and measured as a discrete subset of the marketing mix. So too can distribution. But while the product itself, the price charged, service elements and communication strategies are all part of the 'offer' which is made to the customer, price itself is such an integral part of the offer that it is rarely separated out and put into a plan of its own.

> It is more common to find objectives for a certain group of products or for a particular group of customers, with a pricing strategy attached to it in whatever detail is necessary to indicate what the pricing policy is expected to do to help the company achieve its marketing objectives.

However, we have chosen to address the issue of pricing as a separate element of the marketing mix because this is the only sensible way that all the complex issues relating to pricing can be discussed. We shall, then, refer throughout to a pricing plan as if the intention were to write a separate pricing plan, although it will be structured in such a way that the elements of pricing can be integrated into the individual product/segment plans as appropriate.

The same could, of course, be said for each of the other elements of the marketing mix discussed in this book. How they are all integrated into a total plan is discussed in detail in Chapter 13.

Pricing and accountancy

Many people know the story told on pricing courses of the conversation between the restaurateur who decides to put a peanut rack on the end of his counter and his accountant expert. Essentially the plan is to sell peanuts for 10p a bag, the cost price being 6p.

Unfortunately, the accountant insists that the restaurateur must allocate a proportion of overheads into the peanut operation, including rent, heat, light, equipment, depreciation, decorating, salaries, the cook's wages, window washing, soap, and so on. These allocated costs, plus a rent for the vacant amount of counter space, amount to £1563 a year which, on the basis of a sales level of fifty bags of peanuts a week, amount to 60p per bag, so demonstrating that, at a selling price of 10p per bag the restaurateur would be losing 50 pence on every bag!

Many readers will appreciate the feelings of this imaginary restaurateur and will readily agree that nowhere in an organization are the seeds of potential strife more firmly sown than in the interface between accountants and marketing people, particularly when it comes to pricing issues. Often, however, both parties are equally to blame.

Accountants often fail to understand the essential role that marketing plays in an organization.

> Many accountants know quite a lot about business in general, but very little about marketing, and what little is known tends to be somewhat jaundiced.

One thing is certain. Any team comprising a financially alert marketer and a marketing-orientated accountant will make formidable opposition in the marketplace.

Somehow, marketing is seen as a less worthy activity than the act of producing goods for society. Marketing's more vocal activities, such as television advertising, are not seen in their total perspective, and it is not always easy to understand the complex decisions that have to be made about an activity that is concerned essentially with human behaviour rather than with things than can be conveniently counted. There is, alas, also the issue of marketers who are unprofessional in the way they manage the marketing function. The 1994 Cranfield/Chartered Institute of Marketing survey into the future of marketing was very critical of the lack of professional qualifications and skills in the marketing community. But the blame lies just as much on the side of marketers.

> For their part, those marketing people who fail to understand both the financial consequences of their decisions and the constraints of money on their decision-making have only themselves to blame for the inevitable internecine disputes that arise.

One area where it all bubbles to the surface is pricing. Our intention here is to explain pricing from a marketing point of view, while still recognizing the financial constraints and implications which accountants face. For, one thing is certain. Any team comprising a financially alert marketer and a marketing-orientated account-ant will make formidable opposition in any market. 'Demand exists only at a price', so price is an important determinant of how much of a certain product will sell, although it is obviously not the only factor involved. Given its importance, both as an element in the overall marketing mix, and as a major factor in determining profit-ability, it is somewhat surprising to find just how haphazard the pricing policy of so many companies is. More sophistication might be expected.

> The pricing decision is important for two main reasons: price not only affects the margin through its impact on revenue; it also affects the quantity sold through its influence on demand.

In short, price has an interactive effect on the other elements of the marketing mix, so it is essential that it is part of a conscious marketing scheme, with objectives which have been clearly defined.

Although in some areas of the economy pricing may be determined by forces which are largely outside the control of corporate decision-makers, prices in the market place are normally the result of decisions made by company managements. What should the decision be, however, when on the one hand the accountant wants to increase the price of a product in order to maximize profitability, while the marketer wants to hold or even reduce the net selling price in order to increase market share? The answer would appear to be simple. Get the calculator out and see which proposal results in the biggest 'profit'.

But, possibly, there are some nagging doubts about the delightful simplicity of this approach.

In order to introduce a structured consideration of such doubts, let us first quote in full the Boston Consulting Group on the issue of the almost defunct British motor cycle industry. 'The fundamental feature is its emphasis on model-by-model profits made. It is seen as essential that throughout the life cycle, each model, in each market where it is sold, should yield a margin of profit over the costs incurred in bringing it to the market. With this as the primary goal, a number of subsidiary policies follow:

1 Products should be up-rated or withdrawn whenever the accounting system shows they are unprofitable. Unfortunately, the accounting system will be based on existing methods of production and channels of distribution, not on cost levels that could be achieved under new systems and with different volumes.
2 Prices are set at levels necessary to achieve profitability and will be raised higher if possible.

3 The cost of an effective marketing system is only acceptable in markets where the British are already established and hence profitable. New markets will only be opened up to the extent that their development will not mean significant front end expense investment in establishing sales and distribution systems ahead of sales.
4 Plans and objectives are primarily orientated towards earning a profit on this existing business and facilities of the company, rather than on the development of a long-term position of strength in the industry.'

These are the policies that led to the British industry's low and falling share of world markets, to its progressive concentration on higher and higher displacement models. What is more, profitability, the central short-term objective to which these policies have been directed, has in fact deteriorated in the longer term to levels that now call into question the whole viability of the industry.

We now know, of course, that the British motor cycle industry is, to all intents and purposes, dead, and the above viewpoint of the Boston Consulting Group about pricing and profits must be seriously considered at least as a contributing factor. This view is echoed in the National Westminster Bank *Quarterly Review*, which stated: 'The disastrous commercial performance of the British motorcycle industry has resulted from failure to understand the strategic implications of the relationship between manufacturing volumes and the relative cost position.'

In contrast, the typical Japanese company makes dedicated efforts to increase its market share, and will often achieve this by cutting its prices, despite the possible short-term penalties of doing so. In other words there has tended to be a recognition of the pay-off in the longer term from the sacrifice of short-term profitability.

However, there remain some serious doubts even about this point of view. It is a well-known fact that manufacturers and retailers alike have begun to question the value of price cuts, especially when, against a background of falling profitability, research shows that the average shopper, far from having a precise knowledge of prices, has only a general understanding of and feeling towards value and price.

The idea of a price cut, of course, is to increase the quantity sold, as shown in Figure 9.1. The aim is for area B ($p_2 \times q_2$) to be bigger than area A ($p_1 \times q_1$). Additionally, increased volume should lead in theory to cost reductions through the experience effect (explained in Chapter 5). However, what often happens is that market sales do *not* increase enough to balance revenue and costs, with the result that profitability declines. The result is shown in Figure 9.2, area B being less than area A. It is expressed in another way in Figure 9.3.

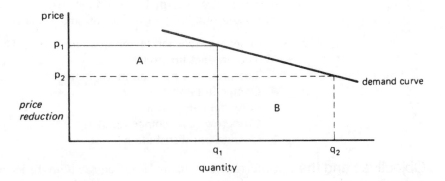

Figure 9.1

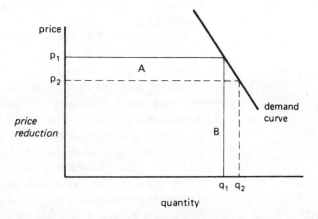

Figure 9.2

> This brings into focus the question of *time*, for the shape of demand curves changes over time, depending on a number of factors. There can be little merit in accepting profit reductions in the *long* as well as the *short* term.

It is appropriate, then, to begin to introduce those factors that should be taken into account when trying to resolve the question

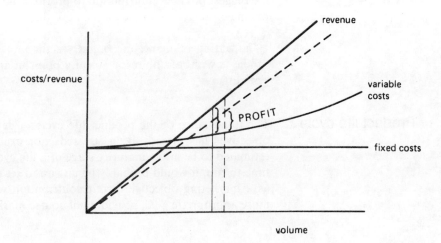

Figure 9.3

raised earlier of whether the objective for pricing should be to increase profitability or to increase market share. These factors are:

○ Objectives (corporate and marketing) and the product portfolio
○ The product life cycle
○ The product's position in the market
○ Competitors
○ Potential competitors
○ Costs (own and competitors)
○ Channels of distribution

Objectives and the product portfolio

Unfortunately, many arguments within firms about pricing take place in the sort of vacuum which is created when no one has bothered to specify the *objectives* to which pricing is supposed to be contributing.

We know now that it is important that a company should have a well-defined hierarchy of objectives to which all its activities and actions, including pricing, can be related. For example, corporate objectives may well dictate that the generation of short-term profits is a requirement. (This may well be due to a particular business unit's position in a matrix *vis-à-vis* other units in the same corporation. For example, a group decision may have been taken to invest heavily in one business unit's growth and to fund this growth from one of their 'cash cow' units elsewhere in their portfolio.)

The point is that in reality *corporate* objectives will have an important influence on *marketing* objectives, which were discussed in detail in Chapter 6. In the same way, a company's marketing objectives for a particular product may dictate a short-term emphasis on profitability rather than market share, and this will obviously influence the pricing strategy. This will be a function of that product's position *vis-à-vis* other products in the portfolio. For example, it may well be that a product is one of many 'question marks', and the company has chosen others, rather than this particular one, to invest in. This would naturally result in a wish to make the biggest possible contribution to profits from the product, and the pricing strategy would seek to achieve this.

> The setting of marketing objectives for any particular product, then, is without doubt the starting point in any consideration of pricing.

Product life cycle

The importance of the product life cycle in determining marketing objectives has already been stressed. For example, for a product estimated to be in the maturity stage of a life cycle, with only a short time to run, it would probably be unwise to set market share growth as a marketing objective. Profit contribution would probably be a more appropriate goal, providing of course market share did not slip to a point below which it would jeopardize the company's ability to introduce a new or replacement product.

The role of pricing will change over a product's life cycle.

On the other hand, if there is estimated to be plenty of life left in the product, it can often make a lot of sense to reduce the price in order to maintain market share.

It will be remembered that when the market reaches saturation level, we could well have a very profitable 'cash cow' on our hands for many years to come.

It is also important to stress that the role of pricing will change over a product's life cycle. For example, during the high growth phase in the product life cycle, price tends not to be the customer's primary consideration, since demand is growing at such a rapid rate and it is still relatively 'new'. Here there are plenty of profit opportunities, which have to be carefully balanced against market share considerations.

It is important, then, not to write one's pricing policy on 'tablets of stone'.

> During the 1980s, the policy of Woolworths of Australia was to enter a market later in the product's life cycle, to price very low, and to promote heavily. However, life cycle analysis indicated to the company that it unwittingly bought some products early in the life cycle, *to which they applied exactly the same pricing strategy*. They quickly realized that they were giving profits away unnecessarily and from then on began to be more thoughtful about pricing, devising pricing policies that were appropriate to the product's progress through the life cycle.

Product positioning

The meaning of the term 'product positioning' was explained in Chapter 4. For pricing, it is a highly relevant concept.

It is clearly foolish, for example, to position a product as a high-quality, exclusive item, and then to price it too low.

Price is one of the clearest signals a customer has of the value of the offer that a company is making him, and there has to be a sensible relationship between the two.

Three simple examples will suffice to illustrate this point.

> One company launched a new pure juice product on the market after tests had indicated an overwhelming acceptance by consumers. When sales fell far short of expectations, research indicated that consumers simply did not believe that the claims on the can about the product could be true at such a low price. So the company doubled the price and re-launched it, and it was a resounding success.

> Jaguar company launched a luxury car in the 1960s and priced it on their standard cost-plus basis. Customers were buying the car and re-selling it immediately at a much inflated price. In other words, the *value* of the car to the customer was much greater than the actual price charged.

> Likewise, some tertiary educational establishments claim their courses are the best in the world, then charge lower prices than their competitors. Research indicates that for directors and very senior managers in industry, a low price is more likely to be counter-productive because in this particular product field it is considered to be an indicator of quality.

Product positioning, then, is another major consideration in the pricing decision.

Competition and potential competition

In spite of product positioning, most products have competitors, and it goes without saying that these must be carefully considered.

It is true, of course, that what are referred to derisively as 'pimply little me-too products' cannot in most circumstances be expected to succeed if they are higher priced than competitive products. It is also true, in such circumstances, that if price is a principal determinant of demand, being higher priced is unlikely to be the right strategy.

This brings into sharp focus again the whole question of product positioning and market segmentation. It will be clear that, wherever possible, a company should be seeking to blend the ingredients of the marketing mix in such a way that their 'offer' to the customer cannot be compared directly with anyone else's 'offer'. For, if two offers *can* be directly compared, it is obvious that the one with the lowest price will win most of the time.

If two products are the same, it is obvious that the one with the lowest price will win most of the time.

Nonetheless, competitive products, in all their forms, clearly have to be taken into account in the pricing decision, as indeed do *potential* competitors.

Some firms launch new products at high prices to recover their investment costs, only to find that they have provided a price 'umbrella' to entice competitors, who then launch similar products at much lower prices, thus moving down the experience curve quicker, often taking the originating company's market away from them in the process. A lower launch price, with possibly a quicker rate of diffusion and hence a greater rate of experience, may make it more difficult for a potential competitor to enter the market profitably.

Costs

Another key factor for consideration is costs – not just our own costs, but those of our competitors as well. There are many cost concepts, and this is not the right medium to go into any detail. However, the two most common cost concepts are *marginal costing* and *full absorption costing*.

The conventional profit-maximizing model of economists tends to indicate that a price should be set at the point where marginal cost equals marginal revenue, i.e. where the additional cost of producing and marketing an additional unit is equivalent to the additional revenue earned from its sale. The theory is indisputable, but in practice this procedure is difficult, if not impossible, to apply. This is largely because the economists' model assumes that price is the only determinant of demand, whereas in reality this is not always so.

In practice, the costs of manufacturing (or provision of a service) provide the basis for most pricing decisions, i.e. a 'cost-plus' method. However, as the example given earlier indicates, the trouble with most such 'cost-oriented' pricing approaches is that they make little attempt to reconcile what the customer is prepared to pay with what it costs the company to be in business and make a fair return on its investment of resources.

An example of the 'cost-oriented' approach is when a company targets for a certain return on costs, i.e. the company will set itself a target level of profits at a certain projected level of sales volume. In fact, this type of approach uses a simple form of 'break-even' analysis as depicted in Figure 9.4.

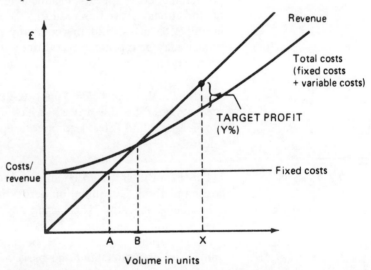

Figure 9.4

In the diagram, fixed costs are shown as a straight line and all other costs are allocated on a cost-per-unit basis to produce an ascending curve. At point A, revenue covers only fixed costs. At point B, all costs are covered and any additional sales will produce net profit. At point X, Y% target profit is being achieved. Obviously, the major problem with such an approach to pricing is that it tends to assume that at a given price a given number of products will be sold, whereas, in reality, the quantity sold is bound to be dependent to a certain extent on the price charged. Also, this model assumes a break-even *point*, whereas in most companies the best that can be said is that there is a break-even *area* at a given level of production.

It is however, quite useful for helping us to understand the relationship between different kinds of costs.

By far the most common way of setting price is to use the cost-plus approach, arriving at a price which yields margins commensurate with declared profit objectives.

When making a pricing decision, it is wise to consider a number of different costing options, for any one can be misleading on its own, particularly those that allocate fixed costs to all products in the portfolio. Often the basis of allocation is debatable, and an unthinking marketer may well accept the costs as given and easily make the wrong pricing decision.

For example, in difficult economic times, when cost savings are sought, unprofitable products are eliminated from the range. Unprofitable products are identified by the gross or net margins in the last complete trading year, and also by estimates of these margins against estimated future sales. However, because conventional cost accounting allocates the highest costs to high-volume products, they show lower margins, so sometimes these are sacrificed. But product elimination often saves only small amounts of direct costs, so the remaining products have to absorb higher costs, and the next profitability crisis appears. Product elimination also reduces the scale of operations, as well as reducing the product mix, so there is less incentive to invest and the company is less competitive. This approach may be repeated several times under successive management teams and sometimes leads to the demise of the company.

> In 1989, the *Financial Times* used the expression '*anorexia industrialosa*' for this process, which describes an excessive desire to be leaner and fitter, leading to total emaciation and eventually death!

This is not intended to be an attack on any kind of total average costing method. Our intention here is merely to advise caution and a broader perspective when using any kind of costing system as a basis for pricing decisions.

Finally, some account has to be taken of our competitors' costs and to try to understand the basis of their pricing policies. For, clearly, everything that has been said so far about pricing applies as much to them as it does to us.

Whatever your pricing problem, however, you will never go far wrong if you sit alongside your accountant and discuss all these issues.

Channels of distribution

Conventional pricing theory does not help much in determining one's policy towards distributor margins. The intermediaries which constitute a particular marketing channel perform a number of functions on behalf of the supplier which enables the exchange transaction between producer and consumer to be fulfilled. In return for their services, these intermediaries seek to be rewarded; this reward is in effect the 'margin' between the price of the goods ex the factory, and the price the consumer pays. However, the total channel margin may have to be shared between several intermediaries and still reach the consumer at a competitive price. Intermediaries, therefore, live or die on the economics of their respective operations. The ideal reward structure in the marketing channel is to ensure that an acceptable rate of return on investment is earned at each level; this situation is often not achieved because of the imbalances of bargaining power present.

There are a number of devices available for rewarding channel intermediaries, most of which take the form of discounts against a nominal price list. These are:

Trade discount	This is discount given against the price list for services made available by the intermediary, e.g. holding inventory, buying in bulk, redistribution, etc.
Quantity discount	A quantity discount is offered to inter-mediaries who order in large lots.
Promotional discount	This is the discount given to distributors to encourage them to share jointly in the promotion of the product(s) involved.
Cash discount	In order to encourage prompt payments of accounts, a cash discount of around $2\frac{1}{2}$ per cent for payment within 10 days is often offered.

In the situation where there is a dynamic marketing channel, there will be constant pressure upon suppliers to improve margins. Because of these pressures, the question of margins should be seen at a strategic as well as at a tactical level. This whole area of margin management can be viewed as a series of trade-off type decisions which determine how the total channel margin should be split. The concept of the total channel margin is simple. It is the difference between the level of price at which we wish to position our product

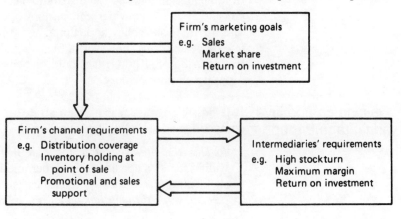

Figure 9.5

in the ultimate market place and the cost of our product at the factory gate. Who takes what proportion of this difference is what margin management is about. The problem is shown in Figure 9.5.

It will be seen that the firm's channel requirements will only be achieved if it either carries them out itself or if it goes some way towards meeting the requirements of an intermediary who can perform those functions on its behalf. The objective of the firm in this respect could therefore be expressed in terms of willingness to trade off margin in order to achieve its marketing goals. Such a trade-off need not lead to a loss of profitability; indeed as Figure 9.6 suggests, the margin is only one element in the determination of profitability, profitability being defined as the rate of return on net worth (net worth being share capital and capital reserves plus retained profits).

Figure 9.6

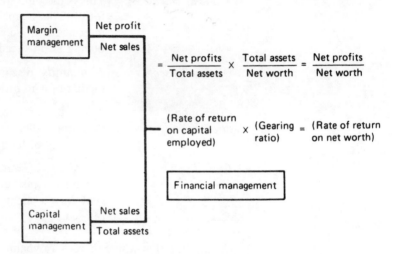

It can be seen that by improving the utilization of capital assets (capital management) as well as by using a higher gearing, it is possible to operate successfully on lower margins if this means that marketing goals can be achieved more effectively.

From the foregoing, it becomes apparent that the question of margins (both the margin retained by the firm and thus by implication the margin allowed the distributor) cannot be examined without consideration of the wider implications of overall marketing strategy and the financial policy and capital structure of the firm.

As a general rule, however, a firm should not give away its profits to a distributor. Rather, it should give away only the costs it saves by using an intermediary.

Gaining competitive advantage through value-in-use

It is possible to use pricing as a strategic marketing tool to gain a competitive advantage. The 'rules' can be listed as follows:

1 *Reduce the life-cycle/alter the cost mix* – customers are often willing to pay a considerably higher initial price for a product with significantly lower post-purchase costs.
2 *Expand value through functional re-design* – for example:

○ A product that increases the user's production capacity or throughput.
○ A product that enables the user to improve the quality of reliability of his end product.
○ A product that enhances end-use flexibility.
○ A product that adds functions or permits added applications.

3 *Expand incremental value by developing associated intangibles* – for example service, financing, 'prestige'.

Preparing the pricing plan

We have so far considered some of the main issues relevant to the pricing decision. We can now try to pull all of these issues together. However, let us first recapitulate on one of the basic findings which underpin the work of the Boston Consulting Group.

It will be recalled that, under certain circumstances, real costs reduce the accumulated experience. Figure 9.7 describes this effect. One of the implications of this is that unless a firm accumulates experience at the same or at a greater rate than the market as a whole, eventually its costs will become uncompetitive. Figure 9.8 illustrates this point.

There is a large range of pricing policies. However, many of these can be simplified into what is referred to either as a *skimming* policy

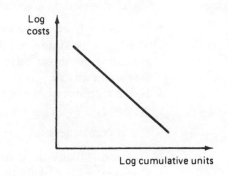

Figure 9.7

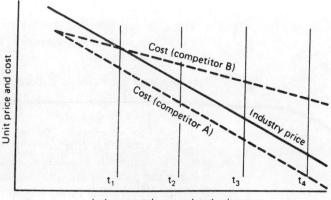

Figure 9.8   t = time period

305

or a *penetration* policy. It is easiest to consider these policies in the context of new product launches.

> Essentially, a skimming policy is a high initial price, moving down the experience curve at a slower rate, while a penetration policy is a low initial price, with a much faster rate of product adoption, hence a steeper experience curve.

Both policies are summarized in Figures 9.9a and b.

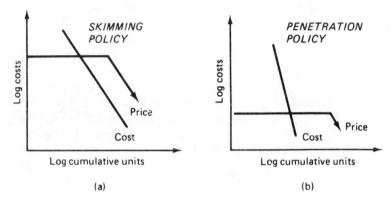

Figure 9.9

(a)   (b)

The circumstances favouring a skimming policy are:

1 Demand is likely to be price inelastic.
2 There are likely to be different price-market segments, thereby appealing to those buyers first who have a higher range of acceptable prices.
3 Little is known about the costs of producing and marketing the product.

The circumstances favouring a penetration policy are:

1 Demand is likely to be price elastic.
2 Competitors are likely to enter the market quickly.
3 There are no distinct and separate price market segments.
4 There is the possibility of large savings in production and marketing costs if a large sales volume can be generated (the experience factor).

However, great caution is necessary whatever the circumstances and, apart from these, all the other factors mentioned above should also be considered.

In conclusion, it must be emphasized that the price charged for the product affects and is affected by the other elements of the marketing mix. It is a common mistake to assume either that the lowest price will get the order, or that we can sell enough of our product at a cost-plus price to give us the required rate of return.

The reality is that pricing policy should be determined after account has been taken of all factors which impinge on the pricing

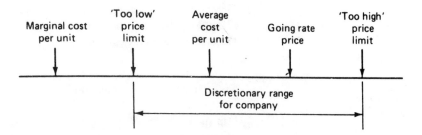

Pricing alternatives for a hypothetical company

Factors affecting price

Figure 9.10

decision. These are summarized in Figure 9.10. The first shows the discretionary pricing range for a company. The second shows those factors we should take account of in reaching a pricing decision.

Application questions

1 When you last introduced a new product or service, how was the price established?
Was the pricing decision correct?

What additional information could you have used to help you with the pricing decision?

What would you do differently given the same circumstances?

2 Describe your pricing strategy for one of your major products. How does it compare with that of your major competitors?

3 Describe how you deal with pricing

(a) in times of high inflation
(b) at each phase in the product life cycle

4 During the past ten years, what trends have occurred in margins in your industry? Are these trends acceptable? What policy has your organization got towards these trends?

5 Are trade margins justified? What is your policy towards trade margins?

Review of Chapter 9

Reasons for a pricing plan

Pricing is a key part of the marketing mix and needs to be managed intelligently, in the same way as the other parts. Generally, pricing is included as part of product/segment plans and doesn't appear as a separate entity. This can disguise some of the complex issues to be found in pricing.

Cost-plus pricing

Traditionally, pricing has been the remit of accountants. Their concern was mainly about the impact of price on margin and hence revenue. The weaknesses of this approach are:

1 Product can be overpriced because of arbitrary loading of production and other overheads.
2 There is no room for strategic thinking.
3 Products can be eliminated from the range, regardless of their synergy with others.

In contrast, marketers look at price in terms of its influence on demand.

Competitive pricing

The possible pricing spectrum is:

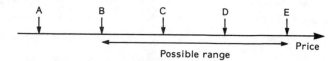

A = marginal cost per unit
B = lowest price limit in the market
C = average cost per unit
D = 'going rate' price in the market
E = top end price limit in the market

Try Exercise 9.1

Pricing and the product life cycle

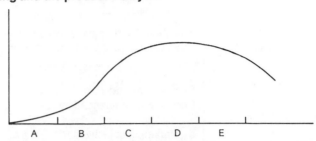

Different positions of the life cycle call for different pricing strategies.

A *Introduction*
   Either
   1 Price low to win high market share.
   2 Price high in recognition of novelty and prestige.
B *Growth*
   Price competitively to win market share.
C *Maturity*
   As per the growth phase.
D *Saturation*
   Stabilize price; consider raising it.
E *Decline*
   Raise price   *Try Exercise 9.2*

Product positioning

Pricing can influence the position of a product in the market, e.g. a high price can convey an image of better quality, design or exclusiveness. Here is one example of product positioning.

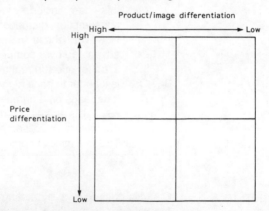

Better positioning beats the competition.

Channel discounts

If there are intermediaries, they have to be rewarded in return for their services, i.e. there has to be a total channel margin allowed for in 'price to customer' calculations. Discounts against nominal price lists can be in the form of:

1 Trade discounts
2 Quantity discounts

3 Promotional discounts
4 Cash discounts

How the total margin is sliced for distributors is a matter of 'trade-offs' of costs versus the added value of using distributors.

Try Exercise 9.3

Factors affecting price
Price can be influenced by:

o Marketing objectives
o The cost structure
o Legal constraints
o Consumer attitudes
o Competition (direct)
o Competition (substitutes)
o Company/product image
o Economic situation

Try Exercises 9.4 and 9.5

Questions raised for the company

1 Q: Is it possible to develop a sound pricing policy if one's costing is suspect?

A: While 'prices' and 'costs' are separate entities, it is essential that a company has an accurate costing system. Without this there is no point of reference to put pricing into perspective.

2 Q: What is the true price of a product?

A: Seen by the buyer it is purchase price and cost of introduction; this can include training costs, maintenance, energy consumption, disruption costs, consumables, floor space, etc. However, these items can be a source of differential advantage over competing products, which in effect provides a 'better price' in real money terms.

3 Q: Is it better to price high or low?

A: It depends on a number of factors, such as market share and so on. It is as well to remember, however, that if you try to have the lowest price, someone will usually try to go even lower. This is a difficult battle to win.

Introduction to Chapter 9 exercises

Clearly, pricing is a marketing 'tool' just as much as advertising, promotions and the use of the salesforce. Moreover, it is generally easier and quicker to change a price than it is to alter an advertising campaign, revamp a sales promotion, or to deploy the salesforce in a different manner.

Pricing decisions not only affect the revenue the company can earn, but also they influence demand, thereby making an impact on the quantities sold. Yet for all this, few companies have a pricing plan. Indeed, rather than a positive strategy, the very topic often becomes a battleground in a war of apparently conflicting interests between marketers and accountants.

Exercise 9.1 looks at how to set a competitive price for a product or service, taking into account a number of different factors which can have a bearing on the pricing decision.

Exercise 9.2 is concerned with selecting the price.

Exercise 9.3 provides some insights into the real impact of price discounts.

Exercise 9.4 is a self-scoring questionnaire which gives you some assessment about your readiness to get involved in aggressive pricing situations.

Exercise 9.5 poses a number of awkward questions about pricing and gives you an opportunity of testing out your expertise.

Exercise 9.1 Competitive pricing

This exercise will enable you to use pricing in a creative way, one which will support your marketing plan. It will use information from your marketing audit and a few new pieces of data to help you to arrive at a sensible Pricing Plan for your products or services.

It goes without saying that unless the company has an accurate costing system, one that realistically reflects its internal situation, then it will be impossible to establish anything like a sensible pricing policy. The reason for this will become self-evident as you provide the information requested below.

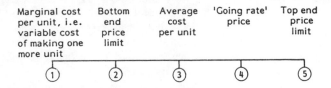

Figure 9.11

Figure 9.11 shows some key positions on the costing/pricing continuum.

Taking just *one* of your company's major products or services, enter on the worksheet the actual figures that correspond to the numbers 1 to 5, in the positions marked in Figure 9.11, i.e. the actual marginal cost, bottom end price limit, etc.

When considering the average cost please remember that costing systems that allocate fixed costs to all products in the range, while being popular, can produce some very misleading results, especially if the basis of cost allocation is somewhat arbitrary. Some products can never survive the cost load they have to carry. Knowing what the customer is prepared to pay for your chosen product/service (the going rate price), consider different costing options, with the objective of getting the average cost per unit as low as possible, thereby providing you with a wider range of pricing options.

Consider other products and services and repeat this process for them. The Worksheet is useful in order to establish the range of discretion open to you, but the more important task will be to identify where exactly on this scale to select your price position.

Worksheet Cost price continuum (Exercise 9.1)

PRODUCT/SERVICE	1 Marginal cost per unit	2 Bottom end price limit per unit	3 Av. cost per unit	4 Going rate price per unit	5 Top end price limit per unit
Example	£6.50	£8.50	£10	£13	£20

Exercise 9.2
Selecting the price

It can be shown that there are a number of factors that can influence your ultimate choice of price. These will be considered in turn.

Corporate objectives

If the corporate objectives dictate that it will be important to generate short-term profits for your chosen product/service, it would be reasonable to select a high price, somewhere between 4 and 5 on the scale established in Figure 9.11. Alternatively, if the aim is to extend market share, then a position between 3 and 4 would be more suitable.

You can see from this example that whatever the nature of the corporate or marketing objectives for your chosen product or service, it is possible to select a position somewhere on the scale which appears to be most appropriate. Now you select a position for your chosen product and record the price on the Worksheet where indicated.

Portfolio matrix

It has been shown that a different marketing strategy would be required according to which quadrant 'housed' your chosen product. Generally speaking, this would mean that prices should be selected as follows:

(a) *'Question mark'* – Price competitively to get market share.
(b) *'Star'* – Price to maintain/increase market share.
(c) *'Cash cow'* – Stabilize or even raise price.
(d) *'Dog'* – Raise price.

With these guidelines in mind, select a position on the 1–5 scale for your product/service and again record the price on the Worksheet.

Life cycle

Your chosen product's position on its life cycle will also be significant when calculating its price:

(a) Introduction stage. Either price low to capture market share, or if there is genuine novelty or innovation associated with the product, price high in recognition of its prestige value.
(b) Growth stage. Price low to get market share.
(c) Maturity. As for growth stage.
(d) Saturation. Stabilize price, consider raising it.
(e) Decline. Raise price.

Using these suggestions, select a position for your chosen product on the 1–5 scale and, again, note the price on the Worksheet.

Product position

Your price will have to take into account the marketing profile you are trying to establish for your chosen product. If yours is the biggest, the best, the most technologically advanced product, then your price ought to echo the fact. Similarly, if your target is just high-income customers, your price should reflect that exclusivity. The converse will be true for down-market economy models, where a lower price would be more consistent with the product position.

Carefully consider your product position and use your judgement to 'score' a position on the 1–5 scale. Record your choice of price on the Worksheet.

Current competition

Analyse the prices charged by your competitors for their versions of your product or service. Will these influence your ultimate choice of price?

Where does this information suggest you position the price on the 1–5 scale? Enter your answer on the Worksheet.

Potential competition

Another consideration you will have to take into account will be the extent to which your chosen price might either attract or repel competitors. Clearly, if you can get away with charging high prices and making correspondingly high margins, then it will not be long before others become interested in your sphere of business.

Estimate the price you can charge using the 1–5 scale as a reference. Note the selected price on the Worksheet.

Channels of distribution

If your business is one where you need to use intermediaries to reach your customers, then, in return for their services, they will expect a reward in the shape of a 'mark-up' or margin on the goods. Thus the price you charge at the factory gate has to be profitable for you, yet still allow the intermediary a fair margin without leading to an excessively high price for the ultimate consumer. What will this mean for your pricing decision?

Choose a position on the 1–5 scale and enter the price on the Worksheet.

Differential benefits

If your product or service provides differential customer benefits which your competitors do not provide, then you could justify a higher price and gain the reward from higher revenue.

Your option for doing this might be limited by some of the other considerations above. For example, it might be better to use your product advantage to gain a larger market share. Nevertheless, if the benefit analysis you carried out in Chapter 4 suggests any room for manoeuvre on pricing, score the new choice on the 1–5 scale and enter the actual figure on the worksheet.

Consumer attitudes

Consumer attitudes to your particular product/service or to your company, because of its name and reputation, might also influence your ultimate choice of price. To what extent will this be the case? Again select a price position on the 1–5 scale that you believe can be justified as a result of consumer attitudes to your product.

Record the price on the worksheet.

You have now looked at nine different factors that are known to influence pricing. These have been considered in isolation and a notional price position for your product has been calculated against each factor.

The price positions were established by using a cost/price continuum, with key positions numbered 1–5. The actual money value of each of these positions was calculated in the Worksheet of Exercise 9.1.

The Worksheet in this exercise is a record of the results you have attributed to the various pricing factors. You will now use this information in the following way:

1 Find the average price position for your product by adding up the column of prices and dividing it by the number of factors you used (an example is shown on the Worksheet). This average figure would seem to be the 'best fit' when taking all the factors into account, and should therefore be selected as the price for your chosen product, unless, of course, there are other factors known to you which would militate against this decision.

2 Now repeat this process for other products or services.

Worksheet Factors affecting price (Exercise 9.2)

	Example (based on example on preceding Worksheet)	Prod. 1	Prod. 2	Prod. 3	Prod. 4
1 Corporate objectives	£18.00				
2 Portfolio matrix	£16.00				
3 Life cycle analysis	£16.00				
4 Product position	£10.00				
5 Current competition	£12.00				
6 Potential competition	£10.00				
7 Channels of dist.	not applic.				
8 Differential benefits	£9.00				
9 Consumer attitudes	£9.00				
Total score	£100.00				
Number of factors	8				
Suggested price average	£12.50				

Critique of example provided on Worksheets

This approach to pricing raises many important issues. In the example provided it is quite evident that the corporate objectives are for the product to generate revenue. The positions on the portfolio matrix and life cycle also appear to support this strategy of pricing high.

But look at some of the other factors. The product position would not appear to justify a high price, there seem to be few differential benefits and consumer attitudes are not very positive. In addition it looks as if the company will have to price below the 'going rate' if it is going to cope with the competition.

Result – a compromise price of £12.50 per unit.
Moral – if the company wants to price high, it must upgrade the product in terms of providing more differential benefits and work to improve customer attitudes.

Alternatively, or in addition, it should carefully re-examine the actual costs and its costing system and by doing so try to improve the margin that would be achievable at £12.50. By these means, it might well obtain results similar to its original objectives of pricing high.

Personal notes

Exercise 9.3 The use of discounts

To give a price reduction, which is really what a discount is, appears on the surface to be a fairly straightforward and easy- to-apply mechanism for stimulating demand. However, it is not always fully appreciated how many extra products have to be sold merely to break even, i.e. to get back to the original situation.

Here is a simple example. Suppose a company had sales of 100 units of a product per week, priced at £10. Thus the total income was £1,000 and this yielded a profit of £200. The marketing director of the company decides that a 10 per cent reduction in price will stimulate a demand in sales. What new level of sales in units would have to be achieved to break even?

Write your answer here . . . .

Probably this was how you calculated your figure:

	Units	Price	Total income	Profit
Original situation	100	£10	£1,000	£200

Since 100 units yielded £200 profit, profit per unit = £2. With price reduced to £9 (10 per cent reduction) new profit per unit = £1.

	Units	Price	Total income	Profit
Therefore new situation becomes	200	£9	£1,800	£200

Thus the company would have to double its sale of units to maintain its existing profit level if it sold at the new lower price. Perhaps some questions would have to be asked about the feasibility of this happening.

To avoid having to make tedious calculations each time you contemplate making a price reduction, Table 9.1 provides an easy-to-use reference.

Table 9.1 Effects of price reductions

If you cut your price	And your present gross profit is							
	5%	10%	15%	20%	25%	30%	35%	40%
	You need to sell this much more to break even							
	%	%	%	%	%	%	%	%
1%	25.0	11.1	7.1	5.3	4.2	3.4	2.9	2.6
2%	66.6	25.0	15.4	11.1	8.7	7.1	6.1	5.3
3%	150.0	42.0	25.0	17.6	13.6	11.1	9.4	8.1
4%	400.0	66.6	36.4	25.0	19.0	15.4	12.9	11.1
5%	–	100.0	50.0	33.3	25.0	20.0	16.7	14.3
6%	–	150.0	66.7	42.9	31.6	25.0	20.7	17.6
7%	–	233.3	87.5	53.8	38.9	30.4	25.0	21.2
8%	–	400.0	114.3	66.7	47.1	36.4	29.6	25.0
9%	–	1,000.0	150.0	81.8	56.3	42.9	34.6	29.0
10%	–	–	200.0	100.0	66.7	50.0	40.0	33.3
11%	–	–	275.0	122.2	78.6	57.9	45.8	37.9
12%	–	–	400.0	150.0	92.3	66.7	52.2	42.9
13%	–	–	650.0	185.7	108.3	76.5	59.1	48.1
14%	–	–	1,400.0	233.3	127.3	87.5	66.7	53.8
15%	–	–	–	300.0	150.0	100.0	76.8	60.0
16%	–	–	–	400.0	177.8	1,144.3	84.2	66.7
17%	–	–	–	566.7	212.5	100.8	94.4	73.9
18%	–	–	–	900.0	257.1	150.0	105.9	81.8
19%	–	–	–	1,900.0	316.7	172.7	118.8	90.5
20%	–	–	–	–	400.0	200.0	133.3	100.0
21%	–	–	–	–	525.0	233.3	150.0	110.5
22%	–	–	–	–	733.3	275.0	169.2	122.2
23%	–	–	–	–	1,115.0	328.6	191.7	135.3
24%	–	–	–	–	2,400.0	400.0	218.2	150.0
25%	–	–	–	–	–	500.0	250.0	166.7

Example: Your present gross margin is 25 per cent and you cut your selling price by 10 per cent. Locate 10 per cent in the left-hand column. Now follow across to the column headed 25 per cent. You find you will need to sell 66.7 per cent *more* units.

Exercise 9.4 Questionnaire

This exercise* is really designed for personal insight, but you won't fail to notice that you could use it equally well to analyse your marketing director or chief executive.

Consider these statements and *quickly* tick the score which most aptly represents your position.

	Very true of me	Usually true of me	No feel-ing either way	Usually untrue of me	Very untrue of me
1 If a rival company is cheaper, I want to match or beat its price.	5	4	3	2	1
2 I would like to talk to competitors about equalizing prices.	1	2	3	4	5

*Note: Exercises 9.4 and 9.5 are based on John Winkler's work on pricing and I am indebted to him for the ideas. Readers are recommended to follow this up by reading *Pricing for Results* (Butterworth-Heinemann 1985).

	Very true of me	Usually true of me	No feeling either way	Usually untrue of me	Very untrue of me
3 I'm prepared to start a discount battle any time; I believe the first one in wins.	5	4	3	2	1
4 Before quoting a special price I will always ask 'Why?'	1	2	3	4	5
5 I'm prepared to lose some deals on price.	1	2	3	4	5
6 I always try to keep it simple if I can! '10 per cent off' is the way to do it.	5	4	3	2	1
7 I try not to publish discounts. I prefer to negotiate them individually.	1	2	3	4	5
8 I am always prepared to offer bigger discounts than I allow those working for me to offer.	5	4	3	2	1
9 I believe that most people will jump at a 10 per cent discount.	5	4	3	2	1
10 I believe that people who start savage price wars often live to regret it.	1	2	3	4	5

Now add up the total score for all your ticks and write it in the box on the right.

Scoring and interpretation of Exercise 9.4

The questions are not very subtle and so very good scores are required from this exercise. The lowest score for each question is the best, but an extremely low score, *of 12 or less*, might show you to be rather inflexible. You might well be used to working in an industry where the quality content of what you offer is very high, with prices that reflect this. In these circumstances you would tend to avoid price fights as much as you can.

A score of 13–16 is a good score – you will hold on and make sensible, profitable deals most of the time. Although you might lose out here and there on high volume, you would rather make the largest profits than the largest sales.

Above 25 – you are a potential warmonger, probably used to working at the bottom end of some very tough markets, with some rapacious buyers. There's one other thing, and you might not like to hear this. These buyers are probably taking you to the cleaners.

Exercise 9.5 Awkward questions on pricing

Here are some hypothetical questions concerning pricing. How would you deal with these situations?

Question 1
You are the Marketing Director of a pharmaceuticals company in a country where there is no equivalent of a National Health Service, and

patients have to pay for the drugs they use. Your company produces a life-support drug. Once patients have been treated with it, they must stay on it continuously to survive. This drug has been outdated by a machine which treats new patients and as a result, your market is gradually eroding.

Should you adopt:

(a) A system based on cost-plus?
(b) A system based on what the market will bear?
(c) A system based on some notion of morality?
(d) A system based on what the competition charges?

Question 2
You have an excess of stock of a poor line to clear. You must shift this stock in order to raise money to invest in better products. What is your view of promotional pricing? Do you:

(a) Actively encourage it all the time?
(b) Offer it only to your best customers?
(c) Refuse to use it at all?
(d) Use it sparingly, outside normal markets?
(e) Use it a little, but create an impression that you use it a lot, through advertising etc.?

Question 3
You want to price aggressively in order to take over a major part of a total market. What level of price discount should you offer in a normal consumer product market, as a minimum, to make the market turn to you in a meaningful way?

(a) 10 per cent off competitors' prices.
(b) 15 per cent off competitors' prices.
(c) 20 per cent off competitors' prices.
(d) 30 per cent off competitors' prices
(e) Between 40 and 50 per cent off competitors' prices.

Question 4
If you average out all the prices of consumer products in a given market, you can arrive at an average price. Yours is the biggest selling brand in this market. Together with your two nearest competitors you share 60 per cent of the market. Measured against the average market price, where would you expect your brand leader product to be positioned?

(a) 10 per cent less than the average price.
(b) On, or closely around, the average price.
(c) 20 per cent less than the average price.
(d) 7 per cent above the average price.

Answers to Exercise 9.5
Question 1
(a) Score +1.
(b) Score −5. They will pay anything to stay alive, but how can you live with yourself?

(c) Score +5.
(d) Score +1.

Question 2
(a) Score 0.
(b) Score +1. A poor tactic because it will make your best customers look for bargains all the time. It might generate some goodwill.
(c) Score +1. Too rigid.
(d) Score +5. Get rid of it altogether if you can, otherwise go for (*e*).
(e) Score +4. A technique used by some supermarkets. A few loss leaders in reality, but all of them promoted very heavily. But you will still be attracting price cutting in your market, and you will have to advertise your price cuts as well as give the discounts away. This can be expensive unless the volume sales justify it.

Question 3
(a) Score 0.
(b) Score +1.
(c) Score +2.
(d) Score +3.
(e) Score +4.

Question 4
(a) Score 0.
(b) Score +2.
(c) Score −2.
(d) Score +5.

Interpretation of scores
15 or more.   You did very well and/or are very experienced.
10–14.   Think a bit harder before making decisions.
Less than 10. Don't engage in pricing decision-making.

10 The distribution plan

Summary

Chapter 10 encourages readers to consider distribution in its widest sense as a critical aspect of marketing management rather than just 'physical distribution management'. It goes on to explore the various components of the distribution mix. Marketing channels are discussed and a method for their evaluation is provided. The essential components of customer service are listed and finally the reader is shown how to prepare a distribution plan.

Introduction

Some readers, alas, will not even bother to read this chapter, because distribution is perceived as outside the scope of marketing.

They would, in common with many businesses, tend to think only of physical distribution, or the transportation of goods, rather than of what distribution is really about. In this chapter, we show why distribution is very much the concern of marketers, and what should go into a distribution plan.

The topic of product distribution involves three main decision areas, each of which will be examined in turn:

1 How is the physical movement of our product organized?
2 Through what marketing channels do we reach our customers (or what channels do our customers utilize to acquire our products)?
3 What level of availability of our product does our customer require (and how well do we meet this requirement)?

Physical distribution

The physical distribution function of a firm provides the place and time dimensions which constitute the third element of the marketing mix. This is depicted in Figure 10.1, which also shows its relationship to the other utility-producing elements. The figures on the diagram are illustrative only, although they are realistic for some industries.

If a product is not available when and where the customer wants it, it will surely fail in the market.

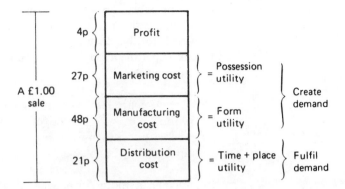

Figure 10.1

To achieve this value-adding function, firms generally have a distributive activity within the corporate organizational structure known variously as physical distribution management (PDM), traffic management, marketing logistics, or, simply, logistics. A generalized model of the entire corporate entity is given in Figure 10.2; this also depicts the position of (finished) product distribution *vis-à-vis* marketing, production, the procurement system, and the financial/accounting systems.

The movement of all materials, both prior to production (raw materials, sub-assemblies, etc.) and after production (finished product) constitutes the total logistics flow of the firm. In this chapter, however, we shall confine our attention to the latter, i.e. finished product distribution.

The distribution mix

In a typical manufacturing company with a formal distribution structure, the responsibility for distribution-related matters is spread across the other functional departments. For example, production

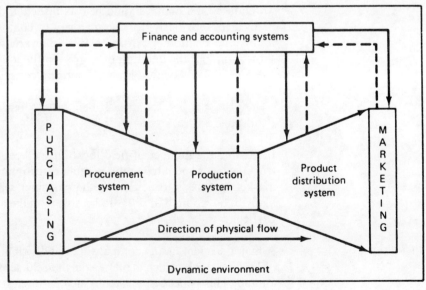

Figure 10.2   Key: ‒ ‒ ‒ ‒ Feedback

may control warehousing and transportation; marketing may control the channels through which the product moves, the levels of service provided to the customer, and inventory obsolescence; and the finance department may control communications, data processing, and inventory costs.

> Such a compartmentalized arrangement leads to each department working to its own objectives, attempting to optimize its own particular activity, oblivious of others or of the good of the whole company.

Introducing a more formalized distribution arrangement into the corporate organizational structure, although not completely eliminating interdepartmental friction, does at least ensure that all distribution-related activities are organized under a more centralized control, thereby gaining focus.

This, then, is the basis of the total distribution concept, because it now becomes possible to seek out potential 'trade-offs', i.e. consciously to incur costs in one area in order to achieve an even larger benefit in another. For example, should a series of field warehouses be maintained, or would one suffice, supplemented by an improved trucking operation? Of course, these types of potential 'trade-off' situations place a heavy burden on the cost-reporting systems of a company.

The professional distribution manager, therefore, has several variables to contend with in the search for trade-offs; taken together these constitute the *distribution mix*. Each of these will now be examined briefly.

Facilities

Decisions in this area are concerned with the problem of how many warehouses and plants should be established and where they should be located. Obviously, for the majority of companies it is necessary to take the location of existing plants and warehouses as given in the short term, but the question does arise in the longer term or, indeed, when new plants or warehouses are being considered.

> The principal marketing task here is to forecast the nature, size and geographical spread of demand.

Increasing the number of field locations will result in an increase in trucking costs and a reduction in retail distribution costs. So, another marketing task is to determine the customer service levels that are likely to be required in order to be able to make a decision about this particular trade-off.

Inventory

A major element in any company's total distribution costs is the cost of holding stock, which is often as high as 30 per cent of its value per annum. This is because of items such as interest charges, deterioration, shrinkage, insurance, administration, and so on. Thus, decisions about how much inventory to hold, where to hold it, in what quantities to order, and so on, are vital issues. Inventory levels are also instrumental in determining the level of service that the company offers the customer.

Transport

The important aspects of the transport decision concern such issues as what mode of transport should be used, whether to own vehicles or lease them, how to schedule deliveries, how often to deliver, and so on. Perhaps of the five distribution variables, it is transport that receives the greatest attention within the firm. It is certainly one of the more obvious facets of the distribution task.

Communications

It must always be remembered that distribution not only involves the flow of materials through the distribution channel, but also the flow of information. Here, we are talking about the order processing system, the invoicing system, the demand forecasting system, and so on. Without effective communications support, the distribution system will never be capable of providing satisfactory customer service at an acceptable cost. It is vital that it should be recognized that inefficiency here can lead to a build-up of costs in other areas of the business, such as, for example, in emergency deliveries, as well as a permanent loss of sales through customers turning to alternative sources of supply.

Unitization

The way in which goods are packaged and then subsequently accumulated into larger unit sizes (e.g. a pallet-load) can have a major bearing upon distribution economics. For example, the ability to stack goods on a pallet which then becomes the unit load for movement and storage can lead to considerable cost savings in terms of handling and warehousing. Similarly, the use of containers as the basic unit of movement has revolutionized international transport and, to a certain extent, domestic transport as well. Mobile racking systems and front-end pricing by means of scanners are other unitization innovations that have had a dramatic effect upon the way goods are marketed.

Together, these five areas constitute the total cost of distribution within a company.

Marketing channels

The fundamental role of a company's distribution function is to ensure that the 'right product is available at the right time'.

This implies some organization of resources into channels through which the product moves to customers. A marketing channel may therefore be considered as the course taken in the transfer of the title of a commodity (which in turn may be either a product or service) from its original source of supply to its ultimate consumption.

It is necessary to consider both the route of exchange (and its administrative and financial control), and the physical movement route of the product – they may well be different.

Many companies use multiple marketing channels through which to reach their customers, often involving one or even several 'intermediaries'. The role of an intermediary is to provide the means of achieving the widest possible market coverage at a lower unit cost. Many intermediaries hold stock and thereby share some of the financial risk with the principal (or supplier). Figure 10.3 shows that using an intermediary carries benefits for the manufacturer, but it also involves significant 'costs', the most important of which is the loss of control which accompanies such a channel strategy.

Often, too, considerable conflict exists between the respective objectives of suppliers and their distributors; this gives rise to conflict and suspicion in the relationship. Nevertheless, suppliers must evaluate the costs and benefits of each marketing channel potentially open to them and decide on a combination which best suits their type of business and the markets they are engaged in. The alternatives depicted in Figure 10.4 quite obviously have different cost/revenue profiles.

Any cost/benefit appraisal needs to be undertaken in the widest context possible. It needs to consider questions of market strategy,

THE DISTRIBUTION CHANNEL

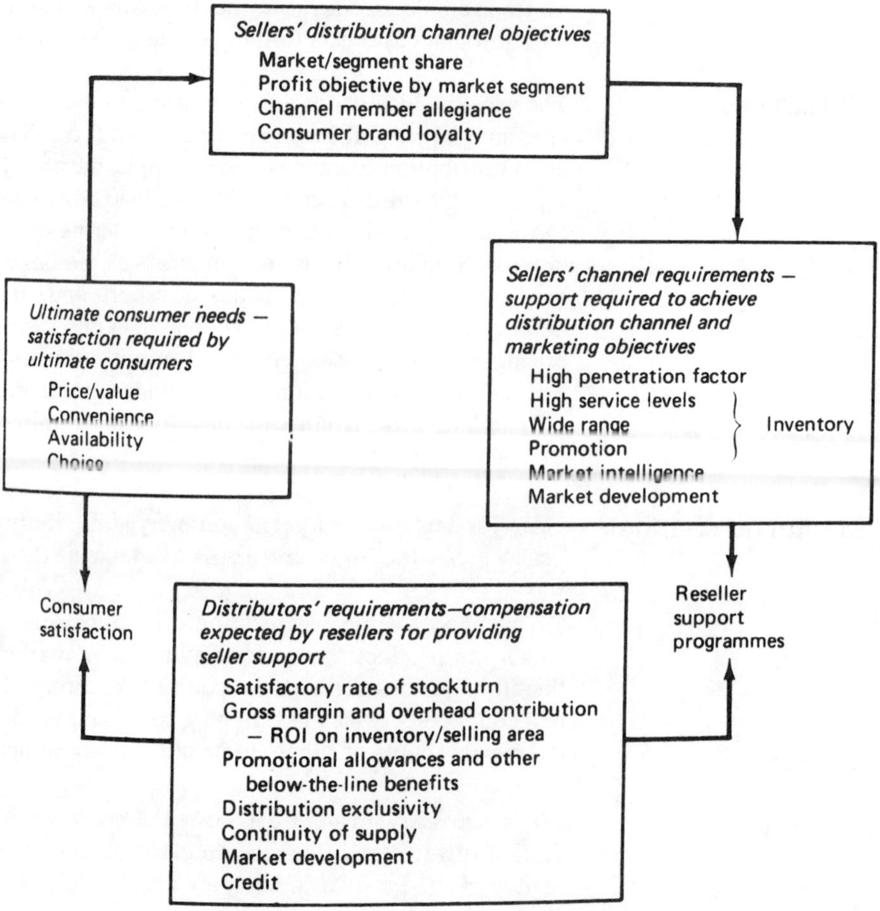

Figure 10.3

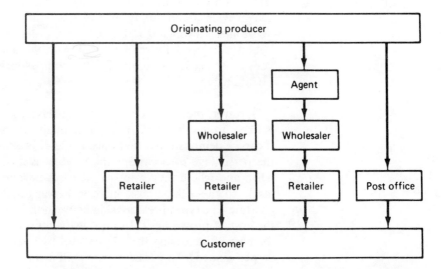

Figure 10.4

the appropriateness of the channel to the product, and customer requirements, as well as the question of the comparative costs of selling and distribution.

> Marketing channel decisions are, therefore, key decisions which involve the choice of an intermediary (or intermediaries) and detailed consideration of the physical distribution implications of all the alternatives. The evelution of intermediaries is, therefore, of significant importance.

Evaluation criteria for channel intermediaries

Regardless of the type of intermediary to be used, there are a number of basic evaluation criteria, for example:

- Do they now, or will they, sell to our target market segment?
- Is their sales force large enough and trained well enough to achieve our regional sales forecasts?
- Is their regional location adequate in respect of the retail (and other) outlets serviced?
- Are their promotional policies and budgets adequate?
- Do they satisfy customer after-sales requirements?
- Are their product policies consistent with our own?
- Do they carry competitive lines?
- What are their inventory policies regarding width, depth and cover?
- Are they credit worthy?
- Is distributor management receptive, aggressive, and flexible?

All the above factors, and others, have to be considered when making specific decisions on choice of intermediaries, which in turn is part of the overall channel selection issue.

Customer service

The output of a firm's distribution activities is a system organized to provide a continuing link between the first contact with the customer, through to the time the order is received and the goods/services delivered and used, with the objective of satisfying customer needs continuously. It encompasses every aspect of the relationship.

However, the provision of customer service in all its various forms is likely to involve the firm in large financial commitments. In fact, it can be demonstrated that once the level of service (defined here as the percentage of occasions the product is available to customer's, when and where they want it) increases beyond'the 70–80 per cent mark, the associated costs increase exponentially. Figure 10.5 demonstrates the typical relationship between the level of availability and the cost of providing it. From this diagram it will be observed that the cost of increasing the service level by a small amount, say from 95 per cent to 97.5 per cent, results in a sharp increase in inventory costs.

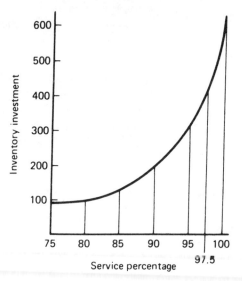

The implications of this cost relationship bear closer examination.

Significantly, many companies appear to be unaware of the level of service they are offering, i.e. there is *no* customer service policy as such. Even where such a policy does exist, the levels are quite often arbitrarily set and are not the result of a careful market analysis.

The question, then, arises: what level of availability *should* be offered? This question is relatively simple to answer in theory, but very difficult to quantify and achieve in practice, since different product groups in different market segments could well demand different levels of customer service.

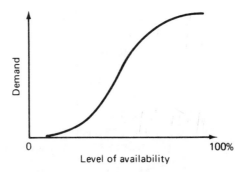

Figure 10.6

In theory, at least, it is possible to say that service levels can continue to be improved as long as the marketing advantage that results continues to outrun the additional costs incurred. Conceptually, it is possible to draw an S-shaped curve (see Figure 10.6) which suggests that at, very high levels of customer service, customers are unable to distinguish between small changes in the service offered. When a company is operating in this region, it is quite possibly incurring more costs than are necessary for the level of sales being achieved.

For example, marketing and sales managers who insist on offering maximum service to all customers, no matter what the profitability and location of those customers, are quite probably doing their company a disservice.

Somewhere between the costs and benefits involved in customer service, a balance has to be found.

By carefully reviewing customer service policy, perhaps even introducing differential service levels for different products or for different customers (at least on a trial-and-error basis), marketing can enhance its contribution to corporate profitability.

Somewhere between the costs and benefits involved in customer service, a balance has to be found. It will be at that point where the additional revenue returns for each increment of service are equal to the extra cost involved in providing that increment. To attempt to ascertain this point of balance, certain information is required, for example:

1 How profitable is the product? What contribution to fixed costs and profits does this product make and what is its sales turnover?
2 What is the nature of the product? Is it a critical item as far as the customer is concerned, where stock-outs at the point of supply would result in a loss of sales? Does the product have characteristics that result in high stockholding costs?
3 What is the nature of the market? Does the company operate in a sellers' or a buyers' market? How frequently is the product purchased? Are there ready substitutes? What are the stockhold-

ing practices of the purchasers? Which markets and customers are growing and which are declining?

4 How profitable are the customers constituting each segment?

5 What is the nature of the competition? How many companies are providing an alternative source of supply to our customers? What sort of service levels do they offer?

6 What is the nature of the channel of distribution through which the company sells? Does the company sell direct to the end-customer, or through intermediaries? To what extent does the company control the channel and the activities of its members, such as the stock levels and order policies?

This basic information is the raw material of the service level decision. To take an example, the level of service offered is less likely to have an effect on sales if, in fact, the company is the sole supplier of the product, and there are no substitutes. This situation is the case in some industrial markets and from a short-term point of view to offer a higher level of service, say 90 per cent instead of 85 per cent, would probably have the effect of reducing the total profitability of the product.

Developing a customer service package

In general terms, customer service is normally defined as the service provided to the customer from the time an order is placed until the product is delivered. In fact, it is much more than this.

It actually encompasses every aspect of the relationship between manufacturers and their distributors/customers. Under this definition, price, sales representation, after-sales service, product range offering, product availability, etc., are all dimensions of customer service, i.e. the total activity of servicing one's customer.

However, it is more traditional to think of customer service in distribution-related terms. Under this more restricted definition the key elements of customer service are product availability, overall order cycle time, and order cycle time variation. Research has shown that many companies have poor product availability due to a variety of reasons, e.g. poor forecasting, production difficulties, inadequate inventory controls, etc.

It is fundamental for suppliers to derive their concept of customer service from a study of their customers' real needs.

Above all else, it is fundamental for suppliers to derive and make operational their concept of customer service from a study of their customers' real needs rather than their own perceptions of such needs. The following list contains the major components of customer service that should be researched.

○ Frequency of delivery
○ Time from order to delivery
○ Reliability of delivery
○ Emergency deliveries when required
○ Stock availability and continuity of supply
○ Orders filled completely
○ Advice on non-availability

- ○ Convenience of placing order
- ○ Acknowledgement of order
- ○ Accuracy of invoices
- ○ Quality of sales representation
- ○ Regular calls by sales representatives
- ○ Manufacturer monitoring of retail stock levels
- ○ Credit terms offered
- ○ Customer query handling
- ○ Quality of outer packaging
- ○ Well-stacked pallets
- ○ Easy-to-read use-by dates on outers
- ○ Quality of inner package for in-store handling and display
- ○ Consults on new product/package development
- ○ Reviews product range regularly
- ○ Co-ordination between production, distribution and marketing

This will almost certainly mean designing different customer service packages for different market groups. At present, very few manufacturers/suppliers bother to do this. Basically, six steps are involved in this process:

1 Define the important service elements (and sub-elements).
2 Determine customers' viewpoints on these.
3 Design a competitive package (and several variations, if necessary).
4 Develop a promotional campaign to 'sell' the service package idea.
5 Pilot test a particular package and the promotional campaign being used.
6 Establish controls to monitor performance of the various service packages.

> Throughout many types of industry, and especially those that are highly competitive, it is increasingly being recognized that, after all the other terms of trade have been tried and exhausted, it will be customer service considerations which will determine who, in the end, gets the order. The distribution function is becoming as important as that.

Developing the distribution plan

Figure 10.7 shows the interrelationship between the process described elsewhere in this book and distribution. Here, we see that product, pricing and promotion decisions are separated from distribution.

Organizationally, it makes a lot of sense to make marketing responsible for distribution, since it is probably in the best position to make the difficult trade-off between very high levels of customer service and the high inventory-carrying costs associated with such levels.

On the other hand, labour relations, wage bargaining, the technical aspects, and so on, of distribution, also demand specialist attention,

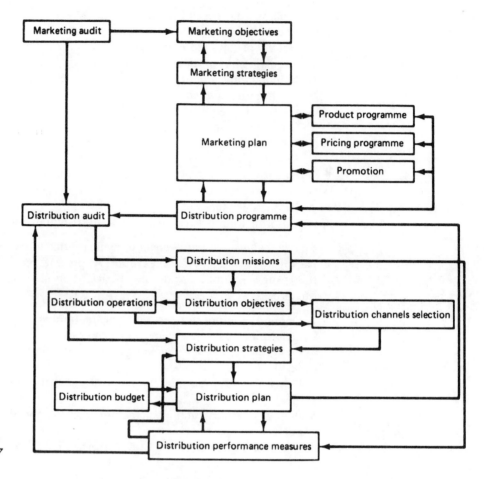

Figure 10.7

and there is a grave danger that such issues may begin to divert too much of the chief marketing officer's attention away from other important marketing areas. The Logistics Director is one possible answer to this problem. Such a role is to view the whole distribution system in an integrated way.

What is integrated distribution management?

Integrated distribution management is an approach to the distribution mission of the firm whereby two or more of the functions involved in moving goods from source to user are integrated and viewed as an interrelated system or sub-system for purposes of managerial planning, implementation and control.

Whatever the organizational solution, however, all of the above issues are relevant and it is necessary to know where to start.

Where to start?

The distribution audit was referred to in Chapter 2. Like the more general marketing audit referred to there, this is in two major parts – *internal* and *external*. Figures 10.8(a) and (b) illustrate the major components of the distribution audit.

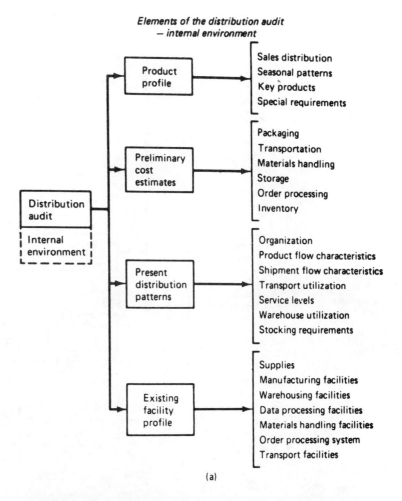

Elements of the distribution audit
– internal environment

Figure 10.8(a)

(a)

Distribution objectives can be many and varied, but the following are considered basic for marketing purposes:

1 Outlet penetration by type of distribution
2 Inventory range and levels to be held
3 Distributor sales and sales promotion activities
4 Other specific customer development programmes, e.g. incentives for distributors

When taking an integrated distribution management approach, it is as well to remember that there are a number of other decisions/trade-offs which need to be specified in the plan. These are depicted in Figure 10.9.

Of course, all of these decisions need not necessarily be located in one plan or be made by one person or department, but clearly they need to be made and written down somewhere in the company's plans.

Finally, the following illustrates a simple iterative approach to distribution planning that should help tighten up what is often a neglected area of marketing management.

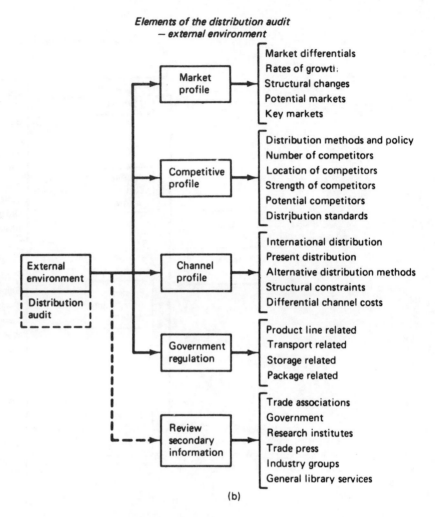

Figure 10.8(b)

(b)

Distribution planning approach

1 Determine marketing objectives.
2 Evaluate changing conditions in distribution at all levels.
3 Determine distribution task within overall marketing strategy.
4 Determine distribution policy in terms of type, number and level of outlets to be used.
5 Set performance standards for the distribution organization.
6 Obtain performance information.
7 Compare actual with anticipated performance.
8 Adjustment where necessary.

Application questions

1 What are the advantages and disadvantages of the channels currently used by your company?
2 Are there any cases where the channels used may not be the most appropriate?
3 If your company were new to the market, what channels would you use?
How would your recommendations differ from existing arrangements?

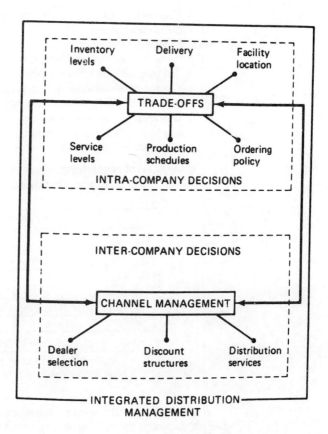

Figure 10.9

What prevents you from making these changes?

4 Is logistics adequately represented at board or senior management level in your organization? How could improvements be made?

5 What coordination takes place between physical distribution management and marketing management? How can any problems be minimized?

6 How are decisions currently made concerning customer service levels?

How does it compare with competitors?

7 Can you see any way of making savings in your distribution system without reducing customer service?

Review of Chapter 10

Physical distribution

This chapter obviously applies only to tangible products.

Physical distribution ensures products get to the right place, on time, and in the right condition. In some businesses, distribution costs can amount to 20 per cent of the selling price. There are five components to manage:

1 *Facilities*. The number, size and geographical location of storage and distribution depots.
2 *Inventory*. The stockholding levels throughout the distribution chain consistent with customers' service expectations.
3 *Transport*. Made up of transport, delivery, schedules, etc.
4 *Communications*. There is also a flow of information, for example, order processing, invoicing, forecasting, etc.
5 *Unitization*. The way in which goods are packaged and assembled into large units, e.g. palletization, container loads, etc.

Considerable savings can be made by innovating in this area.

Channels for reaching customers

There is a range of possible distribution channels, for example:

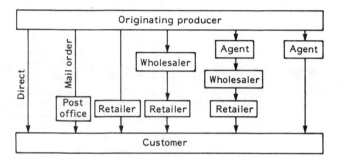

Which one is best for competitive advantage?

Try Exercises 10.1 and 10.2

Availability and customer service package

Customer expectations about product availability will vary from market to market. In theory, 100 per cent availability should be the norm. In practice, a compromise might have to be found, say 95 per cent, because the additional cost of providing that extra 5 per cent can be prohibitive. In addition, often such high levels of customer service are not necessary. Balance the benefits to the customer with cost to you.

Factors which impact on customer service include:

○ Frequency of delivery
○ Time from order to delivery
○ Emergency deliveries when required
○ Accuracy of paperwork
○ Stock availability
○ Reliability of deliveries etc.

Key factors should be identified and researched with a view to improving them.

Try Exercises 10.3 and 10.4

Distribution planning

The approach should follow these steps:

1 Determine marketing objectives.
2 Evaluate changing conditions in distribution at all levels.
3 Determine the distribution task within marketing strategy.
4 Establish a policy in terms of type, number and level of outlets to be used.
5 Set performance standards for distributors.

6 Obtain performance information.
7 Compare actual with anticipated performance.
8 Make improvements where necessary.   *Try Exercise 10.5*

Questions raised for the company,

1 Q: How important is it to have a distribution plan?
   A: It depends on the type of business. In some industries distribution costs amount to 20 per cent or more of sales revenue. Distribution is the Cinderella of marketing, but can often be the area where a competitive edge can be won – through planning.

2 Q: Can services be distributed? After all, they can't be stocked.
   A: No, but services can be franchised. Once a rational decision has been made to use channels, it is the company's responsibility to work at developing a good business relationship based on trust and mutual respect. It is to both parties' mutual advantage.

3 Q: Are there any new developments in distribution?
   A: Franchising is becoming popular. In addition, some transport contractors now also supply warehousing, inventory control and other services, in effect providing the manufacturer with an 'off-the-shelf' distribution facility.

Introduction to Chapter 10 exercises

For many businesses, distribution plays a small part in their marketing plans. When it is considered, the prime concern seems to focus on the physical aspects, the logistics of getting goods transported from the company to the customer.

Distribution, however, embraces a much broader concept than just the delivery of goods. In addition, it takes into account the strategic importance of distribution channels and the potential value of channel intermediaries. It also ensures that 'customer service' is kept in the forefront of the company's deliberations about its marketing policies. The exercises in this section mirror this broad view of distribution.

Exercise 10.1 helps you to decide whether or not intermediaries are required in your type of business.

Exercise 10.2 explains how intermediaries might be selected.

Exercise 10.3 is designed solely to get you to think about your own customer service from the customer's point of view.

Exercise 10.4 looks at the total customer service package and will enable you to check how yours compares with those of your competitors, and, equally importantly, what steps you will have to take to improve your competitiveness.

Exercise 10.5 addresses the physical aspects of distribution.

Exercise 10.6 invites you to use all the information generated in Exercises 10.1 to 10.5 and integrate it into a distribution plan.

Exercise 10.1 Do we need channel intermediaries?

At first sight, the choice of distribution channel is deceptively easy. After all, basically there are only three options from which to choose:

1 To sell direct to the customer/user.
2 To sell to customers/users through intermediaries.
3 To use a combination of 1 and 2, i.e. dual distribution.

Worksheet   Distribution channel algorithm (Example 10.1)

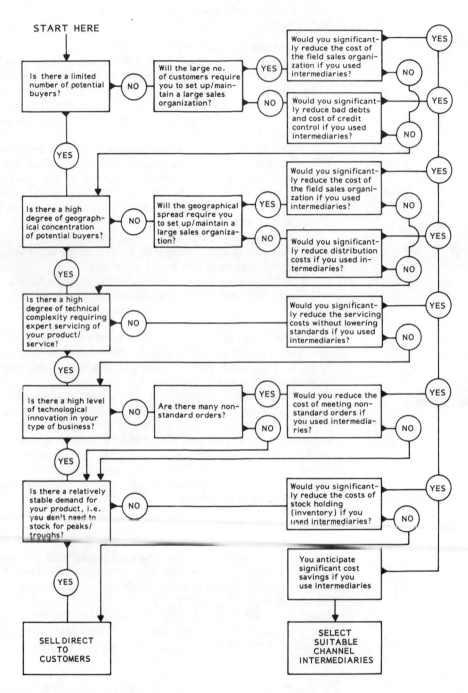

The final choice will always be something of a compromise, with, on the one hand, the desire to keep control of the distribution of one's products or services, and, on the other hand, the practical need to keep distribution costs to a bearable level.

The Worksheet is designed to help you to make a choice about channels of distribution. This is what you do:

1 Take each product/service in your portfolio in turn and subject them to the algorithm given on the Worksheet.
2 Note the decision for each product, i.e. sell direct or use channel intermediaries. Do these seem the best decisions or can you see good reasons for ignoring them?
3 In working through the algorithm, can you see a case for dual distribution for some products or services? For example, do you sell direct to some customers or regions and sell through intermediaries to others. Remember the major problem associated with dual distribution is determining a fair division of the market between yourself (as the supplier) and the intermediary(ies).

Use the space below to record the decisions from using the worksheet or to make any other relevant notes.

Personal notes

Exercise 10.2 Selecting a suitable intermediary

Exercise 10.1 helped to answer the question of whether or not an intermediary is required. Assuming the answer is affirmative, you are now faced with selecting a suitable candidate to play that role.

The Worksheet should help you in your decision-making. Here are the instructions for using it:

1 Make a note of organizations that, on the surface, appear to be possible choices as intermediaries. (You will see that the worksheet allows for comparisons between just three prospective intermediaries. You should, of course, draw up your own form to include as many as you like.)
2 Looking at the list of evaluation criteria, take criterion 1 and apply it to all the prospective channel intermediaries. Place scores in columns A, B and C – a number between 0 and 10, depending on whether the intermediary is a very poor fit against this criterion (zero score) or an extremely good fit (10 points).
3 Continue down the list of evaluation criteria, repeating this scoring process.
4 Add any further criteria that are relevant for your business to the bottom of the list and score them likewise.

5 Add up the scores in each column. The highest total represents the most suitable intermediary.

You may decide that some criteria are more important than others on this list. In this case use a points weighting system which takes importance into account. An example of a weighting system is given in Exercise 4.2.

Worksheet   Criteria for selecting intermediaries (Exercise 10.2)

Evaluation criteria	Prospective intermediaries		
	A	B	C
1 Currently deals with our target market segment			
2 Is prepared to deal with target market segment			
3 Salesforce is sufficiently large			
4 Salesforce is well trained			
5 Regional locations well positioned			
6 Promotional policies consistent with ours			
7 Budgets are adequate			
8 Can provide customer after sales service			
9 Product policies consistent with ours			
10 Does not carry competitor lines			
11 Prepared to carry adequate stocks			
12 Prepared to carry range/cover			
13 Suitable storage facilities			
14 Is creditworthy			
15 Management attitudes compatible with ours			
16 Has suitable reputation (Add others that are relevant)			
17			
18			
19			
20			
21			
22			
23			
24			
25			
26			
27			
28			
29			
30			
TOTAL			

**Exercise 10.3
Customer service
audit***

Before getting into more detail about customer service, start by completing this customer service audit. If you have 'No' in more than three questions, or if you have difficulty answering the open-ended questions, you may have a serious customer service problem in your organization.

*This audit is based on an audit constructed by Professor Martin Christopher of Cranfield School of Management, and is used with his kind permission.

1 Do you have a written customer service policy?

Yes . . . .

No . . . .

2 Is this given a wide circulation within the company?

Yes . . . .

No . . . .

3 Do customers receive a copy of this policy?

Yes . . . .

No . . . .

4 What are the three most crucial aspects of customer service as they impinge upon your marketing effectiveness?

1 . . . .

2 . . . .

3 . . . .

5 Is any attempt made to monitor your customer service performance on these three dimensions?

Yes . . . .

No . . . .

6 Do you monitor competitive customer service offerings?

Yes . . . .

No . . . .

7 Do you believe that within your company there is adequate knowledge of the true costs of providing customer service?

Yes . . . .

No . . . .

8 Which function(s) has responsibility for customer service management?

. . . .

. . . .

9 Where does customer service management fit in relation to the marketing function? (Draw an organizational chart if necessary).

10 Do you have an established method of communications for your customers to contact you about some aspect of their order after the order has been entered?

Yes ....

No ....

11 Do you have (a) a single point of contact for customers or (b) do certain departments handle different types of inquiries/complaints?

Yes (a) (b)

No (a) (b)

12 What do you think are the major areas of weakness in your current approach to customer service management?

....

....

....

....

....

Exercise 10.4 The customer service package

Customer service has been defined as the percentage of occasions the product or service is available to the customer *when* and *where* he or she wants it. Obviously, to operate service levels at 100% might, and often does, impose a crippling cost on the supplier, yet to drop below an acceptable level is to surrender one's market share to a competitor.

Research has shown that to improve one's service level by even a small amount when it is already at a high level can become expensive (the law of diminishing returns). Therefore the marketer will have to be certain about the actual levels of customer service provided and to have a greater understanding of customer expectations and needs. It will be highly likely that different market segments will require different levels of customer service.

The ultimate choice of service level for a specific product will be tempered by other influential factors:

1 The contribution to fixed costs, e.g. can it bear the cost of an upgraded service level?
2 The nature of the market, e.g. are there substitute products?
3 The nature of the competition, e.g. do they offer better service levels?
4 The nature of the distribution channel, e.g. do we sell direct or through intermediaries?

The key to marketing success is for your company to develop a customer service package – one that embraces product availability, with attractive order cycle times, and mechanisms for minimizing customer inconvenience arising from order cycle variations.

The Worksheet is designed to help you to arrive at a more competitive customer service package or, if this is too expensive, to devise an alternative. The instructions are provided on the Worksheet. The space below is for any notes you might wish to make about these issues.

Worksheet Developing a customer service package (Exercise 10.4)

Take one of your market segments and decide what would make the best 'package' by putting a tick against the appropriate items in column 1, i.e. what does your marketing strategy suggest?

In column 2 tick the items that go to make the best competitor package.

In column 3 estimate if the provision of your item is *Better, Equal* or *Worse* than the best competitor.

In column 4 indicate the relative cost of improving where you compete unfavourably with the best competitor, i.e. *High, Medium* or *Low.*

In column 5 list improvement actions to upgrade the service package to match the best competitor.

In column 6 consider alternative packages, i.e. to fight on different grounds.

Repeat this process for all other market segments.

Components of customer service	(1) *Market strategy suggestions*	(2) *Best competitor*	(3) *Better Equal Worse*	(4) *Comp. cost H, M, L*	(5) *Actions to upgrade cust. serv.*	(6) *Alt. package*
Frequency of delivery						
Time from order to delivery						
Reliability of delivery						
Emergency deliveries when required						
Stock availability						
Continuity of supply						
Advice on non-availability						
Convenience of placing orders						
Acknowledgement of orders						
Accuracy of invoices						
Quality of sales representation						
Regularity of calls by sales reps.						
Monitoring of stock levels						
Credit terms offered						
Handling of customer queries						
Quality of outer packaging						
Well-stacked pallets						
Easy to read use-by dates on outers						
Clear handling instructions on outers						
Quality of inner package for handling						
Quality of inner package for display						
Consultation on new developments, e.g. products or packaging						
Regular review of product range coordination between production, distribution and marketing						

(Continued)

Components of customer service	(1) Market strategy suggestions	(2) Best competitor	(3) Better Equal Worse	(4) Comp. cost H, M, L	(5) Actions to upgrade cust. serv.	(6) Alt. package
Add others which are relevant for your business						

Personal notes

Exercise 10.5 Physical distribution

It has been shown that there are five areas to be considered when it comes to physical distribution, the so-called 'distribution mix'. They are: facilities, inventory, transport, communications, and unitization.

Facilities
Having established the level of customer service required by each market segment, you must reappraise the location of your own plants and warehouses in order to ensure they are situated in geographically suitable positions *vis-à-vis* the customers. If the nature of demand and the location of major customers is forecast to change dramatically, then re-locating manufacturing units and/or warehouses is an option that, in the long term, can lead to savings due to reduced distribution costs.

Such decisions cannot be taken lightly. For most organizations their facilities are taken as fixed, certainly in the short term.

Inventory
The holding of stock, whether by design or accident, is always a costly business. Therefore it is important to know the comparative costs of holding stocks of different products in order to arrive at a sensible stockholding policy.

Worksheet 1 enables you to calculate the various components of inventory cost for each of your major products and thereby produce the necessary cost data. Once in possession of this information, it might become necessary for you to revise the customer service package or indeed earlier deliberations about channel intermediaries.

Transport
This is the area that many people are familiar with, and, as such, has traditionally received most management attention. Worksheet 2 shows a typical way of calculating the merits or demerits of various forms of

transporting goods to customers. Try it, using some of your own products as study vehicles.

While cost is an important determinant in the choice of transport, frequency of service and reliability are often just as important. Regular monitoring of transport costs is to be recommended if distribution costs are to be held in check.

Communications

It is often overlooked that accompanying the flow of materials through the distribution channel there is also a flow of information in the form of orders, invoices, demand forecasts, delivery schedules, etc. Each of these 'communications' is likely to be an integral part of your customer service package, and yet, in all probability, they were set up for your own company's administrative convenience.

Look at all your communications associated with distribution and put yourself in the customer's shoes. For example, how sensible does your ordering system seem when viewed from the other end? Get out and speak to some actual customers and seek their views. Anything that can be done to simplify or speed-up communications must be to your company's benefit – and it doesn't have to cost you money to improve the situation.

Unitization

Assess whether or not it is possible to make your products more acceptable to users or intermediaries, e.g. for handling or stacking, by packaging them into different sized units such as shrink-wrapped bulk packs, pallet loads, container loads, etc. It is often possible to win substantial cost savings in terms of handling or warehousing by considering this aspect of distribution.

Worksheet 1 Comparative inventory costs (Exercise 10.5)

Area of cost	Product				
	(1)	*(2)*	*(3)*	*(4)*	*(5)*
Warehouse costs (rent, rates, heat, light, etc.)					
Labour costs					
Losses/shrinkage					
Deterioration/damage					
Insurance					
Interest (on funds tied up in stock)					
Administrative costs					
Other costs relevant to your specific business					
. . . .					
. . . .					
. . . .					
. . . .					
. . . .					
. . . .					
. . . .					
. . . .					

(Continued)

Area of cost	Product				
	(1)	*(2)*	*(3)*	*(4)*	*(5)*
. . . .					
. . . .					
. . . .					
. . . .					
. . . .					
. . . .					
. . . .					
. . . .					
. . . .					
. . . .					
. . . .					
. . . .					
. . . .					
. . . .					
. . . .					
. . . .					
. . . .					
. . . .					
. . . .					
. . . .					

For the purpose of this worksheet take the cost per item, or unit; or you can, if you prefer, just express the costs as a percentage of the book value of the stock.

Worksheet 2   Comparative physical distribution costs (Exercise 10.5)

Method of physical distribution	Product/service				
	(1)	*(2)*	*(3)*	*(4)*	*(5)*
Use own transport					
Contract hire					
Use carriers					
Other forms of road transport					
. . . .					
. . . .					
Passenger rail train					
Freight train					
Red Star Parcel					
Other forms of rail transport					
. . . .					
. . . .					
Boat on deck					
Boat in hold					
Hovercraft					
Other forms of sea transport					
. . . .					
. . . .					
Air parcel					
Air freight					
Other forms of air transport					
. . . .					
. . . .					
1st class post					
2nd class post					
Parcel post					
Other postal methods					
. . . .					

(Continued)

Method of physical distribution	Product/service				
	(1)	*(2)*	*(3)*	*(4)*	*(5)*
Other transport methods					

Use either cost per item or unit, or you can, if you prefer, express the costs as a percentage of the book value of your stock.

Exercise 10.6 The distribution plan

From the foregoing study material you will by now have highlighted several ways of improving distribution in your company or have confirmed that existing practices were well chosen. In order that your effort is not wasted, it will be important to encapsulate your major findings in the distribution plan. Here is a suggestion for how this can be done:

1 Show how, in the light of the company's marketing objectives and strategy, the distribution task needs to be defined.
2 From your work, show where current practice supports this definition of the distribution task and where it does not.
3 Using the data you have assembled, recommend:

   (a) A distribution policy in terms of type, number and level of outlet to be used.
   (b) Performance standards for the distribution organization.
   (c) Where changes in the distribution organization are required.
   (d) Ways of monitoring performance as the plan unfolds.

Personal notes

11 Marketing information, forecasting and organizing for marketing planning

Summary

The first part of Chapter 11 deals with the difference between market research and marketing research, how much to spend on it, what the different forms of marketing research are, database marketing, marketing intelligence systems, and how to organize them. Next, forecasting techniques are briefly covered. Finally, different organizational structures for marketing planning are outlined and discussed and there is a discussion about the cultural implications of marketing planning.

Introduction

In the next chapter, we look at one of the most difficult aspects of marketing planning – actually making it all work in practice by means of a system within the company. This is something that most courses and books somehow seem to overlook. Yet no work on marketing planning can be complete without a fairly detailed consideration of how all the structures and frameworks presented in earlier chapters are to be implemented.

The truth is, of course, that the actual *process* of marketing planning is simple in outline. Any book will tell us that it consists of: a situation review; assumptions, objectives, strategies; programmes; and measurement and review. What some books *do not* tell us is that there are a number of contextual issues that have to be considered that make marketing planning one of the most baffling of all marketing problems.

Here are some of those issues:

○ *When* should it be done, *how often*, *by whom*, and *how*?
○ Is it different in a *large* and a *small* company?
○ Is it different in a *diversified* and an *undiversified* company?
○ Is it different in an *international* and a *domestic* company?
○ What is the role of the *chief executive*?
○ What is the role of the *planning department*?
○ Should marketing planning be *top down* or *bottom up*?
○ What is the relationship between *operational* (one year) and *strategic* (longer term) planning?

Until issues such as these are understood, the other chapters in this book will remain little more than interesting aspects of marketing planning. So, the purpose of Chapter 12 is to help us to pick up all the pieces of the jigsaw puzzle and put them together to form a picture we can all see and understand.

First, however, we need to set the scene, and, in particular, to fill in a few gaps concerning marketing information, and the organizational side of marketing. Our research has shown very clearly that it is important to recognize at the outset what the realistic constraints are likely to be on the implementation of a marketing planning system. Two such major constraints are marketing information and a company's organizational form, which are considered in this chapter. We will then go on in the next chapter to demonstrate how marketing planning can be made to work by means of a system, and will include in this a discussion of the role of the chief executive, and the planning department. In Chapter 13, we provide an actual marketing planning system which will enable you to operationalize the concepts, structures and frameworks described in this book. Finally, there will be a glossary of marketing planning terms.

This chapter, then, is in two parts:

1 Marketing information and forecasting
2 Marketing organization

Marketing information and forecasting for marketing planning

It will, by now, be obvious that without information it is going to be difficult to do many of the fairly common sense things we have been discussing so far.

> Any plan can only be as good as the information on which it is based, which is why we have been making sure that we know the right questions to ask, such as: 'Who are our customers?' 'What is our market share?' and so on.

Throughout this book, we have been stressing that the profitable development of a company can only come from a continual attempt to match the company's capabilities with customer needs. In order that the company can be sure that this matching process is taking place effectively, it is necessary that some type of information flow be instituted between the customer and the firm. This is the role of marketing research.

The difference between market research and marketing research

Put very simply, market research is concerned specifically with research about markets, whereas marketing research is concerned with research into marketing processes.

> We are concerned here with marketing research, which has been defined by the American Marketing Association as the systematic gathering, recording and analysis of data about problems relating to the marketing of goods and services.

347

The words in this definition are important. The process has to be systematic, because it is necessary to have a structured interaction between people, machines and procedures designed to generate an orderly flow of pertinent information collected from sources both inside and outside the company, for use as the basis for decision-making in specified responsibility areas of marketing management.

It will be apparent immediately that data by themselves (such as words, figures, pictures, sounds, and so on) are of little use until they are combined with direction and hence become information. But without some purpose in mind, some marketing problem to solve, information is not much use either. Indeed, research has shown that one of the biggest problems facing management today is a *surplus* of data and information, rather than too little.

> Which brings us to our definition of *intelligence*, which is information consumable and usable by management in converting uncertainty into risk.

Uncertainty, of course, is when any outcome is considered to be equally possible. When a probability can be assigned to certain outcomes, however, we are talking about *risk*, which is just quantified uncertainty. The marketing manager might feel, for example, that a new product has a 90 per cent chance of achieving 30 per cent market share in its first year. Clearly, our ability to make successful decisions is enhanced if we are operating under conditions of known risk rather than uncertainty.

> Conversion of uncertainty into risk and the minimization of risk is perhaps marketing management's most important task, and in this process the role of marketing research is of paramount importance.

How much to spend on marketing research

Before looking at the different kinds of research available to the marketing manager, a book written about marketing planning should surely address the issue of the marketing research budget.

Marketing information has to be produced, stored and distributed, but it has a limited life – it is perishable. Like other resources, information has a value in use; the less the manager knows about a marketing problem and the greater the risk attached to a wrong decision, the more valuable the information becomes. This implies the need for a cost/benefit appraisal of all sources of marketing information, since there is little point in investing more in such information than the return on it would justify.

> But while costs are easy to identify, the benefits are more difficult to pin down. They can best be expressed in terms of the additional profits that might be achieved through identifying marketing opportunities and through the avoidance of marketing failures that could result without the use of information.

It must be stressed, however, that the decision about how much to spend on marketing information is not an easy one. On the one hand it would, generally speaking, be foolhardy to proceed without any information at all, while, on the other hand, the cost of perfect information would be prohibitive. One way of estimating how much to spend is based on the theory of probability and expected value. For example, if by launching a product you had to incur development costs of 1 million ecu and you believed there was a 10 per cent chance that the product would fail, the maximum *loss expectation* would be 100,000 ecu (i.e. 1 million ecu × 0.1).

Obviously, then, it is worth spending up to 100,000 ecu to acquire information that would help avoid such a loss. However, because perfect information is seldom available, it makes sense to budget a small sum for marketing research which effectively discounts the likely inaccuracy of the information. Such an approach can be a valuable means of quantifying the value of marketing research in a managerial context.

Forms of marketing research

Increasing sophistication in the use of the techniques available to the researcher, particularly in the handling and analysis of multivariate data, has made marketing research into a specialized function within the field of marketing management. Nevertheless, any company, irrespective of whether or not it has a marketing department, should be aware of some of the tools that are available and where these may be used.

Marketing research can be classified either as *external* or *internal*.

External marketing information gathering should always be seen as a complement to internal marketing analysis.

The former research activity is conducted within the competitive environment outside the firm, whereas much valuable intelligence can be gained from internal marketing analysis in the form of sales trends, changes in the marketing mix such as price, advertising levels, and so on. External marketing information gathering should always be seen as a complement to such internal information.

Apart from this, there is another basic split between *reactive* and *non- reactive* marketing research.

Non-reactive methods are based upon the interpretation of observed phenomena, or extant data, whereas reactive research involves some form of proactive assessment in the market place.

The most widely used method of reactive marketing research involves the asking of questions by means of a *questionnaire* survey, which is indeed a ubiquitous and highly flexible instrument. It can be administered by an interviewer, by telephone, or it can be sent by mail, and so on.

All of these different methods have their advantages and disadvantages, and all have different cost consequences. For example, the greatest degree of control over the quality of the responses is obtained by getting a researcher to administer each questionnaire personally, but this is very expensive and time-consuming. Telephone interviews are quick and relatively inexpensive, but there is a severe limit to the amount of technical information that can be obtained by this means. The postal questionnaire is a much-favoured method, but here great care is necessary to avoid sample bias. For example, is there something special (and possibly therefore unrepresentative of the population) about those who reply to a postal questionnaire?

But, without doubt, the biggest potential pitfalls with the questionnaire lie in its design. Everyone knows about the 'loaded' question or the dangers of ambiguity, yet these are not always easily detectable. Indeed, even the order in which questions are asked can have a distortion effect on the answers.

Such pitfalls can be reduced by *pilot testing* it; in other words, by giving it a trial run on a sub-group of the intended sample to isolate any problems that may arise.

Sometimes, it may be more appropriate to gather information not by large surveys, but by smaller-scale, more detailed studies intended to provide qualitative insights rather than quantitative conclusions. *Depth interviews* can provide such insights. These are loosely-structured discussions with a group broadly representing the population in which the researcher is interested, in which a group leader attempts to draw from the group their feelings about the subject under discussion. Such in-depth interviews can also take place with individuals, a method which is particularly popular when information is required about specialized products or markets.

The most important of all marketing research methods is the use of existing materials.

Experimentation is another type of reactive marketing research which can provide a valuable source of information about the likely market performance of new products or about the likely effects of variations in the marketing mix. Thus, different product formulations, different levels of promotional effort, and so on can be tested in the market place to gauge their different effects.

Sometimes, market experimentation can take place in laboratory conditions, particularly in the case of advertising. Samples of the target audience will be exposed to the advertisement and their reactions obtained. Eye cameras, polygraphs and tachistoscopes are just some of the devices that can be used to record physical reactions to marketing stimuli.

In contrast with such methods are those that are classified as *non-reactive* in that they do not rely on data derived directly from the respondent.

Best known amongst these are *retail audits* and *consumer panels*, both widely used by consumer companies. Retail audits involve the regular monitoring of a representative sample of stockists. At regular periods, researchers visit the stockists and record the current level of stocks of the product group being audited and the delivery notes for any such goods delivered since their last visit. With the information on stock levels on their last visit, it is now a simple matter to determine sales of the audited items, i.e. opening stock + deliveries between visits – closing stock = sales during the period.

The consumer panel is simply a sample group of consumers who record in a diary their purchases and consumption over a period of time. This technique has been used in industrial as well as consumer markets and can provide continuous data on usage patterns as well as much other useful data.

Finally, and, in many respects, the most important of all marketing research methods is the use of existing materials, particularly by means of *desk research*, which should always be the starting point of any marketing research programme.

There is often a wealth of information to be obtained from published information such as government statistics, OECD, EC, the United Nations, newspapers, technical journals, trade association publications, published market surveys, and so on. Two or three days spent on desk research nearly always provides pleasant surprises for the company that believes it lacks information about its markets. When combined with internal sales information, this can be the most powerful research method open to a company.

Organizing the information to develop sound plans*

The practice of marketing planning is intrinsically difficult. Its main concern is to choose markets to go after and to work out how to win them.

The methods in this book can be applied to make up a plan that describes the marketing objectives and the winning strategies. The trouble is that such a plan could in theory be written without a scrap of supporting evidence; and, in practice, many plans are created upon the flimsiest of evidence.

Two challenges involving evidence and information face executive management.

The first challenge, faced by companies of any substantial size and diversity, is how to manage the complexity of the planning data.

The question arises, how can the planners know very much about what is happening throughout the geographical regions with all of its products and in all the market segments? Auditing the market requires its subdivision into many component parts: by geography,

*The material in this section is heavily influenced by the work of Dr Robert Shaw, of Shaw Consulting. Figures 11.1, 11.2 and 11.3 and Tables 11.1, 11.2, 11.3, 11.4 and 11.5 are the copyright of Dr Robert Shaw and are reproduced here with his kind permission.

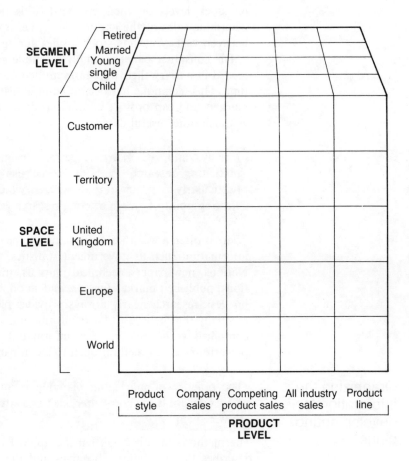

Figure 11.1 One hundred levels of market subdivision and summarization

by product, by segment, etc. Then, portfolio analysis requires the reassembly of these components into a coherent structure.

> The second challenge is how to assess whether a plan is based upon sound evidence, or whether to ignore it as something 'made up', which is neither based on accurate facts, nor believable assumptions.

In the process, planners need to match external facts about the market to internal facts and figures to create a clear and harmonious picture. However, it is rare for the same categories to apply internally and externally, which makes the job of the planner especially difficult.

Fortunately, some large companies have found a way to address both of these problems, thanks to increased availability of information on computer databases, and the power of computer software to make complexity more manageable. Planners must, however, understand the limitations and weaknesses of the databases and master the

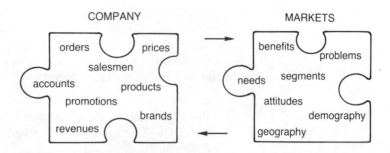

Figure 11.2 Planners must match the internal categories, facts and figures to the external ones

software tools if they are to make the planning decisions sound, as well as easy.

Subdividing the market – data for segmentation

As we saw in Chapter 4, market segmentation is the process that subdivides the market into distinct groups of buyers who might merit separate products and/or marketing mixes. For each segment, a profile is developed, and, very often, a meaningful and memorable name. Segmentation is only effective when it results in realistic commercial opportunities which can be targeted and measured in practice.

> Market segments change over time, as the buyers' needs evolve and as new product offerings become available. The planner must constantly review new combinations of variables to see which reveal the best new opportunities.

Segments are identified by applying successive variables to subdivide the market. As an illustration, a global telecommunications company is interested in stimulating line usage among low users (segmentation variable: *product usage*). Low users consist of those who fear technology, those who are indifferent and those who are positive towards technology (segmentation variable: *attitude*). Among those who feel positive are those with high incomes who can afford to use more (segmentation variable: *income*). The telecommunications company may decide to target high income people who have a positive attitude, but simply use the competitors' networks.

Before discussing data analysis, let us remind ourselves about the steps involved in market segmentation:

1 *Segmentation objectives* The researcher requires a clear brief setting out the business objectives. Different segmentation schemes may result from different objectives. If the objective is market extension, then the key segmentation variable may be income. If the objective is communication, then the key segmentation variable may be attitude.

2 *Desk research and market hypothesis* The researcher collects readily available data and lays it out into a hypothetical map of

the market place. This map contains many gaps, and relies on various assumptions. It suggests areas where more, or better, information needs to be collected.

3 *Data collection and survey* The researcher collects information from and about potential buyers:

○ Buying and/or usage behaviour
○ Buyer attitudes to the product category
○ Buyer characteristics, such as geographics, demographics, psychographics

As we have seen, this can be obtained from:

○ Public databases
○ Proprietary databases (owned by research agencies)
○ Questionnaires sent by mail
○ Telephone research
○ Face-to-face research

Note that internal customer data cannot be used in this context because it is not representative of the whole market, unless the company's customers are representative of all areas of the entire market.

Large data samples often need to be collected to cover all combinations of variables. For example, in a survey where the variables are sex, age (split into 5 categories), geography (10 regions), and products (5 categories), with a minimum sample-per-combination of 10 people, the survey would need to cover at least 5,000 individuals to cover all combinations of segmentation variables.

4 *Data analysis* A wide range of statistical techniques can be used to identify market segments. These include factor analysis, cluster analysis and multiple regression. More recent techniques which go beyond the traditional limits of statistics include neural networks and pattern-finding algorithms

5 *Profile definition* Each segment is defined in terms of the key variables. Often the segments are named on the basis of a dominant characteristic.

Who should be responsible for this segmentation process?

Analysis options – external agencies or internal resources

Market research has traditionally played an important role in segmentation. However, it has often limited itself to 'field and tab' methods, which are severely limited in their flexibility, and do not support the constant reviewing of new combinations of segmentation variables.

Field and tab methods involve the collection of data on 'field' questionnaires, analysis of the data, and presentation of the results as 'tabulations'. This approach is being superseded by in-house analysis, supported by computer systems. There are three reasons for moving in-house: flexibility, competitive advantage and technology.

Flexibility in revising analyses

> The market is changing too rapidly for the traditionally slow process of data collection, data analysis and data presentation. Much data remains unanalysed.

Cost and time limits analysis to the simplest levels – often only hole counts and cross tabulations. There is little opportunity to explore interesting features which emerge from this first stage. As targeted marketing moves closer and closer towards the ultimate market of one person, so the facts produced by the old research are being replaced by models and information on demand.

More than one segmentation scheme will often be needed to fit the strategic objectives at all levels: this covers the advertising and sales promotion plan, the sales plan, the pricing plan and the distribution plan. Cutting the data in many different ways, to explore all the variables, can be prohibitively expensive if done by an external research agency.

Table 11.1   Examples of business objectives and segmentation methods

Business objective	Segmentation method	Information source
Market extension		
new locations	Geodemographics	Electoral roll (consumer)
new channels	Prospect profiles	Companies house (business)
new segments	Survey analysis	Prospect lists and surveys
Market development	Customer profiling	Sales ledger and added profile data
	Behavioural scoring	Models from internal data source
Product development	Factor analysis	Surveys
	Qualitative methods	Panels/discussion groups

> British Telecom operates multiple segmentation schemes in the small business market. For advertising and sales promotion they recognize:
>
> o *Enthusiasts*   These people treat telecommunications almost as a hobby and love to be kept up-to-date with the latest functions and features. All communications with them need to reflect these attitudes.
> o *Luddites*   They hate everything modern and technical. However, give them a few practical examples, and you might get them interested.
> o *Corporate executives*   Managers and directors who respond best to arguments about benefits and competitive advantage.
> o *Shopkeepers*   Shopkeepers have very little use for the telephone, so there is little justification for communicating with them.
> o *Traditionalists*   These people are interested in ease-of-use and easy maintenance.

> For sales planning, their targeting is based on the size of revenue opportunity, which is based on a model which combines:
>
> ○ *Turnover* Larger companies tend to spend more on telecoms.
> ○ *Standard Industry Code (SIC)* Certain industries are bigger telecoms users than others.

Along with inflexibility, lack of control in research is still a problem.

> One company commissioned an agency to research who its customers were. The agency decided, without consulting the client, to do the research during school hours, when field workers would have their children off their hands. Lo and behold, when the results came in, they showed that 1% of customers were under 18 – despite the fact that all previous research showed the figure to be 30–40%. The reason? Most customers shopped during lunch or after school.

Holding the data in-house can enable planners to re-analyse it time after time, without the costs and delays associated with external agencies.

Competitive advantage and unique segmentation schemes

> Standard segmentation schemes bought from external agencies cannot provide significant competitive advantage.

Even if you gain advantage from them today, your competitors can buy them tomorrow and rapidly catch up with you. Unique segmentation schemes are the best solutions to unique problems. Yet many agencies continue to offer standardized segmentation products to all their clients.

Take the automobile industry for example. Henry Ford assumed that price was the dominant segmentation variable, then General Motors started to recognize different income and preference groups in the market. More recently, the Japanese recognized the importance of car size and fuel economy. The success of new entrants into the automobile market has often resulted from discovering new segmentation possibilities in the market.

Yet market research in the automobile market continues to include a widely available off-the-shelf component. The off-the-shelf segments available from agencies are very simple and basic:

○ Small cars
○ Medium cars
○ Large cars

> The traditional automobile segmentation schemes really do not reflect the market very well, and certainly do not offer competitive advantage. Many of the recent products in the market, such as the Rover 200 series or the Renault Clio, have resulted from mould-breaking segmentation schemes.

Other industries, such as financial services, have had their vision of the market blinkered through their adoption of off-the-shelf segmentation. Breaking the traditional rules of segmentation in financial services will almost certainly be a prerequisite to competitive advantage. Customer service is a key characteristic in financial services, and new approaches such as First Direct have been based on mould-breaking segmentation schemes.

Developing customized segmentation schemes is often difficult with external agencies, and some companies are doing such analysis in-house to provide a unique segmentation proposition.

Information technology

Technology has provided the means by which planners can break free of the traditional constraints of relying upon external research agencies.

There are three ways in which information technology supports planners:

○ Databases from external and internal sources are alternatives to the data collected by research agencies.
○ Data collected by research agencies is available on computer databases for clients to analyse themselves.
○ Computer software is available to in-house planners and is making data analysis and interpretation easier, faster and more flexible.

All three of these factors are changing the shape of the research industry. However, the industry often regards the information technology explosion as a threat to its own future, as well it may if it fails to respond to the needs of marketing planners.

The marketing audit

As we saw from Chapters 2, 3, 4 and 5, the marketing audit process requires planners to assemble and organize a great number of estimates of market size, structure and dynamics from external sources, and company share and performance from internal sources.

Two major challenges in conducting a marketing audit are:

○ Getting sound data from external and internal sources
○ Matching external and internal categories.

External data sources

One of the primary tasks in the external audit is to estimate the market size and its breakdown by geography, product and segment.

This should be straightforward, given the vast quantities of market data that do exist.

However, knowing where to begin to collect, store and analyse data presents a real challenge. It helps to differentiate clearly between research on new markets and existing markets. Each presents a very different set of problems in terms of data:

○ For *new markets*, data is comparatively scarce, and extrapolation from surveys is often the main source. Carefully designed analysis methods are necessary to resolve uncertainties introduced by small sample sizes. Models based on limited data and plausible assumptions have to be used to infer market size, structure and dynamics.

○ For *existing markets*, public and agency-owned data sources can provide a rich and detailed picture. Behavioural data is often widely available on buying patterns; often quite detailed information is available on buyer attitudes and characteristics. Sophisticated statistical techniques that rely on large sample sizes can then be used to infer market size, structure and dynamics.

Table 11.2 Consumer markets – major external segmentation variables

Variable	*External source*
What is bought Volume Price Outlets	Government publications provide high-level statistical summaries of many industries. Periodic research by agencies is often published as books of tabulated data. This is obtained by traditional survey methods but also from supermarket scanner data, pharmacy sales data, etc. Such data is often available in computer readable format.

Who buys
Geography
  Postcode
  Population density
  Town or city size
  Driving distance to stores
Demographic
  Age
  Sex
  Income
  Occupation
  Family size
  Family life cycle
  Race/nationality
Socio-economic
  Social class
  Lifestyle
  Personality
	Census data and electoral roll data are the two main sources of geographic and demographic information. The electoral roll can be bought from agencies that collect such data and it covers individual people. Their buying characteristics can be inferred from 'lifestyle' survey databases, built from millions of questionnaires collected from the public over several years. More detailed census data is not available at individual level, but for 100,000 Enumeration Districts (EDs) in the UK. Each ED has hundreds of geodemographic characteristics, which may be of relevance to the planner. Those planners who do not have the time or skill to explore the census data can purchase a pre-segmented coding scheme such as ACORN, which is simpler than the census, but usually less relevant to the user. Most such data can be obtained in computer readable format.

Why Attitude towards product Advertising and promotion Readiness stage Benefits sought Perceptions Brand loyalty Preferences	TV audience data is available from surveys which include a wide range of profiling details. Magazine circulation data is widely available, and often can be broken down into segments. For limited-circulation magazines, individual reader profiles can be purchased. Ad-hoc research can be commissioned and summary data created by a variety of survey methods.

Some examples of sources of data and segmentation variables are given in Tables 11.2 and 11.3.

Table 11.3 Industrial markets – major external segmentation variables

Variable	External source
What is bought	
Volume	Government publications provide a high-level
Price	statistical summary of many industries. Periodic
Outlets	research by agencies is often published as books
	of tabulated data. This is obtained by
	traditional survey methods. There are few
	databases in this area.
Who buys	
Demographic	Companies House data is the main source of
Industry/SIC	information on industrial firms. Only registered
Turnover	companies are included and data can be
Number of employees	out-of-date and incomplete. Private agencies
Financial status	offer alternative sources of data, sometimes
Geography	with added details on specific characteristics. In
Postcode	particular, organizational details such as job
Population density	titles, department sizes, etc. are available. Those
Driving distance (sales	planners who do not have the time or skill to
reps)	explore the data can now purchase a
Organizational	pre-segmented coding scheme similar to
Job titles	ACORN, although its relevance to many
Department sizes	planning objectives is unclear. Most of this data
	can be obtained in computer readable format.
Why	
Purchasing policies	Ad-hoc research is the primary source of data.
Selection criteria	The results of commissioned research can
Attitude towards product	sometimes be obtained on computer media.
Advertising and	
promotion	
Readiness stage	
Benefits sought	
Perceptions	
Brand loyalty	
Preferences	

Internal data sources and MIS

In theory the internal audit should be relatively straightforward. Analysis and reporting of company results by region, product and segment should merely involve a bit of computer analysis of the sales ledger.

> In practice, there are problems. Sales ledgers are owned by finance and designed to facilitate billings and collections. Their purpose does not include supporting marketing, and they rarely do so.

> The information on sales ledgers is incomplete and mis-coded from marketing's viewpoint. Ledgers contain accounts and stock-keeping units, which cannot easily be linked to customers, products, regions or segments.

Collecting, consolidating and using sales ledger information may also be difficult. Ledgers are designed to do accounting consolidations and analysis, not market consolidation and analysis.

An MIS or marketing information system is the solution. Building an MIS involves:

○ Adding codes to the sales ledger to identify customers and products (in addition to accounts and stock keeping units)
○ Summarizing the customer transactions to a level of detail suited to marketing
○ Extracting the customer/product data
○ Storing it on a database
○ Adding extra codes to facilitate segmentation analysis
○ Obtaining software tools to analyse and report on the database

This is easy to describe, but, as those who have tried will know, tremendously hard to implement. The main difficulty to overcome is to manage the expectations of computer staff, financial management (who own the sales ledger) and marketing users.

A problem facing anyone contemplating the development of an MIS is whether to hold data at the lowest level of detail or to hold summary statistics. The extra cost of storing and processing detailed data, at customer level, often deters planners. However, only storing summary data is a mistake in most circumstances, for two reasons:

○ Flexibility to analyse and segment by different combinations of variables is only possible if the data is held at the lowest possible levels of detail.
○ Customer data can subsequently be used for implementing the strategy (i.e. for direct mail, telemarketing and field sales call reporting).

Database marketing – reconciling the tactical with the strategic

Databases have traditionally been too large and expensive, and their performance too slow, for them to be cost-justifiable. Consequently, many of the MIS in use today are summary sales reporting systems. However, with the increased importance attached to direct marketing, telemarketing and sales performance management (using laptop computers), many companies are actively engaged in building customer databases.

Databases often represent a compromise between the strategic requirements of the planners and the tactical requirements of direct marketers, telemarketers and sales managers. Another trouble for newcomers to the world of databases is that they fall prey to the many pitfalls, and believe many of the myths (Table 11.4).

The consequence of these problems is that databases very often hold data that does not fit the purpose of the tacticians, far less the needs of strategic planners.

> The attempt to develop databases that serve both strategic and tactical purposes is often referred to as database marketing.

One of the most acute problems is that of reconciling the internal and external views of the markets. The usual problem is that data retrieved from the sales ledger rarely possesses the details needed to link customer records to market segments. Some of the problems are described in Table 11.5.

Table 11.4 Myths and realities about databases

Myth	Reality
The database collects what we need	We collect what is easily available
The database measures what matters	We measure what is least embarrassing
The database users understand what data they need	We know what we used last, what the textbooks say and what might be interesting on a rainy day
The database needs to hold more and more data	We feel safer with loadsadata, even when we haven't a clue how to use it
The database must integrate the data physically	We like neat solutions, whatever the cost
The database will save staff time	We need more and more staff to analyse data
The database will harmonize marketing, finance and sales	We all compete for scarce resources, and this involves fighting
The database is the one source of our market intelligence	We haven't thought through the business problems

Table 11.5 Problems of reconciling internal and external market audits

External audit – variable	Problem with internal
What is bought	Internal systems have rich detail on accounts and stock-keeping units. However, information about products such as colour, style, etc. can often be missing. Information on the outlets or channels through which they sold is very often lacking.
Who buys	Internal systems record who paid the invoice and who received delivery of the goods. They rarely record who made the buying decision, or who influenced it. Even when the buyer details are on the system, it is rarely easy to determine their characteristics such as age, sex, etc. Reconciling external to internal involves: o matching accounts to customers o matching stock-keeping units to products o matching external variables to internal records o collecting data from other sources than the sales ledger (e.g. from surveys of sales representatives)
Why	Internal sources of information on why people purchase is scarce. Enquiries can be qualified, using survey techniques, to provide some clues on why people respond to an advertising campaign. Customer satisfaction surveys may also yield clues. Call reports from field sales and telesales can also provide valuable clues, especially if survey disciplines can be observed by the sales staff.

Fusing together data from external sources and internal data is becoming increasingly common as a solution to the external – internal problem. This is often referred to as data fusion. Where large volumes of data are involved, computer programs, known as de-duplication routines, are used to automate the matching of the data. However, automation rarely achieves more than 80% accuracy in matching, and manual matching has to be applied to the remaining data.

> The cost of matching external and internal market-coding schemes is driving a few companies to collect customer profiles at source. This is either when they first enquire, or when their sales ledger records are first created.

However, the cost of the changes to the sales ledger, and the fact that it is owned by finance, is often a barrier to success. In the future, marketing will need to work much more closely with Finance and the IT Department, if it is to develop databases successfully.

What is the secret of using information successfully?

Information, in the minds of most marketing managers, lies in a strange no man's land, part way between the nitty gritty stuff of marketing management and the dizzy abstractions of technologists, cyberneticists and boffins. Widely misunderstood, or equated to 'keyboard literacy', or 'technology awareness', the management of marketing information often ends up neglected or delegated to the most junior member of the marketing team.

Information is not the same as technology, nor is it information technology, nor is it necessarily derived from information technology. There are many myths associated with the use of computers to hold marketing data, as Table 11.4 reveals.

The information needs of marketing keep changing as a consequence of the evolution of the marketing strategy.

Information is not all hard, objective data; we will not necessarily become better informed by collecting more and more raw data, and storing it until we end up knowing 'everything'. Accounting systems are often seen as a source of hard facts, since most accounting transactions have to be audited and therefore must be reasonably accurate. Yet most accounting data has little direct relevance for marketing strategy.

What information is needed to support a marketing strategy? The answer to this question is something of a conundrum, since the information needed depends upon the marketing objectives that form the strategy. If you change the strategic marketing objectives, then you may need different kinds of information to support your strategy. Table 11.1, earlier in this chapter, illustrates how different objectives require different supporting information.

This observation goes some way towards explaining one of the great puzzles of marketing information:

> why is it so difficult to specify marketing's information needs? The answer is that, unlike accounting or manufacturing, which have

fixed information needs, the information needs of marketing keep changing as a consequence of the evolution of the marketing strategy.

At this point, the sales or marketing director might feel that, because the situation changes so radically every year, there can be no hope for developing an effective system or procedure for obtaining marketing information. Many at this point delegate the need to an office junior, with the result that they are very ill-informed when they come to develop their marketing strategies.

For all the problems, there are basic underlying marketing issues with which all companies have to contend. Furthermore, the solutions they have adopted can be seen as variations on relatively few themes. The basic model of a marketing system can be visualized as in Figure 11.3.

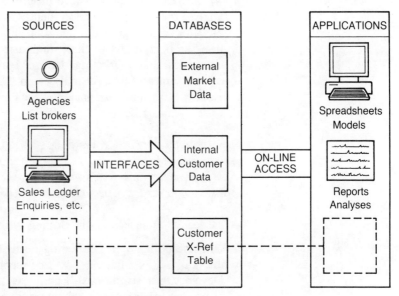

Figure 11.3 Information flows in a marketing system

The main components of the system are as follows:

o *External market data* which is purchased from external agencies. These include governmental agencies, market research firms, list brokers, etc.

o *Internal customer data* which is collected from the sales ledger and other internal sources such as customer service, field sales, telesales, etc. It is coded and segmented in such a way that market-share figures can be created by comparison with external data.

o *Customer reference table* which is needed to make the system work effectively. It identifies customers (as defined by marketing) and provides a cross-reference to sales ledger accounts. Whenever a new sales ledger account is created, the cross-reference table is used to determine the customer associated with that account. This avoids the need for costly manual matching or de-duplication after the account is created. It is also used by marketing applications as a standard reference table for customers.

○ *Database* refers to all three of the above data types. It needs to be structured using a technique known as *data modelling* which organizes the data into the component types that marketing wants, and not the structure that finance or anyone else provides. Usually, the data is held using *relational database* software, since this provides for maximum flexibility and choice of analysis tools.

○ *Interfaces* refers to the computer programs that grab the data from the source systems and restructure it into the components to go onto the marketing database. These programs have to be written by the in-house IT staff, since they obtain and restructure data from the in-house sales ledger, and other in-house systems.

○ *Applications* are the software programs that the planners use to analyse the data and develop their plans. They include data-grabbing tools, that grab the items of data from their storage locations; reporting tools that summarize the data according to categories that marketing defines; spreadsheets that carry out calculations and what-if analyses on the reported summary data. Applications may also include specific marketing planning software such as EXMAR.*

> The critical issue when building such as system is that it is not self-contained within Marketing. It requires interface programs that will alter the systems used by Finance, Sales and other internal departments, as well as data-feeds from external sources.

The secrets of success in developing systems for Marketing are:

○ Understanding what Marketing needs and particularly how the internal and external views will be reconciled

○ Developing a strong cost-benefit case for information systems, given that other systems, including financial ones, will have to be altered to accommodate the needs of Marketing

○ Working continuously with internal IT staff until the system is built. They are under pressure from other sources, especially Finance, and unless Marketing maintains momentum and direction, then other priorities will inevitably win.

> Marketing planners need to become far less insular and parochial if they are to obtain the information they require to plan effectively. Cross-functional understanding and co-operation must be secured by Marketing if they are to develop the systems they need.

*EXMAR is a major decision-support tool for strategic marketing planning. For further information, contact Professor Malcolm McDonald, Cranfield School of Management, Cranfield, Bedford, MK43 0AL, England.

In many companies, Marketing staff are, at best, tolerated by their colleagues in Finance, Operations, IT, and on the Board. Building the interdepartmental bridges to secure data, information and knowledge is one of the greatest challenges facing Marketing today.

Forecasting

Forecasting is one of the most emotive subjects in the whole field of management. Most managers reckon to be experts, or, at least, are rarely backward in expressing an opinion about the subject, and marketing executives are constantly on the rack, because the one task they inevitably get wrong is the forecast.

While in a book of this kind it is not possible to go into any detail, it would be wrong not to attempt to put this subject into a better perspective than it is currently.

Why is forecasting so difficult?

The size and complexity of the marketing task in all kinds of enterprise has substantially increased in recent years.

The growing diversity of customer needs in a rapidly-changing environment has resulted in shorter product life cycles, which have therefore become more difficult to manage profitably.

The growing diversity of customer needs in a rapidly-changing environment has resulted in shorter product life cycles, which have therefore become more difficult to manage profitably. Distribution patterns have changed dramatically in most markets, and competitive pressures have intensified with the geographical dispersion of operations and the growing internationalization of the scale of businesses, the management of which has become more competent as a result of the growing professionalism of management educators. The socio-cultural, legal, political environments in which managers have to operate have become more volatile and subject to more rapid change. The volume of data and information available has mushroomed, and processing networks have become more sophisticated, while the availability of quantitative techniques to the management of the marketing function has outpaced the ability to use them effectively. Added to this is the ever-present difficulty of measuring the behavioural aspects of marketing, such as social, cultural and psychological.

The result of all this is that it is becoming increasingly more difficult to find and develop profitable markets, and with this comes the difficulty of forecasting with anything like the accuracy that was possible when markets were more stable.

Nevertheless, it has to be done, and it has to be done well, because the consequences of being wrong can be very severe indeed for a company.

This is not the place to go into a detailed description of the many forecasting techniques available to a company. However, it could be useful to discuss briefly the major boundaries of forecasting as outlined in Figure 11.4.

From this, it will be seen that there are two major types of forecasting, which can be loosely described as *macro* and *micro*.

Selection of the appropriate technique is dependent on four main factors, the first of which is the degree of accuracy required. It will be obvious that the greater the risk of the decision that depends on the forecast, the greater will be the accuracy required, hence the cost. Second, the method will depend on the availability of data and information. Third, the time horizon is a key determinant of the forecasting method. For example, are we forecasting next period's sales, in which case quantitative extrapolative approaches may be appropriate, or are we forecasting what will happen to our principal market over the next five years, in which case qualitative approaches may be appropriate? Lastly, the position of the product in its life cycle will also be a key determinant of the forecasting method. For example, at the introductory stage of a product's life cycle, less data and information will be available than at the maturity stage, when time series can be a useful forecasting method.

From this, it will be apparent immediately that we must make an important distinction between macro and micro forecasting.

> Macro forecasting is essentially concerned with forecasting markets in total, whereas micro forecasting is more concerned with detailed unit forecasts.

The discussion of the marketing planning process in Chapter 2 makes it very clear that budgets and plans which are based on little more than trend extrapolations are unlikely to be successful in the long run, since the really key strategic issues relating to products and markets are rarely given due consideration through such a process. Likewise, it will be recalled that our discussion of market segmentation in Chapter 4 stressed that there are inherent dangers in running sophisticated budgeting systems that are based on little more than crude extrapolations of past sales trends and which leave the marketing strategies implicit. Such systems are the ones that cause serious commercial problems when market structures change.

> Thus, some form of macro forecasting has to precede the setting of marketing objectives and strategies, while detailed unit forecasts, or micro forecasts, should come after the company has decided which specific market opportunities it wants to take advantage of and how best this can be done.

Figure 11.4 also shows that there are basically two major techniques for forecasting, which can be described as *qualitative* and *quantitative*. It would be unusual if either of these methods was used entirely on its own, mainly because of the inherent dangers in each. What we are really talking about is the need to combine an intuitive approach with the purely mathematical approach.

For example, it is comparatively easy to develop an equation which will extrapolate statistically the world population up to, say, the year 2010. The problem with such an approach, however, is that it does not take account of likely changes in past trends. It would be easy to

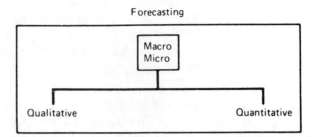

Figure 11.4

list a whole series of possible events which could affect world population, and then assign probabilities to the likelihood of those events happening.

The main point we are making is that it is the task of management to take whatever relevant data is available to help predict the future, to use on it whatever quantitative techniques are appropriate, but then to use qualitative methods such as expert opinions, market research, analogy, and so on to predict what will be the likely *discontinuities* in the time series. It is only through the sensible use of the available tools that management will begin to understand what has to be done to match its own capabilities with carefully selected market needs. Without such an understanding, any form of forecasting is likely to be a sterile exercise.

Organizing for marketing planning

The purpose of this brief section is not to delve into the complexities of organizational forms, but to put the difficult process of marketing planning into the context of the relevant environment in which it will be taking place. The point is that you start from where you *are*, not from where you would like to be, and it is a fact of business that marketing means different things in different circumstances. It is not our intention here to recommend any one particular organizational form. Rather, it is to point out some of the more obvious organizational issues and their likely effect on the way marketing planning is carried out. As a result of the seemingly permanent debate surrounding organizational forms, the author carried out a research study over a two-year period between 1987 and 1989, taking great care in the process to read the literature on the subject of marketing planning.

The interesting fact to emerge was that most approaches to the subject concentrated almost exclusively on the 'medicine' itself and showed relatively little concern for the 'patient' (if indeed the company can be viewed as being ill and in need of attention).

That this should happen makes about as much sense as a doctor dispensing the same drug to every patient, irrespective of his or her condition. Certainly, the treatment might help a proportion of the clients, but for a vast number it will be at best irrelevant and, at worst, perhaps even dangerous.

In the case of those promoting the 'marketing planning nostrum', it is particularly ironic to observe how the product has somehow become more important than the customer. Whatever happened to all that good advice about focusing on customers and their situations?

What must be recognized is that there has to be a symbiotic relationship between the patient and the cure. It is the two working together which brings success. Similarly, the doctor, if the third-party adviser might be described as such, must be more prepared to a take holistic approach to the situation. Instead of writing an instant prescription, the doctor should first find out more about the client.

Since the research study referred to above set out to consider how marketing planning might be introduced more effectively into organizations, let us remember that, like the good doctor, we are going to try to understand more about our patients.

Organizational life phases

At first sight, every organization appears to be quite different from any other, and, of course, in many ways it is. Its personnel and facilities can never exist in the same form elsewhere. Its products, services, history and folklore also play their part in creating a unique entity.

Yet it is also possible to look at organizations in another way and find that instead of uniqueness, there are also similarities.

What, then, is this commonality all organizations share? As companies grow and mature, it seems that they *all* experience a number of distinct life phases. Certainly, our research experience has convinced us that, once the phases of corporate life are explained to managers, they can readily position their own company on its lifeline.

The significance of this is that the senior executives can then understand the nature of their company's growing pains and how these might contribute to current operational problems and even to a particular organizational culture.

Moreover, sometimes this culture will be most receptive to marketing planning, at other times less so. Equally, the marketing planning process itself might need to be modified to sit more comfortably within a given corporate culture.

For now, however, let us look at the way companies grow and develop.

Firstly, as firms grow in sales, so they tend to go through an organizational evolution. Figure 11.5 shows a firm starting off its existence and growing in turnover over a period of time.

When such a firm starts off, it is often organized totally around the owner who tends to know more about customers and products than anyone else in the company.

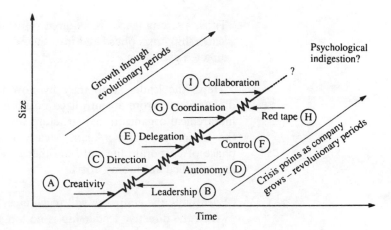

Figure 11.5

This organizational form can be represented as in Figure 11.6, with all decisions and lines of communication revolving around one person. The point here is that formalized marketing planning by means of systems and written procedures will certainly be less relevant than in, say, a diversified multinational.

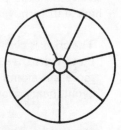

Figure 11.6

However, as this firm grows in size and complexity, as new products and new markets are added, this organizational form begins to break down and the first crisis appears, which is resolved in one of two ways. Either the owner/enterpreneur sells the business and retires or starts up again, or he or she adopts the more traditional organizational form with which most of us are familiar (Figure 11.7) in which certain functional duties are allocated to individuals to manage by means of their own specialized departments. Some aspects of the work will need to be delegated and systems and procedures will have to be developed to replace the ad-hoc arrangements of the initial phase. Above all, organizational loose ends have to be tidied up and a new sense of purpose and direction instilled in the employees.

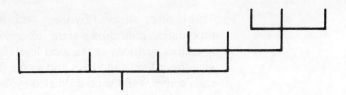

Figure 11.7

Thus, a strong leader is required to bring the company out of the leadership crisis phase and into the next, relatively calm period of directed evolution.

Here, the leader, who may by now no longer be the founder, directs events from a centralized position. He or she presides over a hierarchical organizational structure which is set up to achieve what the leader prescribes. Again, steady growth can accompany this phase of corporate life until another crisis point is reached. This is the so-called autonomy crisis.

Eventually the company will reach a certain size or complexity at which the directive leadership is no longer so appropriate.

Individuals working in their particular spheres of activity know more than the central authority. Not only do they resent being told what to do by someone they perceive to be 'out of touch', they actually want to have more personal autonomy to influence company policies and operations. The struggle for power at the autonomy crisis can be accompanied by a tightening of central control, which, in turn, exacerbates the problem, causing poor morale and even, perhaps, high staff turnover.

The crisis is eventually resolved by the company providing a much more delegative style of leadership which does, in fact, generate more autonomy at lower levels. Again a relatively trouble-free, evolutionary growth period follows from this delegated style.

However, as growth continues, senior management become increasingly concerned about the high levels of autonomy lower down the organization. They experience feelings of powerlessness and sense the need to regain control.

This control crisis can be another very destabilizing phase of the company's development. Understandable though the feelings of impotence might be for senior management, it seems to be very difficult to turn the clock back to a directive style again. Too much has happened in the intervening years.

The solution to the control crises seems to be to embark upon a programme for establishing better co-ordination between the various parts of the organization.

This is often achieved by using such mechanisms as formal planning procedures, centralizing some technical functions, but leaving daily operating decisions at the local level, setting up special projects involving lower-level employees and so on. Thus, another period of relative calm comes with the co-ordinated evolutionary phase of development.

With continued growth, there is a tendency for the co-ordinating practices to become institutionalized, thus planning procedures become ritualized, special projects become meaningless chores and too many decisions seem to be governed by company rules and regulations.

A new crisis point has been reached – the 'bureaucracy' or 'red-tape' crisis. Procedures seem to take precedence over problem solving.

The only solution seems to be for the company to strive towards a new phase of collaboration in which, once again, the contributions of individuals and teams are valued as much, if not more, than systems and procedures.

There has to be a concerted effort to re-energize and re-personalize operating procedures. More emphasis has to be put on teamwork, spontaneity and creativity.

If a company can win through to the collaborative phase of evolution then, again, a period of relatively trouble-free growth can be expected as a reward. However, as we have seen, this pattern of evolutionary growth followed by a crisis appears to be ever-repeating.

Each solution to an organizational development problem brings with it the seeds of the next crisis phase.

Thus it is that the collaborative evolutionary crisis will probably end when there is a surfeit of integrating mechanisms and, perhaps, employees begin to lose the ability to function independently.

This last point is purely conjecture, because not many companies seem to have moved far enough along their biographical lifeline for this to be an issue. But from the work we have completed in a number of companies, this idea of company life phases has helped us to understand much more about a client's operating problems and how we might more suitably provide help.

Within this second phase of growth, there are basically two kinds of organization, which can be described as either *decentralized* or *centralized*, with several combinations within each extreme.

Looking firstly at decentralization, it is possible to represent this diagrammatically as in Figure 11.8.* The shaded area of the triangle represents the top-level strategic management of the firm. It can be seen from this diagram that the central services, such as market research and public relations, are repeated at the subsidiary company level. It can also be seen that there is a strategic level of management at the subsidiary level, the acid test being whether subsidiary company/unit top management can introduce new products without reference to headquarters.

*This section owes much to the original work and thinking of Simon Majaro.

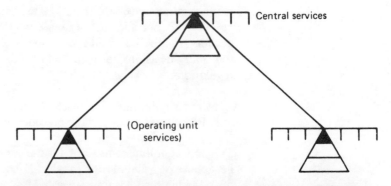

Figure 11.8

The point about this kind of decentralized organizational structure is that it leads inevitably to duplication of effort and differentiation of strategies, with all the consequent problems, unless a major effort is made to get some synergy out of the several systems by means of a company-wide planning system.

One telecommunications company had a range of 1500 products, and one of those products had 1300 different variations, all of which was the result of a totally decentralized marketing-orientated approach in the subsidiary companies. It was not surprising that any sensible economies of scale in production were virtually impossible, with the result that the company made a substantial loss.

The same problems apply to marketing research, advertising, pricing, distribution, and other business areas. When someone takes the trouble to find out, it is often very salutary to see the reaction of senior managers at headquarters when they are told, for example, that the very same market problem is being researched in many different countries around the world, all at enormous expense.

It is this kind of organization structure which, above all others, requires strong central coordination by means of some kind of planning system, otherwise everyone wastes enormous amounts of corporate resources striving to maximize their own small part of the business.

If, however, some system can be found of gaining synergy from all the energy expended, then the rewards are great indeed. The point is, that marketing in this kind of system means something different from marketing in other kinds of system, and it is as well to recognize this from the outset.

A centrally controlled company tends to look as depicted in Figure 11.9. Here it will be seen that there is no *strategic* level of management in the subsidiary units, particularly in respect of new product introductions. This kind of organizational form tends to lead to

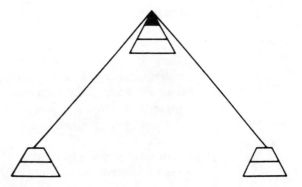

Figure 11.9

standardized strategies, particularly in respect of product management. For example, when a new product is introduced, it tends to be designed at the outset with as many markets as possible in mind, while the benefits from market research in one area are passed on to other areas, and so on.

> The problem here, of course, is that unless great care is exercised, subsidiary units can easily become less sensitive to the needs of individual markets, and hence lose flexibility in reacting to competitive moves.

The point here again, is that marketing in this kind of system means something different from marketing in the kind of system described above.

There is a difference between financial manipulation and business management in respect of the headquarters role. There is a difference between a corporation and its individual components, and often there is confusion about what kind of planning should be done by managers at varying levels in the organization, such confusion arising because the chief executive has not made it clear what kind of business is being managed.

We have looked briefly at two principal organizational forms, both of which consist essentially of a central office and various decentralized divisions, each with its own unique products, processes and markets which complement the others in the group. In enterprises of this type, planning within the divisions applies to the exploration of markets and improved efficiency within the boundaries laid down by headquarters. The problems and opportunities that this method throws up tend to make the headquarters role one of classifying the boundaries for the enterprise as a whole, in relation to new products and markets that do not appear to fall within the scope of one of the divisions.

In this type of organization, the managers of affiliated companies are normally required to produce the level of profit set by headquarters management within the constraints imposed on them, and such companies need to institutionalize this process by providing a formal structure of ideas and systems so that operating management know what they are expected to do and whether they are doing the essential things.

> The point about these kinds of organization seems to be that some method *has* to be found of planning and controlling the growth of the business in order to utilize effectively the evolving skills and growing reputation of the firm, and so avoid an uncontrolled dissipation of energy.

It is probably easier to do this in a centrally organized firm, but, as we have pointed out, both organizational forms have their disadvantages.

Finally, the *financial trust* type of organization needs to be mentioned briefly, in which the primary concern of central management is the investment of shareholders' capital in various businesses. The buying and selling of interests in various firms is done for appreciation of capital rather than for building an enterprise with any logic of its own. Planning in this type of operation requires different knowledge and skills, and addresses itself to kinds of problems that are different from those in the two organizational forms described above.

Before going on to describe marketing planning systems, there are two further points worth making briefly about organizing for marketing.

> The first is that where marketing and sales are separated at board level, marketing planning is going to be a very different kind of activity from a situation in which both functions are coordinated at board level.

Figure 11.10 illustrates these two different situations.

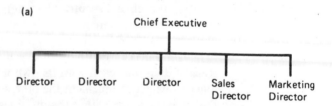

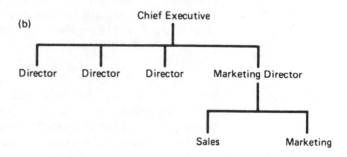

Figure 11.10

374

In the first of these organizational forms, marketing is very much a staff activity, with the real power vested in the sales organization. While a strong chief executive can ensure that the two activities are sensibly co-ordinated, unfortunately this rarely happens effectively because he or she is often too busy with production, distribution, personnel, and financial issues to devote enough time to sales and marketing. The point here is that a sales force is quite correctly concerned with *today's* products, problems, customers, and so on, while a marketing manager needs to be thinking about the *future*. The sales force is also quite correctly concerned mainly with *individual* products, problems and customers, while a marketing manager needs to be thinking about groups of products and customers (portfolio management and market segmentation).

> The two jobs are closely connected, but fundamentally different, and great care is necessary to ensure that what the marketing department is *planning* is the same as what the sales force is actually *doing* in the field. All too often they are not.

The second kind of organizational form tends to make it easier to ensure a sensible coordination between planning and doing.

The second and final part about marketing organizational forms is that there are a number of issues that *all* firms have to address. These are:

○ Functions (such as advertising, market research, pricing, and so on)
○ Products
○ Markets
○ Geographical locations
○ Channels

> Of these, most firms would readily agree that, in most cases, the two main issues are *products* and *markets*, which is why many companies have what are called 'product managers' and/or 'market managers'.

There can be no right or wrong answer to the question of which of these is the better, and common sense will dictate that it is market circumstances alone that will determine which is most appropriate for any one company.

Each has its strengths and weaknesses. A product manager orientated system will ensure good strong product orientation, but can also easily lead to superficial market knowledge.

> Many a company has been caught out by subtle changes in their several markets causing a product to become practically redundant. In consumer goods, for example, many companies are beginning to admit that their rigid product/brand management system has allowed their major customers to take the initiative,

and many are now changing belatedly to a system where the focus of marketing activity revolves around major customer/market groups rather than individual products.

On the other hand, a market manager orientated system can easily result in unnecessary product differentiation and poor *overall* product development.

Ideally, therefore, whatever organizational form is adopted, the two central issues of products and markets constantly need to be addressed. This conundrum can be summarized in the following brief case study.

Northern Sealants Limited manufactures a range of adhesives that fall into two main categories: seals; and sealants. The company supplies these products to a large number of markets. However, the main users come under four industry headings: gas, oil and petrochemical refineries; automative; electrical; and OEM. Advise how the marketing function should be organized.

Figure 11.11 illustrates this case diagrammatically in what is often referred to as a *matrix* organization. Figure 11.12 puts this structure into the context of this particular company. Here, it will be seen that, organizationally, Northern Sealants have both a product management and market management structure. The basic role of the product manager is to ensure that the aspects of the product are properly managed, while the role of the market manager is to pay particular attention to the needs of the market.

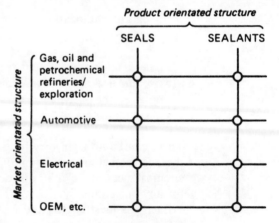

Figure 11.11

Close liaison between the two is obviously necessary and a basic principle of this kind of organization is that ultimate authority for the final decision *must* be vested in either one or the other. Even when this is done, however, communications can still be difficult, and great care is necessary to ensure that vested interests are not allowed to dominate the real product/market issues.

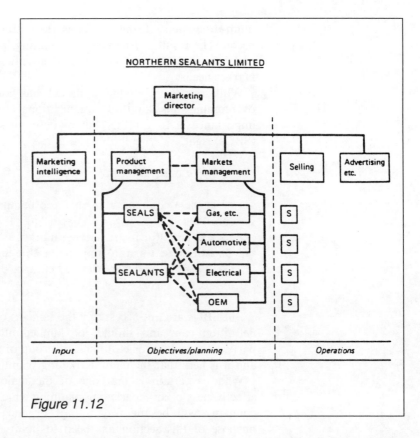

Figure 11.12

To summarize, no one particular organizational form can be recommended, common sense and market needs being the final arbiters. However, the following factors *always* need to be considered:

○ Marketing 'centres of gravity'
○ Interface areas (e.g. present/future; salespeople/drawing office; etc.)
○ Authority and responsibility
○ Ease of communication
○ Co-ordination
○ Flexibility
○ Human factors

The world's leading companies now organize themselves around customer groups and processes rather than around products.

Wherever practicable, however, it appears to be sensible to try to organize around customer groups, or markets, rather than around products, functions or geography. Increasingly, firms are organizing themselves around customers or around processes, such as product development. Quite a large 'industry', known as Business Process Redesign (BPR), has grown up around this issue. The Cranfield/Chartered Institute of Marketing research study into the future of marketing has clearly demonstrated that the world's leading companies now organize themselves around customer groups and processes rather than around products. Computer firms, such as AT&T for example, organize around end-use markets and appoint multi-disciplinary teams to focus their attention on their specific needs. The result is personnel, accounting, production, distribution and sales policies that are tailored specifically to a unique set of market needs.

While this team-building approach has gone a long way towards overcoming this kind of organizational barrier, of much more importance is to get the task of defining strategic business units (SBUs) right.

> A strategic business unit:
>
> o Will have common segments and competitors for most of its products
> o Is a competitor in an external market
> o Is a discrete, separate and identifiable unit
> o Will have a manager who has control over most of the areas critical to success

But SBUs are not necessarily the same as operating units, and the definition can, and should, be applied all the way down to a particular product, or customer, or group of products or customers, and it is here that the main marketing planning task lies.

What is certain is that one of the major determinants of the effectiveness of any marketing planning which is attempted within a company will be the way that it organizes for marketing. The purpose of this section has been to point out some of the more obvious facts and pitfalls before attempting to outline a marketing planning system, to which we can turn in the next chapter.

The influence of the culture carriers

The biographical lifeline described above goes some way towards describing a company situation, but does it go far enough? Is the company culture derived entirely from its past? The answer is negative.

> Certain individuals, the so-called culture carriers, will influence the situation in ways which promote a particular pattern of behaviours and values within the organization.

These will certainly be company-specific in nature, and as such could be described as cultural.

Who, then, are the culture carriers and what do they do to be so influential? Much has been written about influencing behaviours, but there is some convincing evidence about the things that leaders do to transmit and embed culture.

Primary mechanisms

Here are the most influential behaviours that signal and reinforce culture:

1 How the leader reacts to crises or critical events.
2 The criteria he or she establishes for allocating rewards and status.

3 The areas which the leader pays attention to, measures and controls.
4 The criteria he or she establishes for recruitment, selection, promotion, retirement and dismissal.
5 The role model the leader plays to others, by demonstrating certain behaviour, or even by coaching or teaching subordinates.

Secondary mechanisms

1 Organizational systems and procedures.
2 Organizational design and structure.
3 Design of physical space, facades and building.
4 Formal statements about organizational philosophy, creeds and charters.
5 Stories, legends, myths and parables about important people and events.

> One of the main results of the actions of the culture carriers is that they can determine the level at which marketing planning is treated in the organization.

Why they do this seems to depend upon the extent to which they use their positions of power and influence for personal aggrandizement or for the good of the company.

Accordingly, we have identified four levels of acceptance of marketing planning.

○ *Level 1* – marketing planning is deliberately ignored.
○ *Level 2* – marketing planning is treated unthinkingly as a formula and the company merely pays lip service to the end result.
○ *Level 3* – marketing planning is taken moderately seriously and it is recognized that resources have to be allocated to the process if results are to be achieved.
○ *Level 4* – marketing planning is taken very seriously and it is recognized that not only do resources have to be allocated, but also that the plan could fundamentally change the direction and nature of the business (and with it the existing power structure in the company!).

> Thus, it can be seen that marketing planning has to be perceived as not just an economic process designed to use resources more effectively, but also as a change mechanism with 'political' undertones.

Clearly, the level at which marketing planning is accepted by the company is related to the level of risk, or readiness to change, acceptable to the culture carriers.

Figure 11.13 helps to illustrate these points.

How marketing planning impacts on the company can similarly be illustrated as shown in Figure 11.14. Level 1 is omitted for obvious reasons.

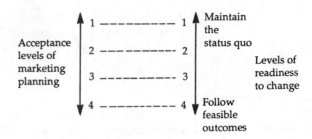

Figure 11.13

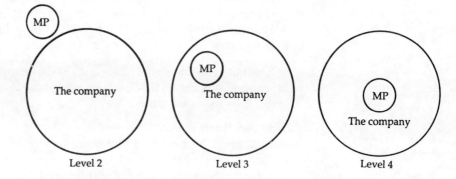

Figure 11.14

The more seriously marketing planning is taken, the more central it becomes in the company's operational life. While it could be argued that the level of acceptance of marketing planning is purely a cognitive problem and that the levels reflect understanding, this does not square with our experience.

> The acceptance of marketing plan-ning seems to be more an attitudinal problem and being prepared to subscribe to the values inherent in a complete planning process.

Equally, when we talk about marketing planning, we are describing a process which requires an acceptance level of 3 or 4 on our scale. Any lower level will, in our opinion, be a complete waste of time for all concerned, be they educationalists or company personnel.

The marketing planning process and corporate culture

Assuming that marketing planning is acceptable at something deeper than a cosmetic level, it becomes possible to see how the process aligns with different phases of the company's lifeline.

Creative evolution phase

In our research, we did not find a single marketing planner at this stage of development. Most of the companies were still really formulating their business ideas and the senior executive (the culture carrier) was in close touch with customers and the company's own staff. The organization had a high level of flexibility to respond to changes in customer needs. In our research, many of these companies were showing high growth and to introduce marketing planning did not appear to offer any additional benefits.

It has to be recognized that some companies do not have a sufficiently good product or service to develop very far along their life path. The infant mortality rate for businesses is very high.

However, if the company successfully negotiates this initial phase, eventually it reaches the leadership crisis. As we have seen, a strong leader is required who will provide the drive and direction which will lead to the next evolutionary phase.

Directed evolution

Companies at this stage of development fall into two camps. Naturally enough, the underlying style behind the marketing planning process was directive in each case, but the impact and effectiveness was significantly different for each type.

The first type we have referred to as 'Directed Marketing Planning Type 1'. Here, the senior executive took responsibility, or delegated the task of producing a marketing plan. This person would then spend time analysing data, performing a situational review and so on, until he or she finished up with a document. Generally, an approving mechanism was built into the process. For example, the board of directors would have to vet the marketing plan before it could be issued, but by and large thereafter the plan acts as a directive for the organization.

The second type – 'Directed Marketing Planning Type 2' – involved the appropriate member of staff being told what information to provide about their areas of work, the form in which the information should be provided, and so on.

Thus, in this case, rather than the plan being directed, the process is spelt out carefully. The resulting information is assembled at a senior level and the resulting planning document is issued as before.

Although in both cases all the creative thinking and control takes place at the top level of the organization, the second method holds a prospect of generating more useful data without sacrificing the directive, power-based culture.

Delegated evolution

As a solution to the autonomy crisis which can develop when directive leadership becomes inappropriate, more delegation becomes an operational feature of organizations.

What seemed to be a problem for marketing planning in these companies was that people in the 'front line', or operating units, of large companies were expected to produce marketing plans, but without very much guidance.

> For example, one company had to send its marketing plans to head office, where they were rigorously examined and then given the corporate thumbs up or down. Only through a process of acceptance or dismissal were the criteria for 'good' plans eventually pieced together.

Our conclusion was that a delegated form of marketing planning can lead to some very high quality inputs and certainly to high levels of commitment on behalf of those involved. Yet, ultimately, the solely bottom-up planning procedures seem to be difficult to integrate and can be demotivating to those involved. Somehow, the sum of the parts is less in stature than it ought to be.

Co-ordinated evolution

At this stage, the lessons of the directed and delegated phases seem to have been learned. There is much more emphasis on a plan for planning and a means to incorporate top-down direction and bottom-up quality.

Equally, a co-ordinated approach enables the company to make best use of its specialized resources and to generate commitment from the staff.

In many ways, the marketing planning processes which are the stuff of textbooks and so on appear to be most suited for a company at this stage of its development.

However, as we have seen, it is possible for the planning process to degenerate from essentially a problem-solving process into a fairly meaningless, bureaucratic ritual. It is at this stage that the planning process will become counter-productive.

Collaborative evolution

Here, the bureaucracy has to make way for genuine problem solving again. At present we do not have very much evidence about what this means in practice. But it is possible to speculate that, as business environments change at an ever-increasing pace, so new marketing planning procedures might need to be developed.

Creativity and expediency would appear to be the passwords to this new phase of development.

Diagnostic tools

We have found it necessary to develop diagnostic tools or instruments to help identify where the company might be on its lifeline and also how the management style reflects the current culture of the organization.

Although these are in a relatively early stage of development, both we and client organizations are finding that the information they uncover helps to make more sense of the company situation *vis-à-vis* marketing planning.

Conclusions

In this chapter, we have shown how the acceptance of marketing planning is largely conditioned by the stage of development of the organization and the behaviour of the corporate culture carriers. Thus it is that different modes of marketing planning became more appropriate at different phases of the company's life.

While the marketing planning process itself remains more or less consistent throughout, *how* that process is managed must be congruent with the current organizational culture. The alternative to this would be to take steps to change the company culture and make it more amenable to a particular planning process.

Since culture tends to act to maintain the existing power structure and the status quo, marketing planning interventions in companies must be recognized as having a 'political' dimension and are not purely educational. Not least among the political issues is the question of whether or not a company's management style can adapt sufficiently to enable the marketing planning process to deliver the rewards it promises.

Can managers who have led a company down a particular path suddenly change track? In other words, is it possible for frogs to change into princes?

The iconoclastic books would claim that they can, because this is a much more optimistic message with which to sell copies. However, those who have carried out academic research, or are experienced consultants, would have some reservations.

We remain open-minded about this issue, believing that, if the business pressures on a company are sufficient, intelligent behaviour will win the day. We might be proved wrong, but, in the meantime, this chapter provides some useful messages for both marketing advisers and senior executives of companies.

While we see our research as being an important step along the road to effective marketing planning, we are also realistic enough to recognize that there is still far to travel.

Application questions

1 Over what period of time do you forecast in your organization? Is it the right period? Do all relevant managers have an opportunity to make a contribution? If not, say how they could become involved.

2 Is there ever a significant variance between forecasts and sales? If so, how do you explain it?

3 What additional information would you like to help you make more accurate forecasts? How could you obtain such information? Why have you not obtained it in the past?

4 Describe any piece of marketing research that in your view has had a major impact on your company's operations.

5 Describe any major decisions taken which in your view required market research before they were made.

6 Describe what your company's major problems are in the way it uses marketing research.

7 If you were to establish a new marketing information system for your company, say what it would contain. Where is it different from your current one and how could such a system be organized and made to work?

Review of Chapter 11

Marketing information
Marketing information is at the heart of the company's ability to plan. *Marketing research* is concerned with research into the whole marketing process (*market research* is research about markets).

Try Exercise 11.1

Types of marketing research
1 Internal – analysis of sales records, advertising levels, price versus volume, etc.
2 External – to complement internal research.
3 Reactive – people respond to questionnaires, structured interviews, etc.
4 Non-reactive – interpretation of observed phenomena, e.g. filming customers in a store, listening to customer panels, etc.

There are pros and cons for each type; therefore, a mix can be useful.

Try Exercise 11.2

How much to spend
Can be based on the theory of probability and expected value. For example, a product costs 100K ecu to develop. There is an estimated 10 per cent chance of failure. The maximum cost therefore = 100K ecu × 0.1 = 10K ecu Therefore, it is worth spending this amount to prevent the loss.

Marketing information system (MIS)
A system to facilitate information flows needs to be developed so that there are appropriate inputs and that correct data get to the users in a sensible form.

Forecasting
Forecasting can be of two types:

1 *Macro* – forecasting markets in total.
2 *Micro* – detailed unit forecasts.

Which to choose depends upon the:

(a) Accuracy required
(b) Availability of data
(c) Time horizon
(d) Position of the product in its life cycle (macro at early stage)

Techniques for forecasting:

Quantitative – based on facts
Qualitative – based on experience and judgement   *Try Exercise 11.3*

Organizational barriers
A number of potential barriers exist:

1 *Cognitive* – not knowing enough about marketing planning.
2 *Cultural* – the company culture is not sufficiently developed for marketing planning.
3 *Political* – the culture carriers feel threatened by marketing.

4 *Resources* – not enough resources are allocated to marketing.
5 *Structural* – lack of a plan and organization for planning.
6 *Lack of an MIS.*

Centralization versus decentralization

For multi-unit/international organizations there are two possibilities.

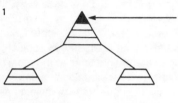

1
Marketing function at head
office; satellites are just
production units

\+ = central control

\- = remote from
local information

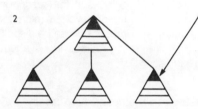

Marketing decentralized

2
\+ = focused, local
identity

\- = duplication of information and effort

Choose an approach where the advantages outweigh the disadvantages.   *Try Exercise 11.4*

Questions raised for the company

1 Q: What influences whether research is carried out internally or
        by external consultants?
   A: There can be a number of factors – speed, timing, cost, nature
        of the research problem, skill requirements, the need for
        anonymity or objectivity, access of information, etc. Each
        decision must be taken on its merits.

2 Q: What criteria should be used to assess external researchers?
   A: Again, there are a number of issues to consider.

   (a) *Reputation* – in general, in the industry, for particular types
        of research, etc.
   (b) *Capability and experience* – how long established, quality
        and qualifications of staff, number of staff, repeat
        business, recommendations and references, etc.
   (c) *Organization* – size, links with sources of information,
        premises, location, geographical coverage, full-time or
        part-time interviewers, terms of business, etc.

Introduction to Chapter 11 exercises

To find, maintain or develop a position in any market, it is necessary to
have the right information about what is happening in that market.
Without having a sensible input of information, the company's decision-
making processes will always be suspect.

However, collecting and storing information can be both difficult and
costly. Moreover, in times of rapid change, information only has a limited

'shelf life'. Generally speaking, companies have an abundance of information at their disposal, either in their own records or from easily accessed external sources such as trade associations and government departments.

Yet, in some ways, having too much information can be just as bad as having too little. It becomes difficult to see the wood for the trees. What is required is to cut through what is merely interesting and home in on the information which is necessary, then ensure that it is presented in a usable form.

Exercise 11.1 will investigate just how much marketing information is needed in your company. In addition, it looks at how to get it to the right people, at the right time, in the most appropriate form.

Exercise 11.2 examines the information-gathering techniques at your disposal, their strengths and weaknesses and how you might select one which best meets your requirements.

Exercise 11.3 looks at forecasting in a generalized way so that any confusion about macro versus micro forecasting, and qualitative versus quantitative approaches, can be dispelled.

Exercise 11.4 provides ideas about setting up the right marketing organization.

Exercise 11.1
The marketing information system

Because all companies are in some ways unique, it follows that there are no easy, 'off-the-shelf', marketing information systems available. Even if they were to exist, the chances would be that they would not work. Instead, the company must assemble its own system, and it must be as simple or as sophisticated as the needs of the situation and the budget allows.

The starting point for any system must be to assess the company's information requirements.

Information requirements
Already, previous work in this book, and the knowledge you have about your company, will suggest certain information requirements to you. However, to ensure that the whole range of possible information requirements is examined, turn to Worksheet 1 which follows and complete it by following the instructions given.

Current information system
The first worksheet will have highlighted the total information requirements for your company. Put this to one side for the moment and now concentrate on your current system.

Turn to Worksheet 2, and follow the instructions.

Proposal for a new system
Compare the information you gathered in Worksheet 1 and that collected in Worksheet 2. Make a note of the following:
1 Information required but not covered by the current system
2 Areas of information in the current system that are redundant
3 Those areas of information that would be more effective if:

   (a) they were presented differently
   (b) they were directed to different people
   (c) they were provided more or less frequently

4 From the above analysis make recommendations about how your company's marketing information system might be improved. See Work sheet 3.

Personal notes

Worksheet 1   Information requirements (Exercise 11.1)

Below is a list of the areas of business that marketing research could be expected to cover. It doesn't follow that you will need information in all of these areas, but, in the light of your earlier study, *tick those that are relevant.*

Then, in the space provided, specify the nature of the information that would be required.

Areas of business	Relevant	Specific information required
Market size		
Market structure		
Market trends		
Market potential		
Market share		
Company communications		
Company image		
Company structure		
Promotion		
Personal selling		
Distribution channels		
Physical distribution		
Packaging		
Profit		
Costs		
Pricing		
Services		
Market research		
Exporting		
New products		
Technical developments		
Competitor activity		
Competitor prices		

(Continued)

Areas of business	Relevant	Specific information required
Competitor processes		
Competitor products		
Competitor services		
User attitude/behaviour		
Governmental factors		
Economic factors		
Demographic factors		
Add your own areas of business		

Worksheet 2   Current information system (Exercise 11.1)

Consider your existing marketing information system and list the various input data, who uses them, for what purpose, the frequency of use and a judgement about whether or not the data are essential, useful or no longer required.

The form below is designed to help you record your findings.

Note: Remember that journals and magazines can be sources of input data just as much as salespeoples' reports and internal control information. You could find it enlightening to include these in your study.

Data input	Used by	Purpose	Frequency	Essential E Useful U Not req. X

(*Continued*)

Data input	Used by	Purpose	Frequency	Essential E Useful U Not req. X

Worksheet 3   Proposal for a new system (Exercise 11.1)

Exercise 11.2
Information-gathering techniques

In this exercise you will make a comparative study of various information-gathering techniques and then decide which ones are best suited to solve the company's information requirements.

Step 1 Study Table 11.6 'Information-gathering techniques', and *only proceed to Step 2 when you have read it carefully*.

Step 2 Consider the information gaps you identified in Exercise 11.1 and decide which type of information-gathering technique will be best suited to provide the missing information. In arriving at your answers, you will have to take into account the level of skill in your company and the likely cost.

Exercise 11.3 will also help you in your choice of information-gathering techniques.

If there were no information gaps as a result of completing Exercise 11.1, then review the current information-gathering techniques used in your company and decide if they could be improved upon.

Table 11.6   Information-gathering techniques

Technique	Main strengths	Drawbacks
Desk research	Can provide quick results, relatively cheap, controllable.	Information. might not be specific enough – interpretation problems. Information can be out of date.
Company sales records	Readily accessible.	Might not be in a form that can easily be interpreted – mainly historical data.
Company financial records	Readily accessible.	Might not be easily translated into the required form. Mainly historical data.
Salespersons' reports	Readily accessible current recent information. about customers.	Interpreting narrative into quantified information can be difficult. Inadequate records.
Journals, etc.	Relatively easy to obtain – libraries, etc.	Information is not exactly what is required, e.g. too general.
Trade associations	Have good understanding of specific trade or industry.	Quality of information and degree of co-operation from TAs is variable.
Government agencies and/or statistics	Vast amount of information, relatively easy access.	Need to know way through government systems. Can be swamped with useless information.
External research	Based on competitive environment – will be current information. Provides confidence for decision-making.	Can be costly/time consuming, samples must be accurate – can be difficult to organize.
Questionnaires, face to face	Questioner ensures questions are interpreted correctly – reactions can be noted.	Time-consuming. Can ask loaded questions. Poor design can give rise to misleading results. Costly. Needs skilled interviewer.
Questionnaires, postal	Reach wide audience, relatively cheap.	Failure to get replies back on time (or at all). Filled in by wrong person. Misinterpretation.
Questionnaires, telephone	Instantaneous response, relatively cheap. Do not take up too much of client's time.	Have to be kept brief and so points can be missed. Person gives on the spot information which might be inaccurate.
Depth interviews	Can get to feelings level about products or services. Good qualitative information.	Needs skilled interviewer. Results can be hard to quantify.
Experimentation	Can provide 'actual' customer reaction under test conditions.	Can be expensive. Customer samples must be chosen accurately.
Retail audits	Good quantitative information about stock movement.	Doesn't explain reasons for stock movements.
Consumer panels	Help to establish patterns of purchases and consumption over a period of time.	Consumers have to be kept motivated to record activities, etc.

(Continued)

Technique	Main strengths	Drawbacks
Use MR consultants	Doesn't use up staff time. Can produce results in easily digestible form.	Can be costly. How do you choose the right consultants?

Add any other techniques with which you are familiar and list their strengths and drawbacks.

Personal notes

Exercise 11.3 Forecasting techniques

There have been many long and heated debates about whether forecasting is a science or an art. The short answer is that it is a bit of both.

If you were asked to forecast what you will be doing in two minutes' time, the chances are you would make a very accurate prediction. The reason for this is obvious, as not very much is going to change in such a short time. Extend the period to tomorrow, next week, a month's time, next year, and your forecasting task would become increasingly difficult.

Companies are forced to look well ahead in order to plan their investment, launch new products and so on. Hence their forecasting task is inherently difficult, unless they operate in some backwater unaffected by mainstream change.

The information they require is sometimes very specific (quantitative) and sometimes fairly general (qualitative). Equally, they need to know what is happening in clearly defined areas of their business (micro forecasting) and sometimes what is happening to total markets (macro forecasting). These aspects of forecasting can be combined, as in Figure 11.15.

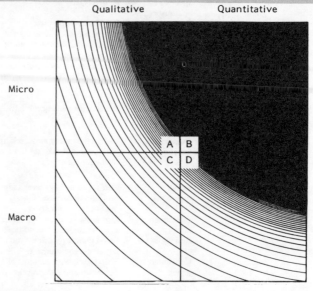

Figure 11.15

The shading indicates the degree of accuracy that can be expected from the various combinations. Thus, the top right-hand corner, quadrant B, demands high accuracy, and calls for scientific rigour, whereas the bottom left-hand corner, quadrant C, relies more on feel, intuition and experience.

Collecting information on which to base a forecast can be a costly business; therefore it is important to recognize the nature of the

forecasting problem with which one is faced before setting out. It is pointless to measure something to three decimal places if only a rough and ready measurement is required.

Here is a list of 'forecasting problems'. Referring to Figure 11.15, identify whether the nature of each problem is qualitative, quantitative, micro or macro, i.e. falls in quadrants A, B, C or D. Write the appropriate letter in the space provided.

1 What percentage change (in volume) is expected in the ice-cream market in 2 years' time? _____

2 What changes in leisure activity are forecast in 5 years' time? _____

3 What percentage increase in total sales can we expect in our key market segment over the next 12 months? _____

4 What would the buyers of our X range want to see as product improvements when we remodel the range next year? _____

5 What changes are expected in our key technology over the next 5 years? _____

6 In what ways will the voting habits of the UK electorate change by the turn of the century? _____

7 How many car-users can be expected to be travelling abroad with their vehicles next summer? _____

8 How many shoppers spending £100 or more can we expect over the next year in our Easthampton store? _____

The answers are as follows:

1 D
2 C
3 B
4 A
5 A
6 C
7 D
8 B

As a general rule, the margin of error has to be minimal in quadrant B, whereas it is least critical in quadrant C. This clearly has implications for the techniques that are used and the cost of assembling the information.

Look at Exercise 11.2 – 'Information-gathering techniques'.

Exercise 11.4 Organizational structure

Business environments are always changing. Demand patterns change, new technology comes in, new legislation is introduced, there is an economic crisis and so on.

Since the key to successful marketing is to have a suitable organization structure, one that can adjust and cope with the environment, it is not surprising that much experimentation has taken place with the different types of structure. Perhaps no one has yet found the perfect answer to this complex problem of getting the organization right. Nevertheless, research studies have shown that, in certain circumstances, some types of structure are going to be more successful than others.

The accompanying worksheet tries to encapsulate these findings in a fairly crude way, showing that structure will to some extent relate to company size and the diversity of its operations. The degree of formality in the marketing planning process will also be related to these factors.

Please answer the following questions:

1 Where would you place your company on the size/complexity of operations continuum?
2 How does your current structure compare with that suggested on the chart?
3 Do the breakdown signals sound familiar?
4 In what ways do you think your structure ought to change?

Personal notes

Worksheet Organizational structure (Exercise 11.4)

Place an x on each of the four lines below to indicate where your organization lies

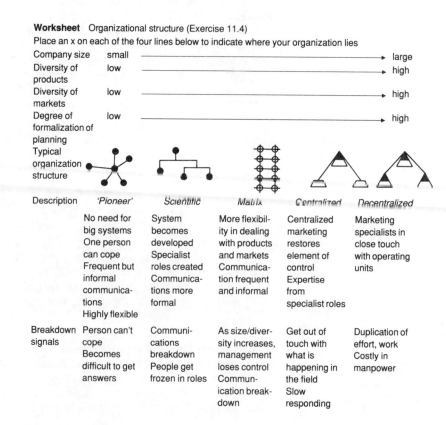

Company size	small	→	large
Diversity of products	low	→	high
Diversity of markets	low	→	high
Degree of formalization of planning	low	→	high

Typical organization structure				
Description	*'Pioneer'*	Scientific	Matrix	Centralized	Decentralized
	No need for big systems One person can cope Frequent but informal communications Highly flexible	System becomes developed Specialist roles created Communications more formal	More flexibility in dealing with products and markets Communication frequent and informal	Centralized marketing restores element of control Expertise from specialist roles	Marketing specialists in close touch with operating units
Breakdown signals	Person can't cope Becomes difficult to get answers	Communications breakdown People get frozen in roles	As size/diversity increases, management loses control Communication breakdown	Get out of touch with what is happening in the field Slow responding	Duplication of effort, work Costly in manpower

12 Implementation issues in marketing planning

Summary

Chapter 12 opens by discussing the implications of size and diversity of operations on marketing planning. This is followed by a summary of the main elements of the marketing planning process. There is a discussion of the role of the chief executive, and the planning department, followed by some thoughts on the marketing planning cycle and planning horizons. Finally, some insights are provided into how the marketing planning process works.

Introduction

In Chapter 3, we explained some of the many myths that surround marketing planning and spelt out the conditions that must be satisfied if any company is to have an effective marketing planning system. These are:

1 Any closed-loop marketing planning system (but especially one that is essentially a forecasting and budgeting system) will lead to entropy of marketing and creativity. Therefore, there has to be some mechanism for preventing inertia from setting in through the over-bureaucratization of the system.
2 Marketing planning undertaken at the functional level of marketing, in the absence of a means of integration with other functional areas of the business at general management level, will be largely ineffective.
3 The separation of responsibility for operational and strategic marketing planning will lead to a divergence of the short-term thrust of a business at the operational level from the long-term objectives of the enterprise as a whole. This will encourage a preoccupation with short-term results at operational level, which normally makes the firm less effective in the long term.
4 Unless the chief executive understands and takes an active role in marketing planning, it will never be an effective system.

5 A period of up to three years is necessary (especially in large firms) for the successful introduction of an effective marketing planning system.

Some indication of the potential complexity of marketing planning can be seen in Figure 12.1. Even in a generalized model such as this, it can be seen that, in a large diversified group operating in many foreign markets, a complex combination of product, market and functional plans is possible. For example, what is required at regional level will be different from what is required at headquarters level, while it is clear that the total corporate plan has to be built from the individual building blocks. Furthermore, the function of marketing itself may be further functionalized for the purpose of planning, such as marketing research, advertising, selling, distribution, promotion, and so forth, while different customer groups may need to have separate plans drawn up.

> Let us be dogmatic about requisite planning levels. First, in a large diversified group, irrespective of such organizational issues, anything other than a systematic approach approximating to a formalized marketing planning system is unlikely to enable the necessary control to be exercised over the corporate identity.

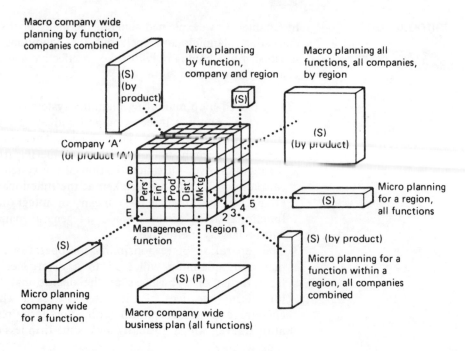

Macro business plan, all functions, all companies, all regions together with constituent building blocks

Key P = parent company
S = subsidiary company

Figure 12.1

Second, unnecessary planning, or overplanning, could easily result from an inadequate or indiscriminate consideration of the real planning needs at the different levels in the hierarchical chain.

Third, as size and diversity grow, so the degree of formalization of the marketing planning process must also increase. This can be simplified in the form of a matrix (Figure 12.2).

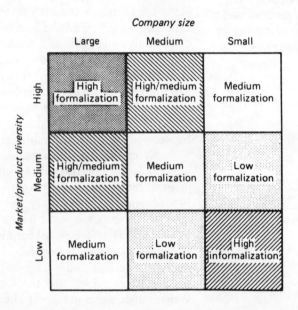

Figure 12.2

The degree of formalization must increase with the evolving size and diversity of operations. However, while the degree of formalization will change, the need for a complete marketing planning system does not. The problems that companies suffer, then, are a function of either the degree to which they have a requisite marketing planning system or the degree to which the formalization of their system grows with the situational complexities attendant upon the size and diversity of operations.

It has already been stressed that central to the success of any enterprise is the objective-setting process. Connected with this is the question of the design of the planning system and, in particular, the question of who should be involved in what, and how. For example, who should carry out the situation review, state the assumptions, set marketing objectives, and strategies, and carry out the scheduling and costing-out programme, and at what level?

These complex issues revolve essentially around two dimensions – the size of the company, and the degree of business diversity. There are, of course, many other issues, such as whether a company is operating through subsidiary companies or through agents, but these can only be considered against the background of the two major dimensions of size and diversity.

Size

Of these two dimensions, size of operations is, without doubt, the biggest determinant of the type of marketing planning system used.

> **In small companies, there is rarely much diversity of products or markets, and top management has an in-depth knowledge of the key determinants of success and failure.**

Size of operations is, without doubt, the biggest determinant of the type of marketing planning system used.

There is usually a high level of knowledge of both the technology and the market. While in such companies the central control mechanism is the sales forecast and budget, top managers are able to explain the rationale lying behind the numbers, have a very clear view of their comparative strengths and weaknesses, and are able to explain the company's marketing strategy without difficulty. This understanding and familiarity with the strategy is shared with key operating subordinates by means of personal, face-to-face dialogue throughout the year. Subordinates are operating within a logical framework of ideas, which they understand. There is a shared understanding between top and middle management of the industry and prevailing business conditions. In such cases, since either the owner or a director is usually also deeply involved in the day-to-day management of the business, the need to rely on informational inputs from subordinates is considerably less than in larger companies. Consequently, there is less need for written procedures about marketing audits, SWOT analyses, assumptions, and marketing objectives and strategies, as these are carried out by top management, often informally at meetings and in face-to-face discussions with subordinates, the results of which are the basis of the forecasts and budgets. Written documents in respect of price, advertising, selling, and so on, are very brief, but those managers responsible for those aspects of the business know what part they are expected to play in achieving the company's objectives.

> Such companies are, therefore, operating according to a set of structured procedures, and complete the several steps in the marketing planning process, but in a relatively informal manner.

On the other hand, many small companies that have a poor understanding of the marketing concept, and in which the top manager leaves his strategy implicit, suffer many serious operational problems.

These operational problems become progressively worse as the size of company increases. As the number and level of management increase, it becomes progressively more difficult for top management to enjoy an in-depth knowledge of industry and business conditions by informal, face-to-face means. In the absence of written procedures and a structured framework, the different levels of operating management become increasingly less able to react in a rational way to day-to-day pressures. Systems of tight budgeting control, without the procedures outlined in this book, are, in the main, only successful in situations of buoyant trading conditions, are often the cause of high levels of management frustration, and are seen to be a major contributory factor in those cases where eventual decline sets in.

In general, the bigger the company, the greater is the incidence of standardized, formalized procedures for the several steps in the marketing planning process.

Diversity of operations

From the point of view of management control, the least complex environment in which to work is an undiversified company. For the purpose of this discussion, 'undiversified' is taken to mean companies with limited product lines or homogeneous customer groups. For example, hydraulic hose could be sold to many diverse markets, or a diverse range of products could be sold into only one market such as, say, the motor industry. Both could be classified as 'undiversified'.

In such cases, the need for institutionalized marketing planning systems increases with the size of the operation, and there is a strong relationship between size and the complexity of the management task, irrespective of any apparent diversity.

> For example, an oil company will operate in many diverse markets around the world, through many different kinds of marketing systems, and with varying levels of market growth and market share. In most respects, therefore, the control function for headquarters management is just as difficult and complex as that in a major, diversified conglomerate. The major difference is the greater level of in-depth knowledge which top management has about the key determinants of success and failure underlying the product or market worldwide, because of its homogeneity.

Because of this homogeneity of product or market, it is usually possible for headquarters to impose worldwide policies on operating units in respect of things such as certain aspects of advertising, public relations, packaging, pricing, trade marks, product development, and so on, whereas in the headquarters of a diversified conglomerate, overall policies of this kind tend to be impracticable and meaningless.

The view is often expressed that common planning in companies comprising many heterogeneous units is less helpful and confuses, rather than improves, understanding between operating units and headquarters. However, the truth is that conglomerates often consist of several smaller multinationals, some diversified, and some not, and that the actual risk of marketing rests on the lowest level in an organization at which there is general management profit responsibility. Forecasting and budgeting systems by themselves rarely encourage anything but a short-term, parochial view of the business at these levels, and in the absence of the kind of marketing planning procedures described in this book, higher levels of management do not have a sufficiently rational basis on which to set long-term marketing objectives.

Exactly the same principles apply at the several levels of control in a diversified multinational conglomerate, in that, at the highest level of control, there has to be some rational basis on which to make decisions about the portfolio of investments. In our research, the most successful companies were those with standardized marketing planning procedures to aid this process. In such companies, there is a hierarchy of audits, SWOT analyses, assumptions, strategies and programmes, with increasingly more detail required in the procedures at the lowest levels in the organization. The precise details of each step vary according to circumstances, but the eventual output of the process is in a universally consistent form.

The basis on which the whole system rests is the informational input requirements at the highest level of command. Marketing objectives and strategies are frequently synthesized into a multidisciplinary corporate plan at the next general management profit-responsible level until, at the highest level of command, the corporate plan consists largely of financial information and summaries of the major operational activities.

The really important issue in any system is the degree to which it enables control to be exercised over the key determinants of success and failure.

> This is an important point, for there is rarely a consolidated operational marketing plan at conglomerate headquarters.

This often exists only at the lowest level of general management profit responsibility, and even here it is sometimes incorporated into the corporate plan, particularly in capital goods companies, where engineering, manufacturing and technical services are major factors in commercial success.

Here, it is necessary to distinguish between short-term operational plans and long-term strategic plans, both products of the same process. Conglomerate headquarters are particularly interested in the progress of, and prospects for, the major areas of operational activities, and while obviously concerned to ensure a satisfactory current level of profitability, are less interested in the detailed short-term scheduling and costing-out of the activities necessary to achieve these objectives. This, however, is a major concern at the lowest level of general management profit responsibility.

> To summarize, the smaller the company, the more informal and personal the procedures for marketing planning. As company size and diversity increases, so the need for institutionalized procedures increases.

The really important issue in any system is the degree to which it enables *control* to be exercised over the key determinants of success and failure. To a large extent, the issue, much debated in the literature, of where in an international organization responsibility for setting marketing objectives and strategies should lie, is something of a red herring. Of course, in a diversified multinational conglomerate, detailed marketing objectives and strategies for some remote country cannot be set by someone in London. It is precisely this issue, i.e. finding the right balance between the flexibility of operating units to react to changes in local market conditions and centralized control, that a formally designed system seeks to tackle.

> Those companies which conform to the framework outlined here have systems which, through a hierarchy of bottom up/top down negotiating procedures, reach a nice balance between the need for detailed control at the lowest level of operations and centralized control. The main role of headquarters is to harness the company's strengths on a worldwide basis and to ensure that lower level decisions do not cause problems in other areas and lead to wasteful duplication.

Figure 12.3 explores four key outcomes that marketing planning can evoke. It can be seen that systems I, III and IV, i.e. where the individual is totally subordinate to a formalized system, or where individuals are allowed to do what they want without any system, or where there is neither system, nor creativity, are less successful than system II, in which the individual is allowed to be entrepreneurial within a total system. System II, then, will be an effective marketing planning system, but one in which the degree of formalization will be a function of company size and diversity.

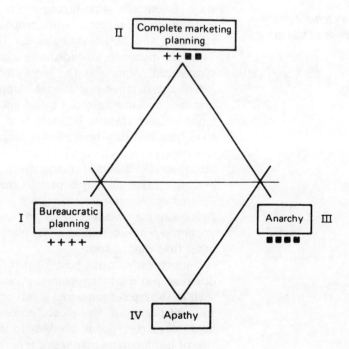

Figure 12.3

+ Degree of formalization
■ Degree of openness

> Creativity cannot flourish in a closed-loop formalized system. There would be little disagreement that in today's abrasive, turbulent, and highly competitive environment, it is those firms that succeed in extracting entrepreneurial ideas and creative marketing programmes from systems that are necessarily yet acceptably formalized, that will succeed in the long run. Much innovative flair can so easily get stifled by systems.

Certainly there is ample evidence of international companies with highly formalized systems that produce stale and repetitive plans, with little changed from year to year and that fail to point up the really key strategic issues as a result. The scandalous waste this implies is largely due to a *lack of personal intervention by key managers during the early stages of the planning cycle.*

> There is clearly a need, therefore, to find a way of perpetually renewing the planning life cycle each time around. Inertia must never set in. Without some such valve or means of opening up the loop, inertia quickly produces decay.

The critical intervention of senior managers, from the chief executive down through the hierarchical chain, comes at the audit stage.

Such a valve has to be inserted early in the planning cycle during the audit, or situation review stage. In companies with effective marketing planning systems, whether such systems are formalized or informal, the critical intervention of senior managers, from the chief executive down through the hierarchical chain, comes at the audit stage. Essentially, what takes place is a personalized presentation of audit findings, together with proposed marketing objectives and strategies and outline budgets for the strategic planning period. These are discussed, amended where necessary, and agreed in various synthesized formats at the hierarchical levels in the organization *before* any detailed operational planning takes place. It is at such meetings that managers are called upon to justify their views, which tends to force them to be more bold and creative than they would have been had they been allowed merely to send in their proposals. Obviously, however, even here much depends on the degree to which managers take a critical stance, which is much greater when the chief executive takes an active part in the process. *Every hour of time devoted at this stage by the chief executive has a multiplier effect throughout the remainder of the process.* And let it be remembered we are not, repeat not, talking about budgets at this juncture in anything other than outline form.

Until recently, it was believed that there may well be fundamental differences in marketing planning approaches, depending on factors such as the type of industrial goods and markets involved, company size, the degree of dependence on overseas sales, and the methods used to market goods abroad. In particular, the much debated role of headquarters management in the marketing planning process is frequently put forward as being a potential cause of great difficulty.

> One of the most encouraging findings to emerge from our research is that the theory of marketing planning is universally applicable, and that such issues are largely irrelevant.

While the planning task is less complicated in small, undiversified companies, and there is less need for formalized procedures than in large, diversified companies, the fact is that exactly the same framework should be used in all circumstances, and that this approach brings similar benefits to all.

In a multinational conglomerate, headquarters management is able to assess major trends in products and markets around the world, and is thus able to develop strategies for investment, expansion, diversification and divestment on a global basis. For their part, subsidiary management can develop appropriate strategies with a sense of locomotion towards the achievement of coherent overall goals.

This is achieved by means of synthesized information flows from the bottom upwards, which facilitates useful comparison of performance around the world, and the diffusion of valuable information, skills, experiences and systems from the top downwards. The particular benefits which accrue to companies using such systems can be classified under the major headings of the marketing mix elements as follows:

○ *Marketing information* – there is a transfer of knowledge, a sharing of expertise and an optimization of effort around the world.
○ *Product* – control is exercised over the product range. Maximum effectiveness is gained by concentrating on certain products in certain markets, based on experience gained throughout the world.
○ *Price* – pricing policies are sufficiently flexible to enable local management to trade effectively, while the damaging effects of interaction are considerably mitigated.
○ *Place* – substantial gains are made by rationalization of the logistics function.
○ *Promotion* – duplication of effort and a multitude of different platforms/company images are ameliorated. Efforts in one part of the world reinforce those in another.

The procedures which facilitate the provision of such information and knowledge transfers also encourage operational management to think strategically about their own areas of responsibility, instead of managing only for the short term.

It is abundantly clear that it is through a marketing planning system and planning skills that such benefits are achieved, and that discussions such as those about the standardization *process* are largely irrelevant. Any standardization that may be possible will become clear only if a company can successfully develop a system for identifying the needs of each market and each segment in which it operates, and for organizing resources to satisfy those needs in such a way that best resource utilization results worldwide.

A summary of the marketing planning process

The purpose of this section is to summarize the earlier chapters, and to ensure that the many threads developed are seen in their correct context, within the marketing planning process.

> There are many checklists of things you have to do to go through the motions of marketing planning. But pages of figures and marketing prose, well typed, elegantly bound, and retrievably filed, do not make much difference.

They make some, because the requirements of writing a plan demand deep thought. However, it is vital that companies must always search for the *requisite level of marketing planning*, just as, in engineering, you will often seek the requisite level of variety in product or services offered.

It is well to remember, above all else, what the *purpose* of marketing planning is, which is to create sustainable competitive advantage. The following sub-sections are intended to identify the main barriers to marketing planning and summarize the main points of a requisite marketing planning system, and to provide the basis for the design of a system suitable for any business.

The process itself

'*How well should we be doing in present trading conditions?*' The answer to this question requires considerable analysis inside and outside the company. Simply looking at the bottom line and saying 'budget achieved' is not enough.

> It is quite possible to achieve budget and still lose market share – if the budget is not developed from a proper qualitative assessment of the market *in the first place*.

Undertaking marketing planning is like 'trying to nail a jelly to the wall'.

The real question we should be asking is '*What sales/gross profits should we be achieving in the current trading conditions?*' To answer the above questions, it is necessary to have available a well argued 'common format' in the organization, i.e. a marketing plan.

Undertaking marketing planning is like 'trying to nail a jelly to the wall'; it is a messy process, which evolves over time. In effect, you are attempting to 'control' the future by deciding *what to do about the possible different trading environments*. In undertaking marketing planning, you join the ranks of those who 'make things happen' in the company. The alternative is to be tossed around like a cork in the sea of competition.

The marketing planning process involves the bringing together of minds within the company/group/department, and a 'trading off' between the difficult issues raised. By definition, the marketing planning process starts from a 'zero base' each year; the 10 per cent syndrome must be avoided at all times.

The marketing planning process facilitates, and indeed depends on, interactive communication up and down the organization. If this does not happen, all that results are forecasts projected from history rather than the development of genuine objectives based on what is actually happening inside and outside the company.

Remember, the planning process is first and foremost to help you to help yourself; it is not something you take part in simply to appease your superiors.

It is sometimes difficult for higher echelons in the organization to synthesize and aggregate the SWOTS from lower levels. However, the task is made easier if, for instance, departments are grouped to reflect the structure of the external market.

Once the marketing planning process has developed through to the agreement of a detailed one-year operational plan, and once this budget is agreed, then commitment must be total. If, however, during the course of the ensuing fiscal year, performance begins to fall behind the budget, it is quite legitimate to manipulate any and all elements of the marketing plan in order to correct the deficit. So, there is flexibility in the way the elements of a plan can be altered and manipulated; the budget, however, remains fixed.

The marketing audit

The marketing planning process starts with an *audit* of the company's operating performance and environment. The marketing audit is essentially a *data base* of all market-related issues with which the company is concerned. The subsequent SWOT analysis lends structure to the audit in order to facilitate on-going planning activities.

The company must provide a list of detailed questions which each manager is required to consider for their own area of responsibility. Each manager carrying out an audit will use sales data and the company marketing information system to complete the audit. If the company has a marketing research manager, it is helpful at this stage to issue to all managers a market overview covering major market and product trends, etc.

It will probably be necessary to customize the audit checklist contents according to the level in the organization to which it is addressed. In this way, each particular checklist is made meaningful and relevant to each level. Some brief explanatory definitions may also be necessary.

The audit will inevitably require more data preparation than is finally reproduced in the marketing plan.

> Therefore, managers should attempt to start a 'product/market bible' during the year, which can also be used as a reference source at verbal presentations of proposals, etc.

What this means is that the marketing audit should be conducted on a *continuing* (dynamic) basis rather than at a particular point in time. In this way, it becomes a useful information source to draw on for decision-making throughout the year.

Do not try to hide behind vague items in the audit, like 'poor economic condition'. Even in overall static or declining markets there will be 'growth' points present. Seek these out and decide whether or not to focus/concentrate your efforts on them.

Incorporate product life cycles and portfolio matrices as an integral part of the audit. The diagrams and the corresponding words should match.

It is suggested that the manager draws a product life cycle for each of the major products and uses the audit information to attempt to predict the future shape of the life cycle. It is also suggested that the manager plots these products on a portfolio matrix and uses the audit information to show the future desired position of the products (e.g. for five years ahead, if this is the planning horizon. The matrix may, therefore, have to include some new products not currently in the range).

> The audit can be a useful 'transfer' device for when one manager moves job and another takes over. For example, the incoming manager can quickly pick up an understanding of that department's business.

SWOT analysis

> It is important to remember that it is only the SWOT analyses, *not* the audit, that actually appear in the marketing plan.

This summary of the audit should, if possible, contain not more than four or five pages of commentary focusing on *key* factors only. It should list internal *differential* strengths and weaknesses *vis-à-vis* competitors and key external opportunities and threats. A SWOT should be completed for each segment or product considered to be crucial to that firm's future.

> The SWOT analyses should be interesting to read, contain concise statements, include only the relevant and important data, and give greater emphasis to creative analysis.

A crucial role for marketing management is to differentiate their company from their competitors. The SWOT analysis is a device which assists us to do that.

A SWOT analysis, well done, helps to identify and pin down the real issues which should be addressed in the future as a matter of priority. Too often, however, the SWOT summary is just a smorgasbord of apparently unrelated points (in which case any underlying theme is difficult to discern).

Having listened to someone presenting a SWOT summary, you should end up with a clear understanding of the main thrust of their business.

> If a SWOT is well done, someone else should be able to draft the objectives which logically flow from it. The SWOT statement

should contain clear indicators as to the key determinants of success in the company/group/department; we can then build on these.

The SWOT statement should, in effect, encapsulate our perception of the market place; summarize what we are trying to do; and point out required future actions. If pursued aggressively, this approach will make competitors into followers

The SWOT is, by definition, a summary of the key issues emanating out of the marketing audit. The SWOT is generated from internal debate; it is not just one person's opinion. The SWOT should provide answers to such questions as:

○ What do customers need?
○ How do they buy?
○ What are our competitors doing?

Generally, the SWOT should be differential, or at least the S and W (internal) part should be. The O and T (external) part of the SWOT is generally non-differential, e.g. the threat of a new sales tax. We have to assess the impact of such a threat (should it happen) earlier than our competitors, and make the appropriate preparations earlier in order to give us the edge.

In writing down each issue in our SWOT summary, we should continually follow with the implied question: 'Which means that . . .?' In this way we are forced to think about the implications of the issue itself.

Finally, agreed budgets (which come at the end of the process) must reflect internal consistency with the issues raised in the original SWOT analysis.

Often, this internal consistency is not evident because budgets are done first rather than last, and the quali- tative content is done last rather than first (in which case it is just rhetoric).

It is difficult to work to a SWOT prepared by another person, unless of course you were involved in the original debate. The quality of a SWOT analysis can suffer if:

1 Each item/issue is over-abbreviated.
2 The writer concentrates on micro rather than macro issues.

Remember, it is a great self-discipline to complete a good, tight, but comprehensive, SWOT.

Assumptions

These also should appear in the marketing plan. List the major assumptions on which the plan is based. If the plan can be implemented irrespective of any assumption made, then the assumption is unnecessary. They should be few in number and key.

Marketing objectives

These should also appear in the marketing plan. Marketing objectives are about products and markets only (*not* about advertising etc.).

The *words* used should reflect what appears in the product life cycle and in the portfolio matrix. Any figures used (such as volume, value, etc.) should also reflect this. Please note that there is a detailed explanation of how this should be done in Chapter 13.

Note that if there is, say, a three-year planning horizon, the three-year marketing plan should contain overall marketing objectives with broad revenue and cost projections for the full five-year period. This plan will be required for the long-range corporate plan. The one-year marketing plan should contain the same overall marketing objectives plus the specific objectives for the first year of the planning cycle. Thereafter, the detailed one-year marketing plan should be about the next fiscal year only.

> Ideally, the one-year and five-year plans should be separate, but not necessarily so.

At an early stage in the planning process, it is likely that managers will have to discuss their major objectives with their superior prior to final agreement, since that person will probably have a better understanding of the broader company objectives.

It is necessary to set objectives in order to articulate what we are in fact committing ourselves to, and to force us to think about the corresponding resource implications.

Marketing objectives flow from the SWOT analysis and should be fully compatible with the key issues identified in the SWOT. Marketing objectives should be quantifiable and measurable for performance-monitoring purposes; avoid directional terms such as 'improve', 'increase', 'expand', etc. There will be a hierarchy of marketing objectives down through the organization. Try to set priorities for your chosen marketing objectives.

> Many so-called marketing objectives are in fact really marketing strategies – do not mix the two up. Marketing objectives are *what* we want to achieve; marketing strategies are *how* we intend to achieve the set objectives.

In some cases, marketing strategies and detailed marketing *actions* are confused. Actions are the short-term list of activities carried out to a schedule which, in aggregate, amount to a particular strategy.

Marketing strategies

These must also appear in the marketing plan. Strategies are how the objectives are to be achieved:

○ *Product* policies, to include functions, design, size, packaging, and so on.
○ *Pricing* policies to be followed for product groups in market segments.
○ *Place* policies for channels and customer service levels.
○ *Promotion* policies for communicating with customers under the relevant headings such as advertising, personal selling, sales promotion, etc.

Programmes

> Detailed programmes (sometimes referred to as 'appropriation budgets') should appear only in the detailed one-year operational marketing plan.

In the three-year strategic marketing plan, all that is required are the financial implications (budget) of the agreed stra-tegies. In a detailed one-year marketing plan, specific sub-objectives for products and segments supported by more detailed strategy and action statements, e.g. what, where, when, costs, etc. Here, include *budgets* and *forecasts*, and of course a *consolidated budget*. The preparation of budgets and sales forecasts *must* reflect the marketing objectives. In turn the objectives, strategies and programmes *must* reflect the agreed budgets and sales forecasts.

Forecasts (in lieu of objectives) are obtained by simply extrapolating past experience. Instead, we should be taking a 'zero-based' view of the current and possible future environments in order to arrive at a viable set of objectives. Unit forecasts then follow.

The above noted zero-based review (in the form of a marketing audit and corresponding SWOT) is necessary in order to identify possible 'discontinuities' in our future trading environment; simple extrapolation of historical data ignores the possibility that discontinuities can (and do) occur.

> Forecasts (and corresponding budgets based on such forecasts) can be self-fulfilling prophecies, e.g. salespeople sell the products they like to customers they enjoy selling to. If we project the resulting numbers by way of a forecast, we are *not* reflecting the real market situation.

A somewhat deeper perception of the market place is needed in order to review and reveal viable marketing objectives and strategies, which are consistent with the company's distinctive competence. Individual budget items must clearly be retraceable to issues identified in the original SWOT. When measuring performance, at all times seek to relate to the outside market as well as to your internal budget.

Marketing plans

A written marketing plan (or plans) is the outcome of the marketing planning process. It is effectively a business proposition containing proposed courses of action which in turn have resource implications.

> Written marketing plans verbalize (and formalize) our intuitive model of the market environment within which we operate. Written marketing plans help to make things happen.

The acid test of any marketing plan presentation is to ask yourself, 'Would I put my own life's savings into the plan as presented?' If the answer is 'No', then further work is needed to refine your ideas.

A good discipline in preparing 'internally consistent' marketing plans is to use the following summary format:

SWOT issues → Objective → Strategy → Specific actions and timing

The role of the chief executive in marketing planning

Our research showed that few chief executives have a clear perception of:

- ○ Purposes and methods of planning
- ○ Proper assignments of planning responsibilities throughout the organization
- ○ Proper structures and staffing of the planning department
- ○ The talent and skills required in an effective planning department

The role of the chief executive is generally agreed as being:

- ○ To define the organizational framework
- ○ To ensure the strategic analysis covers critical factors
- ○ To maintain the balance between short-and long-term results
- ○ To display his commitment to planning
- ○ To provide the entrepreneurial dynamic to overcome bureaucracy
- ○ To build this dynamic into the planning operation (motivation)

> In respect of planning, the chief executive's principal role is to open up the planning loop by means of personal intervention. The main purpose of this is to act as a catalyst for the entrepreneurial dynamic within the organization, which can so easily decay through bureaucratization. This is not sufficiently recognized in the literature.

When considering this in the context of the reasons for failures of marketing planning systems, it is clear that, for any system to be effective, the chief executive requires to be conversant with planning techniques and approaches, and to be committed to and take part in the marketing planning process

The role of the planning department in marketing planning

This raises the important question of the role of the planning department, which is:

- ○ To provide the planning structure and systems
- ○ To secure rapid data transmission in the form of intelligence
- ○ To act as a catalyst in obtaining inputs from operating divisions
- ○ To forge planning links across organizational divisions, e.g. R and D and marketing
- ○ To evaluate plans against the chief executive's formulated strategy
- ○ To monitor the agreed plans

> The planner is a coordinator who sees that the planning is done – not a formulator of goals and strategies.

The planner's responsibility has three basic dimensions. They are:

1 Directive
2 Supportive
3 Administrative

In the *directive* role, the planning executive acts on behalf of top management to supervise the planning procedure to promote orderly and disciplined implementation of the planning process. This function can be performed well only when managers have both the *ability* and *willingness* to make it happen. The planning executive is likely to be more effective by acting in a *supportive*, rather than in a *directive*, role.

A *supportive* role brings the planning executive into service as an internal consultant and advisory resource. In this role, the planning executive:

○ Advises line management on the application of planning principles
○ Assembles background information to provide insight into the economy, industries, markets, investment alternatives, etc., which are relevant to each business served
○ Directs or supports forecasting of the economy, industries and end-user markets
○ Renders assistance in installing progress-monitoring systems and interpreting their output
○ Renders assistance to line executives in applying advanced methods and procedures
○ Provides other internal and consulting assistance to line managers in preparing their plans and monitoring their progress

In their *administrative* role, planners ensure that planning procedures are implemented on schedule and that communications are accurate and rapid. In this role, it is suggested that they have limitations. They can provide co-ordinating and communicating services, but they cannot enforce them. If line management does not participate willingly, someone else with the appropriate authority must take corrective or disciplinary action.

Again, when this is taken in the context of the failures of marketing planning systems, it is clear that an understanding of the proper role of the Planning Department is an important determinant of planning success.

The marketing planning cycle

The schedule should call for work on the plan for the next year to begin early enough in the current year to permit adequate time for market research and analysis of key data and market trends. In addition, the plan should provide for the early development of a strategic plan that can be approved or altered in principle.

A key factor in determining the planning cycle is bound to be the degree to which it is practicable to extrapolate from sales and market data, but, generally speaking, successful planning companies start the planning cycle formally somewhere between nine and six months from the beginning of the next fiscal year.

Planning horizons

It is not necessary to be constrained to work within the company's fiscal year; it is quite possible to have a separate marketing planning schedule if that is appropriate, and simply organize the aggregation of results at the time required by the corporate financial controller.

It is clear that, in the past, one- and five-year planning periods have been far the most common, although three years has now become the most common period for the strategic plan, largely because of the dramatically increasing rate of environmental change. Lead time for the initiation of major new product innovations, the length of time necessary to recover capital investment costs, the continuing availability of customers and raw materials, and the size and usefulness of existing plant and buildings, are the most frequently mentioned reasons for having a five-year planning horizon. Increasingly, however, these five-year plans are taking the form more of 'scenarios' than the detailed strategic plan outlined in this book.

Many companies, however, do not give sufficient thought to what represents a sensible planning horizon for their particular circumstances. A five-year time span is clearly too long for some companies, particularly those with highly versatile machinery operating in volatile fashion-conscious markets. The effect of this is to rob strategic plans of reality. A five-year horizon is often chosen largely because of its universality. Secondly, some small subsidiaries in large conglomerates are often asked to forecast for seven, ten and, sometimes, fifteen years ahead, with the result that they tend to become meaningless exercises. While it obviously makes sense for, say, a glass manufacturer to produce twelve-year plans (or scenarios) because of the very long lead time involved in laying down a new furnace, it does not make sense to impose the same planning time scale on small subsidiaries operating in totally different markets, even though they are in the same group. This places unnecessary burdens on operating management and tends to rob the whole strategic planning process of credibility.

The conclusion to be reached is that there is a natural point of focus into the future, beyond which it is pointless to look. This point of focus is a function of the relative size of a company.

> Small companies, because of their size and the way they are managed, tend to be comparatively flexible in the way in which they can react to environmental turbulence in the short term. Large companies, on the other hand, need a much longer lead time in which to make changes in direction. Consequently, they tend to need to look further into the future and use formalized systems for this purpose so that managers throughout the organization have a common means of communication.

How the marketing planning process works

There is one other major aspect to be considered. It concerns the requisite location of the marketing planning activity in a company. The answer is simple to give.

> Marketing planning should take place as near to the marketplace as possible in the first instance, but such plans should then be reviewed at high levels within an organization to see what issues have been overlooked.

It has been suggested that each manager in the organization should complete an audit and SWOT analysis on their own area of responsibility. The only way that this can work in practice is by means of a *hierarchy* of audits. The principle is simply demonstrated in Figure 12.4.

This illustrates the principle of auditing at different levels within an organization. The marketing audit format will be universally applicable. It is only the *detail* that varies from level to level and from company to company within the same group. For example, any one single company can specify without too much difficulty the precise headings under which information is being sought.

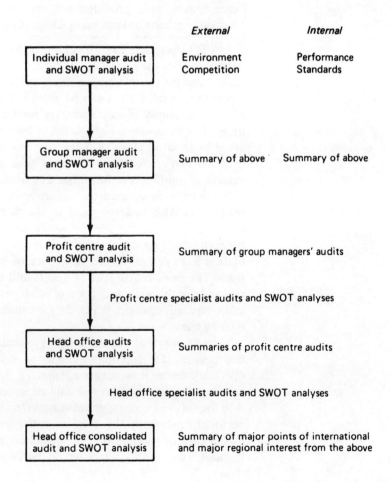

Hierarchy of audits

	External	*Internal*
Individual manager audit and SWOT analysis	Environment Competition	Performance Standards
Group manager audit and SWOT analysis	Summary of above	Summary of above
Profit centre audit and SWOT analysis	Summary of group managers' audits	
	Profit centre specialist audits and SWOT analyses	
Head office audits and SWOT analysis	Summaries of profit centre audits	
	Head office specialist audits and SWOT analyses	
Head office consolidated audit and SWOT analysis	Summary of major points of international and major regional interest from the above	

Figure 12.4

> In the case of an industrial lubricants company, under an assessment of the market environment, information and commentary was required on capital investment schemes, foreign investments, economic growth rates, health and safety regulations (clearly important in this market), inflation rates, tariff protection, etc., together with an assessment of their effect on the lubricants market.
>
> Under the heading 'market', key product groups and key market sectors were defined (in this case the British Standard Industrial Classification System was used). It was left to each subsidiary to specify what the particular key industries were in their particular territories. Data sheets were provided for this purpose.
>
> In the case of the competitive and the internal audit, each operating unit was merely asked to provide, for each major product, its strengths and weaknesses and those of competitive products; likewise for opportunities and threats. To assist with this process, a check list was provided which included, *inter alia*, international approvals from original equipment manufacturers, compliance with health and safety regulations, and so on. Some data sheets were provided for market share analysis by key industry, pricing against competitive products, etc.

At each operating level, this kind of information can be gathered in by means of the hierarchy of audits illustrated in Figure 12.4 with each manager completing an audit for his area of accountability. While the overall format can be universal for a large and diversified group, uniformity is only necessary for units engaged in like activities. The advantages which accrue to the several headquarters levels are substantial in terms of measuring worldwide potential for products and market segments. Without such an information-collecting vehicle, it is difficult to formulate any overall strategic view.

It has to be recognized that information and data are not always readily available in some parts of the world in the sort of format which is required, but given training, resources and understanding between headquarters and units, it is surprising how quickly information links can be forged which are of inestimable value to both sides. The same is also true of agents and distributors, who quickly respond to the give and take of such relationships in respect of audit-type information, which they inevitably find valuable for their own business.

Since, in anything but the smallest of undiversified companies, it is not possible for top management to set detailed objectives for operating units, it is suggested that at this stage in the planning process, strategic guidelines should be issued. One way of doing this is in the form of a *strategic planning letter*. Another is by means of a personal briefing by the chief executive at 'kick-off' meetings. As in the case of the audit, these guidelines would proceed from the broad to the specific, and would become more detailed as they progressed through the company towards operating units. Table 12.1 contains a list of the headings under which strategic guidelines could be set.

Under marketing, for example, at the highest level in a large group, top management may ask for particular attention to be paid to issues such as the technical impact of microprocessors on electromechanical component equipment, leadership and innovation strategies, vulnerability to attack from the flood of Japanese and European products, and so on. At operating company level, it is possible to be more explicit about target markets, product development, and the like.

Table 12.1 Chief executive's strategic planning letter (possible areas for which objective and strategies or strategic guidelines will be set)

Financial	*Operations*
Remittances	Land
o dividends	Buildings
o royalties	Plant
Gross margin %	Modifications
Operating profit	Maintenance
Return on capital employed	Systems
Debtors	Raw materials
Creditors	supplies
Bank borrowings	purchasing
Investments	Distribution
Capital expenditure	o stock and control
Cash flow controls	o transportation
	o warehousing
Manpower and organization	*Marketing*
Management	Target markets
Training	Market segments
Industrial relations	Brands
Organization	Volumes
Remuneration and pensions	Market shares
	Pricing
	Image
	Promotion
	Market research
	Quality control
	Customer service

It is important to remember that it is top management's responsibility to determine the strategic direction of the company, and to decide such issues as when businesses are to be milked, where to invest heavily in product development or market extension for longer term gains, and so on. If this is left to operating managers to decide for themselves, they will tend to opt for actions concerned principally with *today's* products and markets, because that is what they are judged on principally. There is also the problem of their inability to appreciate the larger, company-wide position.

Strategic and operational planning

Top-down and bottom-up

Unit objectives and strategies

Overall objectives and strategies
(strategic guidelines)

Figure 12.5

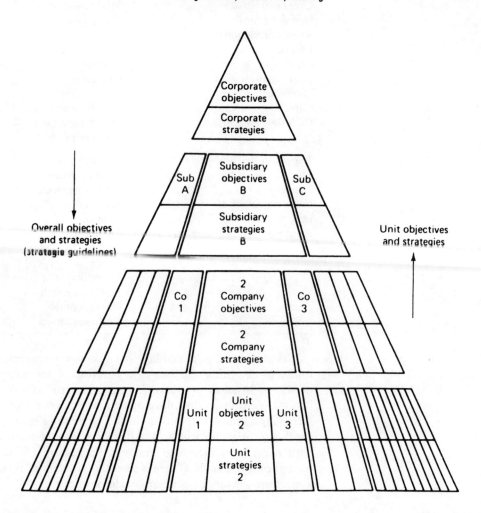

Strategic and operational planning

Corporate
objectives

Corporate
strategies

Sub
A

Subsidiary
objectives
B

Sub
C

Subsidiary
strategies
B

Overall objectives
and strategies
(strategic guidelines)

Unit objectives
and strategies

Co
1

2
Company
objectives

Co
3

2
Company
strategies

Unit
1

Unit
objectives
2

Unit
3

Unit
strategies
2

Figure 12.6

> Nevertheless, the process just described demonstrates very clearly that there is total interdependence between top management and the lowest level of operating management and the lowest level of operating management in the objective and strategy setting process.

In a very large company without any procedures for managing this process, it is not difficult to see how control can be weakened and how vulnerability to rapid changes in the business environment around the world can be increased. This interdependence between the top-down/bottom-up process is illustrated in Figures 12.5 and 12.6, which show a similar hierarchy in respect of objective and strategy setting to that illustrated in respect of audits.

Having explained carefully the point about *requisite* marketing planning, these figures also illustrate the principles by which the marketing planning process should be implemented in any company, irrespective of whether it is a small exporting company or a major multinational. In essence, these exhibits show a *hierarchy* of audits, SWOT analyses, objectives, strategies and programmes.

Figure 12.7 is another way of illustrating the total corporate strategic and planning process. This time, however, a time element is added, and the relationship between strategic planning letters, long-term corporate plans and short-term operational plans is clarified. It is important to note that there are two 'open loop' points on this last

Strategic and operational planning

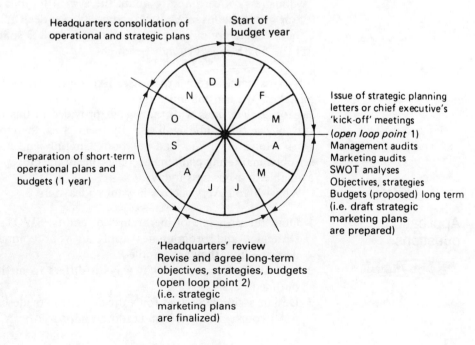

Figure 12.7

diagram. These are the key times in the planning process when a subordinate's views and findings should be subjected to the closest examination by a superior.

> It is by taking these opportunities that marketing planning can be transformed into the critical and creative process it is supposed to be, rather than the dull, repetitive ritual it so often turns out to be.

These figures should be seen as one group of illustrations showing how the marketing planning process fits into the wider context of corporate planning.

Final thought

In conclusion, we must stress that there can be no such thing as an off-the-peg marketing planning system.

> Nonetheless, both our research and our experience have indicated that marketing planning remains one of the last bastions of management ignorance, largely because of the complexity of the process and its organizational, political and cultural implications.

It is for these reasons, and because so many of the readers of the first edition of this book asked for one, that we have added a final chapter which contains both a very brief summary of the main points described in the book and a simple, step-by-step system which can become the basis of your own planning procedures. The system provided has been used successfully in businesses ranging from big international industrial companies to small domestic service organizations.

> In the end, marketing planning success comes from an endless willingness to learn and to adapt the system to your people and your own circumstances. It also comes from a deep understanding about the *nature* of marketing planning, which is something that in the final analysis cannot be taught.

Success comes from *experience*. Experience comes from making mistakes. We can minimize these if we combine *common sense* and *sweet reasonableness* with the *models* provided in this book. But be sure of *one* thing, above all else. By themselves, the models will not work. However, if you read this book carefully and use the models sensibly, marketing planning becomes one of the most powerful tools available to a business today.

We wish you every success in your endeavours.

Application questions

1 Does the principle of hierarchies of audits, SWOTs, objectives, strategies and programmes apply in your company? If not, describe how they are handled.
2 If it does, describe in what ways it differs from the principles outlined here.
3 Design a simple system for your company, or describe in what ways your existing system could be improved.

Review of Chapter 12

Conditions that must be satisfied

1 Any closed-loop planning system, especially if it is based just on forecasting and budgeting, will deaden any creative response and will eventually lead to failure.
2 Marketing planning which is not integrated with other functional areas of the business at general management level will be largely ineffective.
3 The separation of operational and strategic marketing planning will lead to divergent plans, with the short-term viewpoint winning because it achieves quick results.
4 The chief executive must take an active role.
5 It can take 3 years to introduce marketing planning successfully.

Try Exercises 12.1 and 12.2

Ten principles of marketing planning

1 Develop the strategic plan first; the operational plan comes out of this.
2 Put marketing as close as possible to the customer and have marketing and sales under one person.
3 Marketing is an attitude of mind, not a set of procedures.
4 Organize activities around customer groups, not functional activities.
5 A marketing audit must be rigorous. No vague terms should be allowed, and nothing should be hidden. Managers should use tools like portfolio analysis and product life cycle.
6 SWOT analyses should be focused on segments that are critical to the business; concentrate only on key factors which lead to objectives.
7 People must be educated about the planning process.
8 There has to be a plan for planning.
9 All objectives should be prioritized in terms of their urgency and impact.
10 Marketing planning needs the active support of the chief executive and must be appropriate for the culture.

Planning horizon

There is a natural point of focus in the future beyond which it is pointless to plan for. This can differ from firm to firm, depending on its business. Generally, small firms can use shorter horizons, because they are flexible, to adjust to change. Large firms need longer horizons.

Planning paradox

Companies often set out to achieve the impossible. It is not unknown to see planning objectives which seek to:

o Maximize sales
o Minimize costs
o Increase market share
o Maximize profits

Not only are these incompatible, but they damage the credibility of the managers who subscribe to such commitments.

Question raised for the company

Q: Are there different approaches to marketing planning?

A: We believe there are. Please see the following diagram.

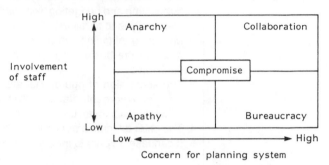

The most successful marketing plans are collaborative. Here, relevant executives take part in the process in a caring way, and at the same time planning is done rigorously.

Introduction to Chapter 12 exercises

As the brief notes have indicated, there are a number of conditions to be met if the marketing planning process is not to become a sterile, closed-loop system. The ten principles of marketing planning listed in the notes go a considerable way to ensuring that the process does not degenerate nto a ritualized, 'numbers game'. However, there are still some problematical issues to be addressed.

Exercise 12.1 looks at the theory issue of how formalized the planning process should be, and how to take the correct steps to get close to the ideal system for your company.

Exercise 12.2 examines how to set up a timetable for planning. This is particularly useful in getting all contributors to the marketing plan working in unison, and coming up with the necessary information at the appropriate time.

In these exercises, you will focus on the marketing planning system best suited to your company. By way of consolidating on all of your work through this book, you will design an appropriate planning system and lay down the 'ground rules' for its implementation.

Exercise 12.1 Designing the marketing planning system

Selecting the appropriate approach

Figure 12.8 shows how the degree of formalization of the marketing planning process relates to company size and the diversity of its operations.

1 Select a position on this figure which best describes your company's situation.

2 In the space below, write down a few key words or sentences that would best describe the marketing planning system you would need for your company, e.g. high formalization, etc.

Company size

	Large	Medium	Small
High	High formalization	High/medium formalization	Medium formalization
Medium	High/medium formalization	Medium formalization	Low formalization
Low	Medium formalization	Low formalization	Very low formalization

Market/product diversity

Figure 12.8 Marketing planning

Identifying the improvement areas

1 Imagine that it is possible to measure the efficiency of a marketing planning system on a scale 0–100, where 100 is equivalent to a 100 per cent efficiency, i.e. the system works well and conforms with your model. How would you rate the current approach to marketing planning in your company? to what extent does it match up with your ideal?

2 Enter your score on Figure 12.9, drawing a horizontal line as shown.

The difference between your scoreline and the ideal must represent where there is room for improvement.

Transfer your score line to the Worksheet, the force field diagram, then complete the Worksheet by following the instructions given below.

3 Identity all those factors that have 'pushed' your actual efficiency line below the ideal. Add them to the Worksheet, showing them as actual forces pushing down. If you can, represent the biggest forces with longer arrows, as shown in Figure 12.10.

You will probably have more than three factors, so list as many as you can. Remember, you should be noting only those that affect the *marketing planning system*, not the company's general approach to marketing. We will call these downward forces 'restraining forces', because they are acting against improvement.

4 Now ask yourself why isn't the actual performance line you have drawn lower than it is. The reason is, of course, that there are several

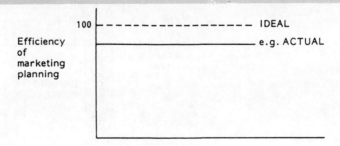

Figure 12.9

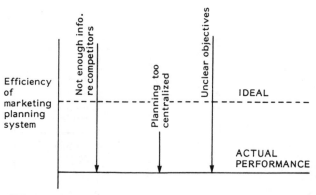

Figure 12.10

parts of the system that work well, or there are other strengths in your company. Identify these positive forces and add them to the Worksheet, as shown in Figure 12.11, again relating the arrow size approximately to the influence of each factor.

Again, the factors shown above are only examples. You will identify many more. We call these 'driving forces' because they are pushing towards improvement.

5 The worksheet should now be complete, showing the two sets of forces lined up against each other. What next? Well, it might have struck you that what you have assembled is somewhat analogous to a ship at sea. Your ship (the marketing planning system) is wallowing below its ideal level in the water but is prevented from sinking by buoyant forces (driving forces). To restore the ship to its correct level, it would be natural to remove or jettison some of the cargo (the restraining forces), not to try to get out and push from below.

As it is for the ship, so it is for your marketing planning system, therefore:

(a) Select the major restraining forces and work out ways that you can reduce their impact, or preferably eliminate them altogether. These will be the source of the greatest improvements, but some remedies might need time to take effect.

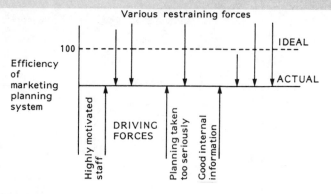

Figure 12.11

(b) So, concurrently, select minor restraining forces and plan to eliminate them also. Although their impact on improvement might be less, you will probably find they respond more quickly to treatment.

(c) Finally, select the smallest driving forces and work out if there are any ways to increase their impact.

6 Assemble your various responses to 5(a), (b) and (c) together into a comprehensive improvement plan, then take steps to get it accepted and acted upon.

Put most of your energy into removing the restraining factors. To focus on the major driving forces, e.g. trying to make highly motivated staff even more motivated, is likely to be counter-productive.

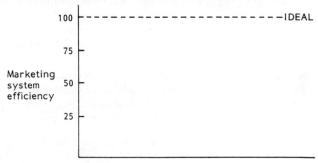

Worksheet   Force field diagram (Exercise 12.1)

Force field analysis theory

The force field analysis, upon which much of designing a system is based, stems from the work of Kurt Lewin (*Field Theory in Social Science*, Harper, 1951). His reasoning, adapted to the programme situation, operates thus:

1 If a company's marketing system is functioning well, then the company could be said to have no problems. Diagrammatically, the efficiency level could be shown at something approaching 100 per cent. See Figure 12.12.

Figure 12.12

2 Few companies reach this happy state of affairs. Without resorting to concise measurement (a consensus of views is generally enough), most companies would 'score' their planning system somewhat lower, as shown in Figure 12.13.

Figure 12.13

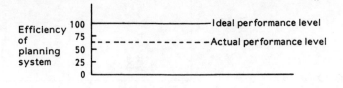

3 Wherever the 'actual' line is drawn, it poses two interesting questions upon which the subsequent analysis hinges, namely:

(a) What causes the performance level to be where it is?
(b) Why doesn't it fall any lower?

4 Clearly the answer to 3(a) is that things are going wrong in the system; that there are missing or malfunctioning areas. Until these are put right, there will always be a drag on the efficiency, holding it down. These negative forces are termed *restraining forces*, because they are restraining improvement.

5 Similarly, the reason that efficiency doesn't drop lower than has been shown is that there must be several parts of the planning system that work quite well. There are many strengths in the system. These positive factors are termed *driving forces*, because they are the forces pushing towards better efficiency.

6 In Figure 12.13, for the efficiency of the planning system to be below the ideal level, then the restraining forces must be greater than the driving forces.

7 Let us take a simple illustration. We are driving a car and it is going more slowly than it ought to because the brakes are rubbing (restraining force). If we want to resume driving at normal speed then we have two courses of action open to us:

(a) We can put our foot down on the accelerator (increase the driving force)
(b) We can free the brakes (remove the restraining force)

We can see that by putting our foot down all sorts of troubles are likely to materialize. Unless something is done to free the brakes, then probably they would overheat, perhaps catch fire or jam up completely.

8 A similar overheating could take place in the company's marketing planning system unless it is tackled properly. To get lasting improvements, it will be important to identify all the restraining and driving forces. Indeed, many of the earlier exercises were designed to do just this. Using this information, it will be important *to plan how to reduce*

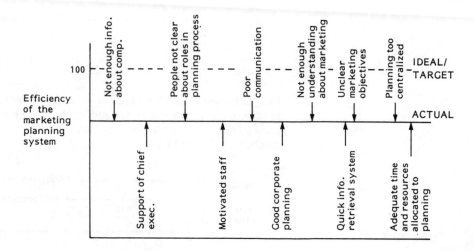

Figure 12.14

or remove the restraining forces and, only when that is done, consider how to plan to boost the driving forces.

9 Figure 12.14 is an example of how a finished force field diagram might look, although most people will have identified several more factors than shown here. Many of the factors identified by you ought to be unique to your company.

Notes

1 Remember that only factors that affect the marketing planning process ought to appear in the force field diagram.
2 It is possible to draw the force arrows proportional in length to their influence.

Exercise 12.2 Implementing the marketing planning system

Perhaps you will be unable to implement a marketing planning system until your improvement plan from Exercise 12.1 has eliminated the more serious obstacles. Nevertheless, from what you have read in this book, you will know that a successful marketing planning system will have to follow these steps.

1 There will have to be guidance provided by the corporate objectives.
2 A marketing audit must take place.
3 A gap analysis must be completed.
4 A SWOT analysis must be drawn up.
5 Assumptions and contingencies must be considered.
6 Marketing objectives and strategies must be set.
7 Individual marketing programmes must be established.
8 There must be a period of review and measurement.

Because of the work required, all this takes time. Various people might have to participate at different stages. There will certainly have to be several meetings or discussions with other functional departments, either to get information or to ensure collaboration.

Figure 12.15

Therefore, in order to keep the planning 'train' on the 'rails', it will be in everybody's interest to be clear about the sequencing of these different activities, to have a schedule or timetable.

As the company gets more experienced in planning, then probably the timetable can be tightened up and the whole planning period shortened. However, to get events into perspective, it is often helpful to present a timetable of the planning activities, as shown in Figure 12.15. The circle represents a calendar year and the time periods are merely examples – not to be taken as recommended periods.

In the second planning year, months 11 and 12 could be used to evaluate the first year's plan and thereby prepare information for the next round of corporate planning.

This diagrammatic approach clearly shows how the planning process is a continual undercurrent throughout the year.

Now, as your final task, try drawing up the planning timetable for your company on Figure 12.16.

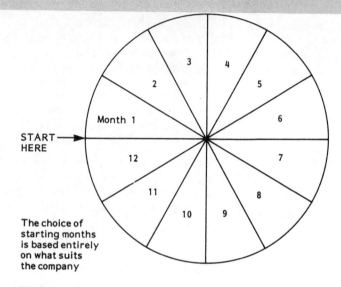

START→
HERE

The choice of
starting months
is based entirely
on what suits
the company

Figure 12.16

13 A step-by-step marketing planning system

Summary

This chapter is in two parts. The first part is a very brief summary of the main points relating to marketing planning. The second part is an actual marketing planning system which operationalizes all the concepts, structures and frameworks outlined in this book in the form of a step-by-step approach to the preparation, first, of a strategic and, second, of an operational marketing plan. Finally, there is a suggested format for senior headquarters personnel who may have the task of summarizing many SBU strategic marketing plans into one consolidated document.

Part 1 Marketing planning summary

The purpose of marketing planning

The overall purpose of marketing and its principal focus is the identification and creation of competitive advantage.

What is marketing planning?

Marketing planning is simply a logical sequence and a series of activities leading to the setting of marketing objectives and the formulation of plans for achieving them.

Why is marketing planning necessary?

Marketing planning is necessary because of:

o Increasing turbulence, complexity and competitiveness
o The speed of technological change
o The need for *you*
    o to help identify sources of competitive advantage
    o to force an organized approach
    o to develop specificity
    o to ensure consistent relationships
o The need for *superiors*
    o to inform
o The need for *non-marketing functions*
    o to get support
o The need for *subordinates*
    o to get resources

○ to gain commitment
○ to set objectives and strategies

Ten barriers to marketing planning

This book has described a number of barriers to effective marketing planning. The ten principal barriers are:

1 Confusion between marketing tactics and strategy.
2 Isolating the marketing function from operations.
3 Confusion between the marketing function and the marketing concept.
4 Organizational barriers – the tribal mentality, for example the failure to define strategic business units (SBUs) correctly.
5 Lack of in-depth analysis.
6 Confusion between process and output.
7 Lack of knowledge and skills.
8 Lack of a systematic approach to marketing planning.
9 Failure to prioritize objectives.
10 Hostile corporate cultures.

The 'Ten S' approach to overcoming these barriers

Figure 13.1 summarizes the 'Ten S' approach developed by the author to overcome each of these barriers. The sections which follow elaborate briefly on each of the 'Ten S's'. Ten fundamental principles of marketing planning are provided.

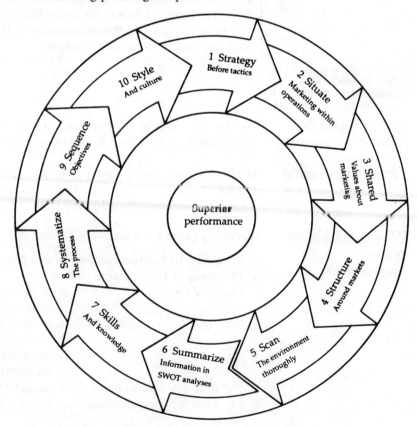

Figure 13.1 Marketing planning for competitive advantage

Marketing planning – Principle 1. Strategy before tactics	Develop the strategic marketing plan first. This entails greater emphasis on scanning the external environment, the early identification of forces emanating from it, and developing appropriate strategic responses, involving all levels of management in the process. A strategic plan should cover a period of between three and five years, and only when this has been developed and agreed should the one-year operational marketing plan be developed. *Never* write the one-year plan first and extrapolate it.
Marketing planning – Principle 2. Situate marketing within operations	For the purpose of marketing planning, put marketing as close as possible to the customer. Where practicable, have both marketing and sales report to the same person, who should not normally be the chief executive officer.
Marketing planning – Principle 3. Shared values about marketing	Marketing is a management process whereby the resources of the whole organization are utilized to satisfy the needs of selected customer groups in order to achieve the objectives of both parties. Marketing, then, is first and foremost an attitude of mind rather than a series of functional activities.
Marketing planning – Principle 4. Structure around markets	Organize company activities around customer groups if possible rather than around functional activities and get marketing planning done in these strategic business units. Without excellent marketing planning in SBUs, corporate marketing planning will be of limited value.
Marketing planning – Principle 5. Scan the environment thoroughly	For an effective marketing audit to take place: ○ Checklists of questions customized according to level in the organization should be agreed. ○ These should form the basis of the organization's MIS. ○ The marketing audit should be a *required* activity. ○ Managers should not be allowed to hide behind vague terms like 'poor economic conditions'. ○ Managers should be encouraged to incorporate the tools of marketing in their audits, e.g. product life cycles, portfolios and so on.
Marketing planning – Principle 6. Summarize information in SWOT analyses	*Information* is the foundation on which a marketing plan is built. From information (internal and external) comes intelligence. *Intelligence* describes *the marketing plan*, which is the intellectualization of how managers perceive their own position in their markets relative to their competitors (with competitive advantage accurately defined – e.g. cost leader, differentiation, niche), what objectives they want to achieve over some designated period of time, how they intend to achieve their objectives (strategies), what resources are required, and with what results (budget). A SWOT should: ○ Be focused on each specific segment of crucial importance to the organization's future.

○ Be a summary emanating from the marketing audit.
○ Be brief, interesting and concise.
○ Focus on *key* factors only.
○ List *differential* strengths and weaknesses *vis-à-vis* competitors, focusing on competitive advantage.
○ List *key* external opportunities and threats only.
○ Identify and pin down the *real* issues. It should not be a list of unrelated points.
○ The reader should be able to grasp instantly the main thrust of the business, even to the point of being able to write marketing objectives.
○ Follow the implied question 'which means that . . .?' to get the real implications.
○ Not over-abbreviate.

Marketing planning –
Principle 7. Skills
and knowledge

Ensure that all those responsible for marketing in SBUs have the necessary marketing knowledge and skills for the job. In particular, ensure that they understand and know how to use the more important tools of marketing, such as:

○ Information	○ How to get it
	○ How to use it
○ Positioning	○ Market segmentation
	○ Ansoff
	○ Porter
○ Product life cycle analysis	○ Gap analysis
○ Portfolio management	○ BCG matrix
	○ Directional policy matrix
○ 4 × Ps management	○ Product
	○ Price
	○ Place
	○ Promotion

Additionally, marketing personnel require communications and interpersonal skills.

Marketing planning –
Principle 8.
Systematize the
process

It is essential to have a set of written procedures and a well-argued common format for marketing planning. The purposes of such a system are:

1 To ensure that all key issues are systematically considered.
2 To pull together the essential elements of the strategic planning of each SBU in a consistent manner.
3 To help corporate management to compare diverse businesses and to understand the overall condition of, and prospects for, the organization.

Marketing planning –
Principle 9.
Sequence objectives

Ensure that all objectives are prioritized according to their impact on the organization and their urgency and that resources are allocated accordingly.

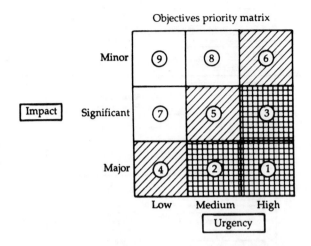

Figure 13.2

A suggested method for prioritization is given in Figure 13.2.

**Marketing planning –
Principle 10. Style
and culture**

Marketing planning will not be effective without the active support and participation of the culture leaders. But, even with their support, the type of marketing planning has to be appropriate for the phase of the organizational lifeline. This phase should be measured before attempting to introduce marketing planning.

Conclusion to Part 1

A summary of what appears in a strategic marketing plan and a list of the principal marketing tools/techniques/structures/frameworks which apply to each step is given in Figure 13.3.

It will be understood from the foregoing that marketing planning never has been just the simple step-by-step approach described so enthusiastically in most prescriptive texts and courses. The moment an organization embarks on the marketing planning path, it can expect to encounter a number of complex organizational, attitudinal, process and cognitive problems, which are likely to block progress. By being forewarned about these barriers, there is a good chance of successfully using the step-by-step marketing planning system which

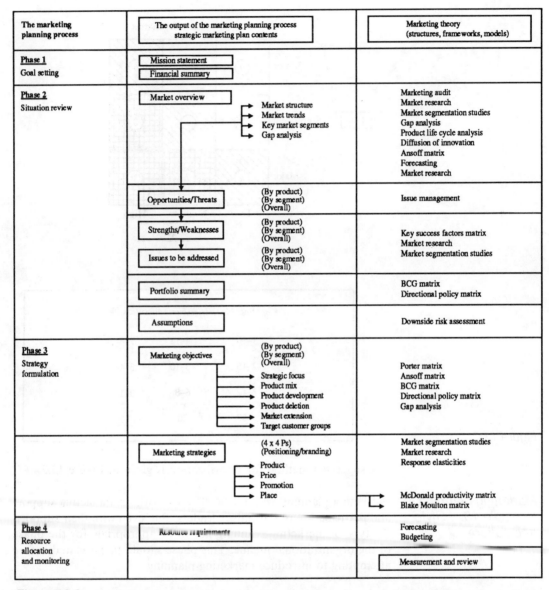

The marketing planning process	The output of the marketing planning process strategic marketing plan contents		Marketing theory (structures, frameworks, models)
Phase 1 Goal setting	Mission statement Financial summary		
Phase 2 Situation review	Market overview	Market structure Market trends Key market segments Gap analysis	Marketing audit Market research Market segmentation studies Gap analysis Product life cycle analysis Diffusion of innovation Ansoff matrix Forecasting Market research
	Opportunities/Threats	(By product) (By segment) (Overall)	Issue management
	Strengths/Weaknesses	(By product) (By segment) (Overall)	Key success factors matrix Market research Market segmentation studies
	Issues to be addressed	(By product) (By segment) (Overall)	
	Portfolio summary		BCG matrix Directional policy matrix
	Assumptions		Downside risk assessment
Phase 3 Strategy formulation	Marketing objectives	(By product) (By segment) (Overall) Strategic focus Product mix Product development Product deletion Market extension Target customer groups	Porter matrix Ansoff matrix BCG matrix Directional policy matrix Gap analysis
	Marketing strategies	(4 x 4 Ps) (Positioning/branding) Product Price Promotion Place	Market segmentation studies Market research Response elasticities McDonald productivity matrix Blake Moulton matrix
Phase 4 Resource allocation and monitoring	Resource requirements		Forecasting Budgeting
			Measurement and review

Figure 13.3

follows in Part 2 of this chapter and of doing excellent marketing planning that will bring all the claimed benefits, including a significant impact on the bottom line, through the creation of competitive advantage. If they are ignored, however, marketing planning will remain the cinderella of business management.

Part 2   A marketing planning system

Introduction

This marketing planning system is in three sections. Section A takes you through a step-by-step approach to the preparation of a strategic marketing plan. What actually appears in the strategic marketing plan is given under the heading 'Strategic marketing plan documentation'.

Section B takes you through the preparation of a one-year marketing plan. What actually appears in a one-year marketing plan is given under the heading 'The one-year marketing plan documentation'. Finally, section C refers to the need for a headquarters consolidated plan of several SBU strategic marketing plans. A suggested format is given under the heading 'Example of a format for a headquarters consolidated strategic plan'.

There are four main steps in the planning process (presented in diagrammatic form in Figure 13.4), which any strategic business unit* interested in protecting and developing its business must carry out:

1 *Analysis* – it must analyse both its marketplace and its own position within it, relative to the competition.
2 *Objectives* – it must construct from this analysis a realistic set of quantitative marketing and financial objectives, consistent with those set by the organization.

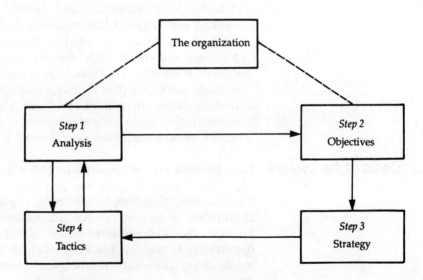

Figure   13.4

*A strategic business unit:
  o Will have common segments and competitors for most of its products.
  o Will be a competitor in an external market.
  o Will be a discrete and identifiable unit.
  o Will have a manager who has control over most of the areas critical to success.

SBUs are not necessarily the same as operating units and the definition can, and should if necessary, be applied all the way down to a particular product or customer or group of products and customers.

3 *Strategy* – it must determine the broad strategy which will accomplish these objectives, conforming with the organization's corporate strategy.

4 *Tactics* – it must draw together the analysis, the objectives and the strategy, using them as the foundation for detailed tactical action plans, capable of implementing the strategy and achieving the agreed objectives.

This process is formally expressed in two marketing plans, the strategic marketing plan and the tactical marketing plan, which should be written in accordance with the format provided in this system. It is designed for strategic business units (SBUs) to be able to take a logical and constructive approach to planning for success.

Two very important introductory points should be made about the marketing plan:

1 *The importance of different sections* – in the final analysis, the strategic marketing plan is a plan for action, and this should be reflected in the finished document. The implementation part of the strategic plan is represented by the subsequent one-year marketing plan.

2 *The length of the analytical section* – to be able to produce an action-focused strategic marketing plan, a considerable amount of background information and statistics needs to be collected, collated and analysed. An analytical framework has been provided in the forms, included in the database section of the 'Strategic marketing plan documentation', which each SBU should complete. However, the commentary given in the strategic marketing plan should provide the main findings of the analysis rather than a mass of raw data. It should compel concentration upon only that which is essential. The analysis section should, therefore, provide only a short background.

Basis of the system

Each business unit in the organization will have different levels of opportunity depending on the prevailing business climate. Each business unit, therefore, needs to be managed in a way that is appropriate to its own unique circumstances. At the same time, however, the chief executive officer of the SBU must have every opportunity to see that the ways in which these business units are managed are consistent with the overall strategic aims of the organization.

This system sets out the procedures which, if adhered to, will assist in achieving these aims.

Sections A, B and C set out the three basic marketing planning formats and explain how each of the planning steps should be carried out. They explain simply and clearly what should be presented, and when, in the three-year marketing plan, in the more detailed one-year operational plan and in the headquarters consolidated marketing plan.

A glossary of planning terms is included at the end of the book. The overall marketing planning format is described in Figure 13.5.

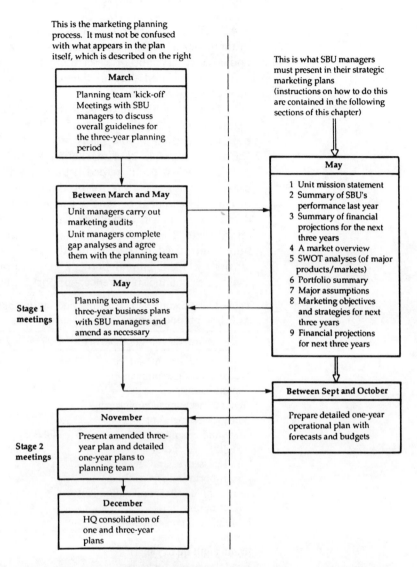

This is the marketing planning process. It must not be confused with what appears in the plan itself, which is described on the right

This is what SBU managers must present in their strategic marketing plans (instructions on how to do this are contained in the following sections of this chapter)

March

Planning team 'kick-off' Meetings with SBU managers to discuss overall guidelines for the three-year planning period

Between March and May

Unit managers carry out marketing audits
Unit managers complete gap analyses and agree them with the planning team

May

Stage 1 meetings

Planning team discuss three-year business plans with SBU managers and amend as necessary

May

1 Unit mission statement
2 Summary of SBU's performance last year
3 Summary of financial projections for the next three years
4 A market overview
5 SWOT analyses (of major products/markets)
6 Portfolio summary
7 Major assumptions
8 Marketing objectives and strategies for next three years
9 Financial projections for next three years

Between Sept and October

Prepare detailed one-year operational plan with forecasts and budgets

November

Stage 2 meetings

Present amended three-year plan and detailed one-year plans to planning team

December

HQ consolidation of one and three-year plans

Figure 13.5

(Note that, for the sake of simplicity, it has been assumed that the organization's year runs from January to December.) The following sections explain how each of the steps in the planning process should be completed.

The marketing audit (for completion between February and May each year)
(Note: not for inclusion in the plan or its presentation)
Every market includes a wide variety of customer groups, not all of which will necessarily provide SBUs with opportunities for servicing profitably.

In order to study those areas of the market which are potentially most favourable to the SBU's operations, it is necessary to divide the market into different *market segments* (hereafter just referred to as 'segments') and to analyse sales potential by type of product within each segment.

All SBUs must, therefore, analyse and evaluate the key segments in their market, plus any other segments which have been identified and selected as being of lesser importance to them.

It is appreciated that all the basic information required for this marketing audit may not be readily available. Nevertheless, an analysis and evaluation of the SBU's situation in each of the selected segments, i.e. a marketing audit, will provide the basis from which objectives can be set and plans prepared.

For the purpose of a marketing planning system, it is usual to provide users with an agreed list so that all SBUs using the system use similar nomenclature for products and markets. In this case, we provide an *example* of such a list in Table 13.1. Please note, more detailed criteria for market segmentation should also be used, where appropriate. For example: geographic location; company organization (centralized or decentralized); purchasing patterns (e.g. price sensitivity, fixed annual budget, local autonomy, etc.); integration level; sales channel preference; support requirements; and so on.

Table 13.1 Example of industrial and marine market segments and industrial product groups

Key industrial market segments	*Explanatory notes*
Primary metal manufacture	
Transportation equipment manufacture	
General mechanical engineering/ fabricated metal products	
Glass and ceramics	Glass, glassware, refractory and ceramic goods
Road passenger and freight transportation (specialists)	
Truck and construction equipment distributors	
Building and construction	
Forestry and timber	
Mining and quarrying	
Food, beverage, tobacco processing and manufacture	
Oil and gas	Extraction and processing of mineral oil and natural gas, excluding off-shore, which is covered in marine
Electricity: power generation and transmission	
Bricks and cement	Manufacture of non-metallic mineral products, excluding glass and ceramics
Textiles	Textile industry and the production of manmade fibres

Table 13.1 (*cont.*)

Key industrial market segments	*Explanatory notes*
Leather	
Pulp and paper	
National defence	
Central and local government	Excludes national defence
Aviation	Excludes military aviation and aerospace manufacturing industries
Industrial distributors	Wholesale distribution of industrial machinery, industrial spare parts and tools, etc.
Rubber, chemicals, plastics	Excludes rubber plantations
Cosmetics and pharmaceuticals	

Key marine market segments

International vessels greater than 4,000 GRT
- o Oil tankers
- o LPG and chemical tankers
- o Containers
- o General cargo vessels
- o Bulk carriers
- o Ferries and roll-on/roll-off vessels
- o Miscellaneous vessels

Coastal/international vessels less than 4,000 GRT
- o Oil tankers
- o LPG and chemical tankers
- o Containers
- o General cargo vessels
- o Bulk carriers
- o Ferries and roll-on/roll-off vessels
- o Miscellaneous vessels

Fishing

Offshore industry
- o Drilling rigs
- o Submersibles
- o Work units, etc.

Miscellaneous
- o Harbour craft
- o Inland waterways
- o Dredgers
- o Military, etc.

Industrial product groups

Automotive products
Engine oils
Transmission fluids and gear oils
Brake fluids
Antifreeze/coolants

Table 13.1 (*cont.*)

Industrial product groups (*cont.*)

Greases
Miscellaneous 'others'
Metalworking products
Cutting oils (soluble)
Cutting oils (neat)
Rolling oils
Heat treatment

Surface treatment products
Corrosion preventives (including DWFs)
Non-destructive testing materials
Industrial cleaning chemicals

General industrial lubricants
Hydraulic
  o fire resistant
  o other
Gear oils
Turbine oils
Heat transfer oils
Compressor oils (including refrigerator)
Grease
Circulating oils
Other (e.g. wire rope lubricants, Ss)

Aviation lubricants
Engine oils
Transmission oils
Hydraulic oils
Grease
Other

Other products
White oils
Electrical oils
Process oils
Textile oils
Leather chemicals
Laundry and dry cleaning chemicals
Mould releasants
Petroleum jelly
Defoamers

All managers carrying out their audit should use internal sales data and the SBU marketing information system to complete their audit. It is helpful at this stage if the various SBU managers can issue to any subordinates involved in the audit a market overview covering major industry and market trends. The audit will inevitably require considerably more data preparation than is required to be reproduced in the marketing plan itself. Therefore, all managers should start a *running reference file* for their area of responsibility during the year, which can also be used as a continual reference source and for verbal presentation of proposals.

It is essential to stress that the audit, which will be based on the running reference file, *is not a marketing plan and under no circumstances should voluminous documents relating to the audit appear in any business plans.*

The contents of a strategic marketing plan

The following sections (1–9) describe what should be presented in strategic marketing plans. These should be completed by the end of May each year.

These sections contain instructions. The actual documentation for the strategic marketing plan is also provided in this section.

1 SBU mission statement

This is the first item to appear in the marketing plan. The purpose of the mission statement is to ensure that the raison d'être of the SBU is clearly stated. Brief statements should be made which cover the following points:

1 *Role or contribution of the unit* – for example, profit generator, service department, opportunity seeker.
2 *Definition of business* – for example, the needs you satisfy or the benefits you provide. Do not be too specific (e.g. 'we sell milking machinery') or too general (e.g. 'we are in the engineering business').
3 *Distinctive competence* – this should be a brief statement that applies only to your specific SBU. A statement that could equally apply to any competitor is unsatisfactory.
4 *Indications for future direction* – a brief statement of the principal things you would give serious considerations to (e.g. move into a new segment.) A statement about what you *will* consider, *might* consider and *will never* consider can be quite useful.

Note: This is Form 1 in the strategic marketing plan documentation.

2 Summary of SBU's performance

This opening section is designed to give a bird's eye view of the SBU's total marketing activities.

In addition to a quantitative summary of performance, as shown in Table 13.2, SBU managers should give a summary of reasons for good or bad performance.

Use *constant revenue* (t–1) in order that the comparisons are meaningful. Make sure you use the same base year values for any projections provided in later sections in your plan.

Table 13.2

	Three years ago	Two years ago	Last year
Volume/turnover			
Gross profit (%)			
Gross margin			
(000 ecu)			

Note: This is Form 2 in the strategic marketing plan documentation.

3 Summary of financial projections

This is the third item to appear in the marketing plan. Its purpose is to summarize, for the person reading the plan, the financial implications over the full three-year planning period. It should be presented as a simple diagram along the lines shown in Figure 13.6. This should be accompanied by a brief commentary. For example: 'This three-year business plan shows an increase in revenue from 700,000 ecu to 900,000 ecu million and an increase in contribution from 100,000 ecu to 400,000 ecu. The purpose of this marketing plan is to show how these increases will be achieved.'

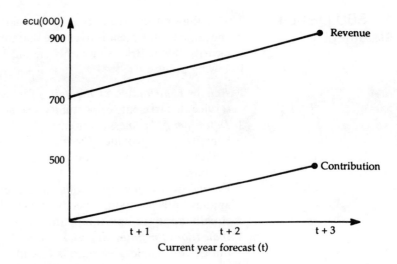

Figure 13.6

Note: There is a form, Form 3 in the strategic marketing plan documentation.

In order to comply with this form, it is strongly recommended that the strategic planning (gap analysis) forms (which follow as Forms 4 and 5 in the strategic marketing plan documentation) are completed first. Note that the 'objective' point should be (as a minimum) that point which will enable you to achieve the corporate objectives set for the SBU. *Ideally, however, it should be set at a point which will make this SBU the best of its kind amongst comparable competitive SBUs.* Note that the sales revenue form must be completed first, followed by the profit form.

4 Market overview

This section is intended to provide a brief picture of the market before descending to the particular details of individual market segments, which form the heart of the marketing plan.

This system is based upon the *segmentation* of markets, dividing these into homogeneous groups of customers, each having characteristics which can be exploited in marketing terms. *This approach is taken because it is the one which is often the most useful for SBU managers to be able to develop their markets.* The alternative, product-orientated, approach is rarely appropriate, given the variation between different customer groups in the markets in which most organizations compete.

The market segmentation approach is more useful in revealing both the weaknesses and the development opportunities than is an exclusively product orientation.

While it is difficult to give precise instructions on how to present this section of the marketing plan, it should be possible (following completion of the marketing audit) to present a market overview which summarizes what managers consider to be the key characteristics of their markets.

In completing this section, SBU managers should consider the following:

1 What are the major products, markets (or segments) which are likely to be able to provide the kind of business opportunities suitable for the organization.
2 How are these changing? That is, which are growing and which are declining?

This section should be brief and there should be some commentary by the SBU manager about what seems to be happening in their market.

It is very helpful if SBU managers can present as much of this information as possible visually (i.e. bar charts or pie charts, product life cycles, etc.) A market 'map' can be extremely useful for clarifying how the market works. (For further details of this technique, see Chapter 4.)

Note: There is a form, Form 6, in the strategic marketing plan documentation.

5 SWOT analyses of major products/markets

Compiling the SWOT analyses

To decide on marketing objectives and future strategy, it is first necessary to summarize the SBU's *present* position in its market(s). This was done in the previous section.

In respect of the major products/markets (segments) highlighted in the previous section, the marketing audit must now be summarized in the form of a number of *SWOT analyses*. The word *SWOT* derives from the initial letters of the words *strengths, weaknesses, opportunities* and *threats*. In simple terms:

o What are the unit's differential strengths and weaknesses *vis-à-vis* competitors? In other words, why should potential customers in the target markets prefer to deal with your organization rather than with your competitors?
o What are the opportunities?
o What are the present and future threats to the SBU's business in each of the segments which have been identified as being of importance?

Guidelines for completing the SWOT analysis

The market overview in Section 4 will have identified what you consider to be the key product/market (segments) on which you intend to focus. For presentation purposes, it is helpful if you can present a brief SWOT for each of these key product/market segments. Each of these SWOTs should be brief and interesting to read. Complete SWOTs only for the key segments.

Section I concerns *strengths* and *weaknesses*. Section II which follows is intended to indicate how the *opportunities* and *threats* section of the SWOT should be completed. Section III summarizes *key issues to be addressed.* Section IV describes the setting of assumptions, marketing objectives and strategies for each product/market segment. Section V summarizes the position of competitors.

I Some important factors for success in this business (critical success factors)

How does a competitor wishing to provide products or services in this segment succeed? There are always relatively few factors that determine success. Factors such as product performance, breadth of services, speed of service, low costs, and so on, are often the most important factors for success.

You should now make a brief statement about your organization's *strengths and weaknesses* in relation to these most important factors for success that you have identified. To do this, you will probably wish to consider other suppliers to the same segment in order to identify why you believe your organization can succeed and what weaknesses must be addressed in the three-year planning period.

These factors are called critical success factors. A layout such as that shown in Figure 13.7 is useful. You should then weight each factor out of 100 (e.g. CSF 1 = 60; CSF 2 = 25; CSF 3 = 10; CSF 4 = 5). It is suggested that you score yourself and each competitor out

Critical success factors / Competitors	Weighting factor	Your organization	Competitor A	Competitor B	Competitor C
CSF 1					
CSF 2					
CSF 3					
CSF 4					
Total weighted score	100				

Figure 13.7

of ten on each of the CSFs. Then, multiply each score by the weight. This will give you an accurate reading of your position in each segment *vis-à-vis* your competitors. It will also highlight which are *the key issues that should be addressed* in the three-year planning period.

Great caution is necessary to ensure that you are not guilty of self-delusion. Obviously, it is desirable to have independent evidence from market research in order to be able to complete this section accurately. If you do not have independent evidence, it is still worth doing a SWOT, because it will at least indicate what you need to know. Also, it is quite useful if you can get a number of managers to complete this independently, as, sometimes, it reveals a lot about what they believe to be the factors for success.

II   Summary of outside influences and their implications (opportunities and threats)

This should include a brief statement about how important environmental influences such as technology, government policies and regulations, the economy, and so on, have affected this segment. There will obviously be some opportunities and some threats.

III   Key issues to be addressed

From I and II above will emerge a number of key issues to be addressed.

IV   Assumptions, marketing objectives, marketing strategies

Assumptions can now be made and objectives and strategies set. It should be stressed at this point that such assumptions, objectives and strategies relate only to each particular product/market segment under consideration. These will guide your thinking when setting overall assumptions, marketing objectives and strategies later on (see section below).

Note: There is a form, Form 7 in the strategic marketing plan documentation. This form incorporates all the points made in I, II, III and IV above and should be completed for all product/market segments under consideration.

V   Competitor analysis

Here you should summarize the findings of the audit in respect of *major competitors* only. For each competitor, you should indicate their sales within the particular product/market segment under consideration, their share now, *and their expected share three years from now*. The greater a competitor's influence over others, the greater their ability to implement their own independent strategies, hence the more successful they are. It is suggested that you should also classify each of your main competitors according to one of the classifications in the guide to competitive position classifications, below, i.e. leadership, strong, favourable, tenable, weak.

Also list their principal products or services. Next, list each major competitor's business direction and current strategies. There follows a list of business directions and business strategies as guidelines. *These should not be quoted verbatim*, as they are only given as guidelines. Next, list their major strengths and weakness.

Competitor analysis					
Main competitor	Products/ markets	Business direction and current objectives and strategies	Strengths	Weaknesses	Competitive position

Figure 13.8

The format shown in Figure 13.8 is useful.

Note: There is a form, Form 8 in the strategic marketing plan documentation.

Guide to competitive position classifications

Leadership	○ Has a major influence on the performance or behaviour of others
Strong	○ Has a wide choice of strategies
	○ Is able to adopt an independent strategy without endangering their short-term position
	○ Has low vulnerability to competitors' actions
Favourable	○ Exploits specific competitive strengths, often in a product-market niche
	○ Has more than average opportunity to improve their position; has several strategies available
Tenable	○ Their performance justifies continuation in business
Weak	○ Currently has an unsatisfactory performance and significant competitive weakness
	○ They must improve or withdraw

The following list includes five business directions that are appropriate for almost any business. Select those that best summarize the competitor's strategy.

Business directions

1 *Enter* – to allocate resources to a new business area. Consideration should include building from prevailing company or division strengths, exploiting related opportunities and defending against perceived threats. This may involve creating a new industry.

2 *Improve* – to apply strategies that will significantly improve the competitive position of the business. Often, this requires thoughtful product/market segmentation.

3 *Maintain* – to maintain one's competitive position. Aggressive strategies may be required, although a defensive posture may also be assumed. Product/market position is maintained, often in a niche.

4 *Harvest* – to relinquish intentionally competitive position, emphasizing short-term profit and cash flow, but not necessarily at the risk of losing the business in the short term. Often, this entails consolidating or reducing various aspects of the business to create higher performance for that which remains.

5 *Exit* – to divest a business because of its weak competitive position, or because the cost of staying in it is prohibitive and the risk associated with improving its position is too high.

6 Portfolio summary (summary of SWOTs)

All that remains is to summarize each of these SWOTs in a format which makes it easy to see at a glance the overall position and relative importance of each of these segments to the organization. This can be done by drawing a diagram in the form of a four-box *matrix* which will show each of the important product/market segments described earlier. A matrix is shown as Figure 13.9. Some

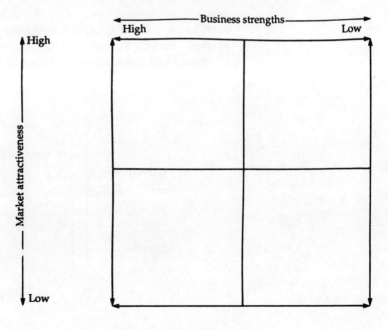

Figure 13.9

445

easy-to-follow instructions follow on how to complete such a matrix. More detailed instructions are provided in Chapter 5.

The *portfolio matrix* (referred to as the directional policy matrix in Chapter 5) enables you to assess which products or services, or which groups of customers/segments, will offer the best chance of commercial success. It will also aid decision making about which products or services (or market segments) merit investment, both in terms of finance and managerial effort.

In this example, market segments are used, although it is possible to use products or services. We recommend that you follow the instructions given below.

This is how you arrive at a portfolio matrix for your SBU.

1 List your market segments on a separate piece of paper and decide which ones are the most attractive. (Note that these 'segments' can be countries, divisions, markets, distributors, customers, etc.) To arrive at these decisions, you will no doubt take several factors into account:

- The size of the markets
- Their actual or prospective growth
- The prices you can charge
- Profitability
- The diversity of needs (which you can meet)
- The amount of competition in terms of quality and quantity
- The supportiveness of the business environment
- Technical developments, etc.

Imagine that you have a measuring instrument, something like a thermometer, but which measures not temperature, but market attractiveness. The higher the reading, the more attractive the market. The instrument is shown in Figure 13.10. Estimate the position on the scale *each* of your markets would record (should such an instrument exist) and make a note of it as shown by the example above. You should use the methodology outlined in Chapter 5 and the example provided in Table 5.3.

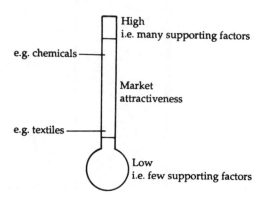

Figure 13.10

2 Transpose this information on to the matrix in Figure 13.9, writing the markets on the left of the matrix.

3 Still using the matrix, draw a dotted line horizontally across from the top left-hand market as shown in Figure 13.11.

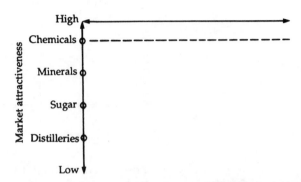

Figure 13.11

4 Now ask yourself how well your SBU is equipped to deal with this most attractive market. A whole series of questions needs to be asked to establish the company's business strengths, for example:

o Do we have the right products?
o How well are we known in this market?
o What image do we have?
o Do we have the right technical skills?
o How close are we to this market?
o How do we compare with competitors?

The outcome of such an analysis will enable you to arrive at a conclusion about the 'fitness' of your unit and you will be able to choose a point on the horizontal scale of the matrix to represent this. The left of the scale represents many unit strengths, the right few unit strengths. The analysis completed in the previous section (Section 5 on SWOT analyses) should be used, since you have already completed the necessary quantification. Draw a vertical line from this point on the scale as shown in Figure 13.12, so that it intersects with the horizontal line. (Be certain, however, to use the quantitative method outlined in Chapter 5.)

5 Now *redraw* the circles, this time making the diameter of each circle proportional to that segment's share of your total sales turnover. (Please note that to be technically correct you should take the square root of the volume, or value.)

6 Now indicate where these circles will be in three years' time and their estimated size. The matrix may, therefore, have to show segments not currently served. There are two ways of doing this. First, in deciding on market or segment attractiveness you can assume that you are at t0 (i.e. today) and that your forecast of attractiveness covers the next three years (i.e. t+3). If this is

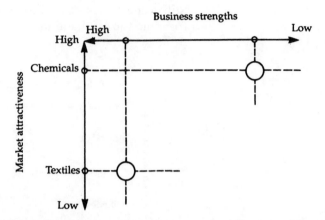

Figure 13.12

your chosen method, then it will be clear that *the circle can only move horizontally along the axis*, as all that will change is your business strength. The second way of doing it shows the current attractiveness position on the vertical axis, based on the past three years (i.e. t–3 to t0) and then forecasts how that attractiveness position will change during the next three years (i.e. t0 to t+3). In such a case, the circles can move both vertically and horizontally. This is the method used in the example provided (Figure 13.13), but it is entirely up to you which method you use. It is essential to be creative in your use of the matrix. Be

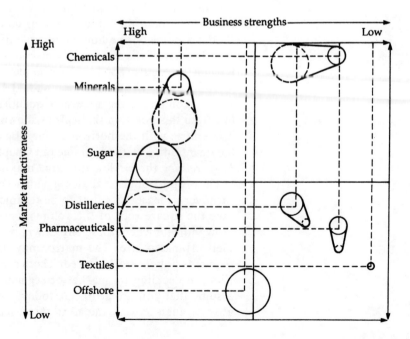

Figure 13.13

prepared to change the name on the axes and to experiment with both products and markets.

Note: There is a form, Form 9, in the strategic marketing plan documentation.

7 Overall assumptions

Each SBU must highlight the assumptions which are critical to the fulfilment of the planned marketing objectives and strategies.

Key planning assumptions deal, in the main, with outside features and anticipated changes which would have a significant influence on the achievement of marketing objectives. These might include such things as market growth rate, your organization's costs, capital investment and so on.

Assumptions should be few in number and relate only to key issues such as those identified in the SWOT analyses. If it is possible for a plan to be implemented irrespective of the assumptions made, then those assumptions are not necessary and should be removed.

You should find that the more detailed lists of assumptions made for each of the principal product/market segments analysed in the SWOT stage (Section 5) will be helpful in deciding what the macro assumptions should be.

Note: There is a form, Form 10, in the strategic marketing plan documentation.

8 Overall marketing objectives and strategies

Marketing objectives

Following identification and statement of key strengths, weaknesses, opportunities and threats, and the explicit statement of assumptions about conditions affecting the business, the process of setting marketing objectives is made easier, since they will be a realistic statement of what the SBU desires to achieve as a result of market-centred analysis.

As in the case of objective setting for other functional areas of the business, this is the most important step in the whole process, as it is a commitment on an SBU-wide basis to a particular course of action which will determine the scheduling and costing out of subsequent actions.

An *objective* is what the unit wants to achieve. A *strategy* is how it plans to achieve it. Thus, there are objectives and strategies at all levels in marketing. For example, there can be advertising objectives and strategies, pricing objectives and strategies, and so on.

However, the important point about marketing objectives is that they should be about products and markets only, since it is only by selling something to someone that the SBU's financial goals can be achieved. Advertising, pricing and other elements of the marketing mix are the means (the strategies) by which the SBU can succeed in doing this. Thus, pricing objectives, sales promotion objectives, advertising objectives and so on should *not* be confused with marketing objectives.

If profits and cash flows are to be maximized, each SBU must consider carefully how its current customer needs are changing and how its products offered need to change accordingly. Since change is inevitable, it is necessary for SBUs to consider the two main dimensions of commercial growth, i.e. product development and market development.

Marketing objectives are concerned with the following:

○ Selling existing products to existing segments
○ Developing new products for existing segments
○ Extending existing products to new segments
○ Developing new products for new segments

Marketing objectives should be *quantitative*, and should be expressed where possible in terms of *values, volumes*, and *market* shares. General directional terms such as 'maximize', 'minimize', 'penetrate' should be avoided unless quantification is included.

The marketing objectives should cover the full three-year planning horizon and should be accompanied by broad strategies (discussed in the following section) and broad revenue and cost projections for the full three-year period.

The one-year marketing plan should contain specific objectives for the first year of the three-year planning cycle and the corresponding strategies which will be used to achieve these objectives. *The one-year and the three-year plans should be separate documents. At this stage, a detailed one-year plan is not required.*

At this point it is worth stressing that the key document in the annual planning round is the three-year strategic marketing plan. The one-year plan represents the specific actions that should be undertaken in the first year of the strategic plan.

Marketing strategies

Marketing strategies should state in broad terms *how* the marketing objectives are to be achieved, as follows:

○ The specific product policies (the range, technical specifications, additions, deletions, etc.).
○ The pricing policies to be followed for product groups in particular market segments.
○ The customer service levels to be provided for specific market segments (such as maintenance support).
○ The policies for communicating with customers under each of the main headings, such as sales force, advertising, sales promotion, etc., as appropriate.

Guidelines for setting marketing objectives and strategies are given in Chapter 6. However, the following summarizes some of the marketing objectives and strategies that are available to SBU managers.

Objectives	
	1 Market penetration.
	2 Introduce new products to existing markets.
	3 Introduce existing products to new markets (domestic).
	4 Introduce existing products to new markets (international).
	5 Introduce new products to new markets.

Strategies

1 Change product design, performance, quality or features.
2 Change advertising or promotion.
3 Change unit price.
4 Change delivery or distribution.
5 Change service levels.
6 Improve marketing productivity (e.g. improve the sales mix).
7 Improve administrative productivity.
8 Consolidate product line.
9 Withdraw from markets.
10 Consolidate distribution.
11 Standardize design.
12 Acquire markets, products, facilities.

Guidelines for setting marketing objectives and strategies

Completing a portfolio matrix (which you have done in Section 7) for each major product/market segment within each unit translates the characteristics of the business into visible and easily understood positions *vis-à-vis* each other.

Additionally, each product/market segment's position on the matrix suggests broad goals which are usually appropriate for businesses in that position, although unit managers should also consider alternative goals in the light of the special circumstances prevailing at the time.

The four categories on the matrix are:

○ Invest
○ Maintain
○ Profit
○ Selective

You may prefer to use your own terms, although it should be stressed that it isn't necessary to attach any particular names to each of the quadrants. Each of these is considered in turn.

Invest

Products in this category enjoy competitive positions in markets/segments characterized by high growth rates and are good for continuing attractiveness. The obvious objective for such products is to maintain growth rates at least at the market growth rate, thus maintaining market share and market leadership, or to grow faster than the market, thus increasing market share.

Three principal factors should be considered:

1 Possible geographical expansion.
2 Possible product line expansion.
3 Possible product line differentiation.

These could be achieved by means of internal development, acquisition, or joint ventures.

The main point is that, in attractive marketing situations like this, *an aggressive marketing posture is required*, together with a very tight budgeting and control process to ensure that capital resources are efficiently utilized.

Maintain

Products in this category enjoy competitive positions in markets/ segments which are not considered attractive in the longer term. Here, the thrust should be towards maintaining a profitable position, with greater emphasis on present earnings rather than on aggressive growth.

The most successful product lines should be maintained, while less successful ones should be considered for pruning. Marketing effort should be focused on differentiating products to maintain share of key segments of the market. Discretionary marketing expenditure should be limited, especially when unchallenged by competitors or when products have matured. Comparative prices should be stabilized, except when a temporary aggressive stance is necessary to maintain market share.

Profit

Products in this category have a poor position in unattractive markets. These products are 'bad' only if objectives are not appropriate to the company's position in the market segment. Generally, where immediate divestment is not warranted, these products should be managed for cash.

Product lines should be aggressively pruned, while all marketing expenditure should be minimized, with prices maintained or where possible raised.

However, a distinction needs to be made between different types of products. The two principal categories are:

○ Those which are clearly uncompetitive in unattractive markets.
○ Those which are quite near to the dividing line.

Products in the first of those categories should generally be managed as outlined above. The others should generally be managed differently. For example, the reality of low growth should be acknowledged and the temptation should be resisted to grow the product at its previous high rates of growth. It should not be viewed as a 'marketing' problem, which will be likely to lead to high advertising, promotion, inventory costs and lower profitability. Growth segments should be identified and exploited where possible. Product quality should be emphasized to avoid 'commodity' competition. Productivity should be systematically improved. Finally, the attention of talented managers should be focused on such products.

Selective

Here, it is necessary to decide whether to invest for future market leadership in these attractive markets/segments or whether to manage for present earnings. Both objectives are feasible, but it must be remembered that managing these products for cash today is usually inconsistent with market share growth and it is usually necessary to select the most promising markets and invest in them only.

Further marketing and other functional guidelines

Further marketing and other functional guidelines which operating unit managers should consider when setting marketing objectives and corresponding strategies are given in Chapter 6.

It should be stressed, however, that there can be no *automatic* policy for a particular product or market, and SBU managers should consider three or more options before deciding on 'the best' for recommendation. Above all, SBU managers must evaluate the most attractive opportunities and assess the chances for success in the most realistic manner possible. This applies particularly to new business opportunities. New business opportunities would normally be expected to build on existing strengths, particularly in marketing, which can be subsequently expanded or supplemented.

Database and summary of marketing objectives

The forms included in the database provide both an analytical framework and a summary of marketing objectives which are relevant to all strategic business unit managers. This summary is essential information which underpins the marketing plan.

Forms included in database

Form 11: *Market segment sales values*, showing, across a five-year period, total market demand, the business unit's own sales and the market share these represent for the various market segments.

Form 12: *Market segment gross profits*, showing, across a five-year period, the business unit's sales value, gross profit, and gross margin for the various market segments.

Form 13: *Product group analysis*, showing, across a five-year period, the business unit's sales value, gross profit, and gross margin for different product groups.

Form 14: Summary (in words) of main marketing objectives and strategies.

9 Financial projections for three years

Finally, SBU managers should provide financial projections for the full three-year planning period under all the principal standard revenue and cost headings as specified by your organization.

Note: There is a form, Form 15, in the strategic marketing plan documentation.

Strategic marketing plan documentation

Form 1

Unit mission statement

This is the first item to appear in the marketing plan.

The purpose of the mission statement is to ensure that the raison d'être of the unit is clearly stated. Brief statements should be made which cover the following points:

1 *Role or contribution of the unit*
e.g. profit generator
service department
opportunity seeker

2 *Definition of the business*
e.g. the needs you satisfy or the benefits you provide. Don't be too specific (e.g. 'we sell milking machinery') or too general (e.g. 'we're in the engineering business').

3 *Distinctive competence*
This should be a brief statement that applies only to your specific unit. A statement that could equally apply to any competitor is unsatisfactory.

4 *Indications for future direction*
A brief statement of the principal things you would give serious consideration to (e.g. move into a new segment).

Form 2

Summary of SBU's performance

This opening section is designed to give a bird's eye view of the SBU's total marketing activities.

In addition to a quantitative summary of performance, as follows, SBU managers should give a summary of reasons for good or bad performance.

Use *constant revenue* in order that comparisons are meaningful.

Make sure you use the same base year values for any projections provided in later sections of this system.

	3 years ago	*2 years ago*	*Last year*
Volume/turnover			
Gross profit (%)			
Gross margin (000 ecu)			

Summary of reasons for good or bad performance

Form 3

Summary of financial projections

This is the third item to appear in the marketing plan.

Its purpose is to summarize for the person reading the plan the financial results over the full three-year planning period.
It should be presented as a simple diagram along the following lines:

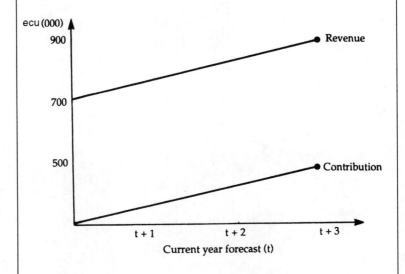

This should be accompanied by a brief commentary

For example:

'This three-year business plan shows an increase in revenue from 700,000 ecu to 900,000 ecu and an increase in contribution from 100,000 ecu to 400,000 ecu. The purpose of this business plan is to show how these increases will be achieved.'

Form 4

Strategic planning exercise (gap analysis)

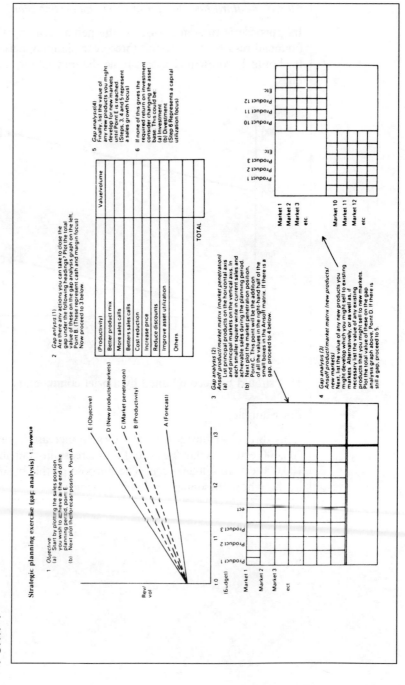

1 Revenue

1 Objective
(a) Start by plotting the sales position you wish to achieve at the end of the planning period, point E
(b) Next plot the forecast position, Point A

E (Objective)
D (New products/markets)
C (Market penetration)
B (Productivity)
A (Forecast)

Rev/
vol

(Budget) I0   I1   Product 1   Product 2   Product 3   ect   I2   I3

Market 1
Market 2
Market 3
ect

2 Gap analysis (1)
Are there any actions you can take to close the gap under the following headings? Plot the total value of these on the gap analysis graph on the left, Point B (These represent cash and margin focus)
Now proceed to 3 below

(Productivity)	Value/volume
Better product mix	
More sales calls	
Betters sales calls	
Cost reduction	
Increase price	
Reduce discounts	
Improve asset utilization	
Others	
TOTAL	

3 Gap analysis (2)
Ansoff product/market matrix (market penetration)
(a) List principal products on the horizontal axis and principal markets on the vertical axis. In each smaller square write in current sales and achievable sales during the planning period.
(b) Next plot the market penetration position, Point C. This point will be the addition of all the values in the right hand half of the small boxes in the Ansoff matrix. If there is a gap, proceed to 4 below

4 Gap analysis (3)
Ansoff product/market matrix (new products/new markets)
Next, list the value of any new products you might develop which you might sell to existing markets. Alternatively, or as well as, if necessary list the value of any existing products that you might sell to new markets. Plot the total value of these on the gap analysis graph above, Point D. If there is still a gap, proceed to 5.

5 Gap analysis (4)
Finally, list the value of any new products you might develop for new markets until Point E is reached (Steps 3, 4 and 5 represent a sales growth focus)

6 If none of this gives the required return on investment consider changing the asset base. This could be
(a) Investment
(b) Divestment
(Step 6 Represents a capital utilization focus)

Product 1
Product 2
Product 3
etc

Product 10
Product 11
Product 12
etc

Market 1
Market 2
Market 3
etc

Market 10
Market 11
Market 12
etc

Form 5

Strategic planning exercise (gap analysis)   2 Profit

1 Objective
(a) Start by plotting the sales profit position
you wish to achieve at the end of the
planning period, point E
(b) Next plot the forecast profit position, Point A

2 Gap analysis (productivity)
Are there any actions you can take to close the
gap under the following headings? Plot the total
value of these on the gap analysis graph on the left,
Point B. (These represent cash and margin focus)
Now proceed to 3 below.

Productivity (Note: Not all factors are mutually exclusive)	Profit
Better product mix	
Better customer mix	
More sales calls	
Better sales calls	
Increase price	
Reduce discounts	
Charge for delivery	
Reduce debtor days	
Cost reduction	
Other (specify)	
TOTAL	

3 Gap analysis (2)
Ansoff product/market matrix (market penetration)
(a) List principal products on the horizontal axis
and principal markets on the vertical axis. In
each smaller square write in current sales and
achievable sales during the planning period.
Next plot the market penetration position,
Point C. This point will be the value
of all the values in the right-hand half of the
small boxes in the Ansoff matrix. If there is a
gap, proceed to 4 below.
(b)

4 Gap analysis (3)
*Ansoff product/market matrix (new products/
new markets)*
Next, list the value of any new products you
might develop which you might sell to existing
markets. Alternatively, or as well as, if
necessary list the value of any existing
products that you might sell to new markets.
Plot the total value of these on the gap
analysis graph above, Point D. If there is
still a gap, proceed to 5.

5 Gap analysis (Diversification)
Finally, list the profit value of
any new products you might
develop for new markets
until Point E is reached
(Steps 3, 4 and 5 represent
a sales growth focus)

6 Gap analysis (Capital utilization)
If none of this gives the
required return on investment
consider changing the asset
base. This could be
(a) Investment
(b) Joint venture
(Step 6 Represents a capital
utilization focus)

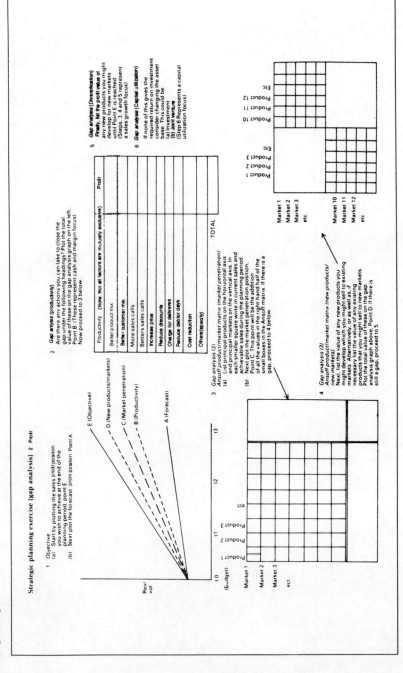

Rev/
vol

E (Objective)
D (New products/markets)
C (Market penetration)
B (Productivity)
A (Forecast)

t0   t1   t2   t3

(Budget)
Market 1
Market 2
Market 3
etc

Product 1   Product 2   Product 3   ect

Market 1
Market 2
Market 3
etc.

Product 1   Product 2   Product 3   Etc

Market 10
Market 11
Market 12
etc

Product 10   Product 11   Product 12   etc

Form 6

Market overview

Strategic planning exercise (SWOT analysis)
(*Note:* This form should be completed for each product/market segment under consideration)

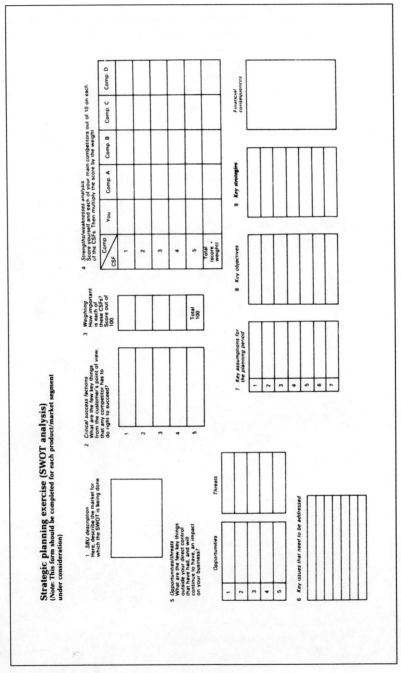

1 *SBU description*
Here, describe the market for which the SWOT is being done

2 *Critical success factors*
What are the few key things from the customer's point of view, that any competitor has to do right to succeed?

1
2
3
4
5

3 *Weighting*
How important is each of these CSFs? Score out of 100

Total 100

4 *Strengths/weaknesses analysis*
Score yourself and each of your main competitors out of 10 on each of the CSFs. Then multiply the score by the weight

Comp CSF	You	Comp. A	Comp. B	Comp. C	Comp. D
1					
2					
3					
4					
5					
Total (score × weight)					

5 *Opportunities/threats*
What are the few key things outside your direct control that have had, and will continue to have, an impact on your business?

Opportunities

1
2
3
4
5

Threats

6 *Key issues that need to be addressed*

7 *Key assumptions for the planning period*

1
2
3
4
5
6
7

8 *Key objectives*

9 *Key strategies*

Financial consequences

Form 8

Note: **This form should be completed for each product market segment under consideration)**					
Main competitor	*Products/ markets and current objectives and strategies*	*Business direction*	*Strengths*	*Weaknesses*	*Competitive position*

Form 9

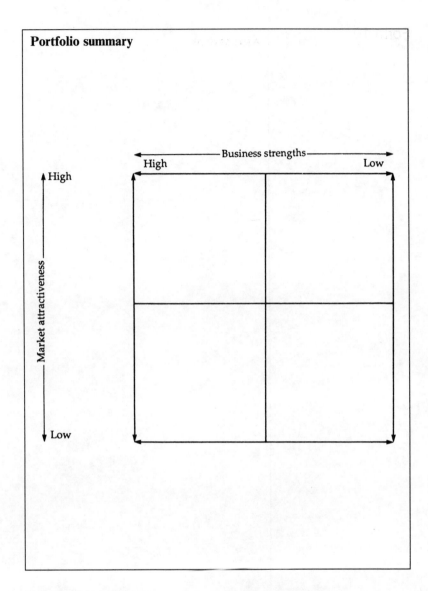

Form 10

Assumptions

Form 11

Database and summary of marketing objectives
Market segment sales values

Sales values	Last year (t–1)	Current year (t0)	Next year (t+1)	(t+2)	(t+3)
Key market segments (list)	Total company market segment sales share	Total company market segment sales share	Total company market segment sales share	Total company market segment sales share	Total company market segment sales share
Total					

Form 12

Database and summary of marketing objectives
Market segment gross profits

Sales values	Last year (t-1)	Current year (t0)	Next year (t+1)	(t+2)	(t+3)
Key market segments (list)	Total company market segment sales share	Total company market segment sales share	Total company market segment sales share	Total company market segment sales share	Total company market segment sales share
Total					

Form 13

Product group analysis

Product groups	Last year (t–1)			Current year (t0)			Next year (t+1)			(t+2)			(t+3)		
	Sales value	Gross profit	Gross margin (%)	Sales value	Gross profit	Gross margin (%)	Sales value	Gross profit	Gross margin (%)	Sales value	Gross profit	Gross margin (%)	Sales value	Gross profit	Gross margin (%)
Total															

Form 14

Summary (in words) of main marketing objectives and strategies

Form 15

Financial projections for three years

**Section B   The
one-year marketing plan**

(This should be kept separate from the three-year strategic marketing plan and should not be completed until the planning team has approved the strategic plan in May each year.)

Specific sub-objectives for products and segments, supported by more detailed strategy and action statements, should now be developed. Here, include *budgets* and *forecasts* and a *consolidated budget*. These must reflect the marketing objectives and strategies, and in turn the objectives, strategies and programmes *must* reflect the agreed budgets and sales forecasts. Their main purpose is to delineate the major steps required in implementation, to assign accountability, to focus on the major decision points, and to specify the required allocation of resources and their timing.

If the procedures in this system are followed, a hierarchy of *objectives* will be built up in such a way that every item of budgeted expenditure can be related directly back to the initial financial objectives (this is known as task-related budgeting).

Thus when, say, advertising has been identified as a means of achieving an objective in a particular market (i.e. advertising is a strategy to be used), all advertising expenditure against items appearing in the budget can be related back specifically to a major objective. The essential feature of this is that budgets are set against both the overall marketing objectives and the sub-objectives for each element of the marketing mix.

The principal advantage is that this method allows operating units to build up and demonstrate an increasingly clear picture of their markets. This method of budgeting also allows every item of expenditure to be fully accounted for as part of an objective approach. It also ensures that when changes have to be made during the period to which the plan relates, such changes can be made in a way that causes the least damage to the SBU's long-term objectives.

Contingency plan

It is important to include a *contingency plan* in the one-year marketing plan. Notes on this are included below.

Guidelines for completion of a one-year marketing plan

Because of the varying nature of strategic business units, it is impossible to provide a standard format for all SBUs. There is, however, a minimum amount of information which should be provided to accompany the financial documentation between September and October. There is no need to supply market background information, as this should have been completed in the three-year strategic marketing plan.

Suggested format for a one-year marketing plan

1 (a) *Overall objectives (see Forms 1 and 2 in the one-year marketing plan documentation)* – these should cover the following:

Volume or value	Value last year	Current year estimate	Budget next year

Gross margin	Last year	Current year estimate	Budget next year

Against each there should be a few words of commentary/explanation.

(b) *Overall strategies* – e.g. new customers, new products, advertising, sales promotion, selling, customer service, pricing. For a list of marketing strategies, see Chapter 6.

2 (a) *Sub-objectives (see Form 3 in the one-year marketing plan documentation)* – more detailed objectives should be provided for products, or markets, or segments, or major customers, as appropriate.

(b) *Strategies* – the means by which sub-objectives will be achieved should be stated.

(c) *Action/tactics* – the details, timing, responsibility and cost should also be stated.

3 *Summary of marketing activities and costs (see Form 4 in the one-year marketing plan documentation).*

4 *Contingency plan (see Form 5 in the one-year marketing plan documentation)* – it is important to include a contingency plan, which should address the following questions:

(a) What are the critical assumptions on which the one-year plan is based?

(b) What would the financial consequences be (i.e. the effect on the operating income) if these assumptions did not come true? For example, if a forecast of revenue is based on the assumption that a decision will be made to buy new plant by a major customer, what would the effect be if that customer did not go ahead?

(c) How will these assumptions be measured?

(d) What action will you take to ensure that the adverse financial effects of an unfulfilled assumption are mitigated, so that you end up with the same forecast profit at the end of the year?

To measure the risk, assess the negative or downside, asking what can go wrong with each assumption that would change the outcome. For example, if a market growth rate of 5 per cent is a key assumption, what lower growth rate would have to occur before a substantially different management decision would be taken? For a capital project, this would be the point at which the project would cease to be economical.

5 *Operating result and financial ratios (see Form 6 in the one-year marketing plan documentation)*
Note: This form is provided only as an example, for, clearly, all organizations will have their own formats – this should include:

o Net revenue
o Gross margin
o Adjustments
o Marketing costs

- ○ Administration costs
- ○ Interest
- ○ Operating result
- ○ ROS
- ○ ROI

6 *Key activity planner (see Form 7 in the one-year marketing plan documentation)* – finally, you should summarize the key activities and indicate the start and finish. This should help you considerably with monitoring the progress of your annual plan.
7 *Other* – there may be other information you wish to provide, such as sales call plans.

One-year marketing plan documentation

Form 1

Overall objectives

Product/ market/ segment/ application/ customer	Volume			Value			Gross margin			Commentary
	t-1	t0	t+1	t-1	t0	t+1	t-1	t0	t+1	

Form 2

Overall strategies		
	Strategies	*Cost*
1		
2		
3		
4		
5		
6		
7		
8		
9		
10		
Comments		

Form 3

Sub-objectives, strategies, actions, responsibilities, timing, cost						
Product/ market/ segment/ application/ customer	Objective	Strategies	Action	Responsibility	Timing	Cost

Total _____

Form 4

	t−1	t0	t+1	Comments
Depreciation				
Salaries				
Postage/telephone/stationery				
Legal and professional				
Training				
Data processing				
Advertising				
Sales promotion				
Travelling and entertainment				
Exhibitions				
Printing				
Meetings/conferences				
Market research				
Internal costs				
Other (specify)				
Total				

Form 5

Suggested downside risk assessment format

Key assumption	Basis of assumption	What event would have to happen to make this strategy unattractive?	Risk of such an event occurring (%) High P(7–10) Medium P(4–6) Low P(0–3)	Impact if event occurs	Trigger point for action	Actual contingency action proposed

Form 6

	t−1	*t0*	*t+1*
Net revenue Gross margin Adjustments Marketing costs Administration costs Interest			
Operating result			
Other interest and financial costs			
Result after financial costs			
Net result			

Form 7

Key activity planner

Date/activity	Jan				Feb				March				April				May				June				July				Aug				Sept				Oct				Nov				Dec			
	1	2	3	4	1	2	3	4	1	2	3	4	1	2	3	4	1	2	3	4	1	2	3	4	1	2	3	4	1	2	3	4	1	2	3	4	1	2	3	4	1	2	3	4	1	2	3	4

**Section C
Headquarters
consolidation of several
SBU strategic marketing
plans**

The author is frequently asked how several SBU strategic marketing plans should be consolidated by senior headquarters marketing personnel. A suggested format for this task is provided below.

Directional statement

1 *Role/contribution* – this should be a brief statement about the company's role or contribution. Usually, it will specify a minimum growth rate in turnover and profit, but it could also encapsulate roles such as opportunity seeking service and so on.

2 *Definition of the business* – this statement should describe the needs that the company is fulfilling, or the benefits that it is providing for its markets. For example, 'the provision of information to business to facilitate credit decision making'. Usually, at the corporate level, there will be a number of definitions for its strategic business units. It is important that these statements are not too broad so as to be meaningless (e.g. 'communications' – which could mean satellites or pens) or too narrow (e.g. 'drills' – which could become obsolete if a better method of fulfilling the need for holes is found).

3 *Distinctive competence* – all companies should have a distinctive competence. It does not have to be unique, but it must be substantial and sustainable. Distinctive competence can reside in integrity, specialist skills, technology, distribution strength, international coverage, reputation and so on.

4 *Indications for future direction* – this section should indicate guidelines for future growth. For example, does the company wish to expand internationally, or to acquire new skills and resources? The purpose of this section is to indicate the boundaries of future business activities.

Summary of the main features of the plan

1 Here draw a portfolio matrix indicating the current and proposed relative position of each of the strategic business units. Alternatively, this can appear later in the plan.

2 Include a few words summarizing growth in turnover, profit, margins, etc.

3 Draw a graph indicating simply the total long-term plan. At least two lines are necessary – turnover and profit.

Financial history (past five years)

Include a bar chart showing the relevant financial history, but, at the very least, include turnover and profit for the past five years.

Major changes and events since the previous plan

Here, describe briefly major changes and events (such as divesting a subsidiary) which occurred during the previous year.

Major issues by strategic business unit

Market characteristics

Here, it might be considered useful to provide a table listing strategic business units, alongside relevant market characteristics. For example:

	SBU1	SBU2	SBU3	SBU4
Market size				
Market growth				
Competitive intensity				
Relative market share				
etc.				

Competitive characteristics

Here, it might be considered useful to list the critical success factors by strategic business unit and rate each unit against major competitors. For example:

Critical success factors/competitors	Our company	Competitor 1	Competitor 2
CSF 1 CSF 2 CSF 3 CSF 4 CSF 5			

Key strategic issues

This is an extremely important section, as its purpose is to list (possibly by strategic business unit), what the key issues are that face the company. In essence, this really consists of stating the major strengths, weaknesses, opportunities and threats and indicating how they will be either built on, or dealt with.

Key strategic issues might consist of technology, regulation, competitive moves, institutional changes, and so on.

Strategic objectives by strategic business unit and key statistics

This is a summary of the objectives of each strategic business unit. It should obviously be tailored to the specific circumstances of each company. However, an example of what might be appropriate follows:

Alternatively, or additionally, put a portfolio matrix indicating the current and proposed relative position of each of the strategic business units.

Financial goals (next five years)

Here, draw a bar chart (or a number of bar charts) showing the relevant financial goals. At the very least, show turnover and profit by strategic business unit for the next five years.

	Objectives	Market share		Relative market share		Real growth		Key statistics				
Strategic business unit								Sales per employee		Contribution per employee		*etc.*
		Now	*+ 5 years*	*Now*	*+ 5 years*	*+ 5 years*	*p.a.*	*Now*	*+ 5 years*	*Now*	*+ 5 years*	
SBU 1												
SBU 2												
SBU 3												
SBU 4												
SBU 5												

Appendices

Include whatever detailed appendices are appropriate. Try not to rob the total plan of focus by including too much detail.

Timetable

The major steps and timing for the annual round of strategic and operational planning is described in the following pages. The planning process is in two separate stages, which are interrelated to provide a review point prior to the detailed quantification of plans. 'Stage One' involves the statement of key and critical objectives for the full three-year planning period, to be reviewed prior to the more detailed quantification of the tactical one-year plan in 'Stage Two' by 30 November, for subsequent consolidation into the company plans.

Planning team's 'kick-off' meetings (to be completed by 31 March)

At this meeting, the planning team will outline their expectations for the following planning cycle. The purpose of the meeting is to give the planning team the opportunity to explain corporate policy, report progress during the previous planning cycle, and to give a broad indication of what is expected from each SBU during the forthcoming cycle. The planning team's review will include an overall appraisal of performance against plan, as well as a variance analysis. The briefing will give guidance under some of the following headings (as appropriate).

1 *Financial*
   o Gross margins
   o Operating profits
   o Debtors
   o Creditors
   o Cash flow
2 *Manpower and organization*
   o Organization
   o Succession
   o Training
   o Remuneration
3 *Export strategy*
4 *Marketing*
   o Product development
   o Target markets

  o Market segments
  o Volumes
  o Market shares
  o Pricing
  o Promotion
  o Market research
  o Quality control
  o Customer service

This is an essential meeting prior to the mainstream planning activity which SBUs will subsequently engage in. It is the principal means by which it can be ensured that plans do not become stale and repetitive due to over-bureaucratization. Marketing creativity will be the keynote of this meeting.

Top-down and bottom-up planning

A cornerstone of the marketing planning philosophy is that there should be widespread understanding at all levels in the organization of the key objectives that have to be achieved, and of the key means of achieving them. This way, the actions and decisions that are taken by managers will be disciplined by clear objectives that hang logically together as part of a rational, overall purpose. The only way this will happen is if the planning system is firmly based on market-centred analysis which emanates from the SBUs themselves. Therefore, after the planning team's 'kick-off' meetings, audits should be carried out by all managers in the SBUs down to a level which will be determined by SBU managers. Each manager will also do SWOT analyses and set tentative three-year objectives and strategies, together with proposed budgets for initial consideration by their superior manager. In this way, each superior will be responsible for synthesizing the work of those managers reporting to them.

The major steps in the annual planning cycle are listed below and depicted schematically in Figure 13.14.

Activity	Deadline
o Planning team's 'kick-off' meetings with SBU managers to discuss overall guidelines for the three-year planning period	31 March
o Prepare marketing audits, SWOT analyses, proposed marketing objectives, strategies and budgets (cover the full three-year planning horizon)	31 May
o *'Stage One'* meetings: presentation to the planning team for review	31 May
o Prepare short-term (one-year) operational plans and budgets, and final three-year SBU managers' consolidated marketing plans	31 October
o *'Stage Two'* meetings: presentation to the planning team	31 November
o Final consolidation of the marketing plans	31 December

Release plan for
implementation

Start
Jan 1

Consolidation

'Stage Two'
meetings and
presentation

Prepare tactical
(one-year)
operational plans
and budgets

Planning team's
'kick-off' meetings

Marketing audits,
gap analyses

SWOT analyses,
objectives, strategies,
budgets (proposed)
three years

Finalize three
year strategic
marketing plans

'Stage One' meetings

Figure 13.14 Strategic and operational planning cycle

Index

LIFT ATTENDANT

LOCAL BANK MANAGER

BRICKLAYER

TOOL-MAKER

SENIOR PARTNER IN A
FIRM OF SOLICITORS

SCHOOL TEACHER

GROUP CHAIRMAN

COMPUTER PROGRAMMER

MACHINE OPERATOR

ELDERLY GRANNIE

SALES MANAGER

SELF-EMPLOYED PLUMBER

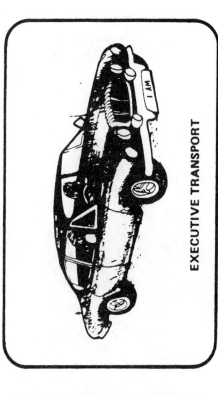

EXECUTIVE TRANSPORT

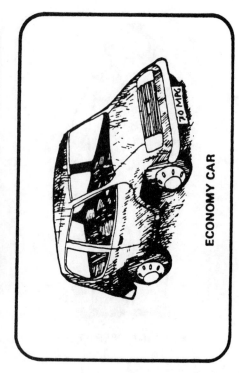

ECONOMY CAR

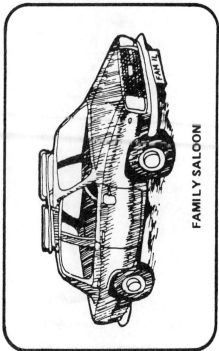

FAMILY SALOON

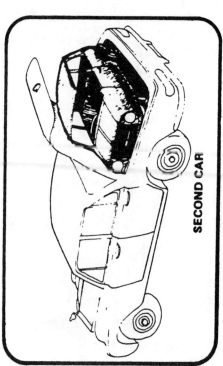

SECOND CAR

ESTATE CAR

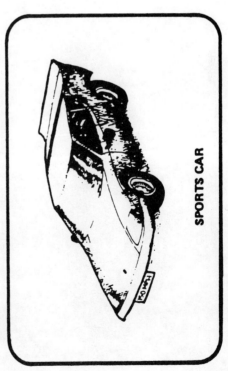

SPORTS CAR

THE MARKETING SERIES

EDITED BY

MICHAEL BAKER

University of Strathclyde Business School

THE Marketing BOOK

AN INDISPENSABLE REFERENCE
WORK FOR PRACTITIONERS

THIRD EDITION

- ■ The authoritative Chartered Institute of Marketing handbook
- ■ Over 20,000 copies sold of previous edition
- ■ Extensively revised and updated
- ■ New chapters include:
  - Strategic Marketing Planning: A review of concepts and their applications
  - Marketing Segmentation
  - Sales Promotion
  - Green Marketing
- ■ Essential text for students (CIM examinations; management and marketing degrees; MBA; DMS; BTEC Higher National and equivalent courses).
- ■ Edited by Michael Baker with contributions from top UK marketing educators and writers

August 1994 860pp 246 x 189mm Paperback 0 7506 2022 6

BUTTERWORTH HEINEMANN

For further information and ordering details, please call
01865 314627
quoting code B502BMFA

Marketing Plans
Interactive Tutor Resource Pack

Malcolm McDonald

Contains chapter-by-chapter tutor guidance notes to help tutors using the *Marketing Plans Third Edition* textbook.

It provides examples of real marketing plans as well as case studies with accompanying tutor notes. There are also two interactive tutorial disks featuring the Boston Consulting Group Matrix and the Directional Policy Matrix.

This is an excellent resource for all lecturers and course leaders to aid their teaching of marketing courses.

- Interactive disks
- 64 OHT masters
- Case studies
- Model answers
- Key terms
- Teaching suggestions
- Revision questions
- Student exercises

0 7506 2304 7   **Ringbound**   **297x210mm**   **June 1995**

☎ For ordering further information – please phone 01865 314627